Déjà Vu

Electronic Mediations
Katherine Hayles, Mark Poster, and Samuel Weber, series editors

Volume 12, Electronic Mediations

DÉJÀ VU

ABERRATIONS OF CULTURAL MEMORY

Peter Krapp

University of Minnesota Press
Minneapolis • London

Parts of chapter 4 were originally published as "Andy's Wedding: Reading Warhol," in *Sensual Reading: New Approaches to Reading in Its Relations to the Senses,* edited by Ian MacLachlan and Michael Syrotinski (Lewisburg, Penn.: Bucknell University Press, 2001), 295–310. A version of chapter 5 was published as "Unforgiven: Fausse Reconnaissance," *South Atlantic Quarterly* 101, no. 3 (2002): 589–607. A section of chapter 6 was published as "Derrida Online," *Oxford Literary Review* 18 (1996): 159–73. All reprinted here with permission.

Published by the University of Minnesota Press
111 Third Avenue South, Suite 290
Minneapolis, MN 55401-2520
http://www.upress.umn.edu

Library of Congress Cataloging-in-Publication Data
Krapp, Peter.
  Déjà vu : aberrations of cultural memory / Peter Krapp.
    p. cm. — (Electronic mediations ; v. 12)
  Includes bibliographical references and index.
    ISBN 0-8166-4334-2 (alk. paper) — ISBN 0-8166-4335-0
  (pbk. : alk. paper)
    1. Déjà vu. 2. Memory (Philosophy). 3. Memory—Social aspects.
  I. Title II. Series.
  BD181.7K73 2004
  128'.3—dc22

                                    2003025477

Printed in the United States of America on acid-free paper

The University of Minnesota is an equal-opportunity educator and employer.

12 11 10 09 08 07 06 05 04   10 9 8 7 6 5 4 3 2 1

CONTENTS

ACKNOWLEDGMENTS

A CADEMIA PREPARES YOU FOR THE PAST. If there are forward-looking statements in this book, they are owed to the peculiarity of the subject matter. As Lewis Carroll wrote,

> "That's the effect of living backwards . . . it always makes one giddy at first—"
> "Living backwards!" Alice repeated in great astonishment. "I never heard of such a thing! . . ."
> "—but there's one great advantage in it, that one's memory works both ways."

I am grateful to Catherine Liu for her generous support. Research for this book in Britain, Germany, and California was made possible by the DAAD (German Academic Exchange Service), the Konrad Adenauer Foundation, the DFG (German Research Foundation), and the University of California. Aleida Assmann, Jacques Derrida, Renate Lachmann, Bettine Menke, Laurence Rickels, Nicholas Royle, Karl-Heinz Stierle, Elisabeth Weber, and Samuel Weber provided critical stimulation. I thank the Electronic Mediations series editors and everyone at the University of Minnesota Press, and dedicate this book to Leo.

BEEN THERE, DONE THAT

[T]he strange feeling (to which, perhaps, no one is quite a
stranger) that all this had occurred before, at some indefinite
time, and that I knew what he was going to say next.
—Charles Dickens, *David Copperfield*

THIS BOOK HISTORICIZES AND THEORIZES déjà vu, from its first
sustained discussions in the late nineteenth century to its latest cultural
effects at the end of the twentieth century. Early theories on mnemopathology between philosophy and psychology yield a pre-Freudian logic of the
cover-up, and later, media theories and cultural history screen each other over
in turn. The French expression déjà vu was popularized in the pages of the
Revue philosophique at the end of the nineteenth century. The psychological
descriptions debated there ultimately prove insufficient for a full account of the
cultural effects of déjà vu, as do the philosophical theories of memory and forgetting offered by Søren Kierkegaard, Friedrich Nietzsche, Henri Bergson, or
Maurice Halbwachs. Yet each contributed considerations that guide the development of the discourse of déjà vu over the course of a century. Subsequently,
we trace it in the thought of Sigmund Freud and Walter Benjamin, in the art
of Heiner Müller and Andy Warhol, in cinematic treatment, and finally in the
high expectations raised by the Internet.[1]

Right in the middle of those hundred years of déjà vu, dictionaries mark a
historical revaluation of the French phrase, which is borrowed in German as
well as in English: a shift occurs in our ordinary language, from an uncanny

experience of reduplicating or foreboding unfamiliarity to a sense of the overly familiar, the tediously repetitive, the already known, the always present.[2] "The naïve subject of *déjà vu* says, 'I vaguely remember experiencing all this before'; the sophisticated subject is not even tempted to say this, but says, perhaps, 'Hm, I'm having a *déjà vu* experience right now.' The experience has changed."[3] It is no coincidence that this discontinuity in the history of an untranslatable phenomenon occurs after the world wars released new media technologies of mass distraction. In this book, we outline what neither the dictionaries nor the history of media technology shows: the cultural effect of déjà vu as well as that of its explanations.

Theodor Adorno already suspected that a generalized, Kafkaesque déjà vu would become our line on place, time, and truth.[4] We have grown used to a kind of context-free conversance with the recognition effects of media and popular culture—indeed a sense of decontextualized familiarity is common where advertising, television, and computer screens transform self-knowledge and the experience of temporality and intersubjectivity. But that does not yet explain the disturbing experience of a situation as new and yet known, nor does it mean that the various interpretations of such unexpected and apparently inexplicable intimacy have been studied sufficiently. Revisiting the history of déjà vu, we have to resist two temptations: faced with a plausible theory of déjà vu, one may all too quickly feel as if one had always already thought so—a fallacy of precisely the type we seek to investigate; and the fact that earlier explanations are hard to reconstruct after Sigmund Freud's highly influential intervention is a variation on this temptation.[5] Thus déjà vu also allows us to historicize psychoanalysis.

Early ideas about déjà vu were contemporary with the invention of media technologies such as photography, telegraphy, and phonography. Granting access to and control over repetition in an unprecedented way, these and later technologies instigate the debates around déjà vu, learn to harness a déjà vu effect, and in the end transform the experience of déjà vu. Thus media technology accelerates a history of déjà vu that complicates our relation with the familiar. The experience of uncanny repetition itself remains unrepeatable: you cannot generate it at will. Whether it is an involuntary memory or a sudden boredom with canned redundancy, how does it allow a vision of the future as if you suddenly remembered it? To tell the story of déjà vu is to deal with such distortions of the frame of reference. Disturbances of cultural memory—screen memories, false recognitions, premonitions—also raise terminological difficulties: strictly speaking, déjà vu is neither a failure of memory nor a form of forgetting. While the humanities tend to celebrate cultural memory and warn against forgetting, often relegating it to a necessary dialectical counterpart, déjà vu figures as a reserve: it is a kind of memory without memory, a kind of forgetting without forgetting.

It may seem obvious for cultural historians to prize memory and to abhor forgetting; holocaust studies and trauma studies heavily emphasize the imperatives of memorial culture. But by the same token, mass media are associated with a detrimental forgetfulness, which they supposedly both exemplify and cause.[6] "Critics routinely deplore the entropy of historical memory," as Andreas Huyssen observes, "defining amnesia as a dangerous cultural virus generated by the new media technologies."[7] For while they make unprecedented forms of storage and access possible, the resulting mega-archive is figured either as fulfillment of ancient fantasies of complete presence, or as the total erasure of all critical criteria. Walter Benjamin supplemented the Hegelian distinction between memory *(Gedächtnis)* and recollection *(Erinnerung)* with a ritualized memorialization *(Eingedenken)*. Yet we seem to have forgotten how to differentiate different modes of forgetting. If cultural history accounted for media technology only by way of exclusion, it would lose track of the slips and accidents that are at their origin; inversely, if media studies ignored cultural history, it would indeed lead into oblivion. Psychoanalysis, although it is often repressed, is a common referent for historical cultural studies as for media studies. Beyond a simple opposition of unfailing memories versus monolithic forgetting, déjà vu allows us to retrieve for media studies a notion of the aberrations of memory, and for cultural history an ethics of forgetting.[8]

In raising critical awareness of the implications of hypostatized appeals against forgetting, Walter Benjamin's media theory of Modernity serves as our guide. If forgetting and memory, and everything in between, are best presented from the vantage point of a dialectic of attention and distraction, any appeal against forgetting is an attempt to dictate what people should think.[9] If I tell you not to forget something, I am really making an ill-concealed attempt to divert your attention from something—or inversely, to distract you from one thing and have you think what I want you to think about another. If we live in an attention economy, it is paramount to protect our freedom of decision on how attention is "paid" and to observe closely how manipulations of the parameters of memory aid a "culture" industry. At the same time, this critical watch is concerned with the perils and payoffs of forgetting.

Too often, forgetting is understood as a disarticulation of the present from the past, or of an intentional object from its field.[10] But if forgetting has a history, then not only as the suffering that is amnesia, Alzheimer's, or aphasia; nor is it simply reducible to an omission, or to uncertainty.[11] Although closely associated with disappearance, the fact is that forgetting returns time and again, and produces certain effects. From before Søren Kierkegaard to after the Frankfurt School, the relation between repetition and forgetting in Modernity is reformulated in all possible combinations: as each other's equivalence, cause, or effect.

To the extent that déjà vu is located in their neighborhood, it may help to circumscribe the scope of our study if we briefly visit the prime addresses. Kierkegaard understood repetition as the same movement as recollection, except in opposite directions: the latter is repetition backward and the former, "genuine" repetition, is recollected forward—and unless one sneaks out of life under the pretense of having forgotten something, one will live between these two poles. For Kierkegaard, forgetting only serves as an excuse—it prevents the commencement of repetition.[12] As such it is an excuse not to shoulder the burden of original sin, not to confront our anxiety.[13] But we must not excuse ourselves at the outset and back away from the task at hand. If these words will have obeyed the law of introduction, one expects comprehensive and comprehensible access to what follows, since it came first. By the same token, what is remembered at the outset also programs what will have followed, making promises and opening lines of investigation.[14] Such apparently paradoxical recall problematizes the bias inherent in our valorization of memory as stacked against forgetting. We tend to predicate learning, thought, and reasoning on the faculty of memory, but in fact we rely on the functions of forgetting: not only for the quantification of memory itself, which we gauge from the fading of recollections, but also for all adaptation to the new by way of loss or suppression of the old. Strict mnemonics of total recall would not only have us suffer the curse of a forgetting of forgetting, but also foil the deictic gesture of any introduction, whose function is to point to what is to come. The task of introduction, after all and before it all, is not to preempt but to indicate, in such a way that it will not appear as if we already knew it all along.

If writing bears the peril of forgetting, according to the duplicitous fable of its invention, this Platonic warning is also valid for the so-called new media. The common assumption is that old memories, habits, and friends tend to interfere with the acquisition and retention of new ones. The many memories and recollections are pitted against the one forgetting, which cannot be pluralized in turn.[15] How can such forgetting become readable? To parse what is hidden behind these presuppositions, consider two strong theories, one allied with Nietzsche, the other with historiography. Subsuming literature in the genealogy of media, Friedrich Kittler defines the truth of forgetting: "In forgetting the word forget, utterance and enunciation coincide. This vertiginous coincidence is truth."[16] However, if forgetting forgets itself in perfect unity of force and meaning, of saying and said, it is impossibly estranged from itself while thought as identical with itself—and when conceived nonidentically, forgetting coincides with itself and thus "covers" itself in more than one way. Harald Weinrich, as a traditional historian of literature, asserts that no definition of the word forgetting is necessary: "one knows always already what this word means and finds it the least forgettable."[17] This assertion, hardly less programmatic than Kittler's, opens Weinrich's account of a historical progression of what we always already knew: it will have been forgetting that inscribed itself at the beginning as unforgettable. But how to decipher its absolutely unprecedented anteriority?

If we considered understandable only what we already understand, we would have no resistance to what returns as familiar yet strange, and indeed much of popular culture symbolizes that loss of critical distance. Tame surprises, slightly confounded expectations, and mild interruptions are welcomed as the last vestiges of something happening. Presenting the story of déjà vu as something we already know would tautologically redouble the very structure we seek to investigate. The unforgettability of what we always already know, or believe to know, cannot simply present itself—it must remain deictic and thus never comes to itself, or else it should find itself already written, said, and known. The investigation of déjà vu can neither pivot around Kittler's coincidence nor around Weinrich's performative contradiction; here, the forgotten will never have taken place, while forgetting remains operative. Forgetting as forgetting cannot escape the self-application in which it loses itself, and therefore its phenomenality is a mere trace. A memory of forgetting remains, irreversibly, a paradoxical recovery: here the originary lapse only shows itself as a lapse into origins.[18] What remains is a screen memory.

It is clear that we will not shake off the defensive stance toward forgetting by simply, conversely, privileging it. Media studies and cultural history need to move beyond the premature identification of memory with culture and of forgetting with loss or regression, and above all, beyond the equation of simplicity with satisfaction. The stakes in both camps are complex and require an awareness of complexity; in déjà vu, both confront the impurity of a forgetting that fails to forget itself, a strange recollection that fails to recall itself. Both media studies and cultural history need to address the loss of critical distance that they see in each other without recognizing it in their own discourse. At stake is nothing less than a dialectical consciousness of culture under the conditions of media that may seem to arrest such critical development. Gianni Vattimo, for one, fears that in our media world, nothing can age anymore, since there is no distance from the past any longer: everything rides on a future history of culture that appears stillborn—and so the past continually returns.[19]

Nietzsche's doctrine of the eternal recurrence of the same is often read as an ethical imperative. In contrast with Kant's categorical imperative, which holds you accountable in every single action, in every moment, to everyone, Nietzsche's suggestion is less impersonal: many times again you shall nurse the same expectations and utter the same words. If the ideal behavior under the Kantian principle is to forget yourself, to forget your interest and your future—overcoming a philosophical loneliness for the sake of the law—then for the Nietzschean, eternal recurrence of the same affirms not the fading of memory, the instrumentalized forgetting of yourself, but a forgetting of forgetting the future of the self. Rather than universalize for others, Nietzsche universalizes the consequences of your action for yourself: there will never come a future moment for any one of your actions when you are not doing it. Once one has contemplated this, one is unlikely to forget it. If we formalize the impulse as a forgetting of forgetting, it is clearly not in the service of memory, nor a mere repression of forgetting. Nietzsche advocates an "active" forgetting that means neither loss nor subtraction but creative gain: forgetting is not instrumentalized in the name of the other—in the dizzying spiral of its doubling onto itself, as forgetting of forgetting, it is transvalued and yet remains elusive. Here, philosophical isolation is overcome by introducing the self to its own subterranean part—and it is not a question of protocol to say that it is unclear who should be addressed first.[20] While Nietzsche considered it possible to live happily almost without recollection, it is altogether impossible to live without forgetting.[21] Nietzsche's warning against a sleepless, incessant mastication in memory of history that puts life itself in peril provides the image that will indeed return in many guises in later theories of the complexity of memory and forgetting: to sleep, perchance to dream.

Presenting "Nietzsche's psychological achievements" in 1920, Ludwig Klages reads the doctrine of the eternal return of the same as neither mythical nor ethical structure, but as a form of déjà vu.[22] This is in stark contrast to common interpretations of Nietzsche.[23] Averse to the insistence on inaugural scenes and returns to them, Klages emphasizes the inaccessibility of the origin, stressing that Nietzsche thought of his doctrine not as an inauguration but as a turning point.[24] Believing in the secret, in the veiled or fetish character of the selection, Klages speculates on the difference between recognition and recollection.[25] Having identified self-deception as one of the fundamental themes in Nietzsche's work, he distinguishes between an easily explicable experience of a return and the inexplicable tremor one experiences when the temporal indication of a banal always already is replaced with a contraction of all time and all recollection to one infinite, but infinitely compressed moment. He points out that in his own experience of déjà vu, he not only felt as if he had seen it already, but also as if all time became at the same time immensely eternal and contracted in the moment.[26]

The contraction and inversion of distance and proximity is a striking structure that we will encounter again: in dissecting the kitsch of souvenirs and ruins, but more directly even in Benjamin (and Warhol) on the "aura." Thus Klages provides a link between the legacy of nineteenth-century discussions of déjà vu as "intellectual aura" and the use of "aura" as a concept by Walter Benjamin. This is not to say that Klages, as a contemporary of Freud, would allow us to skip directly from Nietzsche or the early French psychologists to Benjamin's media theory. For Benjamin's pivotal position for cultural history and media studies is that he juxtaposes insights from philosophy and psychoanalysis. In a book on the "secret history of eternal recurrence," Ned Lukacher claims that "German philosophy and psychoanalysis are 'guises' for the eternal recurrence of the doctrine of the same."[27] Is this double genitive a slip, or is it a reflective twist? Is this guise one for the doctrine of recurrence or for the recurrence of the doctrine? Or are they the same—and if so, what separates the two "doctrines of the same"? We will recognize their difference, if only with hindsight, in the fact that psychoanalysis acknowledges irrationality and its effects. Sandor Ferenczi analyzed the situation of a "supposedly bungled action," where the conviction of having forgotten something—like an umbrella—is objectively false, yet propels one to return and look for it, fully aware that this quest will have been futile.[28] As in Nietzsche's infamous note to himself, the umbrella is remembered only as already forgotten, and thus withdraws from recollection; consequently, the task would be to remember that the umbrella always remains forgotten.[29] Yet to remember this does not yet answer the question of déjà vu.

Although Augustine had already meditated on *falsae memoriae*, the specificity of déjà vu is only taken up in the last decades of the nineteenth century. No longer content to consider it a side effect of reincarnation, psychologists proposed the first sustained descriptions of certain aberrations in phenomena of perception and memory.[30] To describe errors of recollection and forgetting, the term "paramnesia" was introduced in 1874 by Emil Kraepelin.[31] He differentiated deceptive recollections (taking fantasy or dream events as genuine) from associative memory deceptions (e.g., meeting someone for the first time but feeling as if one had met before). Then, he separated the latter, identifying paramnesia from reduplicative paramnesia, where a new situation is experienced as the duplication of an earlier situation. Most of the correspondents taking up such aberrations of memory in the spirit of debate in the pages of the *Revue philosophique* agreed that youth and fatigue are conducive to such experiences, whether or not the uncanny familiarity is limited to a single sense. Distinguishing déjà vu from epilepsy and from what was then called "intellectual aura," they tended to consider the experiences of paramnesia either psychomotoric accidents or "dreamy states," in which escape from reality is combined with a sort of reality-test.[32] Spurious memories or fabrications in psychiatric disorders were considered as pointing toward dreams, but for epileptics, it was observed, déjà vu may persist for hours or even days and can give rise to delusional elaboration; other neurophysiological abnormalities were suggested, originating in a "temporal lobe" of the brain. Yet as it turned out, these complex forms of self-reflective memory loss, though related to brain functions, can be present without organic damage, and cannot be reduced to dementia. Their occurrence among organically healthy individuals rendered the pathologizing of déjà vu difficult; eventually, most inquiries concluded an origin in some partly forgotten memory, fantasy, or dream. Like dreams, which are universal and not pathological as such, déjà vu needs no cure, but allows access to structures of condensation, deformation, displacement, and their potentially pathogenic effects.

Studying the partial amnesia that manifests itself as linguistic disorder, Théodul Ribot, the founder of the *Revue philosophique*, proposed an inversely proportional relation of repetition and forgetting: those things that are most often repeated are the least likely to be forgotten.[33] This sounds obvious and yet soon turned out to be false; as responses documented, there are instances of "motivated forgetting" that call for a different interpretation. Jean Grasset insisted that anxiety is "an integral and necessary part" of the occurrence.[34] Interestingly, Grasset's text incorporates a letter to the author; his correspondent combines reading with self-analysis and then submits his thoughts on *déjà lu* and his anxiety of influence.[35] That this effect works over a distance, in reading, makes the exploration of motivated forgetting a case for media studies. While Grasset sought above all to distinguish his work sharply from interpretations of dream recollection, André Dromard tried to order the new field, not by differentiating between specific cases of *fausse reconnaissance*, paramnesia, déjà vu, *déjà vecu, déjà entendu*, and so forth, but in grouping them broadly into "intellectualist" and "impressionist" theories. Seeking to impress his own view upon his contemporaries, he points out that neither medical-physiological nor philosophical-mystical explanations account for an experience that seems to be "souvenir" and "prevision" at the same time. Where a certain memory and a certain anticipation overlap, the result is neither memory nor anticipation.[36]

When such theories gained popularity, it was no surprise that people suffering mental disorders would pick up on them in turn. Tensions arising from the déjà vu effect, such as a peculiar, estranged familiarity or blasé excitement, can be mimicked or imitated, as in a case discussed by Pierre Janet. A patient of a certain Dr. Arnaud claimed that every event in his life had happened a year before; Arnaud decided that his patient suffered not from disturbance of memory so much as from an obsession with the idea of déjà vu. In his discussion of this case, Janet held that neither dreams nor neurological disorders could be the cause for déjà vu, since the former seemed to him too insubstantial in their nocturnal or waking distortion of reality, and déjà vu also occurred in neurologically healthy people.[37] He decided instead that it was caused by a denial of the present.[38] In pathological cases, defensive stress reduction takes the form of a refuge from temporality, and in fatigued but sane people it appears as a recreative putting on hold of time for a while—usually the while of distraction and entertainment.

Henri Bergson had reservations about this view. To him, the conundrum seemed more a case of a "souvenir of the present," a recollection of what happens where the actual and the virtual overlap. Bergson claimed that since science had eliminated duration, his departure would be to focus on the immediate datum of consciousness.[39] Rejecting the localization of the past, as past, in the brain, he compared the organ to a central telephone switchboard that would connect to the past.[40] He distinguished between memory formed by habit and a memory of unique events that are never repeated. The conditioning by frequent repetition is thus the ground for the appearance of the figure of the unrepeatable.[41] For Bergson, "philosophizing" consisted in inventing the habitual direction of thought, but many of his contemporaries were striving for a more scientific theory.[42] No longer content with ascribing the duplicity of memory to Mnemosyne, they tried to unite the efforts of philosophy and psychiatry.[43] As Michael Roth observes, "such public concerns with memory and with the investigation of it can be considered screens on which a culture projects its anxieties about repetition, change, representation, authenticity, and identity."[44] By the same token, the medicalization of the discourse on memory itself induced a certain amnesia, namely a blind spot to the discourse itself. This is as true today as it was then: Roth assumes a balance of "normality" between too much and too little forgetting, and that forgetting was only studied in order to learn more about memory—but the opposite is just as plausible, as Benjamin's reading of nineteenth-century France shows: memory and not forgetting was the disease of the nineteenth century, and involuntary memories or false recognitions offer some easily overlooked openings in its oppressively overdecorated, stuffy, musty architecture of thought.[45]

The confluence of theories from philosophy and psychology at the threshold of Modernity returns us to an ancient question: why can people act, or believe, against better knowledge? The ancient Greeks called our deficient self-control *akrasia*, translated as "weakness" or "incontinence." For Aristotle, self-control or *enkrateia* and weakness or *akrasia* are the extremes that delimit the characteristic state of most men: some will abide by their own will more and some less than the average man can.[46] Søren Kierkegaard's emendation of this thesis calls "willful ignorance" when you commit a breach of your rational will—it is the opposite of that "purity of the heart" that would allow consciousness to speak with one voice. Irrational acts and beliefs pose such a strong challenge that they give rise to strong border policies such as Kant's—imperatives of reason that are desirable politically, yet impossible intrapersonally.[47] Where reason's claim as the prime adaptive process is rendered questionable, even the most benign self-deception imperils the claim of rationality to be the central mechanism of human negotiations.[48] Philosophers are weary of supposing "that there are *sotto voce* unconscious murmurings, as if the mind were a chatterbox mercifully not listening to itself."[49] Yet only in taking the unification and consistency of my character and my actions as central to my notion of myself am I capable of the self-contradictions inherent in *akrasia* and self-deception.

The distinction between *akrasia* and self-deception is drawn sharply if we understand *akrasia* as a category of action, and self-deception as concerning beliefs. However, it is evident that self-deception can be nonpropositional and behavioral, just as *akrasia* need not manifest itself as an action: I can voluntarily perceive, decide, and intend in ways that go against my better knowledge without being deceived about it, or unconscious of it; and my conflictual predicament may be seen as self-deceived if I am acting out without being fully aware of the fact. One may say that self-deception blocks the rational movement for correction, while *akrasia* merely blocks rational intentions without necessarily precluding its own self-correction.[50] The former would then take the structure of a shifting blind spot caught in interminable hermeneutic suspicion, while the latter indicates that one may indeed uncover and solve the riddle of self-contradictory experience by way of analysis. Rationally, the imperative of reason cannot prescribe its own demise in consensus, yet in performative contradiction it must do so, which means that it is complicit with the coercion that forever prevents consensus from being strictly rational— which is to say that the practice of communication cannot adhere to Platonic or Kantian ideals.[51] If Aristotelian incontinence is due to a kind of forgetting, one distinguishes cases where the *akrates* has two conflicting pieces of information from cases where passion is set against will, as two conflicting desires.[52] Both types of conflicts, however, again reduce the argument to a mental cause and effect, in a rational model insufficient to account for the duplicity of the symptoms. *Akrasia* and self-deception help us delimit déjà vu as an operative concept, without falling into rational topographies of the psyche that never account for irrationality. But to be sure, déjà vu and its analogous paramnesiac symptoms are not simply akratic breaks.

Philosophical ideas on motivated irrationality do not yet account for déjà vu, but they may help to circumscribe what we mean by déjà vu. While one may indeed cover the other, they are not coextensive; we mention them here because they indirectly support our reconstruction of the history of déjà vu. Commentators speak of three types of *akrasia*: first, distraction, attention deficit, or lack of concentration are common, in the visual field as well as other fields of perception, as a defense against overstimulation; second, force of habit or automatism are widely regarded as normal, as inference in the somatic field; and third, the peer group exerts an influence, creating a common libidinal bond

that is a kind of suggestion.[53] All three angles on akratic behavior are easily recognized in our everyday lives, as well as in the products of media culture. These
three types of performative contradiction serve as background against which
one may profile a culture of déjà vu. Thus we will engage the dialectics of distraction and attention, the development of an aesthetics of surprise and habit,
and how déjà vu may elucidate the group psychology of our media society.

If it poses paradoxes for philosophical theories, the possibility of self-
deception is a stumbling block also for sociological theories of memory and
forgetting. In his attempt to formulate a collective memory, Maurice Halbwachs
presents recollection as a collective construction in the present of what is only
called, but not individually experienced as, the past. Moreover, this collective
frame of reference is not retrospective as in Freud's *Nachträglichkeit*, and not
an empty form for combining individual memories; Halbwachs argues that collective memory is a picture of the past that reflects the present sociopolitical
conditions.[54] If there are recollections that feel like hallucinations, then they
may not be reduced to a confusion with reality. Although he cuts this line of
thought off in his discussion of dreams, Halbwachs realizes that in the case of
déjà vu the same is not feasible. He calls it a pathological "exaltation of memory" and takes particular interest in the question of reversibility: if one can come
to a city and falsely feel as if one had seen it before, can one arrive somewhere
for the second time and feel as if one is altogether back in the past?[55] The fact
that curiosity and surprise are irrecoverable in this situation leads Halbwachs
to conclude that such confusion is only possible under conditions of great distraction. Indeed distraction will prove to be a crucial concept: as soon as some
attention is directed to the question, the small differences will be apparent; as
long as attention is diverted from small differences, one can be deceived.

Later, Halbwachs feels compelled to return the déjà vu to the question of
latent childhood recollections—as we will see, most of the theorists of déjà vu
modify at least once what they initially proposed. If there were latent traces
of childhood, they should return, Halbwachs argues, but he insists that they do
not return. While he will not dispute that déjà vu occurs, he concludes that all
such apparent returns are of the same class of phenomena as the paramnesia
one can observe in pathological cases. In order for the moment to recur in an
authentic way, it would be insufficient to forget what one has learned since; one
should also remember what one had in mind just before that past moment
recurred.[56] Halbwachs believed that our collective sense of identity stems from
the frequent repetition of a few scenes of recollection that are molded so as to
form a sense of self; in this constant repetition they lose their past shape and
content and become transformed to serve the present end.[57] Thus for Halbwachs,
true recollection can only be located in that recognition that does not proceed
automatically, while all paramnesia to him is of the order of automatic effects,

be they of familiarity or of its opposite. Thus true collective memory would be largely independent from the evident unreliability of individual recollection.[58] In short, what may be perceived as repetition in one's mind is not reproduced in the collective. Halbwachs formalizes the difference between memory and forgetting sociologically: a collective memory is the richer the more references intersect and cover each other in or on it. Yet this web of intersecting frames of references excludes forgetting, which is explained precisely as the disappearance from such convergences, that is to say, as a deformation of the collective frame of reference.[59] While the association of forgetting and deformation is certainly significant, as a determination it seems insufficient. Indeed it is the curious side effect of Halbwachs's theory that "lacunae in one's own recollection are filled with someone else's memories," as he writes.[60] This means, however, that the construct of collective memory itself is a form of paramnesia. For the sake of its purity, Halbwachs excludes the necessity, significance, and pathogenic role of forgetting.

The facts remain: déjà vu is not shared, and it cannot be remembered or repeated at will. It eludes recall, and at times it will produce false memories in turn. It will necessarily subvert a theory of collective memory, as it subverts ideals of rationality. Its unrepeatable repetition also poses a challenge to media technology. One may argue that the development of media technology is entirely in the service of capturing that which we cannot arrest without its aid. Again, if media technologies granted access to (and control over) repetition in an unprecedented way, they not only instigated the debate around déjà vu, they soon tried to harness the déjà vu effect, and indeed end up transforming the experience of déjà vu. Thus media technology accelerates a cultural déjà vu effect that complicates assumptions about our relation with the familiar. The possibility of time-axis manipulation corroborates that the déjà vu effect itself would be captured in mass media, whereby time has come to be considered as a resource under the conditions of an attention economy.[61] The conundrum of time is that its subjective experience differs from its objective measurement. Although science knows infinity, it does not know the absolute absence of time that would be eternity or timelessness. Yet involuntary recollection is a permanent or timeless possibility: it can occur at any moment without a given date or temporal index fixing its occurrence. Furthermore, the contents of this recollection return from latency as if in their original state, not aged or withered in proportion to the duration of their absence from consciousness. Thus Freud says that the unconscious is timeless.[62] Nietzsche and Freud introduced their systems of thought as lessons about the self that combine measurable time with that other time zone. To talk of déjà vu is to theorize the desire for a return to that Kodak moment just before something happened, since which it may seem as if we had known all along. Without reference to the genealogy of media, it is impossible to reconstruct what the state of affairs was until nineteenth-century technology affected cultural history.

Cultural historians who are disinclined to entertain the genealogy of media technology and its effects may insist that literature has known about déjà vu all along. Arguably, if fiction refers to a past that may never have been, then it shares certain traits with the unrepeatable repetition that is déjà vu. Yet this is not a study of fiction and repetition, and one cannot claim that literary history adequately explicates déjà vu. The saturations of media society can sometimes make it seem as if literature was a thing of the past, but the past is yet to come: if fiction may be described as an extended déjà vu effect, then reading is an exploration of a past that never was, or of a time that never will have been. This is not to suggest that literature runs counterclockwise, as it were, or opens onto a memory of the future.[63] It is a common assumption that the growing reach of teletechnology marks the end of literature, or at least that the ongoing digitalization of cultural memory tolls the death knell of literature. Yet literature's material indeterminacy arguably opens onto a horizon of anticipated disclosure that challenges common assumptions about the capacity and structure of memory itself. Memory is not simply the storage of data, and cultural difference and historical change in a media society are therefore not so much a matter of new media versus old as a challenge to the sheer capacity of storage; thus the question is how the function of memory itself is changed.[64] I. A. Richards wrote in his essay on literary memory, "the partial return of the context causes the system to behave as though conditions were present which are not, and this is what is essential to memory."[65] The always already troubled and troubling memory of the reader of literature may have to be bracketed out, instrumentalized as forgetting, as a corollary of trying to avoid the confusion between people and storage systems. As I. A. Richards demanded, "we have to escape from the crude assumption that the only way in which what is past can be repeated is by records being kept."[66] A mere archiving of archives displaces any particularity with meta-perspective. Of course allusions to déjà vu can be found in Shelley, for instance, or in Dickens.[67] But even where the experience is described as a universal feeling, as in David Copperfield's paramnesia *avant la lettre*, no explanation is ventured:

> We have all some experience of a feeling, that comes over us occasionally, of
> what we are saying and doing having been said and done before, in a remote
> time—of our having been surrounded, dim ages ago, by the same faces,
> objects, and circumstances—of our knowing perfectly what will be said next,
> as if we suddenly remembered it! I never had this mysterious impression
> more strongly in my life.[68]

Certainly it is insufficient to compile a list of fictional characters who revisit familiar locations, repeat actions, face a personal past, and then to claim that protagonists in novels by Charles Dickens or Thomas Hardy, for instance, experienced déjà vu.[69] Such claims are made for the fiction of George Eliot, Walter Pater, William Faulkner, William Burroughs, and John Barth.[70] We need only look at one or two examples of pre- or post-Freudian fiction to establish to what extent one may indeed speak of déjà vu in literature, and to what degree such texts themselves actually offer a sustained explanation for déjà vu. In 1853, Nathaniel Hawthorne arrived in England and immediately felt "as if I might have lived here a long while ago and had now come back because I retained pleasant recollections of it."[71] Approaching Oxford for the first time, he had a strange vision:

> Now—the place being without a parallel in England, and therefore necessarily beyond the experience of an American—it is somewhat remarkable that, while we stood gazing at the kitchen, I was haunted and perplexed by the idea that somewhere or other I had seen just this strange spectacle before. The height, the blackness, the dismal void, before my eyes, seemed as familiar as the decorous neatness of my grand-mother's kitchen; only, my unaccountable memory of the scene was lighted up with an image of lurid fires, blazing all round the dim interior circuit of the tower.[72]

The superimposition of a present view with an inexplicable sort of "memory" gives Hawthorne pause, and he registers this experience as exceptional:

> I had never before had so pernicious an attack, as I could but suppose it, of that odd state of mind wherein we fitfully and teasingly remember some previous scene or incident, of which the now passing appears to be but the echo and the reduplication.[73]

But Hawthorne soon finds an explanation with which he is satisfied: his impossible recollection was taken directly from his recent reading of a kitchen scene by Alexander Pope, where witches labor under the direction of a devil-chef. And he leaves it at that, without pondering how this impressionable kind of *déjà lu*, while offering a degree of "echo and reduplication," does not explain just why some reading leads to such paramnesia and some does not. Moreover, Hawthorne's account betrays no interest in motivation, whether conscious or unconscious.

After Freud, it is that angle that inevitably comes to the fore. As Shari Benstock has noted, there is a scene in James Joyce's *Ulysses* where Stephen, on 16 June 1904, reminisces about a pair of glasses he had broken "yesterday."[74] This apparently naturalistic detail should alert the reader's attention, in a scene where he is occupied with things past, such as the history lesson's riddle, *Hamlet*, and his mother's death: "Must get glasses. Broke them yesterday. Sixteen years. Distance." And indeed it is not the preceding day in *Ulysses*, but the day before Stephen's punishment in *A Portrait of the Artist as a Young Man* where we find the scuffle of school children that results in the broken glasses. There, we also read that this was an incident "he suffered time after time in memory"; once the "spectacles had been broken in three pieces," he received a punishment by Father Nolan, who proceeded to beat his hand.[75] The pain in the hand and the difficulty in lighting a cigarette while drunk bring back the memory of the broken glasses, effectively a scene from another book. Since there is no textual evidence elsewhere in *Ulysses* that Stephen had been wearing glasses, let alone broken them, this insight reframes a chapter that seemed thoroughly familiar to Joyceans.[76]

In both cases, we observe a trans-textual relation. The former shows an effect that may be familiar to voracious readers, but the latter preempts and incorporates that effect. Indeed the history of déjà vu effects is divided between the perception of an unsettling effect and the harnessing of such an effect. In retrospect, such an appropriation may seem self-evident, "as if we had always known," but there is in fact a decisive difference between the first perceptions of uncontrollable effects of uncanny recognition, and an age of marketing and advertising that seeks to *generate* such effects. Yet before as well as after that watershed, memory and foreknowledge of all sorts affect the temporal mode of reading, whether we read a text that mentions the occasional uncanny experience or a text that sets out to mine the possibilities of such effects systematically.[77] In *S/Z*, Roland Barthes goes so far as to claim that, faced with the impure communication or "intentional cacophony" that is literature, one must accept "the freedom of reading the text as if it had already been read"—and he goes further in asserting that faced with the plural text, there is no such thing as forgetting its meaning. Indeed Barthes believes that one truly reads only in such quasi forgetting.[78] Reading would be a certain kind of constructively modified forgetting; inversely, it might mean that one only reads *as if* one had already read.

Havelock Ellis was perhaps more acutely aware than any of his contemporaries that the "reverse hallucination" of the *déjà lu* effect can also extend to scientific exchange.[79] Ellis is the rare early ally of Freud who is neither banished into Freud's footnotes as a rival nor dismissed like others as prescientific.[80] Agreeing with Freud on the importance of dreams, he indicates that "the false memory is an unrecognized true memory." Although the tradition of mnemotechnics held that your memory becomes more capable the more you exercise it, Freud claims that in youth one's memory has more capacity since it is less fraught than in later years.[81] It is important to note that speaking of contemporary media conditions, we do not mean technology causing stimulation overload while presenting itself as an aid to memory. The modifications of memory and forgetting Freud focuses on, in the *Interpretation of Dreams* and elsewhere, are not remembered: "memories—not excepting those which are most deeply stamped upon our minds—are in themselves unconscious. They can be made conscious; but there can be no doubt that they can produce all their effects while in an unconscious condition."[82] And consciousness, as he later added, arises instead of the memory-trace. Ever since he discerned that "hysterics suffer mainly from reminiscences," he could surmise that what is forgotten is recalled in acts.[83] If Nietzsche's intervention in the history of forgetting is that you are held responsible for your forgetting, then the unconscious is the memory of that which it forgets.[84]

In the course of the following chapters, we extract individual and collective déjà vu effects as they disrupt the cultural memory of literature, art, entertainment, and new media. Following Freud along his triple markers of the unconscious, of inhibited or exhibited intent, and of the modification of forgetting that takes place in the face of psychic blockage, we will investigate a trajectory that accounts for phenomena of divided attention or distraction, for resistances and libidinal attachments, as well as for the suggestions of peer pressure. The therapeutic set-up provides a model for the secret without secret, a reserve shared and spilled at the same time. If earlier theories on mnemopathology yield a pre-Freudian logic of the cover-up, then we follow a revaluation of forgetting in reading Freud.[85] Taking cues from various readings of Freud's texts on déjà vu, we will pay particular attention to the language of the cure with regard to the future of the subject and the history of the symptom. One of Jean-Paul Sartre's criticisms of Freud was that for all its anamnetic practice, Freud's psychoanalysis lacked a dimension of the future. This led him to construct an inverted psychoanalysis in *L'Etre et le Neant*, one that would instead work toward the future. But if one had one's posterity in the past, like Sartre, does this inversion not take us toward the symptom? Is it not Sartre's future that he is history? Indicated here is not just a reversal of fortunes, but the possibility of engaging a reversal of irreversibility.[86]

The technical achievements of mass media and their potential for warping and folding time raise the issue of attention and distraction. Spanning more than a century from the first discussions of psychopathology in the late nineteenth century to the present, the déjà vu effect is intricately related to the mass media. If the recurring structures of the cover-up or the secret punctuate all technologies, then the secret effect of the secret, the dynamics of spilling or keeping it, must ground our investigation in the intransparency of social intercourse as it guided Freud. What psychoanalysis describes as "knowledge without knowledge" provides an account of déjà vu as a memory without memory (or a forgetting without forgetting); after World War I, the discussion turns to shock and distraction. Walter Benjamin's media theory is one part Freud-reception and one part resistance to psychoanalysis.[87] Reconstructing the Benjaminian inversion of déjà vu, we analyze his writings on hiding, and on the distracted attention that betrays an anxiousness harking back to the founding myths of mnemotechnology.

What Heiner Müller shares with Walter Benjamin is a disengagement from a ruinous culture of the souvenir, the essence of which is an appeal to memory over and against forgetting (and thus already mired in forgetting).[88] Even when thought is most invested in hope, forgetting is not the opposite of memory or recollection, but rather the mode of deficiency in the order of memory that Ernst Bloch calls a leaving, a betrayal, a lack of faith.[89] Cultural memory revolves around the mourning work that gives rise to mnemotechnology—whether as rhetorical *ars memoriae* and its architectural metaphors, or as mourning the dead and commemorating them with monuments. Heiner Müller demonstrates how the fidelity without fidelity of déjà vu is embedded in the foundation of every war memorial. Heiner Müller's reading of Brecht's alienation effects and his portrait of depersonalized labor offers a highly charged political commentary on the times in Germany, and he demonstrates how the crisis of political representation is a crisis of the conditions of observing political actors under the conditions of mass media. By becoming audible and visible to a virtually unlimited audience, politicians find themselves in the same situation as actors on stage, as radio, cinema, and television transform what is not by accident called "political theater."

Under the conditions of media technology, the past effects that art forms labored toward are more easily achieved, and thus transform the group or mass perception and expectation of the media in turn. Alienation and depersonalization are taken one step further in reading Andy Warhol. The actors in Warhol's cinema, as in the texts produced in his factory, are no longer actors. They are merely *acting out*—in all their iconic glamour, they are reduced to special effects of silk screens, celluloid, or the page. If acting is put to the test of drawing spectators, then film, as Walter Benjamin wrote, exposes the test by turning the exposure of acting itself into a test.[90] Since the actor no longer acts in front of the audience but in front of the machine, the entire apparatus of cinematic labor, the test captures and holds the interest of an audience precisely by virtue of an inversion: while in their work day, they are alienated and dehumanized in front of the machine, now they gather to see one of them maintain a certain humanity—or what passes for it on the screen—with the aid of the machine. Thus an actress does not represent the other on the wall of projection so much as herself within the apparatus. It is the effect of cinema,

Benjamin continues, that the spectator becomes a kind of instant expert.[91] By the same token, every member of the audience may also take the place of the one who is seen. It is possible for anyone to appear in the media—here Benjamin preempts both McLuhan and Warhol in formulating as a general demand that everyone be filmed.[92] Artistic production in the twentieth century is traversed by "time warps" made possible by technical innovation, resulting in infinite loops that extend Warhol's famous fifteen minutes.

As Benjamin knew, it is important to distinguish between nostalgia for what is irreversibly past, and the recall of the irrevocable.[93] If the aestheticization of the past appears as kitsch, the history of cinema offers a different return to that rupture of perception that media technology caused and still represents. Certain conventions of mass media, specifically the treatment of violence and weather, offer access to what is made forgotten in the unforgiving medium of film. Thus cinema can throw into relief the disturbances of cultural memory between fiction, or a past that never was, and the instant replay of "breaking news," or an immediate present that will never have been immediate or present. To screen-test certain exaggerated claims about cutting and shooting in film, we read a movie—a Western that yields access to the history of the medium and its genres. The impossible scene of forgiveness, from its monotheistic origins to the cinema of the Western, marks a break in the linear progress of time. The particular blend of recall and forgetting that is essential to forgiveness exposes and undoes the constant ideological efforts to elide or overcome the multiple modifications of forgetting.[94] This overlap is substantiated as déjà vu effect in television and film in general, and in the Hollywood parable of Clint Eastwood's *Unforgiven* in particular. Stanley Cavell speculated that "psychoanalysis and cinema share an origin as responses to the suffering of women," and the allegation behind this analogy is that they both offer "counterfeit happiness."[95] But Eastwood's *Unforgiven* is no comedy of marriage—here, all women but one are prostitutes, the lone wife turns into a widow halfway into the movie, and the protagonist is himself a widower who tries to protect the fragile memory of his wife from a more vicious recall. The medium of film, after Benjamin, is a violent sequence of cuts, breaks, and blackouts, captivating the attention of audiences to such an extent that such basics are screened over. Rather than organizing our reading around the phallicized gaze that film theory tends to privilege, we will bring into focus certain screen memories that project the cinematic spectacle back onto itself. "The concealment cast around the new improved Freud," as Laurence Rickels warns, must be taken into account: while it is neither possible nor perhaps desirable for us to unveil, in a grand gesture, what is behind such a screening over, it is precisely the screen effect that pulls the argument together.[96] A look behind the mirror-stages of film theory is needed if we are to avoid merely reflecting the already-thought and the always-written.

A critique of the monumentalization of memory needs to open the mediatic field of divided attention, of doubling and copying effects to a rigorous reading of parapraxis as it has informed notions of the subject since Aristotle's critique of Plato under the sign of *akrasia*.[97] Our mass media society certainly knows all three types of akratic behavior: symptoms of distraction or divided attention are reinforced and accelerated; more than ever, habits and automatisms put up a steadily undermined somatic resistance against stimulation; and our peer groups exert influence by way of suggestion and libidinal attachment. Nietzsche already described a trajectory of self-deception, resistance, and control: from an authentic self weakened by contaminations of its self-determination, to the strengthening of the self through resistance against suggestion and peer pressure, to the dialectics of attention and distraction. "Distraction as provided by art presents a covert control," in Walter Benjamin's formula, "of the extent to which new tasks have become soluble by apperception."[98] This inversion indicates that déjà vu is not just an envelope of false recollection, but by logical extension an opening toward the future: if I have been in this situation, I might know what will happen next. As the hyperbolic reception of the Internet demonstrates, historical displacement of earlier interpretations by more recent ones is no simple forgetting. In turn, even a scholarly account of the history of déjà vu will never exhaustively recall, or bring to full consciousness, the entirety of what it ultimately seeks to supplement or replace. In virtual memory—and it has been written that this "was what Benjamin was all about"[99]—we recognize an accelerated culture of déjà vu, as the technologies of storage and archiving multiply in our digital age.

Oscillating between the two extremes of what one might call a process of translation (since what is completely untranslatable into new media will disappear as fast as what is utterly translatable), the Internet may denote scientific progress, but can equally well bode ill for the project of knowledge. Thus the quest for discovery goes along with a desire not to know always already, not to presume too hastily, although horizons of expectation and anticipation certainly help staking a claim. The inversion of this structure in a memory of the future, redesigning the past, reinscribing this uprooted hierarchy differently, will have to avoid revisionism as well as simple identifications with futurist or existentialist modes of speculation. Nevertheless, such an inversion can be recognized in our accelerated mediascape. While some identify the purported novelty of the "new media" with ancient ideas come into their own, at last, there are others to whom the new media spell the end of the canon, of reading and authority, of meaning and coherence—the end, no less, of culture. Electronic media in particular are interpreted either as instruments of forgetting, or as a means of return to the very old—as when the Internet is seen as the implementation of Hegelian *Geist*. Harking back to the mummy effect of Simonides, cultural mnemotechnology is constantly rebuilt on survival and mourning—and their cover-up. Analytic considerations of such double effects must go beyond metaphors of accumulation, annotation, or correction versus loss, dispersal, or oblivion. Arguably, déjà vu is a challenge not to the capacity of cultural memory, but to the very function of cultural memory that takes a double turn. Suspended between live feed and archival mortification, Benjamin's unlucky angel once again faces a heap of rubble—a falling wall of books, piling higher and higher before him, while his back is turned to the wide screen that sucks him into a screaming senssurround.

SECRET AGENTS: SIGMUND FREUD IN RESERVE

It is as easy to deceive oneself without knowing as it is difficult
to deceive others without their noticing.
            —La Rochefoucauld, *Reflexions*

SIGMUND FREUD OFFERED some of the most influential explanations
of failures of memory or of incomplete forgetting, and his ideas have
entered the lexicon of popular consciousness as well as the dictionaries.
But his theories all but cover over the prepsychoanalytic explanations that had
been suggested earlier. And Freud developed several variations on his explanation of déjà vu. Thus for more than one reason, to read Freud closely means
not taking anything as read. We have to account for the degree to which some
of his thoughts may have become commonplace and thus tend to hide their
presuppositions, and we have to take account of the differences in his writing
on déjà vu. In so doing, we excavate both the complexity of the implications
of déjà vu for psychoanalysis and some first reactions to psychoanalytic explanations of déjà vu.

Is it impossible to define, at the outset, what the proper meaning of déjà vu
would be, organizing and subsuming all the variants? The *Chambers* dictionary
defines déjà vu as "a form of the memory disorder paramnesia," and looking

up paramnesia, one finds "a memory disorder in which words are remembered but not their proper meaning."[1] Déjà vu is commonly understood as an illusory feeling of having previously experienced a present situation, but also—more recently—as the impression of tedious familiarity, the correct feeling that something has been previously experienced. In Freudian terms, this fundamental splitting of the concept mirrors the split of consciousness that it is based on. Any attempts to clear up the contradictions inherent in the experience of déjà vu by flattening out a presumed temporal or spatial error of perception or judgment will run the risk of ignoring what is specific to the experience. On the other hand, the seductive self-application of such double vision can result in an inflationary sense of applicability—the déjà vu would become automatic, infinitely transferable, and recyclable; indeed, as Nicholas Royle reads it, it would be "a concept of the recyclable and a recyclable concept."[2] But in reading the historicity of déjà vu as a concept, we will resist this delimitation, precisely because the inversion effect of déjà vu will be repeated, with a difference, in other texts—neither in the sense of recycling Freud nor as Freud recycling the concept (as he found it, for instance, in Grasset). Without surrendering our critical project to an inextricable always already, cultural paramnesia requires a careful analysis that neither oversimplifies nor obfuscates. That the experience of the déjà vu is itself unrepeatable and irrecuperable does not preclude interpretations of its time-warpings. Thus to read after Freud entails an engagement with his concepts of deferral, repetition, and memory under the auspices of parapraxis and self-observation. These assumptions will guide our exploration of Freud's analysis of déjà vu, paying particular attention to the language of the cure with regard to the future of the subject and the history of the symptom.

Freud turns to the question of déjà vu several times. In 1901, "something is touched on which we have already experienced once before, only we cannot consciously remember it because it has never been conscious." In 1914, repression presents itself by way of screen memories. In 1919, without explicitly discussing déjà vu, Freud writes of the urge to return to the womb, the only place of which one can say with confidence, "I have been here before." And in 1936, déjà vu indicates a positive illusion of acceptance that is the inverse of derealization, which keeps something away.[3] Although Freud brackets the phenomena of paramnesia, screen memory, and déjà vu/*raconté*/*eprouvé*/etc. together, we will take a closer look at each of his texts and unfold their implications separately, in an attempt to present an exhaustive study of Freud on the entire class of phenomena known as déjà vu.

In his first published account of parapraxis (1898), Sigmund Freud discussed the "Psychical Mechanism of Forgetfulness" as parallel to what he calls "unconscious hiding"—and when he comes back to it to make it the opening chapter of *The Psychopathology of Everyday Life* published in 1901, he amplifies, but does not revise much.[4] The irritating two-pronged effect of forgetting, he points out, is that focusing, deliberate concentration, or heightened attention prove powerless, and that instead of the forgotten piece of information, another one "persists in coming back," as Freud puts it. Inversely, the therapeutic stance he recommends when faced with unconscious hiding on the part of the analysand is also suspended between forgetting and memory.[5] For the first problem in analysis would seem to be the detailed recollection of the patients' communication; Freud's technique is to "reject the use of any special expedient" or aide-memoire. His advice consists "simply in not directing one's notice to anything in particular," that is to say neither focused attention nor complete distraction, but maintaining what he calls "evenly-suspended attention." It should thus seem logical that to distract oneself from the task could help, that a diversion is even necessary. (Distraction is both a general requirement and an absolute limit to Freudian analysis, and self-analysis in particular; beyond the field of psychoanalysis proper, it influences media studies profoundly.) One might dwell distractedly on how it could be that, as Freud concludes on the topic of forgetfulness, "in my unconscious hiding of the thing the same intention had been operative as in my curiously modified act of forgetting."[6] Here, three notions require our careful scrutiny: the unconscious, intention, and a "modification" of forgetting. We will address them in reverse order, after Freud.

A year after the remarks on forgetting, Freud published an essay on the fragmentary early recollections some patients have, and in this discussion of childhood memories introduces the concept of "screen memories" for the first time.[7] Freud attributes "great pathogenic importance" to childhood, but notes that it is only after a certain age that psychical significance and retention are directly correlated. This sheds light not only on the surprise we feel at forgetting something important or remembering something insignificant, but also on the fundamental split that is so pivotal to Freud's work. Indeed, he writes in a note to the seminal studies on hysteria, "I have never managed to give a better description than this of the strange state of mind in which one knows and does not know a thing at the same time. It is clearly impossible to understand it unless one has been in such a state oneself."[8] The autobiographical tendency does not diminish the import of his position: in fact self-application is essential to the excavation of theoretical knowledge about dissociation on the semantic rather than the syntactic level. The analyst recognizes what the analysand does not recognize precisely because of a prior experience, and thus pays as much attention to his own as to the patient's psychic disposition.

A dozen years later, in "Remembering, Repeating and Working-Through," Freud returns to screen memories by way of forgetting: "When a patient talks about these 'forgotten' things he seldom fails to add: 'As a matter of fact I've always known it; only I've never thought of it.'"[9] Childhood amnesia, to which therapy attributes great importance, is in some cases "completely counter-balanced by screen memories." Although they constitute a resistance to analysis at first, these screen memories yield insight into what they do not quite recall. Inversely, there are fantasies, emotional impulses, and associations that induce a "memory" of something that was never conscious, thus could never have been "forgotten" or shut off; examples might be what Ferenczi called "supposedly bungled actions," where the conviction of having forgotten something—like an umbrella—is objectively false, yet propels one to return and look for it.[10] To Freud, it makes little difference regarding the course of "psychical events"—they all require the kind of "suspended attention" that is psychoanalysis.

Already we find ourselves entangled in paradoxical formulations. How can we assume, much less operate with, a distracted attention, and what is more, a duplicitous attention-distraction to and from oneself? How does knowing and not knowing oneself *at the very same time* complicate the notions of knowledge and self? Before we even get to gender, desire, object choice, and so forth, the concepts become unstable. Given the role recollection plays in psychoanalysis, its volatility must figure as elementary resistance; inversely, despite all tenden-cies toward discharge and displacement, there is always enough inhibition for coherent thought and "memory" to take place. Hence, Freud juxtaposes a desire not to know with a kind of prescience, the "conditions of imposability" in psy-choanalysis.[11] The paradox of not knowing yet while yet being prescient finds one of its most pronounced examples in the screen memory.

If Freud offers a theoretical apparatus for the study of the phenomena of cultural paramnesia, this also raises questions about the status of the "theoret-ical" vantage point that our analysis of the culture of déjà vu assumes when including Freud's writing among its objects.[12] This is not to surmise that in the final analysis, everybody will agree to disagree and all post-Freudian theories converge on dissension. On the contrary, the very mode of seeking to over-come and leave behind a theory has come to constitute the very figure of the "post" in its spatiotemporal sense, and each theoretical formation may gain a perspective on its own post-isms when confronted with the ineluctably spaced out, timed out, antithetical doubling that unfolds itself not as pure repetition, but as *Nachträglichkeit* and deferred effect in each field. Writing after Freud, therefore, must engage with this complication openly.

Displacement, repression, secondary revision—hindsight governs Freud's vocabulary, and yet what is brought out in analysis (founded on diversions from that which is always coming back) cannot obey a simple law of returns. If the interest in childhood memories consists in the assumption that "an unsus-pected wealth of meaning lies concealed behind their apparent innocence," then what constitutes such meaning, how is it concealed, and why, indeed, is it un-suspected? Can one seek what one does not know? The unsuspected wealth brought to light—to consciousness, that is—is another childhood memory that was covered up, screened over. But what is the veracity, the validity claim of the second kind of childhood memory, the one excavated by a string of associations and eliminations, reductions and inductions? "Now that you have raised the question," Freud's patient answers, "it seems to me almost a certainty that this childhood memory never occurred to me at all in my earlier years."[13] In other words, one may suspect, one fallacy is replaced by another. However, when the patient concludes "what I am dealing with is something that never happened at all but has been unjustifiably smuggled in among my childhood memories," Freud decides to "take up the defense of its genuineness."[14] In short, a screen memory is genuine to the extent that it presents not its own content as valuable, but the relation between it and some other memory that exists in repression. The screen memory is thus no mere counterfeit, but the temporal folding of two "memories": it represents as the memory of an earlier time data that in fact are connected to a later time, yet are transported back by virtue of a symbolic link. In concluding, Freud touches on the possibility that the relation between screen and screened can also be pushing forward instead of being regressive: "it is to be anticipated that screen memories will also be formed from residues of memories relating to later life as well."[15] If the uncovering of a repressed memory invariably presupposes the *falsified* memory we first become aware of (by no means a necessary presupposition), this not only raises the question of whether we "have" any childhood memories at all, but more specifically whether or not the structure of memory is in fact a relation to the past—and this question is anticipated, but not addressed in Freud's text.

Readers of Freud will notice, as the editors of the *Standard Edition* note, that the type of screen memory mainly considered in 1898 and 1899 disappears from later literature.[16] Freud's *anticipation* of an extension of the structure he described in such detail is taken up fifteen years later, in a very short study on "*Fausse Reconnaissance ('déjà raconté')* in Psycho-Analytic Treatment."[17] This text opens with a remarkable therapeutic setting: if a patient recounts a memory and adds, "But I have told you that already," the analyst may feel sure that this is not the case, but also knows that to contradict the analysand will only elicit energetic resistance. "To try to decide the dispute by shouting the patient down or by outvying would be a most unpsychological proceeding," Freud writes. So even if the analyst hears of this memory for the first time, one of the two must be in the wrong, and thus "the analyst will admit as much to the patient, will break off the argument, and will postpone a settlement of the point until some later occasion." This conscious disjunction warrants some attention. Although it may be the analyst who is the victim of *déjà raconté*, it is still the analyst who dominates the situation, if only by postponing the dispute, even in admitting this possibility. This break, one might feel, is hardly less coercive than "shouting the patient down." Freud makes a statistical argument, according to which sometimes the therapist may find some "far-fetched reason" that led to temporary forgetfulness—there is apparently no question here that memory will return. Conversely, "the great majority of cases" finds the patients in the wrong, and in their cases, the reasons are less far-fetched: they had the intention of telling, but were blocked and protest in futility until they can be "brought to recognize the fact" in the analytical practice. Among such cases, Freud then advances a few that he considers "of special theoretical interest." Of interest to him are not those phenomena where one assumes that something unavailable is validly remembered as unavailable, but rather those where in dealing with a false memory it is the analyst's task to discover "how this paramnesic error can have arisen." Excluding hypnosis, neuromotor problems, or religious assumptions about rebirth, the phenomenon can be reduced to *déjà raconté*, which Freud considers "completely analogous" to what he described earlier as déjà vu.

Thus *déjà raconté* is treated as undeniably symptomatic; here, denial does not impinge much on Freud's mnesic therapy. A skeptic may suspect that the "not infrequent" occurrence of this "completely analogous" confusion is the confusion of analogy. Despite Freud's argument, his analogy still amounts to an "effacement of the patient's experience." If denial simply served to buttress the point it is directed against, then how are we to interpret Freud's implicit use of the debate about paramnesia in dreams in the pages of the *Revue philosophique*, where Grasset first published his theory just before Freud wrote his earlier treatise on the topic, without ever mentioning it until his defensive return in 1914? Like Grasset, Freud incorporates a letter from a reader as evidence for *déjà lu*. Finally acknowledging Grasset, Freud insists: "I proposed an exactly similar explanation for this form of apparent paramnesia without mentioning Grasset's paper or knowing of its existence." This is surprising, since in a footnote in part VI G4 of the *Interpretation of Dreams*, Freud explicitly acknowledges the debate in the pages of the *Revue philosophique* where Grasset's theories first appeared.[18] To complicate matters even more, in his reference to the rewritten version (which found its way into the second edition of *The Psychopathology of Everyday Life* in 1907), Freud erroneously predates his first case history by three years.[19] Surely these slips of attention and memory are not completely insignificant. Is this Freud's own *déjà raconté*—and if so, may we analyze him here as he did?

Having decided that déjà vu is only the "name" for a "whole class of phenomena, such as *déjà entendu, déjà eprouvé* and *déjà senti*," Freud offers a case of *déjà lu* that demonstrates not the analogy, but the inverse of *déjà raconté*. It is based on written material provided by someone Freud does not know when he presents those notes of self-analysis, interspersed with minimal commentary, to the reader. The structure of protest in the analytic situation is taken a step further here: this person had read Freud's study of Leonardo da Vinci and was first "moved to internal dissent." This is no patient of Freud's, but a reader who feels an effect, *from afar*. Despite his dissent, the reader persists and finds himself amazed: "such amazement as one feels when one comes across a fact of an entirely novel character." Struck by this amazement, the reader then remembers something which makes him reevaluate not only his counterassertion to what he had read (prior to the effect the "novel fact" had had on him), but which in fact leads him, to his own surprise, to the realization "that the fact could not be by any means so novel as it had seemed." Once he has accepted this new light on himself, "another recollection occurred to me"—thus he is led, by reading, from a reconsideration of his resistance to Freud's claim that male children harbor a strong interest in their own genitals, to remembering his mother, who had died while he was still little. He had often tried, Freud's reader writes, to interpret the misdemeanor for which, in this childhood memory, his mother slaps him, after which he sees his little finger fall off. The letter closes: "It is only now, after reading your book, that I begin to have a suspicion of a simple and satisfying answer to the conundrum." This case not only impresses upon us the importance of reading, of reading closely, and perhaps most importantly of *reading on*, but also demonstrates the relation between the initial satisfaction of a simple answer and the value of subsequent suspicions. Before returning to the function of the surprise that folds into one event the effect of novelty and its unraveling as something so "old" that it seems primary and irreducible, we must turn to the paragraph Freud appends to his long citation from his correspondent. The last twist of the discussion with which Freud closes his treatment of the déjà vu is curious enough to quote it here in full:

> There is another kind of *fausse reconnaissance* which not infrequently
> makes its appearance at the close of a treatment, much to the physician's
> satisfaction. After he has succeeded in forcing the repressed event (whether it
> was real or of a psychical nature) upon the patient's acceptance in the teeth
> of all resistance, and has succeeded, as it were, in rehabilitating it—the
> patient may say: "Now I feel as though I had known it all the time." With
> this the work of the analysis has been completed.

The tone of this paragraph resounds with several surprises. Apart from the fact that surely the "physician's satisfaction" cannot signify the completion of psychoanalytic treatment, the point Freud made at the outset—deferring the validity claims and avoiding direct confrontation—seems to be completely renounced by this closure. Forcing an interpretation in the teeth of resistance will surely result in the build-up of another resistance, and thus "rehabilitating" the repressed event cannot possibly work in the teeth of *all* resistance, since it requires the collaboration with the analysand.[20] All qualifications notwith-standing, the moment when I say to myself, "I knew all along that X is Y" can count as the turning point of screen memory; beyond this characterization, though, definitions, let alone sincere accounts of the symptoms of screen mem-ory, still remain elusive. These phenomena occur at a hidden fold where for-getting and memory overlap, and perhaps to analyze them is to suppose an originary concealment that is already an effect, rather than a cause, and that shows itself only as that symptom—that effect—of concealment.

The last text in which Freud returns to the problem of déjà vu is a letter to Romain Rolland on the occasion of the latter's seventieth birthday, published in 1937. The declared double aim of this text is to pay homage to the younger friend's "love of the truth" and to offer something that would sum up "the aim of my scientific work," which, as Freud writes, was "to throw light upon unusual, abnormal or pathological manifestations of the mind" by boldly extending the findings of self-analysis to private practice and then "to the human race as a whole."[21] Indeed, in this late text, Freud refers to an episode he had alluded to, ten years earlier, in *The Future of an Illusion,* and arrives at a diagnostics of general culture—and yet he ends again by putting his analytic conclusions in reserve.[22] He recounts a trip to Greece, taken in the company of a brother who is of the same age as Rolland. Athens, it turns out, had not been their original destination; they were both in low spirits upon their arrival in Trieste and were dissuaded from taking a ferry to Corfu. In their ambivalence, they booked passage for Athens without really having discussed this change of plans with each other. Once Freud is in Athens, standing on the Acropolis, he catches himself thinking: "So all this really does exist, just as we learned at school!" Surprised at this notion, he feels "divided, far more sharply than was usually noticeable." Both parts of him are surprised, but for different reasons. One "person," as Freud writes, is surprised as if having to take cognizance of the existence of the Loch Ness monster. The other "person" is surprised that the existence of the Acropolis could ever have been in doubt—the foiled expecta-tion of an expression of delight or admiration.

Freud proceeds to analyze his split, reasoning that he may have thought he was convinced in school but unconsciously never really believed in the exis-tence of the Acropolis—and only when faced with it did he acquire a conviction that reached the unconscious. But he immediately repudiates this explanation, since it is exposed to theoretical reproach and "easier to assert than to prove." Instead, he surmises that the event must be connected to the dejectedness felt at Trieste. This state of mind, he reasons, already indicated that he was of two minds about this trip: it appeared too difficult actually to go see the Acropolis, and at the same time this seemingly insurmountable difficulty was depressing.

Thus Freud proceeds to search for the cause of his incredulity that might also have been the point of production of this split. Denial of a reality that is displeasing is not unexpected, but to disavow a reality that promises pleasure is a different case. In a swift move, Freud establishes the double effect of ascribing either to fate or to a severe super-ego the punitive withholding of that which is "too good to be true." It is significant that Freud does not write of déjà vu but only alludes to that untranslatably French phrase, while the mention of something "too good to be true" occurs twice, cited as an English phrase in the original German. The English citation holds the place of that French foreign body in the thought of psychoanalysis that Freud has already rewritten and repeated several times, only to return to it here, once more, in a different guise, twice repeated.

Freud then asks himself why the meaning of the surprising thought on the Acropolis would have appeared in "such a distorted and distorting disguise": namely, as a derealization. He recognizes a double displacement: a shift back into the past—school days—and a transposition from his relation to the Acropolis to the existence of the Acropolis. The tension of the thought and its splitting force arise from the fact that he remembers not doubting the existence of these ruins, or at least does not remember doubting their existence. The disbelief, he concludes, is not a past but a present one and only projected into the past. In fact, Freud relies on his memory to clear up the confusion that the incident had caused in memory. He concludes that within his scientific system of unusual, abnormal, or pathological manifestations of the mind, the derealization felt in Athens represents the negative counterpart of *fausse reconnaissance,* déjà vu, *déjà raconté,* etc., "illusions in which we seek to accept something as belonging to our ego." The derealization, by contrast, throws into relief pathologies of memory Freud lumps together in repudiating something "we are anxious to keep out of us." But at this point, Freud stops himself and issues an interdiction that will halt the sliding of analogies and positive-negative switches: "all of this is so obscure and has been so little mastered scientifically that I must refrain from talking about it any more to you." (A more accurate translation would be "I must forbid myself to expound it any further in front of you.")[23] Is this policing injunction the return of the punitive force whose workings have been exposed? Which one of the two personalities on the Acropolis is addressing whom?

After an advertising break for his daughter Anna Freud's forthcoming book on a related topic, Freud proceeds by putting the concept in reserve.[24] "It will be enough for my purposes" to return to general characteristics, he concludes his letter to Rolland. This turn away from pathology and toward theory requires our attention. A certain repression and subsequent reliance on the past—to shed light on disturbances and falsifications of memory—are established already, and it is also clear that a sense of guilt was attached to the imminent satisfaction: thus we have reason to scrutinize the bashful way Freud backpedals to the general concept of disavowal. All Freud indicates is that the brothers' father had not enjoyed any secondary education and was not well traveled; hence their incredulity upon finding themselves on the Acropolis, cathected with educational significance, had to give way to a "feeling of filial piety" that interfered with their learned enjoyment. In a final gesture of self-abasement, Freud ends with a hint that he must have known would provoke further speculation: the reason why this incident from more than three decades ago had recently recurred more frequently in his mind is that his own advanced age and infirmity increasingly kept him from traveling.

On the heels of the suspicion that the reader is witness to another disavowal (since Freud holds his thoughts in reserve), an alternative explanation is indicated here. Perhaps this is another kind of filial impulse, only indirectly towards the father, that divides the mind of the son. The Acropolis of course was the governing center of ancient Greece, and for Freud, the mother of Western culture. That is to say, it is the symbol of the autonomous state, of self-determination (*enkrateia*) and the power to maintain borders; it is also a maternal symbol.[25] The unsuspected shift to his daughter—"the child analyst"—might represent a bashful aversion from the sight of mother, and at the same time return him to childhood. Self-control falls into ruin at the forbidden sight—mother in the nude, up close, again and for the first time. We need not speculate whether or not Freud had literally seen his mother thus and was once again disavowing the sexual implications of this impression in his old age; his fondness for Greek antiquity and his collection of relics indicate some plausibility. This reading, alluding to Freud's fetish for Greek antiquity, in fact does not contradict the reading he offers; filial piety forbids him to go where the father should go, or could no longer go, and the thought recurs later when Freud himself is old and infirm.[26] But we are less concerned literally with his life, and more with the conceptual problem of a déjà vu that metaphorizes itself.

A simple psychoanalytical formula for the structure of déjà vu was offered by Otto Fenichel: "The ego does not want to be reminded of something that has been repressed, and the feeling of *déjà vu* consists of its being reminded of it against its will."[27] But we need to subject the simplicity of this explanation to a rigorous examination of its ramifications. Indeed one would assume that we tend to deceive ourselves when it is not pleasant to face the facts, but as Freud pointed out, it is equally plausible that we are able to convince ourselves of something unpleasant that is not true. This is probably not to be expected from a perfectly rational being, but is as possible as its opposite. Two further distinctions can be helpful. In terms of responsibility, we distinguish between delusions and self-deceptions: a deluded mind suffers no conflicting belief, whereas a self-deception implies a countervailing belief.[28] It is important to differentiate between make-believe, or pretense, and self-deception; the former is based on a suspension of disbelief, while the latter potentially affects a person's judgment. Superficially there may be nothing paradoxical about holding contradictory beliefs, yet when they commence to have contrary effects that tend to block one another, we are no longer able to dismiss the symptoms as consequences of being naive or careless. A screen memory is never founded on plain ignorance; rather, it consists in a covert operation: the superseding of one memory by another, but so that the latter is not erased or "forgotten." It continues to have an effect; one might say that the superseding cover-up in fact *is* that effect. This may not be entirely cleared up in Freud's late self-analysis, but it was the stated aim of his analyses of others.

Close analysis of the language of the talking cure offers one way to explore the resistance of linguistic material, whether offered in session, by correspondents, or in other texts. When the recognition of the cover-up is established through therapy, the analysand might comment that he or she feels as if having known it all along. Several possible interpretations of this scene hinge on the assumptions made about that speech act and its sincerity.[29] Is it perhaps just a new deception or a repetition of the same deception, and if so, who is deceived? Such an utterance may seem like a new ruse, a pretense, but in that case it could simply constitute an attempt to deceive the therapist. It might also be an attempt on the analysand's behalf to negotiate—half-aware—the earlier failure of realization, to cover up the previous state, to repress it instantly. The patient, in other words, may try to get the therapist to relent, or may be taken in by his or her own pretenses.[30] While we cannot exclude that possibility, we may still assume, for the sake of the argument, that the analysand sincerely feels "as if." Whether or not the analysand is or was deceived in the past or in the present, or behaves deceptively at one point or another, and whether or not this pivotal utterance is motivated by successful transference, as Freud would put it, or a ruse of any kind, all that remains undecidable at this point.

Yet it may not be completely impossible to formulate the structure of favoring one belief at the expense of its coexistent but contrary belief without blatant logical contradiction in both believing and not believing something—if we accept, on the basis of the above, that screen memories are not simply cases of self-deception. Whether or not analysands are honest to themselves or the therapist one cannot possibly determine from this vantage point. The transition between pretending to oneself and believing oneself is not merely a question of sincerity; suffice it to say that the possibility of contamination touched on above cannot be excluded.[31] This difficulty can be sidestepped if we assume, for a moment, that all speech acts are equally meaningful for the situation.

Surely the issue, for the sake of a discussion of screen memory, is not whether or not one can be, or has been, honest to oneself. Such an avowal would signify both in *what* is said and in *how* it is said that the speaker acknowledges the act of saying without distancing herself from it by the same token. In a word, it requires the identification with the stability of the statement—that is to say, with truth. Since psychoanalysis never claims to deal with unchanging truths, it is feasible to argue that any of the aforementioned possibilities is "sincere" in terms of psychoanalysis, in that they constitute and demonstrate successful transference.

If the analysand has indeed "learned" something from the encounter, or has come, or been brought, to the point where something happens and the utterance becomes possible, then the dilemma posed by the ruminations above poses itself in a different light. The identification with the statement—whether it was elicited by the therapist or arrived at on one's own, calculatedly disingenuous or in startled honesty—returns us to the paradox of a duplicity that operates in retrospect, without keeping two "selves" apart. One possibility to avoid blatant paradoxy would be the assumption that one never holds both beliefs at the very same time, but at different, that is to say successive, times. Another possibility seems to be the assumption that one belief occupies the mind while another is present in a latent state. Yet while both spatial and temporal deferral may appear to be apt descriptions of the phenomenon, they can both lead the discussion astray. The paradox remains, it is once again the very same person who held contradictory beliefs before therapy and now does again after therapy. If the analysis of therapeutic speech acts founders in this attempt to clear up the paradox, we should try to tackle the problem from another vantage point. How is it possible at all to hold contradictory beliefs in such a way that they fold on one another in the spatiotemporal paradox of déjà vu?

Let us draw some preliminary distinctions between screen memories and similar phenomena that also have their cultural effects. Without telling screen memories from what an analysis of the language (and the intra- as well as interpersonal implications) of symptomatic cultural phenomena will have given us to understand by lying, self-deception, or bad faith, we would be in peril of deceiving ourselves about our frame of reference. Consequently, we cannot simply change the terms of the riddle and call one of the two contradictory beliefs that make up the symptom Freud called screen memory a doubt, for instance, or a lie. Even though we cannot exclude the possibility that the analysand is lying, this question will be misleading; upon careful examination, even though the moment of "satisfaction" where Freud ends his account might be said to give the lie to the earlier protests, it seems unhelpful to equate contradiction with the lie. Such liars, it seems, would be their own first victims: the true hypocrite is the one who ceases to perceive his counterfeit, "the one who lies with sincerity."[32] However, this commonsensical assumption turns out to be just as paradoxical upon closer examination. For if "lying with sincerity" were possible, how to keep lying and sincerity apart? And what does the question of verification or falsification tell about screen memories?

If a self-deception covers a truth with a falsehood and a lie cloaks falsity in the appearance of truth, it is the specific trait of the screen memory that it adds at least one more layer. We hasten to admit that, of course, the lie also has a troubled relation to history.[33] Already in elaborate early modern discourses on *simulatio* and *dissimulatio*, the ways of feigning are multiple and irreducible to one structure, and these are exactly the symptoms of that which is cleft in such a way that unity comes to designate the impossible origin of confusion.[34] How could there be a true history of the lie? To ask this is to declare oneself unable to tell the whole truth about the lie, and to cast doubts on whether or not telling the whole truth about the investigation of the historicity of the lie is even possible.[35] Moreover, if we were prepared to entertain the analogy of *fausse mémoire*, self-deception, and lying, we should return to Augustine's distinction between belief and opinion.[36] We would have to distinguish the use of the lie in the interpersonal relationship from the liar's paradox and its self-application.[37] Such commonsensical distinctions notwithstanding, the Kantian invective against the lie is not translatable into the increasing contamination of truth in psychoanalysis.[38] As Adorno concurs, "the untruth of truth has a core which finds an avid response in the unconscious." However, access to this mode of response is shrouded in a rhetoric of exaggerated oppositions. Writing of a "conversion of all questions of truth into questions of power," which he sees attacking the very heart of the distinction between the true and the false, Adorno concludes that "only the absolute lie now has freedom to speak the truth."[39] But as soon as the lie is absolute, there can be no intralogical solution, in the psychoanalytic sense, of the problem of declared untruth. Guided by the structure of untruth as it shows itself in screen memory, we will sidestep a historicizing eschatology of the absolute lie and opt, for the purpose of this study, for the weaker concept of the cover. For in the final analysis, analogy cannot help to clarify the *temporal* conundrum of *fausse mémoire*. So we content ourselves with pointing out that lying and deceiving are not equivalent: deception involves an intention only to the extent of its effect, and it might be possible to deceive unintentionally. Lying, on the other hand, is a speech act where the intention is part of the meaning, and it remains a lie even if it is not believed by the addressee.[40] If you lie to me and I believe you, I am deceived; but if I do not believe the lie, I am not deceived. It follows, therefore, that we distinguish between self-deception and lying to oneself. In self-deception, I believe something although I know, on some level, that it is false, and no reply to the questions about sincerity one could ask can be satisfactory for settling the issue, regardless whether or not the self-deceptive belief is really held. Both positive and negative answers are possible, since self-deception is a conflict-state.[41] The necessary logical qualification of *believing and not believing* something is the introduction of levels of awareness—which is not yet psychoanalytical.[42] However, at no point does this vortex release an explanation of the specific difference between false memories and self-deception or lying. This is not to say that the would-be liar or potential self-deceiver cannot proceed from an original belief that is false. Rather, screen memories are not simply reducible to an error or a lie, because of the compression of two times in the moment of turnaround, of déjà vu, while both the error and the lie can be corrected with reference to time, to history. In other words, for errors and lies, verification or falsification become available at least with hindsight; matters are not so simple for déjà vu.

If we come to accept, after all this, that it is hard to think of a better explanation of these specific forms of irrationality and parapraxis than Freud's, it might be because his explanation proved superior. However, we will entertain one last doubt: we may still exhibit undue credulity, owing to the impact of his ideas that, acting like extensive screen memories in their turn, prevent one from remembering alternative theories or developing other solutions. Although Freud's *Introductory Lectures* drew a distinction between cases where both the operation and the existence of a wish are kept out of consciousness and cases where only their operation is covered up, the question will have been whether everything in a person's consciousness really proceeds rationally unless it is disturbed by an unconscious desire, as Freud seems to assume. In other words, the point of production of parapraxis and irrationality might be located outside unconsciousness. Methodically speaking, we cannot appear to be always already satisfied with the psychoanalytical account, for two reasons: it is, on the one hand, not merely a question of one point of production giving rise to multiple effects, but rather of the many locations from which effects can arise; and on the other hand, paramnesia is not something that starts or stops with psychoanalysis. Hence we seek to outline its distinctions from self-deception and bad faith; after looking at attempts by analytic philosophy to incorporate psychoanalysis, we turn to Sartre's attempt to update Freud.[43] This is necessary not only for testing déjà vu vis-à-vis its false friends, but particularly so that the interest, declared and undeclared, of our analyses may not be covered over by the logic of the cover-up inherent in any screen memory.

Let us return to the scene once more, for nothing has been said as yet about how we take Freud's curious statement about concluding analysis. If we assume he is aware, at the time of writing and editing his study, that what is at stake in psychoanalysis cannot be "the satisfaction of the analyst," then his presentation poses a problem. On the other hand, it could be that it is indeed the satisfaction of the analyst he wishes to foreground at this point. Why would that be plausible? Either he could be of the opinion, at the time of the exchange or later in representing the case, that the analysand is entering a new circle of error and inquiry—analysis interminable, effect without a pause. Or he might be "playing" the role of the analyst, "playing" with the case, precisely giving pause by pretending that it is the satisfaction of transference, after all, that is at the heart of analysis. Either way, this would pass off the object of analysis, the déjà vu, as the effect of analysis, which short-circuits the inquiry altogether. Therefore, it is more productive for us to assume that Freud did not hold that the satisfaction of the analyst was the driving force when he put this case study into writing. However that may be, we cannot completely dismiss the possibility, deeply unsettling as it is for the very readability of the scene, that Freud might have considered himself deceived in the text on screen memories that became part of the *Psychopathology of Everyday Life* when he came back to the question of *fausse mémoire* later, and that he committed this text to publication as supplement to the earlier one.[44] If this were the case, there is no reason to assume this could not have happened again *after* the publication of the essay on *fausse mémoire*. Nevertheless, faced with the unfathomable abyss of these considerations, we may decide that Freud's conclusion is most plausibly a remark intended to leave the question in suspension for reasons of method and presentation.[45] In fact it is this very suspension that, instead of arresting the scene, lends its energy to Freud's complex formula for the psychopathological slip that hides behind amnesia.

With the assumption of irony and possibly self-irony, we return to the "sincerity" of any such conclusion. We ought therefore to entertain the question whether the structure of screen memories corresponds with (or can be reduced to) what Jean-Paul Sartre called bad faith, in his attempt to update Freud. "Hiding a displeasing truth or presenting as truth a pleasing untruth," Sartre says, bad faith "has in appearance the structure of falsehood."[46] It may seem difficult to make ourselves believe something that we know to be false, but intend to trick ourselves into adopting as true, but Sartre intends to demonstrate that it occurs, and that it is undesirable. Sartre analyzes *mauvaise foi* in terms of the anguish humans experience when confronted with freedom. The burden of responsibility is too great, and we seek to evade it by tricking ourselves. Among the devices we use, such as irony, is above all what he calls bad faith, a pretending-to-ourselves that something is inevitable when it is in fact a matter of existential choice at any given time. Such bad faith shows itself in three temporal aspects. It expresses itself as an embeddedness in the past, and thus to live in the past means to refuse all past potential by treating it as something that never was actual—as if enclosed in amber. This results in the second aspect, a scattered present that is projected into the future; for the one who "is" in bad faith, the present is neither the result of past action nor the potential commencement of action that would decide the future. Therefore, it results also in a disengagement from the future as an end of action or decision, and is perceived as already determined.[47] What Freud had diagnosed as postponement, delay, deferral, displacement, and so forth is for Sartre an existential trap. Tomorrow is known as tomorrow but never lived. The belief that no experience of time allows access or involvement results in bad faith, in the denial of any correspondences between past, present, and future. "One puts oneself in bad faith as one goes to sleep and one is in bad faith when one dreams. Once this mode of being has been realized, it is as difficult to get out of it as to wake oneself up."[48] Since Sartre maintains that identity is not constitutive of human reality, the supposedly ineluctable choice will only show itself folded over in bad faith, as a concealed secret.[49]

If one were to agree at this point with Sartre, who points out that "there is a truth in the activities of the deceiver," but its meaning has yet to be uncovered by analysis, then self-analysis should pose a yet more acute problem, akin to Münchhausen's levitation by lifting himself by the hair. Insofar as analysis requires the mediation of another, detached observer who distrusts the analysand's intuitions and proceeds according to a set of assumptions about therapy, it places the one who wants to conduct a self-analysis in the same relation to the self as to the other, so that it might be possible for him or her to lie, or to be lied to, without lying to him- or herself; "psychoanalysis substitutes for the notion of bad faith the idea of a lie without a liar," Sartre deduces. Accordingly, he proceeds to force the analogy of self and other onto the structure of id and ego, only then to conflate that duality of deceiver and deceived in a dialectical move. Sartre's pivotal accusation against Freud is that of prizing apart the constituents of the psyche. Indeed the logic of the akratic, self-deceived subject must be applied to oneself first and foremost; the assumption of hegemony for partial observers could otherwise allow them to count each denial as further proof against the other as deceived about his or her self; such ideological and un-self-critical observers would never once assume that the other's denial might be self-reflexive, self-informed, and honest—in a word, that the person denying to be self-deceived or in bad faith indeed might not be self-deceived or in bad faith. Such an ideology of unilateral diagnosis would thus become a coercive method of intervention, imputing hidden intentions and lack of self-knowledge nobody could disprove.[50]

In short, Sartre's interventionist reading of Freud finds itself caught in the structure for which it tries to fault Freud. If bad faith makes one be what one is (in the mode of not being what one is), or not be what one is (in the mode of being what one is), then one finds simply no resistance to bad faith in positing sincerity, although it is still a necessary concept. "Affirming at once that

I am what I have been . . . and that I am not what I have been," living in bad
faith necessarily requires that one have a concept of sincerity, which Sartre calls
"the antithesis of bad faith" and an ideal impossible to achieve, since it is in
contradiction with the structure of consciousness. Sartre sought to continue
Nietzsche's preludes to a philosophy of the future by inverting old "truths"—
not in order to present their questionability, but rather their decidability, "as if
a second will had grown inside." Thus existential psychoanalysis criticizes Freud
not from the linguistic vantage point on sincerity as we explored above, but
from a philosophical one. "In order for bad faith to be possible, sincerity itself
must be in bad faith," Sartre writes, and then goes so far as to assert that "the
essential structure of sincerity does not differ from that of bad faith since the
sincere man constitutes himself as what he is in order not to be it." In other
words, sincerity as an effort to adhere to oneself is by the same token the way
one differs from oneself; thus, in sharp contradiction to Nietzsche's exhortation
to become who you are, for Sartre I am always already what I have to be.[51]

Furthermore, even if the resistance of the analysand presents a deeply
buried secret to the analyst, "its root in the very thing which the psychoanalyst
is trying to make clear," Sartre argues, it must still be known to the analysand,
for it is within his other psyche that it is hidden. Rejecting the Freudian split
subject, Sartre redefined the "censor" as an instance in the psyche that "in order
to apply its activity with discernment must know what it is repressing." For how
else could the repressed drive disguise itself, or hide from itself the repression
that it exacts? While Freud, according to Sartre, breaks up the conscious unity
of the psyche, Sartre's own concept of bad faith seeks to affirm the identity
of contradictory concepts while preserving their differences. As Sartre put it,
"I must know the truth very exactly in order to conceal it more carefully—and
this not at two different moments, which at a pinch would allow us to reestab-
lish a semblance of duality—but in the unitary structure of a single project."[52]
Such behavior, which he holds to be characteristic of humans as free conscious
beings, serves to show how nothingness is brought into the world as an essential feature of consciousness. The essentially nihilating freedom harbors the
potential rejection of any and every future; but then again, for existentialism
there is no given, nothing is known in advance, or predetermined—existence
precedes essence. On the one hand, I must discover what I have been, and what
my potentiality had already been before I started writing this; on the other
hand, nothing can compel me to follow the trajectory that a past might point
out for me.[53] The permanent possibility for abandoning this project is the very
condition, therefore, of proceeding with it. That split between action and reflection marks Sartre's definition of anguish as the reflective apprehension of freedom.[54] Bad faith, in turn, has two patterns: pretending to be inert, a thing, or
pretending to be whatever someone else may see in one.[55] But the reaction from

Freud's analysand, convinced, finally, of the existence of a screen memory, folds both patterns into the irreducible pattern of the screen memory: one covers the other, and the covering appears only in the privileging of the cover-up. What bad faith and screen memories have in common is a certain structure of self-application: "We must note in fact," Sartre admits, "that the project of *mauvaise foi* must itself be in *mauvaise foi*."[56] Hence, it is only in suppressing their duplicity that screen memories remain recognizable and yet indecipherable as such.

Skeptics will again raise the possibility of differentiating between holding a belief that runs contrary to one's general mind-set, and speaking one's mind or acting on the inner contradiction. To believe is to know that one believes, yet to know that one believes is no longer to believe—in other words, to believe is not to believe that one believes, and not to believe is in fact not to believe that one does not believe: this is what Nietzsche, copying Dostoyevsky, called the logic of atheism.[57] This second-level observation is both the path of and the resistance to analysis. As Nicholas Royle formulates, "déjà vu can only ever be a question of belief, but it is necessarily belief in quotation marks, in suspense, a suspension of the very subject of belief."[58] At this point it may be useful to distinguish between a certain automatism of consciousness and the act of volition behind speech, and to accord to the latter a higher degree of reflexivity and of defensive formation. Other cultural forms, surely, will be analogous. Since we all too quickly forget how we had to learn to walk and talk, we tend to take those skills for granted. Similarly, if the unconscious gets ahead of itself, as it were, to the extent of hiding from consciousness not only the defense but also the means of repression, trying to cover its traces, then how shall we account for this latter defensive maneuver of keeping from consciousness the initial defensive maneuver? To adopt such a covering of the cover is thus never to make the cover-up itself explicit, thus hiding the cover-up better than what is to be hidden by it in the first place. From the point of view of analytic philosophy, the predictable result of such an "automatically self-covering policy" must be that there will be "breaks" or gaps as one comes near the "hidden" area in question.[59] This echoes precisely Freud's complex formula for the psychopathological slip that hides behind amnesia: the reduplicating paramnesia and amnesia are in a complementary relation to one another. One will find few false memories where amnesia takes sway; but the other way around, Freud found that false memories can cover up the existence of amnesia at first sight.[60] This logic of the cover, or to be precise, of the cover-up of the cover, thus turns on itself.

How do concerns over sincerity, belief, deception, or bad faith open our discourse to its future dimension? The anticipated resolution of such complex observations may just be a matter of "therapy," a term derived from the ancient

Greek word for service. In *therapeia*, the craft of one person meets the needs of another person; what occurs is not so much a mode of production, but the realization of a use value in an object.[61] Such object relations therapy, therefore, is the beginning of specialization and of the division of labor: specific technical solutions serve one goal, not many.[62] Our contemporary understanding of the word derives from this use; its medical connotations of nurture and maintenance are present in the Greek root, although the notion of treatment surely has undergone historical transformations. Arguably, this service in which *téchne* is only an extension of natural poietic ability, a service that is interesting less for its form than for its application, differs from a production of meaning (as an invention of differences), which often characterizes analytic activity. Psychotherapy retains but covers its Greek roots in maintaining a clear distinction between the techniques of therapy and the theories of those techniques, as Freud writes "On Beginning the Treatment."[63] But when we invoke therapy, it is not simply to discuss techniques in their relative or isolated merit regarding the treatment of someone who experiences déjà vu. Rather, it is to alert the reader that technical issues are attendant from the outset. We flag the intricate connections between the history of technology and the history of therapy that accompany our readings throughout, between media studies and cultural history. Specialization, division of labor, object relations, therapy, and technique— and specifically, the latter two together—form a knot of anticipations readings try to unravel. Sigmund Freud's stipulations about "The Future Prospects of Psycho-Analytic Therapy" offer several clues as to how therapy, not theory, is the anticipated continuation of his work.[64]

Addressing an audience he presumes to be past an early "enthusiasm at the unexpected increase in our therapeutic achievements" and also past a "depression" about the remaining obstacles, Freud outlines prospective reinforcements. An increase in knowledge, from experience with patients, will permit a new division of labor between analyst and analysand: what used to be "inexorable and exhausting," because "the patient had to say everything himself," has changed by 1910: Freud states that "to-day things have a more friendly air." Although this friendlier atmosphere is the direct result of a shifting of the burden away from the analysand to the analyst, for Freud this shift to a treatment in "two parts—what the physician infers and tells the patient, and the patient's working-over of what he has heard" holds the promise of a less inexorable and exhausting treatment, precisely because it increases the scientific "authority" of the therapist. Increased experience and knowledge from past cases lead to specialization, and so analytic labor is divided in a decisive shift away from the analysand to the analyst, once he has overcome enthusiasm and depression about the treatment. Without forgetting the issue of a friendlier atmosphere in analysis, note the anticipatory nature of Freud's shift:

the mechanism of our assistance is easy to understand: we give the patient the anticipatory idea and then he finds the repressed unconscious idea in himself on the basis of its similarity to the anticipatory one.[65]

This *anticipation of anticipation*, therefore, is the new law in the practice; it puts the very urgency of technique to work in the analytic relation. This is not to dispute that Freud sought to establish analysis as radically different from a treatment by suggestion. Seeking neither to "prove" nor to "discredit" psychoanalysis, we merely attempt to pay exacting attention to its effects.

Furthermore, Freud sees as the dual aim of psychoanalysis "to save the physician effort and to give the patient the most unrestricted access to his unconscious." The patient, who no longer says everything himself, will be granted access to his own unconscious, and the analyst will be less "exhausted," since one can increasingly suggest the right structures; Freud indicates a turn away from symptoms to a general system of complexes as the future direction of therapy. This marks a return to the end of the *Interpretation of Dreams*, where Freud, although considering "unthinkable" the possibility of "supplying an awareness of the future," still opens a loophole by adding, as a qualification, that wish fulfillment in dreams represents a present future that is molded "into a perfect likeness of the past."[66] Among the anticipatory appeals Freud dreams up at the putative end of his own achievements is the direct advertisement that this *Interpretation of Dreams* as yet "awaits amplification" from other researchers.

The problems arising from transference and countertransference, moreover, will be addressed by stipulating that every analyst "shall begin his activity with a self-analysis and continually carry it deeper while he is making his observations on his patients."[67] This corollary to the creation of a friendlier air in the practice, Freud insists, will bolster the authority of the analyst. In pitting his own powers of suggestion—the anticipation of anticipation—against the waning suggestive powers of religion and social authority, the analyst seeks to enhance the credibility of therapeutic promise by countering "men's emotions and self-interest" with the power of the intellect, which is able to bring certain illusions to the light. Thus Freud bets on enlightenment in the face of resistance from emotions and self-interest, seeking to replace suspicion, on both sides, with knowledge. Instead of casting doubt on this stance with the easy benefit of historical hindsight, we raise the profile of resistances to what we will still call therapy. The future prospects of our explorations will also address what Freud raises as his third anticipation—that of a "general effect." What Freud calls the "general effect" is the translation of the desired therapeutic effect on the patient onto the entire society. The constellation Freud proposes "will appear strange to you too at first," he admits, "until you recognize in it something you have long been familiar with."[68] Ultimately, therefore, the very constellation of psychoanalysis is in fact the constellation of a déjà vu.

Freud compares its effect to the power that is broken as soon as you speak its secret name. One will do well to heed what light the history of the secret can shed on the general effect we seek to establish as an object of knowledge. To a degree, Freud's writing implicates itself in something scholarly texts customarily distance themselves from. While in the "earliest days," Freud had taken an "intellectualist view" and set "a high value on the patient's knowledge of what he had forgotten," therapy soon moved away from hasty disclosure of such "knowledge," since it might more likely than not lead to failure, denial, even simulated memory loss. Thus psychoanalysis came to recognize the "strange behavior of patients in being able to combine a conscious knowing with not knowing."[69] In short, even though the analyst may gain knowledge with experience, this is on the order of scientific interest and the systematic formulation of analytic principles; in the practice of therapy, it is always a matter of not knowing already. In his pivotal study on Freud, Samuel Weber expresses this innovative risk relating to the psychoanalytic object of knowledge in terms of the Kantian distinction between thought and knowledge. While knowledge must directly refer itself to an object, thought need not prove the existence of a corresponding object, as long as it avoids contradiction; this, however, implies a distinction within knowing itself.[70] This curious knowledge without knowledge is at the threshold of psychoanalysis, and from the *Studies on Hysteria* onward, Freud introduces a systematic exploration of how one can both know something and not know it at the same time. Once again we return to the awareness of a knowledge that one cannot or does not wish to acknowledge.[71] It is worth noting that Freud and his translators use the future perfect at this turn: "Disclosure of the secret will have attacked, at its most sensitive point, the 'aetiological equation' from which neuroses arise—it will have made the gain from the illness illusory."[72]

In his justification for the concept of the unconscious, Sigmund Freud posits it as necessary in two ways: primarily due to the observation that there are gaps in the data of consciousness that one has to account for in some way; and second, while the repressed "does not cover all that is unconscious," it is not erasing, but only keeping something from becoming conscious, for reasons to do with the limited capability of the mind and the limited tolerance of the internal censor. This topological model of secrecy within the human psyche hinges on the assumption (inferred "without any special reflection" from the fact of communication, of interpersonal relations) that we *cannot not* attribute our own constitution to everyone else. In other words, since we cannot possibly know the contents of another person's consciousness, we draw certain conclusions from their utterances and behavior, and to Freud, this inference is the sine qua non of understanding. Nevertheless, this does not mean that one could short-circuit analysis in telling someone what he or she is repressing, for it would make no difference to the analysand's mental condition: "all that we shall achieve at first will be a fresh rejection of the repressed idea," and in fact, the analysand will now harbor the conscious memory of the auditory trace of what the analyst said, which could cover the unconscious memory of what is being repressed.[73] Through performative utterance, patients may reasonably be expected by the analyst to externalize, objectify, or even exorcise what was restive but unobserved. But if the analyst—the one who is supposed to know—deflects this transferential expectation, with good reason, the distinction between what is said and what goes unsaid is again made in the same manner. Self-censure, silence, repression, or other symptomatic mechanisms of hiding pivot around the theoretical possibility that something remains unsaid. It need not be unspeakable to be that which I will not or cannot say; it may simply be what the other cannot hear. My secret is secret precisely because of the other; privacy and secrecy are born precisely of the separation established when someone is shut off from that truth.[74] The knowledge and the secret of the self derive each from the other. Their limitation is the mark of the other on the discourse of the subject.[75] This fundamental asymmetry characterizes the analytic situation.

Therapy requires patients to share conscious secrets with the analyst so that their unconscious secrets may ultimately be revealed; the contents of the secret are seen as related to secrecy itself, that is to say, they are considered either shameful or valuable: "a patient's decision in favour of secrecy already reveals a feature of his secret history."[76] The ambivalence between their expulsion and retention revolves around the basic structure of the secret, and the pressure it exerts is less due to possession and more due to the temptation to spill it, insofar as the moment of disclosure not only attracts attention but also offers intense relief in the sacrificing of ego defenses; by the same token, full disclosure would give away more than just the secret, insofar as it would dispense with the whole apparatus of secrecy altogether. In analytic practice, this can lead to two scenarios. On the one hand, there is the secret that is consciously retained and hidden from the analyst, but confided in a friend; Freud warns about this temptation and insists on confidentiality. On the other hand, he coyly alludes to the fact that if patients want to keep their treatment secret, "in consequence the world hears nothing of some of the most successful cures."[77] The latter scene repeats the strict division between the therapeutic and scientific interests of the analyst, while the former stresses the detrimental effect of a divided attention on behalf of the patient. This double distinction has several consequences for friendship and secrecy, some of which we will defer for subsequent chapters to address. Above all, one should not misunderstand any of this to mean that the analyst will occupy the place of a friend and confessor, despite the fact that the former scene revolves around a theory of friendship. Indeed to the many definitions of "friend" could be added, "the person to whom we tell all, with impunity." Nevertheless, the tidal pull of repressed memories may be even stronger than even the most dangerous and vigilantly guarded secret of which one is conscious.[78] The clandestine, transferential resistance to the analyst, then, is readily understood as a patient's repetition, via identification, of the secrecy of parental intercourse, for instance, which is brought to bear on the analysis in the mode of transferential retribution. On the other hand, though secrecy may endanger the process of analysis, the therapeutic task is to retain enough of the secret self, as Theodor Reik recommends, to remain independent, while becoming enough of a sharer of secrets to be capable of relating to others.[79] Therapy is thus an analysis of transference as well as of resistance. While the informed analysand, not unlike the good student, might strive to help things along by offering no resistance, trying to be as "intelligent" as possible at any one moment about the process, this is nothing but a resistance to resistance in the name of sublation or "intellectualization" and shies away from the encounter with the transference.[80] Conversely, a resistance one might call "stupid" is an integral part of working through, since it aids the analysis in more than one way.[81] Hence, fast and apparently "intelligent" appropriations of Freud's texts in an academic mode often fall short if they ignore the integral place of resistance in theory and analysis, and such hypocritical good faith is the spitting image of what Sartre calls bad faith.

It is striking that the questionable "physician's satisfaction," in the scene we are still not done reading, would consist exactly in the overpowering of all resistance, without reserve. This "success" of stoppage, coming "at the close of a treatment," therefore achieves just another cycle of symptom production instead of a solution—opening to compulsive repetition. Such bad faith about analyzing in good faith may or may not be originary, and the complications that repetition and duplicity necessitate are but open secrets. One may consider the interpretation of the analyst a secret until it is "given at the correct time," and then "the patient generally experiences the interpretation as if it were something he has known all along."[82] Positing an origin of the structure of secrecy in biblical fable, Ekstein and Caruth write of a post-Edenic capacity of secrecy that gives away that there is a secret: as Adam and Eve eat from the tree—although God had admonished in Genesis 2:17, "of the knowledge of good and evil you shall not eat"—they acquire not only the capacity to make distinctions, such as the one between their genders, which makes them ashamed of their nakedness, or the one between good and evil, which might have prevented them from transgressing the commandment, but also the ability to lie, and a limited capacity to distinguish between veracity and mendacity. As they hide in the Garden, their original sin brings on them and their kin to come the *punishment* that is the human predicament. It could be speculated that, like all traumatic events, this leaves us repeating the moment just before the impact of the trauma in order to cover the (shameful or valuable) secret, in order to make forgotten what had happened; telling a fable of the history of an error would cover the fact that the notion of truthfulness inherent in it is in fact a secondary confabulation.

There are those who declare or reveal, in analysis and elsewhere, that their secret is that they have no secret; the empty feeling expressed is a desire to be filled up, a demand for communion, and so the role of the analyst or interlocutor in these cases would be to restore the secret core to them, to help reconstitute the primary process. Suffice it to indicate just one major difficulty with the situation: to schizophrenics, speech can be an intrusion in the mode of an annihilating invasion and, at the same time, an isolation from inevitably separate objects. Silent communion can therefore become operative. The secret of the human condition, as Ekstein and Caruth describe it, is "to seek constantly for the object, *with and through whom* one regresses and restores oneself, while also seeking incessantly for independence *from* the object, *apart from whom* one can and must progress and fulfill oneself."[83] We may trace this duplicitous move as feed-back and feed-forward. The symptomatic screen memory, as a prototypical structure of the secret, contains both a forbidden impulse and the defense that keeps it hidden, in such a way that its concealment is simultaneously its revelation. After screen memories have been worked through, what will have been uncovered can be integrated in a nondefensive way, instead of being repressed or replaced by another screen memory—or so one might expect. But that would assume a linear progression, from the primal secret before individuation via the period of latency where the secrets are repressed, to a betrayal of secrets in adolescent acting out, and finally the (fiction of a) mature adult who neither requires nor hides secrets. Just as memory and forgetting are folding over in the structure of déjà vu where the unforgettable and the irrecoverable converge, it is questionable that we can follow such simple directions, and it could even be argued that such an expansion of the process in time would find itself ultimately caught in the spiraling repetitions of déjà vu once again.

In "The Splitting of the Ego in the Process of Defence," one of the last papers Freud worked on shortly before his death, published only posthumously, he offers a restatement of the facts presented in his two prior, incomplete attempts to write the definitive scientific description of psychoanalysis. He opens with the observation that he found himself "for a moment in the interesting position of not knowing whether what I have to say should be regarded as something long familiar and obvious or as something entirely new and puzzling."[84] Freud insists that the processes of the unconscious are timeless, neither ordered

nor altered by the process of time, and in fact without reference to time altogether, which is bound up with the reworking of the conscious system. Yet the
case of *fausse mémoire* comes to complicate this central tenet of his doctrine
of the unconscious forcefully. One may try to reduce the problem and state
that screen memory is in fact the byproduct of just this stripping bare of every
spatiotemporal reference, the remainder that drives the multiple mutual contradictions inherent in the process of analysis home with a vengeance. With
paramnesiac symptoms, the law of noncontradiction does not apply. Whatever
the conceptual contradictions inherent in the assumption of an unconscious, a
negotiation of intentions, and a positing of memory as pitted against forgetting,
there are the cultural effects that beg to be analyzed along the fault lines of
reduplicating paramnesia, by way of a reduction of reduction. The underlying
paradox from which none of the arguments of and around psychoanalysis can
be extricated is that the symptom can all too easily be turned into a concealed
memory, and thus apparently into a memory, but really into a form of oblivion; either way, we risk compromising our ability to diagnose its effects as
precisely suspended between recollection and forgetting, if we treated them as
coextensive or indistinct. We ought to beware of this effect—the risk of being
deceived "less by a secret than by the awareness that there is a secret," in Michel
Foucault's words.[85] Moreover, the necessary assumption of a divide—of an outside and an inside—breaks down if we see ourselves forced to think of them as
simultaneous in the common structure of lying to oneself, self-deception, and
screen memory. The same goes for the distinction, apparently so fundamental
to our media society, between the new and the old, when a surprise, felt as a
novelty, turns out to hark back to what is older than old. The intrusion of new
stimuli as we abolish more and more safety zones of perception has given rise
to a defensive mechanism that spaces out what cannot be temporalized, and
temporalizes what deforms and breaks down the space around us. The spacing
out of simultaneity thus goes hand in hand with a deferral of complexity; the
result is the projection into time or space: déjà vu.

The division of inside and outside goes hand in hand with the invention of
the secret self. It is the basis for any active distinction between that which is
said and that which is not said; of necessity, not only in the analytic situation,
we need to strike a balance, as it were, between spilling the secret and keeping
it. This division, however, can lead directly to an anxiety of performance, to a
blockage of the performative act that threatens to close communication down
before it is even established preliminarily. This bifurcation between keeping
and spilling the secret leads to a conflict of interests. On the one hand, society
is fascinated with every appearance of secrecy, and thus has an interest in
preserving secrets and proving discretion. On the other hand, the desire for
interpretation and explanation is strong enough to weaken the attraction of the

hidden, and of course the fascination with the secret stems in no small part from the thrill of finding out. Negotiating the conflicting desires for transparency and secrecy, revelation and concealment, explication and seduction, one may be tempted to take the easy way out and choose negation, the Freudian *Verneinung*, which would conceal or efface the symbolic split we do not want to acknowledge. That way, repression is denied, yet still manifests itself; a rationalist point of view, as we have seen, does not overcome all contradictions; attempts to exclude the psychic will not abolish feelings and desires; and a negation of the unconscious will simply mean a return to the old, unreconstructed self-interest by way of regression.[86]

An attempted literary application of Freud to depersonalization is offered by Arthur Schnitzler, whose affinity to psychoanalysis was acknowledged by Freud. In the play *Die Frau mit dem Dolche*, a young married woman called Pauline is on the brink of entering into an adulterous relationship with Leonhard. They meet in a museum, where Pauline intends to tell Leonhard that they cannot be lovers; she has confessed her temptation to her husband, and he has made arrangements for them to depart for Italy the next day. However, her mind begins to wander and she asks Leonhard which one of the Italian paintings around them she resembles; he picks one that shows a woman with a dagger. Momentarily, Pauline sinks into a kind of absent-minded daydream, and imagines herself, as the Italian woman Paola, having an affair with the young man, now called Lionardo. After one night of passion, they are discovered by her Italian husband, now called Remigio. Terrified of the consequences of her adultery, Paola kills her lover with a dagger and stands transfixed, just like the woman in the painting; the dream wraps up with her husband painting it. At this moment, Pauline comes out of her trance and realizes she has not declined her lover Leonhard's insistent temptation. Although she had come to the museum to decline, now she changes her mind and consents, resigned that her vision has preordained events for her. In short, she interprets the daydream as déjà vu in the future. Friedrich Kainz maintained that this is the core of the play: "*Die Frau mit dem Dolche* puts the psychological problem of *déjà vu* (of *fausse reconnaissance*) into the center of the dramatic plot."[87] Several decades later, Schnitzler studies still assent that the dream is explicable as déjà vu. However, there are good reasons to interpret the trance not as a dream that foreshadows subsequent events, but as a self-hypnosis, and indeed the tension is not alleviated by the fantasy, but merely brought to consciousness. Thus one may conclude that her trance, caused by the conflict between being faithful and being adulterous, results not in negating her desire, but in her abdicating her responsibility. If the subsequent events are preordained, she is inescapably compelled to follow in their steps. However, this is her fantasy, and unless we suppose the dream had been created by someone other than her, we cannot agree with her convenient self-interpretation. Since this is a piece of fiction, that may be literally true—Schnitzler created the dream for her; but again, what we said regarding fiction and déjà vu remains correct: while it may share traits with the symptom, it does not offer a sustained, intrinsic explanation.

Freud knew about observing oneself as if the actions belonged to someone else: "Psycho-analysis demands nothing more than that we should apply this process of inference to ourselves also—a proceeding to which, it is true, we are not constitutionally inclined."[88] Freud admits that "this process of inference, when applied to oneself in spite of internal opposition, does not, however, lead to the disclosure of an unconscious"—rather, it leads him logically to the assumption of the "existence of psychical acts which lack consciousness." This assertion does not only aim at establishing the existence of an unconscious, it also specifies the particular convenience Schnitzler's self-deceiving heroine allows herself, mixing wish fulfillment with depersonalization. Like most popular explorations of depersonalization, Schnitzler's writing falls short of a complete analysis of this connection. It is not a matter of a distraction from oneself, as in Pauline/Paola's daydream. Adaptation psychoanalysis in particular, as Laurence Rickels writes on the work of Owen Renick, portrayed "depersonalization (via analogy with Freud's notion of the 'screen memory') as a restriction of attention through hypercathexis of an unthreatening program."[89] Freud's early formulation of a "primary thought defense" consists in a withdrawal from preconscious disturbances. Owen Renick claimed that the symptom of derealization "protects against an action or a disorder of reality testing that would otherwise take place to the detriment of adaptation." The image of a limited quantity of attention, whereby one can withdraw from one perception by hypercathecting onto another, thus ultimately yields to another, similarly mechanical simile, which shows adaptation to reality as normal and distortion of reality as the aberration.

Close attention to the type of self-relation entered in depersonalization (observe yourself as if from a distance) will allow us to distinguish it from screen memory in the strict sense, because the latter does not so much alter your sense of reality as the possibility of being in contact with any reality, distorted or not. The unreal feeling of observing yourself as if from a distance is not just a hypercathexis of perception, but a judgment passed on yourself, a feeling of not only being not at one but acutely at odds with yourself. This enables you to appear on the screen of self-observation, and your increased leverage of judgment can increase powers of decision, once the hindering bind to a fixed sense of self-identical reality is being shed. Thus the self is mediated and mediatized; as Rickels comments, "recalling or fixing only on the gloss—'it was a dream,' 'it was this or that show'—lets one forget to say what can be recalled of the situation itself." While such depersonalization is less restrictive than the obverse defense strategy mentioned by Freud, that of isolation, depersonalization does not cover up the repressed: it produces an estrangement that serves to detract attention precisely from the *failure* of repression. If this structure shares symptoms with the structure of the screen memory, the latter may indeed be another alternative to depersonalization, besides isolation: the screen memory in the strict sense would be the recall of the present as a memory as well as a critical perception of its constructedness. None of this is to say that there is no pathogenic potential in heightened self-observation. The defensive mechanism can serve to construct a new stimulus in turn: "At bottom," as Rickels concludes, "one should reach in the course of analysis a memory in which looking away, while it had a defensive purpose, also permitted (like the fetishistic object) the partial gratification of a scopophilic impulse." As expounded at length in film theory, this divided attention to the screen (which finds its logic in analogy to fetishism) calls the audience into a relation to a ubiquitous screen that is both critically observant and distractedly deflecting.

Generalizing all types of aberrations of memory in conjunction with media saturation would not aid our careful scrutiny of cultural phenomena; on the contrary, a discerning typology fanning out from the spectrum of psychoanalytic observations can only be useful if it preserves all intrinsic differences. To recoup, if attention is not a limited quantity, distraction must be conceptualized other than as the simple addition or subtraction of it here and there. It is questionable whether adaptation to a reality perceived as stable is healthier, psychically, than an awareness of its group-psychological fabric and media construction. Consequently, we cannot pathologize the mediatized subject in portraying the complex reactions ranging from the mundane to the extreme cases of media junkies and supernerds. What Renick's argument tends to conflate under a general rubric of defense against unwelcome, preconscious contents—and what Rickels's reading points toward—is the potential opening of a spectrum of observations, from depersonalization and isolation to fetishism and screen memories, that can gainfully accompany cultural history and media studies when engaging failures of forgetting and aberrations of memory.

The duplicitous possibility of a mental distraction, a splitting of attention, could be one key to the symptoms of media society. According to Otto Pötzl, the "metapsychology of déjà vu" comprises two characteristics that are themselves nothing new: a trance-like experience of depersonalization and a defensive stance toward the new.[90] Something that "actually belongs to the future" is transported into the past in the same moment in which it is experienced. Unwittingly, Pötzl recounts the Dickensian "feeling of déjà vu" in Venice as his own, once again confirming that its effects extend into the personalized realm of reading (whether Freud or Dickens). In every paragraph of his essay, Pötzl repeats his assertion that all he has to say is already known. The experience of the new, he sums up, has its virtual reference in a projection into the past, the experience of which is only now complete—just as the writing of the article itself may simply be Pötzl's Freud, *déjà lu*. But Pötzl's article is remarkable for another reason, namely for the experiments with media technology he mentions in support of his view that screen memories are like superimposed slides in the mind. He recounts treatment of "traumatic hysteria" with the aid of slide projection, and relies on the visual unconscious to elicit further information from the patient's dreams, which in turn serve to elucidate the patient's "interrupted intentions" from a past that is not manipulated by the analyst's slide show. Finally, Pötzl finds the felicitous formula of an inverted perspective, where the projection of a "mental image" onto the canvas is momentarily interrupted, or barred; the déjà vu would be an "inversion of the perspective of consciousness." This inversion of the gaze, Pötzl speculates, owes itself to an antagonism that is analogous to the one between dream work and interpretation. This is indeed where Walter Benjamin will continue the discussion.

2

FUTURE INTERIOR: WALTER BENJAMIN'S ENVELOPE

Recollecting: a look into the past? Dreaming could be so
described, if it shows things past. But not recollecting; for even
if it showed us scenes with hallucinatory clarity, it only teaches
us that this is the past.
—Ludwig Wittgenstein, *Über Gewißheit*

"**D**EJA VU," WALTER BENJAMIN MUSES, "has been often described. Is the
designation felicitous at all?"[1] It is the tedious familiarity of the descriptions that raises his doubt as to whether the term is at all apposite for
the phenomenon. To him, déjà vu is not merely that which has already been
seen, or is falsely recognized as what has already been seen, it is something else
altogether. The secret of the experience is not the tedium of an unwelcome
familiarity of vision: one should speak instead of incidents, he recommends,
that come upon us like an echo of an event that has already passed. The echo of
a word, a thud, a rustle that has receded into the darkness of the past is the
"shock with which a moment enters our consciousness as already lived." Ascribing to such synesthetic impulses the power to transport us back into the cool
crypt of the past from which the present only reverberates as a faint echo,
Benjamin muses how curious it is that nobody has investigated the inverse phenomenon: "the shock with which a word gives us pause like a forgotten muff
in our room." Just as a forgotten muff would allow us to deduce the past visit

31

of a lady, there are words or pauses that permit, by analogy, the assumption of a visit from Lady Future, like an inverted echo.

This brief passage from the *Berlin Childhood around 1900*, one of only two where Walter Benjamin explicitly addresses déjà vu, telescopes crucial points whose importance for his thought we need to unpack. That a blanket term for tedious familiarity would itself soon become tediously familiar is hardly ironic, least of all to those who live in Yogi Berra's country: "it's déjà vu all over again!" But for Walter Benjamin, the core of the experience of déjà vu represents something that it tends to cover over: it can show itself as an inversion of assumptions about the perception of time and space. Such a flash of insight, irreducible to an error about the past, may point to a remnant of the future. This poignant insight, reverberating throughout a number of Benjamin's other writings, will organize our reading: déjà vu as an inversion of common assumptions about space and time will itself bring about an inversion of assumptions about déjà vu.

This double inversion in Benjamin's thought has been observed first by Peter Szondi, in what is still the best account by far of the clear contrast between *mémoire involontaire* and Benjamin's memory of the future, despite Benjamin's elective affinity with Proust.[2] While it is often assumed that Benjamin's declared addiction to Proust's writing put him wholly under the spell of the *Recherche*, Szondi locates the limits of that fascination, and demonstrates that Benjamin's own writing is not dictated by Proust, but is productive in its opposition.[3] The happiness of Marcel's remembrance is mixed with the terrifying recognition that he is not outside time, but subject to passing and oblivion himself. Thus he wishes to avoid the dangers of the future that lead to unavoidable death. For Proust, the pursuit of lost time is directed towards the past, only to escape the circle of time altogether in a kind of recuperation of the past that is the coincidence of past and present: the search for the lost time aims to lose time altogether. Benjamin, however, is invested not in an ahistorical perspective but in historical experience; he seeks the future in the past.[4] The places to which he returns bear the traits of that which is to come, "die Züge des Kommenden." If Proust listens for the echo of the past, Benjamin pricks up his ear for an echo of the future. Historical knowledge is gained from a past that is not fixed, but open toward the future, and Benjamin's time is not the perfect tense of three thousand pages, but the future perfect of a few short prose pieces. Admittedly, there is déjà vu also in Proust, but it is the kind of discomforting aberration that cannot open up toward a future, as it does for Benjamin in his metaphorical double formulation. Szondi does not compare the intention of the two writers, but explores the consequences of their closely related, but ultimately diametrically opposed directions. Proust idealizes the past as that zone that is preserved and does not change while it remains inaccessible. For Benjamin the future can only be recognized where it is already past, since the world, as he indicates in his study of modernism, is becoming increasingly technologized, which means a transformation of cultural memory, or "Nachweltuntergang." However, Szondi's commentary focuses exclusively on messianic hope. Although he recognizes Benjamin's inversion of déjà vu, as does Howard Stern, both commentators ignore the actual childhood anecdote and "Todesnachricht" that accompany the rumination on inverse echo.[5] And despite stating that déjà vu is in fact the principle underlying the *Berlin Childhood*, Christiaan Hart Nibbrig does not pursue the concept and its ramifications across the rest of Benjamin's writings.[6]

The short pieces of the *Berlin Childhood around 1900* introduce precursors or early forms of new technologies; at the same time, they reflect Benjamin's poignant insight regarding accelerated technologization: the effect of a new form that is not understood differently from the old will be déjà vu. His concept of technology is not as negative as Adorno's, but utopian; thus he criticizes not technologization itself, but the way in which it misses its utopian potential. Hence Benjamin reflects less on the latent destructive potential of contemporary technology than on the time it first opened up certain possibilities on the future horizon. Yet from the childhood of technology on, as it were, he observes a resistance against the immediate past as that which appears most outdated and invalidated, like yesterday's news:

> Images in the collective consciousness in which the new and the old
> intermingle correspond to the form of the new means of production that
> initially is still dominated by that of the old (Marx). These images are
> wishful images, and in them the collective seeks to sublate as well as to
> glorify the insufficiency of the social product as well as the deficiencies of
> the social order of production. Moreover, in these wishful images an
> insistence manifests itself to differentiate against the old—which means
> above all against the most recent.[7]

Denial of the most recent past takes the form of a screen memory. Because insight into the present conditions is barred and utopian perspectives are almost lost, futurity is only recognizable in the past. Benjamin's philosophy of history insists that the past comes with a temporal index that refers it to the future.[8] It may be worth noting that childhood played a role in Benjamin's writing since 1918, partly because of his disappointment with the youth movement, and partly because he set certain hopes in children's culture from that year onward. Childhood figures as a prefiguration or anticipation that is not nostalgic but as a concern that will be replayed and renewed in future reflections on the past.[9] Like the realization of the meaning of a childhood memory, futurity may lie hidden in latency for many years, only to present itself like a surprising gift; as Benjamin notes, "there is a preconscious knowledge of the past, and its production has the structure of awakening."[10] Knowledge of the past that is not yet conscious can still be unearthed, but it requires that one awaken to its potential.

Focusing on the motif of awakening that is found throughout the *Berlin Childhood*, we can corroborate what Szondi had not yet been able to cross-check in Benjamin's letters. Benjamin had read Freud since taking a seminar in Berlin in 1918, but we know from letters to Adorno that in 1935, he was looking for a "psychoanalysis of awakening."[11] Benjamin himself calls this interest in a transitional awareness a turn in his thinking, toward topography and memory. This turn is mentioned, staged, and discussed in several of Benjamin's recollections of his childhood, parents, schooldays, holidays, and visiting relatives.[12] "Like a mother who breastfeeds the newly born without waking it, life for a long time treats the still tender memory of childhood."[13] Whether it is in the park, in associations in front of the dark pantry, during a fever, or on a winter morning, every scene of the *Berlin Childhood* harbors premonitions of adult life: the awakening of sexual desire; the cruel fulfillment of a childhood wish to sleep in that results in unemployment; the realization that once one has learned to walk, one cannot repeat that experience. Unrepeatability of experience is directly linked to the technological crutches of memory; later, in an entry in the *Passagen-Werk*, Benjamin recalls: "Just as Proust begins his life story with awakening, so every account of history must begin with awakening, indeed it must not treat of anything else."[14] The task of writing would be to collect precisely those irrecuperable transitional moments that a progressive and constantly renewed technologization serves to repress industriously.

The short entry in the *Berlin Childhood around 1900* with which we began continues abruptly, and not insignificantly, with a childhood recollection—a story told by the father that is recognized by the child as a cover-up, the truth of which has to be retroactively added. This twist is often overlooked; while Szondi simply omits it, Howard Stern directly dismisses it. Yet in Benjamin's last version, the anecdote is all that is left, and the meditation on déjà vu is omitted.[15] The parental bedside apparition itself does not leave a deep impression on the child, who reasons that the father probably just wanted to say good night; he bores the child with details about the death of an older relative the child never knew, rambling in great detail about heart failure. With distracted alertness, the child hardly listens to the details of the father's story, but vows to commit the room and bed to memory "like a place of which one surmises that one day one has to return to it in order to retrieve something forgotten." Years later, this childhood suspicion is confirmed when it turns out that the cousin in question in fact died of syphilis—a fact that was studiously hidden behind rebarbative talk of heart failure when the very fact of his death hardly concerned the child. The effort to conceal something is so evident that the child has a premonition of the future secret that will have been covered over by a false childhood memory.[16]

Walter Benjamin assigns to the distracted memory of the present covering for the future the role of signal-splicing between historical continuity and interpretation: his déjà vu is the spaced out time of the fragment, a frozen moment, a synthetic reality of perception stretched and deformed by forces of distraction and displacement in a complex attention economy. A persistent focus on the role of close-ups of the forgettably small not only punctuates Benjamin's analyses of film and photography, but also emerges as organizing principle from the childhood vignettes of *Berlin Childhood around 1900*. The scenes explore the mutability of forms, spaces, and thresholds under the mimetic gaze of the child wrapped up in them. The section cited above, entitled "Todesnachricht," death notice, reflects on the notion of déjà vu as it shifts from the visual to the acoustic, an echo awakened by a call, "a sound heard somewhere in the darkness of past life," or indeed the silence of an omission. While sound "may be endowed with the magic power to transport us into the tomb of long ago," he then shifts his focus to the sudden reencounter with a word forgotten in our space by the future, as if it were a muff left behind by a lady visitor. This shift commands our attention, for no other commentary on déjà vu ever speculates about the weak force emanating from the possibility that a relic of the future has been left in the space of the present.

The shock of the new, the intrusion of ever new media stimuli that abolish more and more safety zones of perception, gives rise to defensive mechanisms that space out what cannot be temporalized and temporalize what penetrates, deforms, and breaks down the space we assume around us. The deferral of unmanageable simultaneity goes hand in hand with a deferral of spatial complexity; the effect is a projection into time or space, the splicing up of space-time. Thus the duplicitous possibility of a mental distraction, a splitting of attention, arguably becomes key to the symptoms of media society: "Distraction as provided by art presents a covert control," as Benjamin wrote, "of the extent to which new tasks have become soluble by apperception."[17] This inversion is analogous to the way in which déjà vu for Benjamin eventually pushes the envelope of *fausse mémoire* and, by extension, becomes an opening toward the future: if I have been in this situation, I might know what will happen next; there might be a clue left for me of what is yet to come. Indeed, it will be Benjamin's assertion that déjà vu turns from the pathological exception it is considered in everyday life into a magical capability. The clues soon multiply and proliferate: the secret tradition that runs alongside and partially under the cover of modernism and innovation (on which the fragmentation of collective experience is blamed) is recognizable in the mass-produced small objects that will occupy every nook and cranny of familial space after the turn of the century.

Benjamin's observations on kitsch (as a nineteenth-century idea surreptitiously entering twentieth-century thought) bring us to his second explicit reflection on déjà vu, in a short piece on folk art and kitsch. "Behind the back of what is called great art," he sees kitsch being handed down like contraband. Locating the difference between new art, demanding a reaction to the ever unfamiliar, and kitsch in its appeal to familiarity, in its simple appeal to "human response," Benjamin observes that folk art and kitsch elicit the feeling that "this same room and place and this moment and location of the sun must have occurred once before in one's life."[18] And so the seduction of kitsch is "like the feeling of wrapping oneself into an old coat," appealing to a sense that unconsciously experienced situations can be called up "in a flash" of insight. This flashlight into the darker realms of real or imaginary experience momentarily illuminates the allure of the hidden; it takes you back to a magical, childlike experience of space. Benjamin's list of associations covers primitive art, children's books, and folk song. Confronted with them, we "find our way into the situation as into a familiar one, comparing this moment with an earlier one." Whether or not that earlier moment that is evoked had actuality or not is irrelevant for the effect of these works and situations; what counts is that the "arsenal of masks" that can aid us in reliving unconscious experiences thus becomes accessible to the adult, as it once was to the child.

Benjamin argues that this experience of a return to this sense of space (a room and situation in a specific, always already familiar time) converts what had hitherto been considered a "pathological exception" into a veritable "magical capability." This is possible because déjà vu, according to Benjamin, is "something fundamentally different from the intellectual insight that a new situation is similar to an old one." "Closer," he adds, "would be to stipulate that fundamentally it is the old one, but that too is erroneous." At stake is thus not a rational repetition and recognition, but rather a different experience of space-time—"for the situation is not experienced as by an outsider: it has come over us, we have enveloped ourselves in it." The warped space that wraps around it has to surround and neutralize the intruder; but in its internal differentiation, the wrapper can also be wrapped in its turn, as Fredric Jameson would later concur with regard to postmodern architecture.[19] This inversion of the envelope is the generic effect of what one may call the architecture of déjà vu; both inversion and the envelope are called *Umschlag* in German, and here they converge, masking the banal, as Benjamin defined kitsch: "It comes down to the primal fact of the mask" that would allow us "to take the power of the extinguished thing-world into us."[20] At the same time, it releases the secret potentiality that lurks in each monument erected, that which is hidden in the appearance of the present.

The insistent latency of the hidden recurs in Benjamin's writing, no doubt harking back to his on-again, off-again engagement with Freud's negotiation of conscious and unconscious intent in terms of habit and resistance.[21] In their relation to forgetting and memory, habit and resistance are key to Benjamin's dialectics of attention and distraction. In a short character sketch, Benjamin offers the chiastic inversion of forgetting and memory in terms of habit and resistance: a certain unhappy, but very orderly person of his acquaintance is punctuality herself. She never forgets anything; everything in her life goes according to plan; time-space for her is a solid, monolithic volume; there is "not the slightest crevice where time could have gone another way."[22] But with an improved mood, the same person gets rid of his watch, makes a point of missing appointments, and becomes more and more messy in work and life, to the extent that nothing is achieved anymore; he forgets things and thoughts and people. However, everything takes a fortuitous turn for this hapless, absent-minded, forgetful character: friends who visit when he least thinks of them come at just the best of times, and his presents in turn, to which he seems to give little attention, strike their recipients like God's gifts. In this time of distraction, the acquaintance was doing visibly better than in the orderly, organized, unhappy phase of his life, although he "does little and considers little done." (The gender crossing from a female personification of punctuality to a male personification of distraction in Benjamin's text probably warrants commentary; but we defer all hypothetical interpretation for a moment, until we arrive at another discussion of closet space.) In a subsequent prose note, Benjamin takes up the same dialectic, introducing it with a quote from Goethe, whom he quotes as insisting that attentiveness is first among all character traits. However, as Benjamin hastens to add, that rank is shared from the first day with habit, vying for position—and so they enter into a dialectical relationship: "All attention must end up in habit, if it does not tear one apart; all habit must be disturbed by attention if it is not to hem one in."[23] This image sums up much of Benjamin's media theory and anthropology, and he goes on to put it in the language of so many of his dialectical images: of wind and sea. Attention and habit are "like the crest and the valley of a wave in the sea of the soul," and there are moments when the wind ceases to blow; heightened attention to a detail, such as pain, can all too easily distract one from a sound, a murmur, or an insect; inversely, that extreme end of attention is not its end but its utmost deployment, when attention produces a sluggishness of habit, a distracted, absent-minded reception of the world. However, to fall into commonsense assumptions about the fabric of space-time or to stay in the habit of thinking time, space, and history in continuity is not to think them at all; conversely, once they cease to be part of a distracted, absent-minded reception of tradition and culture, as they must for the writer and intellectual, they will immediately begin to disappear under critical attention. Furthermore, as pain and attention are complementary insofar as they must go together, so are habit and sleep: "In dreams there is no astonishment and in pain no forgetting, because both already carry their opposites in them, just as the crest and the valley of the wave lie close to each other when the wind does not blow." What happens when we dream is a different kind of attentiveness, emerging from the middle of the deepest habit, where the quotidian dredges of waking existence are suddenly thrown into relief. Walter Benjamin distinguishes with Baudelaire between mnemonic dreams and mantic, hieroglyphic dreams that are the product of intoxication and may point toward the future. In either case, the subject has no control over the dream images, although they are created by the subject; this observation, which already vexed de Quincey and Baudelaire, found its first theoretical elaboration in Freud's *Interpretation of Dreams*.[24] Lack of control over the production of dreams is explained as the fulfillment of unconscious wishes—their production knows no control or censorship. But the primary processes of the unconscious are condensed and displaced, and these transformations necessitate an interpretation. Benjamin's focus is on the second complex of transformations: if dreams are remembered upon waking, they have passed through the censorship of recall. In this step, the dream images are cast into a syntax that departs from the dream itself. The becoming-conscious of what was unconscious also puts the functions and failures of memory into question; and it becomes even more complicated once there is remembering, or failed remembering, within the dream.

Although criticizing surrealism as an anachronistic, sentimental, romantic resistance to Modernity, Benjamin reads the surrealist protest against Freud attentively. His understanding of dreams does not presuppose any truth in them, but seeks to make them legible alongside their contemporary modes of interpretation, as strategies of historical meaning. We might formalize this by venturing that where Benjamin proposes a negative hermeneutics of waking, Lacan reads the modification of the primary processes as a kind of poetics, by applying the distinction of metaphor and metonymy (the insistence of the letter in the unconscious). A Lacanian dream interpretation might try to take dream images only as signifiers, without yoking them to what appears to be signified; in repeating a chain of signifiers, one would decode the repressed trace of the unconscious without the working-over of memory. Benjamin's radicalization of the dream, by contrast, almost proposes the opposite and pays less attention to the signifier, since there is no reliable comment to be made on them without the historical signified. Hope lies in the verbalization of the moment of waking:

> The language of the dream is not in its words, but beneath them. In the
> dream, words are arbitrary products of the sense that lies in the wordless

continuity of flux. In the language of dreams, meaning is hidden as in a rebus. It is even possible that the origin of the rebus is found in that direction, as a kind of dream stenograph.[25]

The memory of a dream only becomes legible in recall; in order to remember the memory of the dream and reflect on it, one must wake up. Memory is content both of the dream and of the reconstruction of the dream:

> Should awakening be the synthesis of the thesis of dream consciousness and the antithesis of waking consciousness? Then the moment of awakening would be identical with the now of recognizability, in which things put on their true mien.[26]

At stake is ultimately an inversion: "For who could invert the envelope of time with one move? And yet dream recollection is nothing else."[27] Telling dreams means turning the lining of time inside out in one gesture: here, the dialectical inversion is the moment of recognition. The key to Benjamin's twist is neither the logic of the day nor the transformations of the night, but their momentary constellation in the instant of awakening.

However, if one were to dream of a *fausse mémoire*, matters reach an impasse. Not only would this mean that there is no true dream content on two levels, it adds to the difficulty of mediation upon waking in two ways: the result is a split or reduplication of the dreaming self. In writing about having dreamt, remembered, and observed this memory, Benjamin calls a group of his dreams self-portraits of a dreamer. As Freud observed, childhood memories often show the self as a childlike figure, which is surprising since adults do not visualize themselves as adults in later dream memories.[28] The imaginary self-recognition stages a screen memory that for Benjamin becomes poetic program: I see myself.[29] The dream is the place of involuntary memory that bars the inspection of the past; memories of the self constitute and lose themselves in the illegible text of the dream image, and what remains is the gesture of textualizing the dream.

> On *mémoire involontaire*: its images not only come without being called up, but they are images we never saw before we remembered them. This is most evident in those images that show ourselves, as in some dreams. We stand before ourselves, as we have stood somewhere once, in the dim past, but never before our gaze.[30]

"Dream Kitsch," Walter Benjamin's first essay on surrealism, admonished that dreams participated in history, and had too often given orders to wage war; more often than not, the dreamscape opens onto a battlefield. As technology had already captured the outer appearance of things, dreams allowed a last tactile inspection of them. But the side of such inversion and inspection of things in dreams is that which is covered by commonplace sayings, the side that is worn: it is the side of kitsch. "Just as the dreams of the night belong to the household of the soul," as Walter Killy speculated, the household of the soul "appears to require also the daydreams (the kitsch)."[31] Kitsch at first specifically denoted sentimental Victoriana, referring to artifacts that were perceived as being of poor quality or in poor taste; later, of course, it turned into a category of sentimental or perverse enjoyment. In the latter sense, it attracted a wealth of scholarly attention. Several points bear emphasis at this juncture. Kitsch achieves heightened sentimentality due to wholesale substitution of beauty by recognition, emotion by romance, the sublime by pathos or mere pose, tragedy by sensationalism or an escapist happy end. The disfigured imitation of an established work of art appears pretentious in its affected artificiality, repetitive in its clichés, trivial in its construed symbolism. However, as an always already accepted perspective on kitsch, this notion needs to be interrogated: inherent in such switching is a cultural logic of high and low art, which in turn has undergone interrogation this century. Although kitsch is an interesting case in the history of aesthetics, to reflect on its historical determination is to acknowledge that it is historically explicable as a phenomenon of aesthetics, and thus neither a mere deficiency of "good taste" nor an anthropological category that would mark those who crave kitsch as inferior.[32] To blame the problem on mass reception as a sociological figuration would be skirting the issue, since that figuration is in turn in a dialectical relationship to polemical defenses of high versus low. Furthermore, to claim that kitsch will not allow for tragedy or catharsis commonly results in a stand-off between elitist connoisseurship and the cheap thrills of kitsch. This presents a false dichotomy of art versus pseudo-art, since it would imply that art adheres to absolute principles that define once and for all what is and is not comprised in its sphere.[33] Here, Benjamin's dispersed thought on the space of kitsch and its distractions allows us to proceed.

Assigning kitsch status to an object is not in itself a critique, but it changes the field of reception, and it suddenly seems as if we knew all along, since childhood at the very least, that rather than constituting mere hindsight, this is an insight that has long served its clandestine function: "Whereas art teaches us to look into things," as Benjamin characteristically puts it, "kitsch and folk art teach us to look out from within things."[34] Sentimentality and obsession with the banal make surrealism a rival science to psychoanalysis in Benjamin's eyes: the latter seeks to "ferret out" things about the soul, whereas the former would rather investigate the soul of things. What was called art has to be seen from a distance, "two meters away from the body," while kitsch, the "last mask of the banal," hides on the inside of things, and offers a clue to why Heiner

Müller will have found himself in such uncanny agreement with Benjamin. "The repetition of the child's experience," Benjamin writes, "gives to ponder that when we were little, there was no protest yet against the oppressive world of our parents."[35] Elsewhere, Benjamin writes of the arsenal of masks associated with childhood and the magical capability of inversion. In various reformulations, he portrays the return of childlike cunning in hiding, an art that masters uncanny space and turns its vicissitudes into capabilities and opportunities. Conjuring childhood moments that harbor a premonition of the future, Benjamin prized the kind of kitschy glass paperweights that enclose a winter landscape; once shaken, they come alive in renewed snowfall.[36]

For Benjamin, there were two privileged forms of kitsch: the souvenir and the ruin. Both fetishize a past rendered inaccessible by a certain inversion that makes the ruin of beauty the beauty of ruins, familiarizes the exotic and exoticizes the familiar. On a phenomenological level, kitsch indicates a reduced transcendence of consciousness, intermingling self and object, figure and ground. Its uncannily immediate affect pivots around a strong identification.[37] Kitsch makes no effort to present a smooth, coherent, artistic whole; its attraction lies in its falling apart, cumulating the effects of its fragments. In its economy of wish fulfillment, the audience prefers to enjoy themselves, to enjoy their enjoyment, rather than to enjoy the work for its proper attributes. Its most immediate result is a technics of total synesthesia that generates a "mood." If the artificial generation of moods functionalizes the recall of past experience, as Ludwig Giesz argued, for whom "the past as such is a panoramic mood," then kitsch, in sum, is a gesture that is perceived "as if" it depicted itself, offering itself up to enjoyment.[38]

Benjamin's destructive character calls for the inversion of the bourgeois, kitschy "envelope" (or womb) of the furnished room full of knickknacks; thus while the destructive character would "efface the traces" and even efface the traces of effacement, the bourgeois dwells, like the living dead, by filling his space with kitschy tchotchkes and dark furniture: "The soulless richness of the furniture becomes true comfort only for the corpse."[39] Covering uneasiness over as coziness, these are accommodations fit only for a corpse; they are brandished as a crime, not least because they force inhabitants into habits that are more suitable to the interior space than to the inhabitants themselves. Evenly suspended between the murderous situation of the furnished, stuffed space and the total clearing by the destructive character, kitsch points to a third way. As an aberration of mourning, kitsch is the defensive trick that turns this warped space into a tight-fitting "envelope," to use Benjamin's word, into which one can wrap oneself.[40] This sentimentalized humanization of inhuman space is the last holdout of the bourgeois against the commodification of everything, including the person. It is as if, in a primitive impulse, one would make an atrocity disappear by hiding oneself—or inversely, try to make oneself invisible by covering one's eyes, as children do.

The secret of the art of hiding is to spot the cracks between the objects that seem to fill space, and even the cracks in them—analogous to a perception of cracks in time even when it seems to flow evenly and without interruption. Rather than cede to the excremental kitsch object the places where a lack, or a crack in the material of space, manifests itself and subsequently requires filling in or stopping up, one can occupy it oneself. The child does this by way of exploring, fearless and yet fully aware of the fissures of space and time, and out of such hiding places can grow the self-confidence of an adult who can confront his space and time without being phobic about it.[41] Writing, of course, is one of the ways in which such an emotional memory, a deeply rooted childhood affect can be hidden—neither erased or forgotten, nor forever booked into a sequence of recollections, but rather planted in a stratum that will be the future key to a realm where death notices are delivered as half-truths, to be analyzed and understood by way of a delayed, later return. The specific inversion in the relation of inside and outside, observer and participant, attention and distraction was addressed by Ernst Bloch on kitsch writing that flips the switch: "The inside of the readers is itself squashed here," he wrote, "the outside which they perceive as theirs is not the one in which they really are."[42] Such spatial self-deception makes the reader "grope in the dark"; for the kitsch market and the space from which kitsch writing issues can be equally musty. Bloch considered kitsch "a hieroglyph awaiting its interpretation" and surmised that it provokes polemical opposition because of its "uncanny twilight that simultaneously encodes and exposes the object"—an object to which, significantly, he assigned the status of a displacement, a bungled action.[43] Bloch's essay on "Images of Déjà Vu" is clearly influenced by Benjamin; in fact, it ends with a postscript that reconstructs a conversation on the topic with Walter Benjamin on the island of Capri.[44] As an early exponent of academic Benjamin-kitsch himself, as one might say, Bloch inserts a Benjaminian twist into his ruminations on kitsch, dreaming and awakening, shock experience, and childhood. Although déjà vu exemplified for Bloch the popular "metaphysics" of his contemporaries, he considers that its least interesting aspect. Along with Benjamin, he would rather focus on the premonition of the next moment that déjà vu enables, a "brighter shock that comes not from forgetting, but from anticipation." After Benjamin, media technology alone allows you to keep the forgotten token from the future, which will allow for a tilt in perspective that may open and contain the secret and make legible half-truths of history writ large.[45] What is hidden with great effort will only have served to advertise its being hidden; and what is covered over by a feint, a distraction, will become the spring of that "productive disorder of involuntary memory" diagnosed in Proust: by contrast with the wilfull, voluntary recollection that makes the object disappear ("We must have been there"), déjà vu allows the memory to persist and reappear when time is ripe: we will have been there.[46]

Such arcane knowledge can only grow out of an awareness of the crevices, suspensions, and extensions of memorial space-time; access to those hiding places will eventually be triggered, in the manner of a déjà vu. Benjamin's account of Easter egg hunting establishes three basic principles of an art of hiding. First, the principle of the clamp. This would be the use of interstices and chasms ("Fugen und Spalten") to slip Easter eggs "between handles and levers, between picture and wall, in a keyhole as well as between the pipes of central heating." Second, the principle of "filling in": Easter eggs as bottle stops, as lights on a candlestick, in a flower arrangement, or instead of a bulb for an electrical lamp. Third, the principle of height and depth: "as is well known, people first perceive what is at eye's height; then they look up, and lastly they care about what is at their feet." Thus small eggs can balance on a picture frame, larger ones on a chandelier, but this is nothing against the "plenitude of clever asylum" found just five or ten centimeters above the ground: in city apartments, table legs, carpet rims, or piano pedals resemble the grass into which the Easter bunny lays its eggs. And Benjamin's postscript offers modern solace to those who live in rationalized, gleaming environments of mirror-smooth walls and steel furniture: "they may look attentively at their gramophone or their typewriter, and they will notice that they comprise just as many holes and hide-outs in small quarters as a seven bedroom apartment in Makart style."[47] The close-up reveals what lies hidden in technology; the truly modern place to hide one's treasures is modern media technology. With this, we can return to the opening statements of Benjamin's short essay, where he defines hiding as the leaving of invisible traces—the kind of sleight of hand that only technology will have been able to retrace.

The hiding child is one of the recurring motifs in Benjamin's short prose—found again in at least two other, chronologically related pieces. In all of them, it is directly associated with belatedness and reading. In *One-Way Street*, the hidden child that knows all the haunts in the apartment can return to them, sure of repetition without difference, unlike Kierkegaard.[48] Yet in the revisiting of the already experienced, Benjamin does not see a forgetful turn away from happiness so much as a decoding of the overdetermined adult world through a distracted double take.[49] The "arsenal of masks" that is the children's world has intense material implication for the one who is hiding: just as the clock's chime could freeze a grimace, gesture, or posture forever, so being detected in a corner or under a table could mean being doomed to stay there forever, becoming part of the surroundings into which the child tries to blend. In peril of being banned into the inanimate world of commodities, the child preempts detection by crying out and releasing the demon, beating it to the moment of revelation, so that it is once again the demon that remains booked into the material world ("Stoffwelt"). Suffice it to point out that for the child in Benjamin's account, the magic of inversion becomes science once a year when all the uncanny haunts become places where presents and surprises are hidden, and the child "demystifies as its engineer the dark parental dwelling and seeks Easter eggs."[50] The very same story from *One-Way Street* is later included in the chronicles of *Berlin Childhood around 1900*, only that time told from a first-person perspective rather than in the third person.[51] It, the child, becomes I, the one who hides, who writes.

There is a third and recurring use of these structures in Benjamin's writing. While it is less explicit, it appears in central passages in Benjamin's works and thus corroborates what we have surmised so far. Indeed, the hidden appearance of déjà vu is arguably the most significant. It is recognizably the same thought of double inversion, and appears as a dwarf with a hunchback. It is the hidden player inside the chess automaton at the opening of the *Theses on the Philosophy of History*, and there indicates that which is at work in oblivion.[52] It appears as Odradek, the return of "the shape things assume in oblivion" in both Kafka essays.[53] Finally, at the end of *Berlin Childhood around 1900*, the prose collection that served as our guide, there it is, the same figure. The form things assume in oblivion is the form that will have returned as the imp, Odradek, the hunched dwarf.[54] How could these imp possibilities not have been noted? In a moment it will seem as if we knew it all along, and yet in the massive secondary literature on Benjamin, relatively little attention is paid to the fact that this figure of distraction and hiding returns repeatedly. Of course, given its reputation, it is not obvious that it will yield any more to our critical attention. But although the difference between attention and distraction is small, it nevertheless makes all the difference. It was Irving Wohlfahrt who noted that it is only logical and appropriate that little attention would have been devoted to the hunched dwarf—for he is indeed first and foremost the personification of Benjaminian distraction.[55]

What is forgotten and hidden never counts as lost for Benjamin. Inside the chess automaton, theology is represented as an ugly hidden dwarf, because "as it is known," Benjamin says, it is forgotten nowadays—that is to say, the only force that may save mankind from forgetting is itself forgotten. This doubling over is legible also in the fact that Benjamin's thesis splits ideology and history: a self-interpreting figure on the one hand, and on the other hand an allegorical challenge. In one reading, then, the "historical materialism" puppet is the hidden serf of theology, since the dwarf is the invisible "master of the game," guiding the puppet. In another reading, however, historical materialism can take on any opponent if it enlists the help of the invisible dwarf. Consequently, the chess automaton and the dwarf inside may stand for an allegorical triumph over ideology for some, and may signify the subjection of the automaton to ideology for others.[56] Either way, they appear together and should perhaps be interpreted less as a rebus of "either-or" than in fact a logic of "both-and" that inverts common assumptions about historical inheritance. Indeed if either reading is always already contained in and informed by the other, they cannot have meant (or aimed for) the overcoming of either term. Keeping in mind that the unforgettable, as Benjamin put it, would still exist even after everybody has forgotten it, neither theology nor historical materialism is the forgetting of the other term.[57] Rather, since the unforgettable is nothing but the injunction against forgetting, it persists in theology as well as in history. Thus Benjamin reminds his readers that the hunched, hidden, invisible theology is nothing but the memory of the injunction against forgetting in its forgotten shape.

In the penultimate part of Benjamin's longer essay on Franz Kafka, he recognizes his dwarf in Kafka's uncanny spool-creature. Benjamin associates this text with the messianic to-come that will manifest itself as a slight but crucial backwards shift of the disfigured. Odradek is the personification of guilt and of a damaged life that is above all guilty of forgetfulness. But contrary to a popular reading of these texts, Odradek is not already a messianic figure itself. Gershom Scholem wanted to recognize in him a theological messenger of messianic potential, and Benjamin quotes Scholem in this text—as the great Rabbi who surmised that the coming Messiah will change the world not violently but by a small adjustment.[58] Yet apparently, it is easily overlooked that the same essay offers a stern warning against two modes of nonreading that proceed too fast, one psychoanalytic, one theological. The chiropractic adjustment of the world is taken up again in the second essay on Kafka, where Benjamin stresses that the precise defacement or disfigurement that is so typical for Kafka's world stems from the fact that the future is a rueful reparation only as long as the past has not come to itself. The hunched dwarf therefore combines the burden of the past with the new burden of guilt about the past, or more precisely the guilt of forgetting the past. To Benjamin, the figure is familiar from childhood, as something "we once knew and then it had its peace," but now that we no longer remember it, it returns and bars the way into the future.[59] The future is not only barred to those who are oblivious to the past; since the imp is personified forgetting, he simultaneously bars the future by distracting us from it, putting it in peril of oblivion.

Moreover, the dwarf who stands for the form things assume in oblivion can appear at will on every floor of the house, inside, outside, anywhere—a constant worry to the inhabitant. Commenting on Odradek, the creature from

Kafka's "Die Sorge des Hausvaters," Benjamin recognizes in the enigmatic, disfigured figure what he calls the primal image of defacement. Unraveling the curious time-axis manipulations and sudden exits and entrances of the imp at the end of *Berlin Childhood around 1900* requires special attention to the contraband from the nineteenth century, the communal past, smuggled behind the back of history and dropped on the threshold between present and future. Adorno, in a curious turn of phrase, had warned those who would pin it down, "kitsch impishly slips out of any definition like a goblin." The imp of kitsch may well be related to the hunched dwarf who waits in the work of art, as Adorno puts it, for those recurring occasions to burst forth from its inside:

> Kitsch is not, as believers in erudite culture would like to imagine, the mere refuse of art, originating in disloyal accommodation to the enemy; rather, it lurks in art, awaiting ever recurring opportunities to spring forth.[60]

The double interpretation of the dwarf inside the automaton translates also to the reading of the imp of distraction we meet at the end of *Berlin Childhood*, here in the guise of the clumsy kind of a distraction. While it first appears personified but nameless, with hindsight an offhand remark by the narrator's mother decodes it for him: "ungeschickt läßt grüßen." Hannah Arendt took this gnome to be the emblem of Benjamin's lifelong clumsiness.[61] Of course, Scholem and Arendt may not be wrong, but it seems that the recurring appearance of this figure harbors more than associations about Benjamin projected onto one of his most enigmatic images. Although we do not deny that the strange imp indeed stands for that which one has already assumed—indeed it seems to confirm and even personify the already-thought, the already-read—we need to take another close look at the text from which he once more emerges.

This time it is not the puppet of historical materialism or the dwarf of theology, but the outer husk of quotidian habit and memory that is interrupted and undermined by the apparition of what is beyond the range of everyday attention. This dwarf seems invisible because it is disfigured and responsible for hidden, deceptive workings; it is disfigured because its responsibilities have been neglected and forgotten. It emerges at the end, in a prose piece that revisits the stations of the *Berlin Childhood*, and from each memory, it demands half for itself, as if by way of an exorbitant taxation. Here, Benjamin transfers the architectural and spatial aspects of his childhood memories into a subterranean milieu; the narrator pursues a curiosity about the "souterrain" during the day until one night, in a dream, gnomes with pointed hats turn the tables on him and look back. This inversion of the gaze happens in an instant and summons all the opposites in the preceding text into a dialectical image.[62] This image clearly aligns aura and paramnesia: the inversion of the gaze is akin to what Benjamin writes elsewhere of aura, and of the reification of the object as kitsch

or fetish. If the aura produces a shock of recognition, and shock in turn com-
mences the decay of the aura, then here we observe a negative aura that inverts
common assumptions about the distracted attention of the observer, as well
as about the visibility and recognizability of the object.[63] The observer feels a
déjà vu, that is he feels observed, and this inversion of the gaze makes him look.
"To experience the aura of a phenomenon," Benjamin asserts, "is to invest it
with the power to open the eyes." In his scenario, however, that which one does
not look at, or hardly pays attention to, is invested with the capacity to prevent
the gaze. In this sense, the uncanny taxation of half of everything by the imp
may be proportional to the semi-attentive way he is perceived—or lets himself
be perceived. The narrator continues with the remark that as a child he did not
make sharp distinctions between daytime and nocturnal apparitions, and so he
was not surprised to read about his own dream-character in a children's book,
or to encounter him in a basement. Then again, the absence of surprise is only
an effect of hindsight, since the imp appears suddenly—he is the surprise,
because his appearance is barely noted until later, when it is quickly assimilated,
usually by way of repression.

If it is only with hindsight that Benjamin's narrator understands whom
he had before him, then it is remarkable that from then on, the figure from
the dream reappears as if it had always already been known: as clumsy,
"ungeschick," after the mother's invocation of a habitual phrase, "ungeschickt
läßt grüßen." The key to understanding the situation, then, already lay with the
prior generation, with the unmemorable, repeatable word of the mother, or
more precisely with the sourceless source of the adage cited by the mother
again and again—until it suddenly reveals its significance. Once more, the muse
of the flaneur ambles before the strolling writer, each street leads down "if not
to the mothers so into a past which is not only the author's own."[64] The covering over and return of maternal knowledge has to do less with the fact that
women are forgotten in history than with Benjamin's intuitive formulation,
associating women with what is repressed and forgotten. Here, we return to
the question of closet space and gender. Just as you may remember a dream
upon waking, as Benjamin suggests in a dialogue on the metaphysics of youth,
in conversation you remember the ruins of the past. Again, gender is associated
with a tension of present and past, reminiscent of his sketch on distraction—
only here the roles are reversed.[65] Whereas the speaker is possessed by the present, women appear as the keepers of the past. The creative one, oblivious to
time and cursing his memory in the process of creation, ends up clueless about
the past; women, by contrast, possess the past, but are without presence.[66] This
is not an eternal feminine that gestures toward the altogether timeless; rather,
the women point toward a past that was lost but will return again, as the past.
In his Kafka essays, Benjamin associates the submerged world of the forgotten

past with the maternal, and Kafka's feminine figures with the kind of oblivion that is extant in the present. In this recurrence of the past, one may recognize the dialectical countertime to a future anterior that is the time of desire, the historical time of the subject. Defining recurrence as the essence of an antimythology of the nineteenth century, Benjamin sought to subvert its bad infinity by dint of history, while subverting history with messianic inversions.[67] Ingeniously, he recast the thought of recurrence as the prophetic dream of impending breakthroughs of technological reproduction.[68] Thus, the quasi-mythical structure of the returning past drifts past the present into the future and turns into the desire for a repetition of that which has never been yet: and this is, in short, Benjamin's inverted déjà vu. It is no longer a matter of access to what already happened; rather, it is that which returns *in the guise* of the first time.

"Ungeschickt," in German, can also indicate the unsent, the uncalled-for. What was never sent for now arrives; it has not taken its post precisely because it only appears *post facto*. Since angels are literally the sent ones, the messengers, Benjamin's semantic play allows "ungeschickt" to appear as a kind of ambivalent name that would mark him as the opposite of an angel. But what is expressed in this inversion? As Benjamin's memorialized child recognizes, belatedly, in the folk wisdom invoked by a maternal figure, greater presence of mind would only result in yet another failed encounter with the nonangelic imp. Greater punctuality would only mean that the always already delayed encounter will be missed every time. Yet the sudden energy derived from the first encounter compacts the return of the forgotten future and the explanation from the distance of a literary past, and it is contained most intensely in Benjamin's two-faced definition: "Wen dieses Männlein ansieht, gibt nicht acht." The imp causes forgetting and is itself brought forth as the personification of forgetting. It appears precisely there where one is distracted—and thus one almost does not see it. More precisely: you never see it, it only sees you, and indeed the better the less you see of yourself.[69]

Distraction and forgetting, as Benjamin writes elsewhere citing Goethe, are closely related, and may appear as two sides of the force of habit: one that habitually overlooks what is hidden in plain sight, and one that hides desires and wishes from conscious awareness in order to preserve and protect the regularities of habitual behavior. While the former is a necessary weakness that Benjamin also addresses in his text on the Easter egg hunt, the latter is more directly aligned with the defensive structures of modern existence. It is just as well that what is forgotten cannot be entirely recovered, Benjamin warns, for if it were to be recovered fully, the shock might be so great that it would interrupt our understanding of desire. Inversely, the more deeply our desire is sunk into oblivion, the better we understand it—thus distance becomes a function of interpretation. Yet forgetting weighs heavily on us, as heavily as the self-imposed training weight of the stones on Demosthenes' tongue: the promise of remembering is thus aligned with liberation from a burden.

For each one of us, habit may arise from different things. For Benjamin, undoubtedly, it was the habit of reading that was formed early and then determined much of his life. It is an attentive habit that comes with its particular set of distractions; the fairy-tale creature of the hunchbacked dwarf, for one, is of course not Benjamin's invention—he took it from Clemens Brentano's canonical collection of tales, *Des Knaben Wunderhorn*.[70] In the non-self-identical apparition that is this Odradek-hunchback-dwarf, one may recognize a mythological motif of belatedness that doubles as premonition: "Wo es erschien, da hatte ich das Nachsehn." Where the imp appears, only hindsight remains for me, including the perception, with hindsight, of what had appeared: a compound personification of a certain guilt, a certain modification of forgetting, a certain barred recollection that returns precisely as a guilty, forgotten, barely recognizable entity. "Das Männlein kam mir überall zuvor." The imp preceded me everywhere I go; it is always already there. "Zuvorkommend stellte sich's in den Weg." While in an ordinary sentence, the word "zuvorkommend" would simply translate as "courteously," here it takes a strangely uncanny turn: it is obstructive and obliging, forthcoming and preempting. The messianic augur of remembrance is, at the same time, the "supremely guilty instance of forgetfulness."[71] In this sense, what is forgotten is never lost but misplaced, or displaced. The personification of guilty forgetting shows itself as displacement, "Entstellung"—as a small and ugly creature. However, even if the narrator claims to have been oblivious to the differences between the nocturnal realm and that of daylight, the figure of the hunched dwarf is marked by a certain division that is caused, no doubt, by his doubling over. Since he always already precedes you wherever you go, he has always taken the carafe of wine, eaten half of your meal, and broken the pot. Since the "main feature of forgetting," as Benjamin writes, "is that it forgets itself," it follows that the figure of the hunchback is both small and ugly, disfigured and distorted; he doubles over in the forgetting of forgetting, the repression of repression.

Regardless whether one blames galloping cultural paramnesia on progress or on tradition, in either case it refers us to the distracted dialectic of memory. Curiously, just as the imagery of the imp pivots on an inversion and a doubling over, so does the entire staging of its apparition. For how is it possible that the personification of forgetting would come to constitute the sum and summary of childhood recollections? At the end, the imp has collected images of the narrator in the various hiding places, in the park, on the phone, at the train station, and sick in bed; the entire project of the *Berlin Childhood* is rapidly replayed as if in a slideshow, until the hunched dwarf "has his work behind him." How is such recollection possible, if the distracting imp was always already there all along, spreading forgetting and destructive clumsiness before the child? Either the child is able to recollect regardless, or it is, in fact, the imp itself who collected and wrote. Whether or not it is true for the literary *mémoire involontaire* of the narrator, it certainly is incontrovertible for the reader that these complex images are not visible until remembered, arriving like souvenir postcards never sent.

With an uncanny gaze that resembles that of a camera lens, the imp of distraction takes snapshots in the dark room of the optical unconscious.[72] It is in this sense that the small images are both repeated and new, both always forgotten and already remembered, creating an overall impression that is tinged with kitsch, like the photographs of Venice for Proust.[73] In presupposing a lost time that is regained in instances of déjà vu, a certain modification of forgetting turns out to be the condition of all healing remembrance, in two ways: not only as its opposite that is remedied, but also as the condition of possibility of remembrance. Here, we are confronted neither with *mémoire involontaire* that arises out of the unconscious, nor with the equivalent of Nietzsche's active oblivion that would shake off (some of) the burden of memory. Arguably, Benjamin stages an inversion of assumptions about time and remembrance that was not conceivable before the widespread introduction of mass media. Benjamin scholars seek to align him in this respect either with Nietzsche on forgetting, or with Heidegger on guilt, or again and again with Proust; of course such elective affinities may exist, yet here, it is neither a question of nostalgia nor of moral philosophy, but a very material question of the conditions of experiencing the impossible—that is, experiencing under the conditions of mass media. Back to back with the imp, it may become clear how it messes with the conventions of distance and proximity in directly textual ways. Its diminutive size is directly proportional to the diminished presence in the mind of what is forgotten. The work it has behind him is itself a kind of memory: calling up and listing the locations and motifs of the preceding prose pieces comprised in the *Berlin Childhood*. As the narrator indicates, the imp has such snapshots "of us all," and can make them appear in a flash before one's eyes. It is as if the imp edits the film flashing before your eyes just before dying from these images—here rendered as a kind of textual remembrance by way of self-citation.[74] Benjamin's take on déjà vu is that testamentary film of early memories, compressed and summed up as a presentation of the forgotten. Like the mnemotechnical list of places visited at the end of *Berlin Childhood*, Benjamin's *Theses on the Philosophy of History* are readable as a montage of self-citations. When Benjamin announced the *Berlin Childhood* to Adorno, his emphasis on the diminutive size of his project, seemingly already inserted but as an afterthought, induces us to warn in turn that our reading is but a small part of an even smaller project.[75]

Lastly, the disfigured back of the dwarf invites scrutiny. The back is the side that is turned to what is invisible in the place of the obvious, underexposed in plain sight. The same goes for what is behind you in the sense of a past, or inversely what is before you when your gaze is fixed on the past while you drift into the future that is barred to inspection. Only if you no longer turn your back on the past will you not carry it on your back anymore. Insofar as forgetting and other psychopathological slips are only recognized with hindsight, they are already carried on the back, like the hump on the back of the imp. Moreover, after the scenes from the *Berlin Childhood* are revisited, the hunched dwarf has his work behind him, since he is not only identified with forgetting, but is also the accomplice of remembrance, aiding the adult by bringing the child's past back. This duplicity mirrors the apparent contradiction between Benjamin's earlier use of the disfigured figure in the Kafka essays, where he represents the damaged life that will disappear once the messianic promise is fulfilled, and in the thesis on the philosophy of history, where he seems to serve as a stand-in for messianic expectation itself. In both roles, he puts the reader in mind of the *angelus novus*; his hump "grows to heaven" behind him like the heap of broken dishes and split portions he leaves in his wake.[76] Thus at the end of the *Berlin Childhood,* the narrator stands before ruins, "verstört vor einem Scherbenhaufen," resembling the rubble piling high before the luckless angel. Moreover, Benjamin's Kafka shifts the world into a backward position, "eine rückwärtige Stellung," in order to recuperate the forgotten; yet, as Benjamin insists, the fact that it is forgotten does not mean that it is not still extant in the present, for it is present precisely as oblivion.[77] This world is ours, it turns out, because we have repressed and forgotten what we should have worked through.[78] Thus Benjamin aligns Proustian *mémoire involontaire* expressly more with forgetting than with remembrance; the labor of remembering a past forgetting that is recovered from the unconscious goes along with an affirmation of present and future forgetting.[79] As Adorno concurs, "the erasure of recollection is the achievement of an all too alert consciousness," and so the working through of the past is contingent upon the success, but also the failures of this rational effort.[80] It is an inevitable corollary to this rule that the uncanny prescience of the imp, the question "what the forgotten knows of us," cannot be solved by heightened attention, but only by means of mediatized distraction: precisely because Benjamin, unlike Proust, is concerned not only with a past that almost allows you to drop out of time, but with the returns of the future anterior that Szondi pointed toward in his grammatical remark on the difference between Proust and Benjamin.[81] In short, the reserve of déjà vu, the hump, holds both a promise past the future and the peril of futures past.

3

POSTHISTOIRE IN RUINS: HEINER MÜLLER'S HYDRAPOETICS

"All truth is simple."—Is that not twice a lie?
—Friedrich Nietzsche, *Götzendämmerung*

MORE DIRECTLY THAN THE WORK of any other German playwright or poet, Heiner Müller's writing commented upon the political theater and cultural debates of Germany, both in the splits of the postwar, preunification era and around post–Berlin Wall, post–cold war tensions. Paramount among his convictions was the determining force of our relations with the dead. He observed sharply how in the past, history and politics had galvanized around the repression of mortality.[1] Art, by contrast, was to cultivate its heritage in communication with the dead. To allow the dead a place in society was in his eyes an absolute precondition for the future. A love of the future, he concluded, would have to be a love of the dead. In the course of such a necrophiliac conversation, Heiner Müller indicated that history and memory had parted ways, and that "great texts are recognized by a sort of déjà vu: they say what one knows and sought to forget or repress."[2] Despite or because of this, the cross of labor and the double-cross of betrayal in the politics of cultural memory form the core of his texts. Although much more pessimistic than

Walter Benjamin about the potential of technology, and sometimes forced to curb or encode his commentary on issues close to his heart, he always found ways to put it on stage or on the page.

Indeed, Müller's texts repeatedly state what he thought the two German states were repressing, or trying to make forgotten. One of his best-known theses was postwar Germany's continuity with Prussia, both being marked by their lack of any relation to femininity.[3] Analyzing the iconography of war monuments in particular and memorial culture in general, Müller recognized what lay behind feeble efforts at redecoration by states and regimes. He had learned to read the screen memories generated by officious state imagery as the folding-over of two time zones, where the false memory can always reveal an unrecognized true memory. However, Müller's embrace of déjà vu does not express alignment with psychoanalysis—rather, in its alignment with déjà vu, it puts the creative privilege of writing into reserve. Müller's labors of writing opposed dialectically reflected modes of mindless production. Indeed, he felt that technology constituted a threat of counterproductive forgetting and repression to cultural recollection, and he defined his art as the "opposite of psychoanalysis," insofar as self-analysis and the drive to self-recognition would be fatal for the creative process. Writing was his attempt to delay insights, to build up resistance to technology's annihilating process; we must not kill the dead once again, but keep them in mind. Solidarity with ancestors is not psychoanalytic, Müller insisted, but something that "can be described as flight from self-analysis." Equating the drive to interpret with the death drive, he considered art an endeavor to slow down the closing time of recognition, to dull the sense of interpretation and build up desperately impossible resistances against it.[4] By the same token, he exhibited a well-informed suspicion of the comforts of official history, and against the rewriting of history by pre- and post–cold war ideologies.

Reading Müller is therefore not simply a matter of an archeological dig in the rubble of the past, in literature and history; it is the labor of identifying the locations and intended locations of his textual memory work. Walter Benjamin stipulated that literature could be based on an experience that has normalized the reception of shock, and is accompanied by a political calculation. In conscious alignment with Benjamin's proposal, Müller featured monuments, tombstones, and war memorials as frozen moments of normative commemoration; his writing was to offer a countermemory, a motivated modification of cultural forgetting.[5] The notion of "lieux de mémoire" is the cornerstone of an immense collection of articles under the direction of French historian Pierre Nora.[6] This tome illustrates the rupture between memory and history after the end of great institutions (church, school, family, state) and tries to turn the loss of historical memory into a new historiography. For Pierre Nora as for Bergson, the vitality of a culture depends on a timeless presence of all memories. Where they ossify and become monument, museum, souvenir, or ruin, they fall out of that continuum. Heiner Müller's writing seeks to document this. Configuring history as opposed to memory, Nora argues that certain "places of memory" bear witness to history's mistrust of memory. If the global village is consti-tuted in a synchronicity of media and events, the result is total historicization, the end of all memory.[7] For Müller as for Nora, memory would be the com-prehensive form of that which we can no longer remember. This forces the mnemopathology of our time into archiving everything. As a result, the trans-fer of memory from the historical register to the psychological, from the social to the individual, materializes the trace of memory's destruction—from conti-nuity to déjà vu and similar ruptures. The memorial cult lapses into the index of its own ruin, as Nora suggests to fellow historians of this shift, and memory now shows the epistemological age of historiography.

In Heiner Müller's writing, the motif of the ruin is pervasive. Walter Ben-jamin's x-ray vision of the ruin is for Müller the trauma of *passé vecu*, but while Benjamin zoomed in on the miniature, Müller went for the big picture.[8] Where the consequences of a dramatic plot are themselves in the past, new writing must cause an "explosion of a memory" within the dead structure; Müller considered this vision of exploding ruins as descriptive of his own writing.[9] The rubble of literature, of history, and of cultural memory can only be worked over by blow-ing it up; at times, his protagonists have it in their back, as a pile of literary rubble in *Traktor* ("Die Schutthalden der Literatur im Rücken"), as the ruins of Europe in *Hamletmaschine* ("im Rücken die Ruinen von Europa"), and as a ruin in "The Luckless Angel."[10] Time and again, Müller writes of the impossible labor of that position, exploring and exploding the déjà vu of great texts.

In *Herakles 2 oder die Hydra*, a dense prose piece from 1972, we find one of Müller's most pervasive figures—the impossible labor of fighting off and revers-ing the traumatic embrace of a maternal, destructive, cannibalizing power.[11] It begins with a grammatical sleight of hand that introduces a self-deceived pro-tagonist in pursuit of a beast. "For a long time he believed he was still crossing the woods"—the beginning of a sentence of forty-nine words, interminable cadences offering clues: a barely visible trail of blood, heaving ground, an in-toxicatingly warm wind from all sides that makes the trees move like snakes. There is no heaven to orient him in time, days or hours pass, he begins to won-der why his movements become more difficult, slower, his feet heavier. Before he can decide whether there is a suction from the ground or his feet are sim-ply tired, he realizes a loss in blood pressure, the branches of the trees grasp at him, he is entangled in them, they seem to take his measure with an irritating automaticity—and before he realizes that he is in fact not hunting a beast in a forest but holding onto the surface of the beast and already at its mercy: "years hours minutes" have passed, the monster has "transformed time into an excrement in space." Grappling with this technological beast that annihilates time and is about to do him in too, he recognizes that the blood that leaves the trail he was following is in fact his own. In panic and pain, he adapts to the destruction by adapting and not adapting to its rhythm, resisting and not resisting this uncanny union of battleground and enemy, preempting and attacking by neither attacking nor preempting the Hydra, countering with inversions and the opposite, changing or repeating unchanged the movements that are still possible. To the sound of a sentimental song, the maternal beast almost suffocates him and cracks his ribs. And to the degree he is taken apart by the sinister machinic opponent, he rebuilds himself, sometimes wrongly, sometimes correctly, having turned into a machine himself when the labor of survival became the only thing possible. Sometimes, however, he delays the reconstitution, as if hoping for total destruction, "greedily anticipating the total annihilation in the hope for the nothing, the infinite pause, or in fear of victory which would come only by way of the complete destruction of the beast which was his dwelling place." The constant shock gives the lie to divisive thoughts that would separate him from the ground. In this battle, neither of the combatants can afford to win, they have become so locked into one another that they cease to be separable. In the white silence that is a premonition of the last round of this interminable dying labor, he learns to read the constantly changing blueprint for the machine that he is, stops being, and again becomes in a different way, and he learns that he writes the plans himself with the inscription of his labors and deaths.[12] Significantly, it is not white noise but white silence that announces the beginning of the end, a veiled allusion to Benjamin's messianic vision of the Last Judgment not as the silence before the storm, but the storm of annihilation preceding the white-out of silence. Here as in most of his other texts, myths crystallize collective experience, and their repetition with a difference is Müller's preferred vehicle for political theater, taking repetition with a dialectical twist. When Benjamin proposed that a certain literature could be based on an experience that has incorporated the reception of shock, he hastened to add that it would require a high degree of self-awareness, since it would have to evoke and adhere to a master plan.[13] With Baudelaire, he compares it to a rationale of political calculation addressed more or less explicitly in "traumatophiliac" literature. When the stabilizing, normative plan manifests itself in the frozen, crystallized public images of commemoration, we are confronted with the question of the monument, the tombstone, the war memorial. In the *Passagenwerk,* which Benjamin worked on both before and after the writing of the *Berlin Childhood around 1900,* he pushed the envelope of déjà vu to encompass a theory of warped space.

In theater division of labor institutes an inversion of hierarchies, a heightened attention to the violence that crystallized in the clear separation of groups of people from other groups. In this sense, the invention of theater replaced a vicious circle of violence with an awareness that allows the fatal pattern of imitation to be broken. While watching, you observe your own acts in the action on stage, and thus the socializing force of theater is the reinscription, on an abstracted level, of antagonistic structures in a confined space. Müller shared with Bertolt Brecht an interest in shattering that space of confinement in order to bring back the forgotten energy behind a theater caught in the fatal embrace of the institutions of the stage professions. Müller tried to invert or at least subvert its divisions, playing with Brecht's utopian motto, "wie es ist so bleibt es nicht" (it will not stay as it is); he inverted Brecht programmatically: "so wie es bleibt ist es nicht" (it is not the way it stays). Behind such wordplay is a theatrical program; epic theater as conceived by Bertolt Brecht no longer accepts the division of labor between laypeople and actors. It would therefore also erase the distinction between the audience and the actors. Müller concluded that after the end of professional make-believe, fear and terror are the only options theater has left, because they are the shape of the new on stage and in texts.[14] In the figure of the forgetful mnemonist reduced to a cipher, he stages déjà vu as the mishap that is a traditional actor's nightmare: "I start to forget my text. I am a sieve. More and more words fall through. Soon I will hear no other voices than my own, asking for forgotten words."[15] Even if Müller's inversion and subversion of the structures of the theater only result, again, in theater, their return will be marked by the constitutive differences. Just as Brecht's actors were to display that they were "only acting," Müller's texts aim to foreground what used to be covered over.[16] The labor of Herakles will not have been to hunt down the Hydra, but to recognize that he only survives in history and cultural memory as long as he keeps fighting it. In this manner, Heiner Müller stages figure and ground, juxtaposed and merging.

The official attitude toward the war-dead always played a crucial role in the constitution or reconstitution of states; however, with ever new means of warfare, the foundation of the nation can resemble a dream-like hallucination. It was Napoleon III who claimed, according to Paul Virilio, that for the warrior, "memory is the science itself"—not in the sense of collective memory as in a popular culture, but as "a parallel memory, a paramnesia, that is to say an erroneous localisation in time and space, the illusion of déjà vu."[17] Shell-shocked by the information implosion, the first victim of war is the concept of reality. Any attempt to come to a posthumous defense of destroyed memories must confront the question of mechanical reproducibility. Critical theory offers a therapeutic account of this loss of the future and its return as a forgotten past

that will have culminated in the war memorial. The culture industry fused
advertising, manufacturing, and the state, but the human body was ill suited to
experience war, as Adorno writes: the First World War had already taken a long
while to process, and when the first memoirs came out, they seemed fake and
impotent, due to the difficulties of reconstructing feeble memories. World War
II, however, was as foreign to the body as the motions of a machine. War leaves
no room for history, it begins again with every moment: "with each explosion,
it has breached the barrier against stimuli beneath the experience, the lag
between healing oblivion and healing recollection forms."[18] The breakdown of
the barrier makes not only healthy recollection and healthy forgetting impossible, but above all their dialectical relationship. Instead of a continuity of experience, there is a timeless series of shocks, punctuated by paralyzed intervals.
This kind of dysfunctional present constantly incinerates the past and consigns
it to being forgotten all over again: as Adorno formulates, "even the past is
no longer safe from the present whose remembrance of it consigns it a second
time to oblivion."[19] If the media create an informational present, fabricating
each day separately without regard to past or future, then everybody who is
included in their structure will receive the same present at the same time even
at the farthest points of the globe. This global present serves to coordinate
action and speed up the transmission of messages in fractions of a second.
Traumatic experience is the result of a generalized shell shock, and of the transformation of space first by pilots and later by rockets that carry cameras. However, from this enveloping experience emerges a notion not of something so
resistant as to be extra-medial—which could only be invisible and ineffective,
immaterial and inconsequential—but rather a notion of literature as a reserve.

Right after World War II, Müller had come across some book reviews by
Walter Benjamin; when the first two-volume selection of Benjamin's writing
appeared a decade later, he was able to consolidate his reading impressions.[20]
Müller's prose poem "Der Glücklose Engel" appeared in 1958, transcribing the
figure of Benjamin's angel of history into the context of divided, postwar Germany. He later went on record quoting Benjamin, expressing his admiration for
his work, reading and recording Benjamin's texts; his unlucky angels and utopic
fragments are often compared and rarely contrasted with Benjamin's.[21] The
luckless angels in Müller's two inversions of Benjamin's allegorical angel of history share with their counterpart not only their figurative helplessness, but also
the spacing out of time into the dimensions and directions of a timeless expansion; while Benjamin's *angelus novus* would drift into the force field of the
future and Müller's angels are still waiting for history to begin, they all oppose
historicism and the idea of an end of history.[22]

In Müller's first variation, the angel is grounded and weighed down by the
rubble of history, but while he is thus petrified, the ground also anticipates his

flight: interlocking of angel and ground offer a Benjaminian dialectical image, and the momentum of history arises anew.[23] But while Benjamin's angel does not allow for any optimism, Müller gestures toward hope—not as an effect on the addressee, since his first variation seems to have none, but as the potential of the medium that opens our eyes to a perspective that would otherwise not be accessible to us. The angel looks back into the past and counters our fixation on the future. Thus he promises to open history. Müller's reading of the tensions extant in ruins and war memorials will provide a key to the arrest and animation of the dialectical image. The angelic figure also appears in *Hamletmaschine*, where Horatio is facing backwards, in *Der Auftrag*, where an avenging angel appears as the angel of despair, and in *Die Einsamkeit des Films*, where the revolutionary angel lives in a graveyard until his flight is about to commence.[24] After the fall of the Berlin Wall, however, Müller felt compelled to rewrite the angelic topos once more—this time in personal apostrophe: "Der Engel ich höre ihn noch / aber er hat kein Gesicht mehr als / Deines das ich nicht kenne" (The angel I hear him still / But he no longer has any face but / Yours that I don't know).[25] This angel now looks neither into the future nor into the past, but into the present moment; his personal address seems all the more significant as it has been perceived by most critics as untypical for Müller. At the same time, once the critic's perspective is invoked, it is evident that this text looks back at least to the earlier luckless angel, if not past Benjamin's *angelus* to the theological connotations of the courier figure. After the fall of the wall, only the afterthought remains of what already in 1958 had no future. What is now irrevocably past thus returns to fall into place, but only by way of a distracted recollection; we no longer see the angel, nor do we see what he sees; we merely hear an echo of his wings flapping desperately. Hoping to be luckier, in the end, than Benjamin's luckless messenger, Müller depicts himself as the prophet of a release.[26] If history presents itself on the stage of literature as the contemporaneity, if not simultaneity, of past, present, and future, then the drift of this art of memory goes "backwards from the past into the present, for the past lies before us and the future, which was enclosed in the present, behind us."[27] This release of the future from the confines of the present where it lies hidden is the secret mechanism Müller inherited from Benjamin.

Literature, for Heiner Müller, is "something like a memory," but a memory of the future: recollection of what does not exist yet. Literature, he insists, is not only the remembrance of a past and the acknowledging of a present, but also reminiscent of a future.[28] This future, however, is under immemorial threats: Müller shares Adorno's conservative fear for culture in his surmise that the entire range of modern technology aims directly at the annihilation of memory.[29] Forgetting therefore had to appear counterrevolutionary. In open allusion to the first modern poetics of memory, which Baudelaire's *Salon de 1846* constitutes (and executes fragmentarily) for Benjamin, Heiner Müller profiles the ambiguity of Mnemosyne as daughter of permanence and change, heaven and earth, and her progeny, the muses whose function is to distract, to help commemorate or forget. By the same token, Müller performs a paradigm shift by replacing the mimetic and fantastic points of reference for the creation of art with those of recollection and oblivion. Increasingly suspicious of technology the newer it is, he pits the creative imagination of recollection against any utopic order of mnemotechnics, imitation, and repetition; recollection is to be the sole measure of his art.[30]

Monuments in particular are supposed to demonstrate the semiotic and transformative mechanisms that institute collective national and cultural representations of memory. What they program and prescribe is problematized as the attempt to manipulate political signification without actually confronting the symbolics of historical and contemporary politics themselves. Müller's obsessive labors of imagination obey Benjamin's demand that true recollection simultaneously ought to offer an image of who is remembering.[31] This image, however, may remain unavailable to the remembering writer, if and when for him the main thing is not what he has experienced, but the weaving of his recollection.[32] As war memorials continue to command public and critical attention, it is significant how Müller's reading of them was shaped by one screen memory. It is this screen memory, harking back to childhood, that Müller keeps returning to, both in his writing and in interview and journalistic interventions, and it also influenced his own effort to collaborate with Daniel Libeskind in a war memorial of sorts, toward the end of his life. If the Hydra text was an endless battle without war, Müller called the fictional dialogue of his autobiography a war without battle. As his privileged childhood memory that monumentalizes that war, Müller exhibits nothing more and nothing less than an instance of Benjaminian déjà vu: "as ghosts used to come from the past / now they also come from the future."[33] In intertexual echoes of Benjamin and Brecht, Müller joins in a haunted present the splinters of a past that receive their electrifying charge from a surge in the future.

In his autobiographical dialogue, *Krieg ohne Schlacht*, Heiner Müller exhibits a childhood memory as his first recollection. It is the recollection of a moment that already made the child surmise that there will have been more to it than was evident at the time, and that time would tell the true story. From this primal scene of suspicious faith in the future and distrust in the appearance of the past, Müller builds the edifice not only of his memoirs, but of his entire dramatic and poetic program. Trenchantly aware of nationalist grandeur and political bad faith, he traces his perceptive critical distance back to what is hidden in a scene from childhood. It would be wrong to claim, before we interrogate

Müller's fictional strategy, that he was on the run from analysis or therapy—that would be to fall into the autobiographical trap he seeks to circumnavigate. The complex tactics of psychoanalytically informed resistance to psychoanalysis are part of his artistic program.[34] Thus Müller sets the scene for a performative defense and simultaneous inclusion of psychoanalytic thought. As he indicates in his autobiography, this was his "only chance to forget" his texts: a liberating act.[35] Memory work is not something that can be contemplated; it has to be performed, it is a labor of meaning, withdrawn from the moment into the effects of posterity and futurity. The self-reflective effort of recollection, the inevitable inclusion of the writer of autobiographic work, entails a frame of reference for the past that may or may not stand up to "factological" inquiry, as Müller admits. Even where it does not, it nevertheless generates "something like the real memory" in formulations that both cover and expose the *apres-coup* of secondary revision.[36] The crystallized moment that both invites and fends off Freudian and Benjaminian associations is a childhood memory in which a war monument, "a mother" as Müller says, becomes uncannily emblematic for the child, and that perception grows into the foundation for an entire architecture of memorial inscriptions. Considering his childhood recollections, Müller writes:

> the first one is a walk to the cemetery with my grandmother. There was a monument for soldiers fallen in the First World War, of porphyry, a gigantic figure, a mother. For me, this war memorial was cathected for years with a purple maternal image, with fear, perhaps also fear of the grandmother who led me across the cemetery.[37]

The memorial exhibits a silence, a telling omission: it cannot show why the dead died. If monuments in general and war memorials in particular are to present history symbolically, then they are prone to manipulative strategies of omission and disingenuous ideological filtering.[38] And so of course the installation of a petrified mother can come to signify not loss in general and the failure to pass life on to a next generation in particular, but also a militaristic apotheosis of sacrifice. The uneasiness the child may have felt later explains itself as premonition of an affirmative stance toward war that leads from the aftermath of World War I into German fascism and National Socialism. The monument as the child remembers it (or as the adult reconstructs it) thus oscillates between a Christian image of loss and a murderous maternal beast of war. What the child instinctively may have taken exception to, in the presence of his grandmother, is nothing less than the archaic political iconography of death; and while the child is not as lucid on these matters as the dramatist will be, the experience brings forth the future Heiner Müller.

In this labor, Müller's writing shuttles back and forth between the show-and-tell of theater and the hide-and-seek of that drama's operating principles;

in Benjaminian terms, we would speak of the dialectics of attention and distraction in alliance with forgetting and memory. Müller's numerous dream-texts testify to his fascination with that mode: they allow articulations of skewed spaces and times that grant access to things that remain invisible or are overlooked in waking. Similarly, the trauma of an unforgettable pain will haunt the overalert faculties of reason and undermine its efforts to solidify the space of experience. Following Klaus Theweleit's associations in his meditations on Heiner Müller's last prose piece, "Traumtext," about the gaze that forms what is seen, adds desire, and covers the blind spot of projection, one might be tempted to recognize in Müller's déjà vu the gaze of a Lacanian *déjà regardé*.[39] Then again, the most complex play of the gaze has always accompanied theatrical material.[40]

Müller's mode of operation revolves around the theatricality of trauma, articulating and interweaving phantasmatic and interpretive perceptions of a set scene. It shows in repeating and repeats in showing what the dynamics of recollection are owed to: "masks and roles" on the stage of his text; memories as staged and dressed up and artificial as any theatrical scene.[41] The works of Heiner Müller, the playwright who reduces his own autobiographical deformations to being a mere object of history and of politics, put the contents of his individual past in conjunction with those of a collective experience of the past, as history or politics, just as Benjamin observed in Proust.[42] This frames the traumatic material of biography in a context that can only be written by including one's own situation in turn, as Müller postulates. Writers must not "exempt themselves" because all objectivity had become voided. Thus in a double turn away from the realm of any "factual" recollection, the playwright seeks to legitimize his artistic cover-ups in a political and historical appeal to a veracity that goes beyond what really happened.[43] Any family secret and its effects across the generations straddles a crypt into which the writer consigns anything that is not plainly historical or political at the time of rewriting. Conspicuously, this encryption hides the forgotten pact with the dead: in order for the dead to remain dead and in their place, secure and without possibility of their return, Müller's memories must function as obituaries, summoning all available models of death management between mourning and melancholia, to the extent of mortifying a certain personal history in the name of what will rise out of the cemetery of letters.

In this manner, Müller's work operates on two levels: exposing the sometimes artistically productive, but politically ambiguous modes of revisionism, and injecting them with the psychoanalytically informed work of mourning, negotiated in writing. This double strategy ensures a steady resistance to assimilation, reading, and understanding in the hermeneutic modes that Müller's theater would preempt. Borrowing from Theodor Reik's Freudian take on surprise, he holds that the function of literary recollection is not the defensive preservation of impressions in a stable memory, but the destructive, transvaluating labor that gives rise to the memory trace.[44] The privileged position accorded to childhood memories had become such a commonplace notion that it serves to hide a reflection at the same time, and therefore Müller's traumatophiliac literature grows out of a self-awareness that knows, and seeks to show, that the power of the hidden is greater than the attraction of the obvious.

If Müller's awareness of psychoanalysis as a discourse that would afford a certain faith in the power of the hidden is evident, his debt to a political philosophy that articulates a complementary point is perhaps less obvious. Müller's admiration for Ernst Bloch's philosophical project was recognizable in the way he mediated between the apparently diametrically opposed poles of faith and treason, memory and forgetting. Grounded in a philosophy of history, Müller allegorized memory by extricating himself from simple binary conceptions such as that of faithful recollection versus the hope for delivery from the treason of forgetting. For Bloch, forgetting is not the opposite of memory; both forgetting and treason are a lack of faith and memory when faced with what remains historically unresolved, with which we have not come to terms. With Bloch, the cultural semiotics of memory and forgetting can be inverted and recoded:

> Forgetting is not the opposite of recollection, for its opposite would be complete breakdown, one that no longer concerns anyone, that offers no admonishment, and to which no consideration can lead. For the same reason, forgetting is not the opposite of hope-reminiscence, rather it is a mode of memory as of reminiscence, it is that lack, which is called absence in memory, treason in recollection. Forgetting is a lack of faith, and here again not a lack of faith to ashes, but to unfinished business.[45]

Arguably, the architecture of Müller's take on history is built on the foundation of these lines. It is the realization that the overcoming of the dichotomies of victor and victim is an unattainable illusion, and that what remains are the dead.[46] To remember them faithfully is the minimal requirement without which no mode of mere living-on is feasible; but that alone does not necessitate monuments. Müller explodes their ruins in writing; his intertextual arrangements, collages, and montages, his polyphonic juxtapositions demonstrate that just as the writing subject is implicit, so is the meaning of the product.[47]

Even if we took Müller's mode of production as a prophylactic defense against forcible interpretations of anything even faintly autobiographical, we would still admit that his first, galvanizing recollection assumes programmatic status only if taken literarily, not literally. His concern is neither with truth nor with history, and so we are bound to take the exhibited first memory seriously, beyond historical veracity, for again, even as a false memory it may cover unrecognized true memories. Other autobiographical material would seem to offer itself up readily: suicides loom large on the horizon of his work, rewriting Rosa Luxemburg, Ophelia, Alcestis. Critics inevitably speculate about the role his wife Inge Müller's suicide might have played, how her texts haunt his before and after her death, and whether in the wake of the day he came close to being arrested for political reasons, he may have developed a literary habit of continually setting one scene in many ways, by way of a therapeutic experience.[48] Certainly his dialogue with the dead is led under the sign of poetic remembrance, and the many marked and unmarked citations from his wife's writings cannot cover the fact that her death has irrevocably cut something off and yet set something else in motion: the interaction of the lovers gives way to textual play, to the unmarked textual grave of intertextual practices that go beyond mourning and/or melancholia.[49]

Notably, there are no female warriors in Müller's drama. An early piece, *Medeaspiel*, shows military women, albeit in a patriarchal society.[50] Medea, who cut up her brother to gain time on those who would capture her but stop to pick up each piece from the sea, escapes with Jason. Intertextually, Bertolt Brecht's *Maßnahme* (1930) is radicalized here: a gang attack toward a young man is transformed into a kind of Pietà of several killers holding their victim; Medea herself appears as a cruel caricature of the Pietà. Yet Heiner Müller injects a complication into the apparent reduction to the one-on-one of mourning woman and dead man: Antigone is only a mask of Medea. The status given to the first, masked memory of a statue not unlike this figure—a killer, apparently mourning, as the kernel from which everything else could grow—affords the scene its programmatic power, a power that is confirmed by a cursory look at Müller's other dramatic work. One scene on this trajectory in Müller's writing is found in *Verkommenes Ufer Medeamaterial Landschaft mit Argonauten*: "But on the ground Medea, the cut up brother in her arm, a specialist in poison."[51] While Antigone had to die, Medea manages to survive: again, the survivor holds the victim in her arms, in the guise of the ethical gesture of the mourner, though she was in fact his killer. The deceptive gesture goes back beyond the programmatic screen memory from Müller's autobiography. Behind the logic of this superimposition, we recognize a taboo of socialist literature in East Germany.

Between Brecht's rendering of Sophocles in 1947 and the fall of the wall, there were no Antigones in East German literature.[52] For four decades, the GDR had Medea, Cassandra, Penthesilea, but no heroine who, like Antigone, is opposed to utopian deferrals. The dead must be buried here and now, Antigone admonishes; no deferral is ethically admissible. Her act of disobedience to Kreon demonstrates that she values forgiveness and mourning over the pride of her polis; accordingly, she is tried for treason just like her brother. Müller, conscious of this taboo, worked toward a continuing emphasis on femininity, in its relation to a time that is not dissected into units of measurement, but opens onto an ethical dimension, as in Nietzsche. Where the ideologically inadmissible topos of mourning was not excluded entirely under socialist rule, Heiner Müller's superimposition defamiliarizes it and once again throws his own primal topos into relief—that of the murderous mother whose mourning is false. The numerous recastings of Lysistrata, Ophelia, Elektra as vengeful goddesses of memory, such as in *Hamletmaschine*, eventually give way to the maternal figure as cemetery, Tamora for instance in *Anatomy Titus, Fall of Rome.*[53] Once the mother serves as a burial ground, her cannibalistic enjoyment of sacrifice turns her into a function of war. As Klaus Theweleit analyzes this male fantasy, a disturbed maternal bond gives rise to the psychical makeup of the warrior son who wants nothing but to be reunited with her in a fatal regression into death.[54] The despair that stems from the breakup of a primal pair thus fuels the war machine, and the depiction of a mother holding her fallen soldier-son cannot detract from the fact that she stands for the society that sent him into his death. To Müller, it seemed therefore only logical that the large sculpture by Käthe Kollwitz in front of Schinkel's "Neue Wache," a Pietà dedicated to the fallen son, would be surrounded by bronze statues for warriors Scharnhorst, Blücher, Gneisenau, and Yorck.[55] As one of the most central German war memorials, this set-up exemplifies exactly what Müller's childhood memory of the cemetery gestured toward. Feminine gestures of mourning may expose the cruelty of war and provide a sympathetic survivor identity, but they can just as well be seen to legitimize war.[56] In a similar vein, Müller criticized the underhanded strategy of the Verdun memorials, which he considered legible neither as commemorative nor as admonishing, but as blatant lies that erase the cruelty of battle, as dishonorable attempts to excuse having sent soldiers into certain death, as a futile effort to lend meaning to meaningless war.[57] He derided their monumental patriotic "kitsch" as appealing only to the dead, protesting that real art should be produced for the living.[58]

Müller's evocation of the notion of kitsch helps to elucidate the hidden nature of the hollowed-out figure of history.[59] Repeating his denunciation of memorials as nationalistic "legitimating kitsch," he analyzed them as phantasmatic "ersatz" and symptoms of bad conscience.[60] Indeed, the mask of the banal that Heiner Müller exposes, the mask with which a society may cover its shameful past, is the other side of Walter Benjamin's definition of kitsch: "it comes down to the primal fact of the mask" that allows us "to take the power of the extinguished thing-world into us."[61] Already as a child, Müller had felt that the Pietà does not symbolize mourning, but offers the perverse enjoyment of the death of others in a cannibalistic mode of survival. If it seems as if he knew all along, since childhood at the very least, then his readers will have known all along that this is an insight that served clandestine functions, and does not constitute mere hindsight. Benjamin wrote, "kitsch and folk art teach us to look out from within things."[62] This touches on Heiner Müller's central concern: to release what is hidden in the appearance of the present, the secret potentiality that lurks in each monument. A general suspicion of a systemic fabrication of memories allowed Müller to develop his means of exposing bad faith; in literary texts as in interviews, Müller takes recourse to the imagery of screen memories designed to expose the bottomless pretexts of political rituals of commemoration.[63]

The war memorial thus turns from a focal point of political and historical consciousness into a kernel of untruth, around which the playwright arranges the entire iconology of bad faith of the state and its duped citizens. If might indeed makes memory, Müller warns, then their fatal alliance must result in a severely crippled cultural collective—in totalitarian regimes, but also in any other society that does not unmask this strategy. For how could a statue even begin to account for death by starvation, by poison gas, or by shock?[64] Against this manipulation of cultural commemoration, Müller's texts summon resistances that reject all usurpers of the role of the keeper of memory, denouncing the tasteless survivalist pact between the dead and those who got away.[65] In interview after interview, Müller protested that state and mother, depicted as holding the dead in their grasp, forfeited any right over the dead.[66] In *Mommsens Block*, Müller extends the line that began before the First World War into the oblivious present after the fall of the Berlin Wall.[67] While practically everybody feigned the continuity of a cleansed, western self-image of Germany, Müller wanted it exposed as the crass attempt to silence all recollection of the German Democratic Republic and its political iconography. As he knew, it was an attempt doomed to failure due to heavy loans from the imagery of officious state memorials that are supposed to galvanize cultural memory.[68] The doomed art of collective forgetting that Müller diagnosed in memorial culture cannot shed its heritage of exclusive gestures and architectonic exorcisms, and the new hegemony covertly inherited it from the regime that resulted in the division of Germany in the first place. Müller exposes the monumental displacement that sealed German reunification with the ideological mark and scar of the Third Reich. The same structure was recognizable after 1989 behind efforts to make the Berlin Wall a symbol of unification and pacific tendencies. Müller's critical loyalty to the communist system of East Germany notwithstanding, he coldly diagnosed its continuity with Prussia, both being marked by their lack of any relation to femininity. Müller harbored no illusions about the paramnesia that calculatedly dehistoricizes political semiotics by hardly even redecorating, for want of another symbolic iconography, in order to mask the scars and traumatic traces as pure desire for eternity beyond all reproach and ideological discussion.

Heiner Müller's criticism of historical reasoning converges with a Marxist ideology of labor, and of the postwork characteristic of media society, in a uniquely
skewed space-time in which all teleological history is about to evaporate: "time
is the hole in creation, all of humanity fits into it."[69] Against any backward projection of a unified time-space that stabilizes history for delayed consumption,
reading Müller is to confront the diminishing relevance of personal and collective history as a frame of reference.[70] Müller exhibits his childhood memory
as symptomatic of the loss of critical distance, calculating that it will placate
and invite psychoanalytical readings as well as serve to deflect their interpretive
intervention by commingling historical and political concerns and reflections.
Indeed, Müller's laconic commentary was that this particular memory only
takes its rank as primary because in school, little Heiner was assigned an essay
about just such a "first memory." If the unstable privilege of the childhood
memory deflects and invites psychoanalytical and autobiographical interpretations, it is only due to the writer's sleight of hand, hiding the most vulnerable
secret right in the place of the obvious. Thus woven into the fabric of writing,
the fragmentary architecture of work built upon this precarious foundation
rises up as an architecture of déjà vu and is reinforced by a terminology that
both allows and deflects certain aberrations of memory.

In one of the last interviews before his death, Heiner Müller again distances
his conception of memory from a recollection of factual sequences of events, a
faculty, as he says, that machines ultimately execute much better. As if by return
to his programmatic, retroactivated beginnings in that first unsure premonition that he was to turn into the first memory, Müller pulls together his politics and poetics in the cover-ups and delays of a memory that would not obey
ideological peer pressures.[71] Müller thought that history and politics in the end
boil down to mechanisms of repression, and insisted that art, instead of being
complicit in the repression of death, is in fact rooted in communication with
the dead. Thus the future could only begin in a dialogue with the deceased.[72]
Suspecting that the history of facts is written, that is to say manipulated, by the
winners, Müller locates the difference between empirical and historical reality
in that events often only manifest themselves belatedly:

> For people who make art, memory is something quite different. It is not
> primarily a matter of remembering events. In the end, machines do that
> better: remembering facts. It is a matter of recollecting emotions, affects,
> that are related to events. Of an emotional memory. And that is what makes
> recollections material in the sense that one can build traditions and pass on
> experiences through this emotional memory. It is not at all a question of
> facts. This is the point where it basically becomes irrelevant whether a
> historical novel or drama depicts events in the order they occurred, or

whether one changes the chronology: the difference between empirical and historical truth. At times, the historical one is not identical with the empirical one, because the events are over before they become manifest. They already happened; the motion has already taken place.[73]

What Müller called his "Altgier" was a curiosity for that which is old, which sprang from a fear he often expressed in interviews: that technology ultimately cannot fail to erase memory.[74] To feed the constant hunger of the theatrical business of entertainment, he kept reformulating the sobering memento mori of his historical work: "Our task will be the work of difference, or the rest will be statistics and a matter of computers."[75] Compressing labor into a Benjaminian dialectical image, from *Herakles 2 oder Die Hydra* to the many superimpositions of female figures onto the cannibal mother, he continuously sharpens it for pointed impact. Such images require the collaboration of memory to space out what is compressed into their heightened tension. In this manner, the war monument crystallizes the discourse of mnemotechnics and the shock of mortality with which it is inextricably linked.

Benjamin, contemplating war memorials, appointed Karl Kraus a guardian of empty monuments of language on the "gigantic battlefield of bloody work."[76] Müller may have inherited that mantle. But if we read labor as the only red thread through Müller's work—whether as mothers bearing children or as male heroic stance, whether as Marxist organizing principle of history or as textual self-reflection—we risk neglecting what Hans-Thies Lehmann rightly calls its opposite pole on the elliptical trajectory of Müller's thought, and that pole is betrayal.[77] Indeed Müller's writing betrays his faith to Bloch's concepts of faith and treason, and many commentators have picked up on these keywords. Wolf Biermann's "Müller-machine" rips into the oedipal-institutional net of the near-miss anagram of father (*Vater*) and treason (*Verrat*) that caught an infinite number of doctoral dissertations.[78] But as Lehmann points out, even for Marx the utopian concept of labor was already contaminated in questionable ways with a violent insistence on presence and discipline that would later turn into state terror. The concept of labor includes, at its limits, the willingness to die, and the readiness to kill, in the name of the state. These labors mark the suffering and subjection of human existence. It is only logical that Herakles, above and before all other mythological figures, galvanized Müller's thought. Aside from *Herakles 2 oder die Hydra*, we should name the cleansing labor of *Herakles 5* (1964), fighting the systemic stench of mismanagement; *Die Befreiung des Prometheus* (1972), where his liberation by Herakles is unwelcome since Prometheus arranged himself with torturous repetition; and *Herakles 13* (1989), resonating with the fall of the Berlin Wall. Like Herakles, who at times wants to stop time and reverse his work, return the fur to the Lion and the heads to the

Hydra, Müller returns to his texts and rewrites them. Here is also a resonance with Müller's 1958 poem, "Der Glücklose Engel," a text Müller rewrote twice more. An overwhelming pile of rubble rises up behind the angel; inconceivable pressures from beyond are on the angel, whose eyes are gouged by the storm of the future, since unlike Benjamin's *angelus novus* he faces not the past but the future.

> Behind him, the past washes up, heaps rubble onto wings and shoulders
> with noise as if from buried drums, while the future backs up before him,
> gouging his eyes, exploding his eyeballs like stars, turning his word into a
> resonating gag, strangles him with his breath. For a while, one can still see
> his wings beating, listens to the rush of the stones coming down before over
> behind him, the louder the more violent his futile motions, isolated when it
> slows down. Then the moment closes over him: the luckless angel comes to a
> rest on the quickly covered platform, waiting for history in the petrification
> of flight gaze breath. Until the renewed rustle of mighty wings ripples in
> waves through the stone and indicates his flight.[79]

4

ANDY'S WEDDING:
READING WARHOL

It's the sound, heard by all, that lives in her
—Ovid, *Metamorphoses*

ANDY WARHOL USED ANY AND EVERY AVAILABLE TECHNOLOGY to communicate, and above all to communicate the fact that he was communicating,   but he never worried about the success or failure of communication—it was going to be repeated anyway.[1] "Non-communication" was not a problem—"I think everyone understands everyone," he said; yet he remained detached, even remote: "I don't want to get involved in other people's lives . . . I don't want to get too close . . . I don't like to touch things . . . that's why my work is so distant from myself . . ."[2] So how are we to read Andy Warhol—from afar? In recycling our unfulfillable desires, the culture industry invites us to enjoy our own lack and props it up as a mass deceit. For Adorno, who focuses on the downside of group psychology, the culture industry mechanism confirms the Freudian repetition compulsion, since culture is seen as the reduction of tension at all costs. Yet Andy Warhol's considerable body of work, strongly marked by repetition, cannot be dismissed as tedious silk screens, infantile drawings, and unhappy soup cans. His contribution to twentieth-century thought should not be underestimated: he was, after all, one of our foremost thinkers on such topics as repetition, kitsch, and aura—and perhaps the one who originally debunked originality.

If Heiner Müller was a technophobe who did not blink when it came to confronting contemporary conditions, Warhol was an all-out enthusiast who exploited a range of technologies. But if we accept his self-description, which combines an immediate transparency vis-à-vis the other with an insurmountable mediatic distance from the other, his own position disappears behind the machines. Warhol tried to see and record everything, though he knew this to be impossible, even with all the technological help he could get: "'But it's impossible,' he said, 'it's impossible! I tried, but it is impossible. It's impossible to carry with you a movie camera, a tape recorder, and a still camera at the same time. I wish I could do it.'"³ Reading Warhol in his obsession with remote sensing might offer an experience of the impossible. Arguably, all technologies are there to serve as means of stalking and preserving the moment in order to repeat it, and to preserve it as repeatable—not in timeless storage, but with a difference. Thus the repeatability granted by technology converges with, and confirms, the irresistible power of iterability. But if repetition, in Warhol's world, comes to constitute everything, what would the unrepeatable be?

The victory of technological innovations leads not only to ever more obsessive documentation and surveillance—omnipresent reduplications entail a palimpsestic cultural déjà vu. This effect goes hand in hand, as psychoanalysis helps us diagnose, with depersonalization and derealization—or as Adorno wrote about the doubles and revenants in Kafka's technifying, collectifying literature: "the permanent déjà vu is everyone's déjà vu."⁴ This kind of repetition, as an agent of repression, is understood as existential unhappiness in the tradition of the Frankfurt School.⁵ In the same logic, the unrepeatable is a peculiar singularity that cannot be subsumed, or rather that disappears when it is subsumed under generality. And if singularity precisely does not consist in its being indivisible, not in a recollection or gathering, but rather in the sealed mark of division or doubling in the medium, then it does not depend on a conceptual nature or an essence, but can only appear, in its disappearance, as that which is radically nonconceptual. This fury of disappearance depends on an obsession with repetition, and is conceivable only as a disappearance of repetition, as a negative function of repetition.⁶

From the earliest shoe drawings to the final painting of the Last Supper all in kitschy red, the incessant repetition in Warhol's work and the relentless industrial naivete of the "Factory" have given more than one critic the impression that in many ways this work is placed firmly under the sign of déjà vu.⁷ Indeed Warhol's use of movie cameras, tape recorders, and still cameras applies itself to the arrest, the capture, of what we could not perceive without technological aid. This application illustrates the inversion of perspective, the recording of voices, the experience of the unrepeatable, the returns of kitsch. His use of modern media technology did not stop at works on silk screen, paper, canvas, or the projection screen; he also produced a novel in the factory, a tape that—once transcribed—returns the question of writing anew. For writing, far from being reducible to mechanical repetition, exhibits a certain "mechanical" resistance to presentation or analysis. Thus reading, in turn, can end up having to deal with tape-recorded speech, despite Hans Georg Gadamer's protestations to the contrary. A real text, Gadamer protested, should be written for the reader, not merely a fixation of voice, tone, and gesture by means of tape-recording. Consequently, Warhol's texts would be impossible to understand. The ideality of the eminent text as an extension of the reach of communication, as that which "wants to be read," would have to remain linear and unchanged, untouched by reading.[8] Its sense would be prescribed, only to be voiced by the reader. To consider writing a mere addition to speech, on the other hand, would mean to admit that our sense of speech had fallen short of itself, from the beginning— riding the ripples of auto-affective feedback all the way into literacy.[9] Navigating between the extremes of a hermeneutic gesture that would exclude Warhol a priori and the journalistic amusement his sensational work was greeted with, we will try to map out a way of reading Warhol, attending to what he called his wedding with the machine.

Warhol's texts require the reader to decode the specific hiatus, the asymmetry of deferred communication: traditionally, voice and aura are considered inimitable and unrepeatable, and the task of technology would be to capture their moment, preserve the voice, reproduce the aura. Here, communication is neither impossible nor truly possible—it is caught up in the loops of replayed recordings and replications. Warhol was so bonded to technology that eventually he considered himself married to it. Practically living by proxy, always on the phone, watching TV, he relentlessly recorded his Factory personnel on tape or on video. In his first book, *The Philosophy of Andy Warhol from A to B and Back Again*, he confessed to enjoying certain kinky bedroom plays:

> So in the 50s I started an affair with my television which has continued to the present, when I play around in my bedroom with as many as four at a time. But I didn't get married until 1964 when I got my first tape recorder. My wife. My tape recorder and I have been married for ten years now. When I say "we," I mean my tape recorder and me. A lot of people don't understand that.[10]

Therefore, when the *Andy Warhol Diaries* came out after his death, consisting of carefully edited transcriptions of tapes by Pat Hackett, we may say that his wife had written his memoirs while he was still alive—only their publication lagged behind. Once again, we return to the figure of the impossible couple—

the female part restricted to repeating, but changing in deferral, what is spoken. From its improper origin, this altering echo produces meanings, but Warhol's production of reproduction was not a monogamous affair: when he started recording interviews for his book *POPism*, he would bring two tape recorders and run one while changing the tape in the other, so that nothing could escape.[11] And in the same manner, Warhol—who spent much of his time on the phone, while trying to take in everything that went on around him—produced the book published in 1968 as *a. a novel*, consisting of 451 pages of taped, transcribed Factory activities and telephone conversations, as in a cumulative collect call.[12]

Since the status of the telephone and its attachments in writing is hotly contested, some unlikely alliances are formed. One party, siding with Gadamer at least on this question, warns that "we can continue writing and reading, adding phrase to phrase without interruption," as Niklas Luhmann wrote, "except by the telephone"—for once finding himself on the same side as Ernst Jünger, for whom telephone and tape recorder were detrimental to conversation.[13] The other party, led by Marcel Proust, encourages you to embrace the new means of communication: "since one cannot telephone all the time, one reads. One does not read til the last moment; above all, one phones a lot"—one reads only when one cannot talk on the telephone.[14] While the first alliance will protest the dignity of literacy and the richness of the word, the latter group states soberly that the audio-visual contact made possible by technology ought to be confronted without phobic defenses. Frank O'Hara stopped writing poetry because he could phone his lines in, others claim that "literature no longer allows you to telephone," reasoning that "only writing (in the intransitive sense) disconnects you."[15] The telephone book used to be one of the few volumes an academic does not wish she had written; yet this may no longer hold true after Avital Ronell's popular advertising copy in the yellow pages of her best seller.[16] We cannot let such party lines take over this text. They will have left their messages, as if on an answering machine.[17] We are interested above all in Andy Warhol's tapes:

> I did my first tape recording in 1964 . . . I think it all started because I was trying to do a book. A friend had written me a note saying that everybody we knew was writing a book, so that made me want to keep up and do one too. So I bought that tape recorder and I taped the most interesting person I knew at the time, Ondine, for a whole day.[18]

Warhol and his "wife" SONY had been following Robert Olivio, or "Ondine," one of the first Factory stars, and simply recorded him everywhere. Olivio aka Ondine had appeared in Warhol's *Vinyl* (1965), *Chelsea Girl* (1966), and *The*

Loves of Ondine (1967) before he was cast in this first of all radical reality shows. As Olivio recalls three years later:

> We tried to do 24 hours at one stop, and it became . . . it was just too much. I mean, Andy followed me into the toilet room when I was taking a shit. It was just impossible. It was literally impossible. It was literally like crawling up the walls. Have you ever had anyone do that to you? It's just . . . It's a fabulous book, isn't it? I mean, it is a totally fabulous book, but . . . but how can you say that to anybody?[19]

Warhol's intrusive witness protection program does not relieve the senses, nor does it heighten them; it offers love and attention, but only on condition of total control in repetition and recall. The impossible Factory experience starts like this:

> Rattle, gurgle, clink, tinkle.
> Click, pause, click, ring.
> Dial, dial.
> ONDINE—You said *(dial)* that, that, if, if you pick, pick UP the Mayor's voice on the other end *(dial, pause, dial-dial-dial)*, the Mayor's sister would know us, be *(busy-busy-busy)*.
> DRELLA—We should start for the park, right? Okay. Hmm. *Coin drops. Money jingles as coins return. car noises in the background.* You're a clunk. Are there any way stations on the way that we have to *(honk, honk)* like uh, I, wha—*(noise)*. If we go through, through the park, is there ANY place we can keep calling your uh, I mean right through the, uh, phone call. Is there any place where we can keep call him if we— Answering service . . . Are you *(cars honking, blasting)*. Are there difFER-ent places—are there different places where we can call your ans—oh. (1)

When *a. a novel* was sold for ten dollars a copy in 1968, complete with carefully preserved typing mistakes, the reception was very reserved; it was read mostly as a frivolous portrait of sixties drug culture. The only good review it ever got was from *Playboy*, praising its "microcosm of words, mutilated sentences, grunts, giggles and blah blahs surrounding us."[20] All subsequent attempts to elicit further comment on the time, the project, or the perceived conundrums and juicy secrets of this clumsy roman à clef were futile, since Warhol appeared oblivious or at the very least indifferent to what readers might make of the book. But it is too easy to argue that such polished provocations play with the sheen of the surface and its refraction, and Warhol's manifest interest in the marginal may have been an attempt to stage the return of a repressed aesthetic. We can infer that Warhol was hardly bothered when confronted with the question whether or not there was any "realism" in it, for seven years after publishing *a. a novel*, he explained:

Nothing was ever a problem again, because a problem just meant a good
tape, and when a problem transforms itself into a good tape it's not a
problem any more. An interesting problem was an interesting tape.
Everybody knew that and performed for the tape. You couldn't tell which
problems were real and which problems were exaggerated for the tape.
Better yet, the people telling you the problems couldn't decide any more if
they were really having the problems or if they were just performing.[21]

At stake here is the very distinction between observer and observed: the other
of interiority is not simply its opposite, it works the interior, from the interior,
and yet is not itself inside. Suddenly, reading takes place within a much altered
frame of reference: there is no "outside the media," no detached vantage point
of the observer, after Warhol. This inversion echoes Benjamin's déjà vu, only in
this case, it is less a matter of time and its passing than of the dialectics of seeing or being seen, under the conditions of the machine.

Accordingly, the challenge posed to us is to figure out the conditions of
possibility for reading a text produced not by an original, inspired author, but
by the means of repetitive, automatic, senseless technology. The technological
innovations of the twentieth century have allowed mankind to break the limitations of space and time and to extend the means of understanding, "mass-
producing the moment."[22] Timing, efficiency, automated production rule; on
the other hand, the spontaneous is in increasing demand: just reach out and
touch someone. As fleeting images become recordable, food portable, experiences repeatable, so it does not require a cunning technical apparatus to realize
that reading already telephones: it summons distant voices. The invention of
the telephone rose out of attempts to create a telegraph that would be able to
send more than one message at once over a single line. The logic of the machine
is its power to invert, at least potentially, the traditional notion of time. In a
more abstract formulation: the machine produces anachronisms.

One of the earliest Bell Company advertisements for the telephone presents
a prescient user's manual for the novel of indistinctly articulated repetition that
Warhol would publish decades later: "Conversation can easily be carried on after
slight practice and with occasional repetition of a word or sentence. On first
listening to the Telephone, though the sound is perfectly audible, the articulation seems to be indistinct, but after a few trials the ear becomes accustomed
to the peculiar sound."[23] Of course, one voice alone may already constitute
sensory overload in exceptional cases. The synesthetic memory of Luria's mnemonist seemed so inexhaustible that it took him decades to learn about forgetting: "I got so interested in his voice," the patient recalls, "I couldn't follow
what he was saying." Frequently experiencing trouble recognizing someone's
voice over the phone, he found it was not because of a "bad connection," but

"because the person happens to be someone whose voice changes twenty to thirty times in the course of a day." Despite bad connections, he eventually succeeds, as Luria reports proudly: "he automatically screened off excess details by singling out key points of information."[24] In short, we had to learn the art of distraction and filtering to cope with the new medium, before attaching peripherals to it. The threat of a fail-safe automatic memory to the much older technology of writing has had to do with the fact that the inscription of the live and spontaneous quality of the voice was much delayed. Considering the enormous effect the telephone had right away, it is surprising that it took as long as it did before it was supplemented by the tape recorder to form a small surveillance unit: already in 1877, Thomas Alva Edison had considered the possibility of what he called a "telephone repeater." Afraid that the high cost of telephoning might deter people from using it widely, he hoped to profit from offering a device that people without a phone could use to record their voice and then have the message replayed over a central voicemail box to the prospective addressee.[25] But nothing became of his plans. Radio and television captured the attention until the question of recording returned during World War II for the purposes of cryptology and propaganda. Although Alexander Graham Bell was the first to suggest the possibility of magnetic recording devices, it took until 1898 for Valdemar Poulsen to develop a "telegraphophone" in Denmark that could be used as a dictaphone, but was not loud enough for entertainment use. In the 1930s, magnetic recording on coated paper was developed in Germany and turned to commercial use, and soon canned voices could withstand even the heat, cold, or vibrations that disk recording could not take. Tape cassettes were introduced in the early 1960s, and outsold open-reel players for the first time in 1968, just when Warhol decided to use them to "write" his novel.

Perhaps only the word gadget—derived from the French *gachette*, meaning a piece of machinery—comes close to describing Warhol's relationship with technology. Although in this context it may appear to be another anachronism, since Warhol's antics predate its widespread use in English, the gadget has since come to stand for a particular kind of fetishism. The telephone of course was originally a gadget, and today's secondary gadgets attach themselves to it, up to the Internet and beyond. Call waiting, call forwarding, beepers, quick-dial, cordless extension phones, and conference calls became available in the late 1960s; recording devices have been in particular demand, as preferable to operators. In the mid-seventies, answering machines that replayed a prerecorded message, then took incoming messages and could be accessed remotely by the owner, became available for home use. In 1974, the Phone Mate, the Remote Mate, and the Automatic Electric Speaker Phone sold for several hundred dollars; for considerably less money, the anxious could not only monitor incoming calls without answering immediately, but also record every conversation that went over the phone line.[26] At the time, such surveillance was legal as long as one party was informed of the call being recorded.[27] As motivations for such relentless surveillance, we consider three proposals: paranoia, narcissism, and mourning.

If, as Freud has it, we ourselves are creating the gaps that we consequently have to bridge with the help of gadgets such as the telephone, this goes back all the way to the invention of writing as one of the first technologies, substituting for the voice of an absent person. The telephone becomes an image of the transference, a projection of our earliest connections. As Roland Barthes pointed out, Freud did not like the telephone's separation lines: "the other departs twice over, by voice and by silence."[28] The telephone is also hooked up to the occult when it seems to connect to that which belongs to the past. The desire to get in touch with "the other side" frequently manifests itself in the early reception of new technologies; one could cite spiritistic photography as a prime example, and radio was regarded, in its infancy, as a possible means to contact the dearly departed. Edison, the inventor of the phonograph, was also working on a device that was to enable him to communicate through a telepathic channel that he surmised between the long and the shortwave frequencies, and Guglielmo Marconi believed he could capture Christ's last words on the cross by wireless transmission.[29] The voice is the other, more primal connection to mother, and it remains a direct connection to the one who is far away and so close; over the telephone, the voice always comes life-size, no bandwidth restrictions detract from its primal associations. The phone is very good at conveying apparently unmixed intentions, for we cannot see the conflicting nonverbal message that could accompany the voice; in this way, too, the phone gives rise to the fantasy of emotional directness. But the same anonymity and invisibility that offer relief can be very scary, since the phone always reanimates the earliest connections. In short, Warhol's motivation might be traced back to childhood, and in particular, to his relationship to his mother.

However, in an interview Warhol claimed: "I've had no childhood, I may have it later."[30] This inversion, which we must neither take at face value nor dismiss out of hand, raises another possibility besides mourning for mother. Media theorists like Friedrich Kittler opine that the possibility for endless repetition on the basis of automatic recording was only one more reason to keep speaking: "to speak in particular about what writing is, and what it means psychoanalytically to be able to read one's own speech, even what is merely spoken off-the-cuff."[31] This odd scene of technified speech is staged in Warhol's *Diaries* as well as in *a. a novel*. If only for comparison's sake, consider Richard Matheson's short story "Person to Person," where the protagonist has to deal with a phone ringing in his head.[32] As he proceeds from one diagnosis to another, from stress to schizophrenia to telepathy to a secret NSA operation

experimenting with hypnosis to possession with an earthbound spirit, it tran-
spires that every time he answers the ring, the voice gains more control over
him, merely by making him lose himself. Whether the voice returns as that of
his father, that of a spy, that of a Martian, or that of a lonely inventor trying to
make contact, neither the protagonist's physician nor his analyst nor a psychic
can figure out that, in fact, it is an acoustic mirror of the loser protagonist who
kills himself a little every time he answers, only to return within himself in
the end as a more empowered, less frightened self; and it is only that new self
that is strong enough to yank out the wire to that internal telephone. Regardless whether one calls it conscience, superego, or soul, in our teletechnological
world, the pivotal repetition without which there would be no such thing as
recognition will have always been deranged, as it were, by a mechanical double,
an internal telephone; to capture and replay is also to reply.[33] However, reading Andy Warhol has nothing to do with persecutory internal voices; he was
simply fascinated with the capture of the other, and with the mechanisms of
repetition, in an obvious attempt to control people, actively and passively:

> You know? And that I was the only one that could use the bell that way: BIZZ!
> BIZZ! BIZZ! And that everyone would eventually get up. You know?[34]

Thus while some of his entourage may have been paranoid (or driven to act
out as if they were), as witnessed at various stages in Warhol's book, there is
little indication that Warhol himself was even marginally paranoid; even in his
deepest gadget-love, he maintained an impregnable mask.

Then one day, Warhol was shot by Valerie Solanas. This intimation of mortality, perhaps the one undeniably singular event in Warhol's life as an artist,
was seized on for various approaches to the question of his originality and its
undoing. But for Warhol and his inner circle, it was soon absorbed in a strange
logic. Valerie Solanas, as it turned out, was not the first to fire a gun in the Factory, but she did so on the day Robert Kennedy was assassinated on the other
coast, and she was prepared for the celebrity to come with her SCUM manifesto. Since in Warhol's world there is neither infamy nor notoriety, celebrity
is all. When Dorothy Podber aimed a gun at Warhol long before Solanas, she
then turned away and shot a stack of six Marilyn portraits on the wall. After
she quietly left the building, it was quickly declared a "happening." The authenticity of Warhol silk screens is questionable, because his dislike for any kind of
touch at times would prevent him from signing them; as Ultra Violet reports,
it became normal for anyone else in the Factory to sign Brillo Boxes, Marilyns,
and soup cans as "Andy Warhol." However, the shot Marilyns came to be considered more valuable since the bullet holes made them more "authentic."[35]
Here may be a connection to Warhol's relationship with the dead; after all, this
enigmatic vampire of the art world of his time was nicknamed Drella, a cross

between Cinderella and Dracula. Warhol's book had provoked the pessimistic judgment of the *New York Review of Books,* concluding in a characteristically dismissive review "that in its errant pages can be heard the death knell of American literature."[36] Then again, writing can be about taking calls from the dead. In literature, as Northrop Frye wrote, repetition is "not the simple repeating of an experience, but the re-creating of it which redeems or awakens it to life."[37] Thus here is a possible distinction between actively stalking repetition and an uncanny, uncalled-for, ghostly return.[38] In both cases, psychoanalysis can serve as a user's manual to mankind's ongoing technologization.[39] It is not just a question of automatic machine effects—predictable or unpredictable, the very idea of using the telephone for communing with the other side invites the posthumous, uncanny return.

However, to read Narcissus without Echo or vice versa will miss the point: the story of Echo's strangely spectral and yet amplified voice already established how she serves to hide both the meaning and the source of repetition.[40] This is mildly revised in Walter Rathenau's story "Resurrection Co.," where telephones are installed in each grave to ward off the fear of being buried alive in a graveyard in an American town.[41] Soon enough, a lady who had been buried for several months calls up the switchboard, demanding to be put in touch with another grave. It turns out that it is precisely the technology that is supposed to offer the solace of salvation that can transform a whole society into a wired, technologized graveyard. Electronic recording, as a logical consequence, must practically offer itself up to similar investigations. "The experimenter must develop his hearing by constant listening to tapes," as one gadget lover warned: "What at first seems like atmospheric buzzing is often many voices. They have to be analyzed and amplified, of course."[42] This is exactly what happens in Andy Warhol's book:

> I'm going to the . . . we are now, oh look . . . Oh uh, what happened? Oh it's just ruined just signaled. I don't bel- . . . Ondine. Oh here, I have it. No, I mean I just have, it's not armed. *Ondine sings—Phaedra jalous. Kids in the background.* Oh stop that noise. Basta with the noise. *(Ondine mutters.)* Stop the eternal racket, my ears are killing me. *(Pause.)* Maybe we're doing the right thing without doing anything. Do you think I should try a tape? Uh maybe you should wait til Bill comes. This is always there. W-wait . . . *(pause).* Turn it louder. (72)

As a double of the living voice, the recorded one must appear uncanny, canned, straining to erase itself in order to shake its technological constraints. In order to remain the live voice, it would rather die and disappear than be forced into repetition. At the same time, repetition can also mean cathexis onto the same, or narcissism in all its different forms. Interestingly, New York artist Kenneth

Goldsmith imitated Warhol's project, and also put out a book entirely produced by round-the-clock tape recording, printed unedited. However, he claims not to have known of Warhol's *a*.[43] But perhaps the sincere flattery of imitation is no less sincere as a repetition of Warhol's debunking originality.

Andy Warhol was also a collector, and the discovery of his hoard after his death was a surprise. While he was good at generating a group dynamic, he did not seem to be defined by the company he kept—or its factory. Although Warhol let it be known that sexually he preferred men to women, it seemed as if he needed no completion, felt no lack, since he was already completed by the machine. At times, his behavior certainly resembled the narcissistic disturbance of falling for the seduction of pure surface, where the secret is not what is hidden inside, but an excess on the surface. In this regression, one is no longer libidinally connected to anything other than the ego; consequently, any stimulation at all, whether in the form of a demand from another person or an impulse from within oneself, is perceived as technological. But unlike Daniel Paul Schreber, Warhol did not engage in paranoid overinterpretation—he never interpreted anything. Everything was plain, circulating on the surface. And Warhol never accepted responsibility for anything, least of all the writing published as "his." Whenever someone would bring up the typographic and other errors in *POPism* or *a. a novel*, he would invariably claim neither to have written nor in fact to have read it, and so none of it could have been his fault.[44] Echo was condemned to absolute irresponsibility since she could not answer in words, phrases, signs, or even silence. She could only echo, register, repeat, and so stands for iterability and recordability. But strictly speaking, absolute irresponsibility is the only possibility of responsible answerability, the structure of an answering machine, because it does not dictate an immediate response to the living voice. It allows for a delay, for storage; it gives time. In this sense, Warhol's work expresses the desire of a narcissistic art world to overcome its own encryption in specular repetition.

Certain screen memories are carried over in lapses, and such reminiscence-by-symptom shows the difference between what Jacques Lacan called symbolic recognition and imaginary reminiscence.[45] In his seminars, Lacan dismisses the "ambiguous phenomenon of *déjà vu*," opting for a focus on the gaze and its inversion.[46] Nevertheless, the reality testing to which he reduces Freud's ambiguities does not prevent the structure of déjà vu from appropriating the notion of the gaze (in reverse) with which he screens over the complexity. Regarding the notion of recollection in analysis, Lacan claimed "categorically" that full speech was intrinsic to the process: "in psychoanalytical anamnesis, it is not a question of reality, but of truth, because the effect of full speech is to reorder past contingencies by conferring on them the sense of necessities to come"—

and this conception of veracity in the future anterior of *la parole vraie* realizes the subject's history with the future in mind.[47] The voice, moreover, is supposed to be directly identical with that of which it speaks, live and immediate. But what happens to the "live voice" after it becomes technologically repeatable? Without allowing for retransmission or recording, a Lacanian reading of the Freudian scene of *déjà raconté* becomes doubly impossible: namely, impossible to analyze from afar on the basis of letters of correspondence, and intrinsically insoluble as the folding away of the live voice since it seems to arrive only as its own originary repetition.[48] To this extent, Andy Warhol presents a "Lacan in reverse," offering one of the most original discourses on unoriginality. More specifically, reading Warhol's gadget love shows how the erasure by technology is bound to the incessant recall of its historical interventions. In reading Warhol, we encounter a voiceless voice that is activated on the surveillance tape of his answering machine.

In Lacan's seminar, the tapes were running along with the stenographer, creating media links between tape recorder, headphones, and typewriter, feeding every noise back into the loop of what had already been said. The attempt could be made to draw parallels between the tape reels of Warhol and Lacan, the master whose seminars had to be "written" by tape, since he was addressing an audience that understood nothing, as Friedrich Kittler put it.[49] But to make this comparison so is to elide one crucial difference between their positions toward the machine: where Lacan with heroic gestures offers himself up as spectacle, indicating nothing but depth and difficulty, the impresario of the Factory uses the machine only to make superstars of others, never directly of himself.[50] What is more, as Warhol told interviewers time and again, "If you want to know all about Andy Warhol, just look at the surface of my paintings and films and me, and there I am. There's nothing behind it."[51] As a consequence, Warhol's insistence on flat superficiality had to be tested by a gun, while Lacan was never shot at. Inversely, this distinction is also borne out by the fact that Lacan's inheritance is bitterly fought over by sectarian factions, while Warhol, during his lifetime as well as in death, remained supremely in control; as Thomas Crow puts it, "it would be difficult to name an artist who has been as successful as Warhol was in controlling the interpretation of his own work."[52] What would a "successful" interpretation be of this artist so deeply obsessed with success, and so successful at deciding the success of others? If our reading is not to be programmed by Warhol the machine, we may need to get around the mechanism it sets up, without repeating Valerie Solanas.

Despite all his obsession with loops of repetition, Warhol was fully invested in the present, in its circulation and its ever renewed powers of seduction. Psychotics know nothing about the present, they make no distinction between inside and outside and so have no interiority; despite a certain structural kinship it is not tenable to portray Warhol as a psychotic. Warhol dismisses models that build on depth and interpretation and opposes to them the notion of superficial seduction. (As Jean Baudrillard would argue, Warhol saw that the secret is not what is repressed or hidden in an inside—it is an excess on the surface.[53]) More precisely, it is that which is outside the self to such a degree that it draws away from the self and plunges into the abyss, absorbing everything around it.[54] In the cultural logic of late capitalism, Jameson sees "an extraordinary sense of déjà vu and a peculiar familiarity one is tempted to associate with Freud's 'return of the repressed.'"[55] In Warhol, he recognizes a return of the repressed, something that looks back at you:

> we must surely come to terms with the role of photography and the photographic negative in contemporary art of this kind; and it is this, indeed, which confers its deathly quality to the Warhol image, whose glacéd X-ray elegance mortifies the reified eye of the viewer in a way that would seem to have nothing to do with death or the death obsession or the death anxiety on the level of content.[56]

Therefore, only appearances are in fact secret, because they do not yield to interpretation; they are only there for the sake of the seductive effect. This effect means that seduction ultimately promises to return the secret—more precisely, "to circulate and animate appearance as secret."[57] This theory takes as its basis a kind of acting out. It would be grounded in an interruption of communication that displaces from speech to surface appearance. However, this mere gesture of seduction will in turn demand from the other that it be interpreted, however seductively it beckons the addressee without giving any further indication of how channels are to be opened to negotiate its effect or meaning.[58] This may seem like an appropriate description of Warhol until we remember that this seduction is a displacement onto the circular, the repetitive, and the ritualistic; and we recognize that this scenario, though advertised as an alternative to psychoanalysis, in fact proposes nothing but an inversion of psychoanalysis.

In this inversion, we return to the structure of the secret. Of course, taking into account Warhol's influence, Baudrillard's reading of narcissistic secrecy may in fact have been invited by Warhol's dissociation from psychoanalysis. Suffice to point to the relation between a desire to be filled, and an acting out that makes you believe that plenitude is already achieved, that there is no depth that would need filling. When a disappearance into the utmost depth, or the total surface, is staged as the end of communication, one may well suspect that it has to do with the tidal pull of that last disappearance, death. Of course, the anxieties, displacements, forms of denial and self-deception that cling to ideas about death, or to fear of death, are vanishing points for theory. The thought, however dim and secretive, of finitude in the ultimate suspension of all symbolic exchange brings out the need for continuity, for renewal and return; and in such forced new beginnings, we again encounter the bending back of time onto itself that would remark all present and future as already past: déjà vu. In short, déjà vu performs a certain acting out of resistance to the absolute lines of division between life and death, self and other, and thus helps bridge the gap. One would rather experience repetition than the end, if it were possible to experience the end that would not already be the end of experience.

Although Freud rarely considers the possibility of a resistance that is heterogeneous to all analysis and hence nonsubjective, it seems necessary to consider it here. It would be a force that is not of the order of dissimulation, not simply a veiled or hidden meaning. Nor would it fit the categories of the five types of resistance Freud accounts for in the appendix to "Inhibition, Symptom, Anxiety," because it would remain irreducible to a product of the ego, super-ego, or id. Not owing, but indeed lending its force to the process of analysis, this built-in resistance can be called repetition.[59] What, however, would the end of repetition be? As we know from Benjamin, Kafka, or Cocteau, the power of the voice from the other side of the line is irresistible; one suspects that the structures materialized in the machine have to do more with an automatic forgetting than an automatic memory. Indeed Warhol joked in interviews that his head is like a tape recorder with only one button: to erase.[60] Thus repetition in Warhol would be circumscribed by two kinds of forgetting. He who claims to have no memory since he got married to a magnetophone, since he had technology in his head to substitute for memory, never actualizes repetition or reproduction, since he forgets right away—and thus, ironically, experiences difference in repetition. As Warhol said, he would watch a show on TV one night, and then again right away with the same tension, because he simply did not remember what happened. To lose the capacity to recognize or identify two similar events or objects is to achieve an impairment that Marcel Duchamp visualized as the impossibility of memory.[61] But Warhol exhibits his amnesia less as an ascetic exercise of artistic virtue than as a humorous provocation that would make him the inverse of Luria's mnemopathic patient. Before returning to the question of the unrepeatable, take a closer look at what Warhol leads us to understand by repetition.

What is sensation, and what is the voice, when technological repeatability and reproducibility intrude into the realm of perception in such a way that Warhol could consider himself literally wedded to the machine? It is under these conditions, in response to this initial call that we must read. "We had to wait for the machine. It's just been delivered. It just got here."[62] Is the book an answering machine? In what sense can one claim that the reader must also be an answering machine? As in Samuel Beckett's play *La dernière bande*, set one day in the distant future, memory and future become questionable when the last conversation can be recalled by means of a tape, and when the postmortem lies in the archive for decades. Warhol's *a. a novel* confronts the reader with all the sounds of the Factory, but mainly with the half-recorded telephone conversation between people who call each other "Rotten Rita" or "The Duchess," "Billy Name" or "Tiger Morse." There is an impressive amount of drug-taking and a depressing length of tape, the book being the result of almost complete technical surveillance. Everything happening in the Factory is stored on tape, video and audio, and while some audio tapes are being transcribed, the next ones are being recorded with the clatter of typewriters in the background producing the book: "O—I had everything I wanted including *telephone rings typewriter writes telephone rings* O—I'll get it; no I won't" (405). The book produced in this manner is utterly automatic in that it contains its own principle of movement; and while it does not erase but self-consciously foregrounds its own means of production, it would like to do away with forgetting.

> No it's novel that it's being a novel as a matter of fact—vut do you mean by a novel? uhhhhhh   I know it just . . . there's no other brush stroke. 12 hours of Ondine   a novel? quo're not going—are you going to put it in a book or what make it one whole book. (100)

This unity is of course forever postponed by means of the ongoing tape recording. The penultimate chapter of Warhol's novel is a soliloquy that begins like this: "This is a supposedly long m-o-n-o-logue about whatever it is that I talk about uh—I'm no brain—and I never have had a brain—and I don't want one; I dun know what else to say—this tape should be finished—I wish I were a brai-n" (405). In this parody of post-Joycean monologue, Warhol confounds not only the apparently so easy distinctions between ear and phone; even the spiritual is no longer opposed to the mechanical, but the mechanical comes back to haunt the spiritual: "Hello may. I'm making love t o th e taperecord er. Hehh Hehh Hehh I don't know what to say to i t. Uhh—religiou s" (445). And this marriage with the mechanical bride, made in technological heaven, does not allow for a divorce, because writing and reading presuppose the technological to such an extent that they are inseparable. The history of memory and of mnemonics is commonly divided into a rhetorical tradition that constantly invents technical models, and a psychological one that holds them to be mere metaphors unable to represent either incorporation or hypomnetic excarnation. However, if speech is communicated above our heads, we will have needed the ferro-heads of tape recorders, as Kittler put it, to make speech "immortal."[63] In passing through circuits and terminals, the voice will have been terminated.[64] But it survives: the short-circuiting of the voice results in a technologized text, a computerized telephone, that is to say, an answering machine.

How to respond to this kind of antihermeneutical teletext that automatically creates itself and has already swallowed the reader? An approach to Andy
Warhol's book must take into account the way in which the phone is already
off the hook; the receiver dangles in front of us and we have to respond as we
are sucked into the telephonic structure of the book, remembering and foiling
all recall. When we speak of technology, we speak of repetition and of memory:
but is this use of technology against forgetting not also an attempt to forget
about forgetting by means of technology? If there could be no literature without the technologies of writing, we also need an anamnesis of that which is
erased and forgotten. The last words of *a. a novel* are: "Out of the garbage, into
The Book" (451). The recycling of the voice in writing is figured, here, as the
return of remembrance in forgetting. As Kittler put it, "after all, tape recorders,
television cameras and radio microphones were invented for the very purpose
of recording gibberish (Blabla). Precisely because they 'understand nothing.'"[65]
It is an attempt to use tape and paper against forgetting, while at the same time
covertly trying to forget about forgetting. And yet, a memory of forgetting only
turns the forgotten into something phenomenal and thus betrays forgetting in
turn. It would seem that an "automatic forgetting" is redundant—yet how could
forgetting be anything else? The materiality of the act of reading itself is all too
easily forgotten, as on the tape of incoming messages on an answering machine,
erasing older messages. The automatic keeps erasing itself automatically, and
intervenes in order to facilitate a forgetting of forgetting; it automatically functions like a cover-up, and I have momentarily forgotten who told me that—it
might have been left on my ansaphone. The case of Andy Warhol's *a. a novel*
demonstrates that the delayed answerability, the very structure of responsibility in literature calls for an answering machine. Nothing, this pervasive use of
technology seems to promise, can be lost anymore—everything is collected. Yet
this amassing presupposes disappearance, a loss against which one must guard.
Here, the archive is a cover-up for the inevitable, necessary forgetting that contaminates all commitment to memory. In the Kittlerian spin that is replayed
on all such discursive occasions, the phonograph makes memory possible and
thus unconscious.[66] Media theory, citing Kafka's clairvoyant audio-vision that a
parlograph could pick up the phone in Berlin and chat with a phonograph in
Prague, will have to groove with Warhol's scratchy provocations by combining
Freud's with Benjamin's insights on matters of collecting and kitsch.[67]

As part of the prehistory of the museum, one may understand collecting as
rationalization of the empiricism of science or as a compensation in the sense
of a constant but mostly unreflected drive for completion that stems from some
kind of early loss or trauma. In a certain psychoanalytic setting or session,
the choice can be seen as lying between depression and the manic pursuit of

compensation. In addition, one may focus on the intensity and subjectivity of collecting and situate it in the context of innovation in modernity. Boris Groys argues that the logic of collecting has led to a privileging of the new and different; in preserving artifacts from the past, the museum in effect creates the demand for innovation and for the incorporation of the new into the existing collections. Museum collections, seen that way, should be the real motor behind the drive for artistic and cultural innovation in modernity by creating an ever greater demand for what is different and new.[68] But there is little to suggest that Warhol collected either by way of rationalizing an objectivist, scientific spirit or due to childhood trauma, nor did he specifically collect contemporary art, or old art. From the contents of his townhouse that were spilled after his death, it seems rather that he collected coffee mugs and shopping bags, vases and figurines, anything and everything, especially that which was not valued in any existing market. This collecting is the last reserve of disinterested interest— ordering the world of objects in a kind of unprejudiced physiognomy or taxonomy that Walter Benjamin describes in his stamp collecting or the unpacking of his books.[69] Warhol desired the undesirable, but only to have it join other objects of its kind, from which it differed ever so slightly. Ultimately, this inflected desire disappears into the quasi-interior realm of remembering by way of a curiously modified forgetting. The motivation for collecting is unthinkable and irrecoverable with hindsight; the meaning it has assumed since can no longer be separated from the objects; it lies hidden in the cracks of their small differences and interrelations. It can only be summoned by media recollection.

Now that Warhol's works are almost never bought or sold since they all entered museums or private collections at prohibitively high prices, it is intriguing to figure out what motivated his own collecting, and perhaps to what extent it may go toward an understanding of his own production. Although Warhol's work (and his behavior, insofar as it is reconstructible) may elude diagnostic categorization, as collector he evokes what Walter Benjamin observed not only in the Easter egg hunt, but also in postal stamp collections, for instance. The collector stuffs objects into time-space, shifting away from any use value to a collector's appreciation of the object. This may indeed be the shift in the history of art for which Warhol is popularly held responsible: he recognized this tendency and made it the basis, in turn, for the production of art objects. In the collector's world, as Benjamin wrote, things are liberated from the enslavement to usefulness and service. This liberation means that for Benjamin, collecting is the exact opposite of using; as a corollary, completion is the ideal aim of the collector.

For the Andy Warhol who felt completed by the machine, for the Warhol who collected uncountable objects that were only discovered after his death (some of which now reside in a less imaginary Warhol Museum in Pittsburgh),

for Warhol as for Benjamin, collecting may be a form of "practical remembering." *Gedächtnis* or "the stockpile of memory," according to Benjamin, "is that
which consciousness, in order to shield the apparatus from shock attack, must
not receive. Instead, *Erinnerung*, the internalizing German word for remembering, must record in place and thus erase: consciousness contains shock by 'in-
corporating' it within the register of *Erinnerung*." And what is more, "shock
defense quarantines the traumatizing event by assigning it an exact time and
place *(Zeitstelle)* in consciousness."[70] Laurence Rickels, who develops this pivotal difference into a theory of gadget love, points out that "with gadgets, each
moment comes equipped with a trigger, which (everyone's share in) *Erinnerung*
pulls." The incident inflicts momentary shock; the apparatus captures the
moment and awards the delay that kills time—until time returns, all bent out
of shape and fully mediatized, under the guise of so-called real time. For Benjamin, natural beings and historical events both suffer a time lag separating them
from paradise, a temporal difference that is effaced by the time-traps of technology, since preserving the instant severs the event from future and past rever-
berations. The traumatic experience thus generates a feeling of déjà vu; it grows
out of the shock of witnessing the moment being devoured by the machine, the
loss of an irretrievable future that will be revealed in a forgotten past.

> Listen you—Listen you—You called, didn't you? You're divine *(typewriter
> writing)* Not net. There is no PHONE *(Typewriter writing.)* No, it's not too
> new—there's no phone. As you ho *(tap tap tap)* You know don't you realize
> what what happened? *(tap tap tap)* NEM BU TOL. It wa- Huh—Are you
> serious? (405)

More so than drugs and other distortions on the line, gadget love becomes "the
password for a genealogy of media," as Rickels proposes after Benjamin, "in
which modern group psychology can be followed up and out through the internalization and technologization of trauma."[71] In this logic, the structure of
cover-up is already in place. To the extent to which fetishism detracts from
itself, Rickels continues, it is "the overdetermined received notion or ready-
made" par excellence. Indeed, Warhol's work follows the itinerary from perver-
sion via disavowal to what Freud called defensive splitting. The fetishist avoids
those other twin phenomena, the isolated rock of melancholia and the hard edge
of castration anxiety, and slides into the installation of screen memories. This
substitution is a happy one, as long as its foundation remains securely covered
over. As Freud succinctly puts it, "when the fetish is instituted some process
occurs which reminds one of stopping of memory in traumatic amnesia"—
the curious circumnavigation of a possible self-reflexive turn in this phrasing
covers up the question of who the subject able to diagnose such a stoppage
would be. In other words, the traumatic halting of memory occurs, perhaps, to

none other than the one who is then reminded of the institution of the fetish instead of the trauma. Freud continues: "As in this latter case, the subject's interest comes to a halt half-way, as it were; it is as though the last impression before the uncanny and traumatic one is the one retained as a fetish."[72] Déjà vu is this half-arrest of interest between attention and distraction.

Warhol's collecting of moments, objects, and people is no auratic restitution; it is bringing the far-flung into proximity. In Benjamin's thought, the trace is the appearance of a proximity, while aura is the appearance of a distance, however close that which provokes it may be. Aura is only diagnosed in its disappearance, and the trace recollects that disappearance. To experience the aura of an appearance, Benjamin writes, is to endow it with the capacity of the gaze.[73] In the final analysis, Benjamin's dialectical image of trace and aura becomes the "ingenious turning point to a dialectical recovery of the commodity" in fetishism.[74] The *now of recognizability* yields access to a sunken past by way of tracing new experiences to industrial commodity production. Warhol's beginnings in shoe design signal fetishism even to the most casual observer, and his gadget love would certainly seem to be the most reliable indicator.[75] The Frankfurt School understood the fetish character of commodities as a dialectical effect, not already given in consciousness, but producing consciousness. This production answers to unconscious fears and wishes that cannot be directly represented as in a dream.[76] Benjamin sought to prove how the new aura of the "commodity soul" captures the attention of the flaneur: if the trace allows us to capture the thing, then in the aura we are captured by the thing.[77] This inversion corresponds to the relation between the apparition of proximity and distance under accelerated conditions of an industrialization, and Warhol's industrial art may be the test to show whether the categories still hold. While industrial art is arguably an attempt to recover the negative trace that marks the appearance of proximity, the aura of autonomous art in high capitalism can be described as a loss that accompanies the development of art as commodity, and of an imaginary museum. But is the story simply a history of loss? Hans Robert Jauss tried to balance the books in making Benjamin a prescient forebear of a hermeneutics of reception aesthetics that is "always already retrospective."[78] Yet this is not Benjamin's but Jauss's déjà vu. As Karlheinz Stierle quickly corrected, the recognizability of the past for Benjamin is precisely not a continuous process of reception, but refers to the privileged moment of an almost idealized historical distance.[79] What kind of distance is this, and how does it carry over from Benjamin to Warhol?

Benjamin's use of the term fetish returns to Marx's suggestion that old means of production initially dominate any new form of production, and that therefore collective wishes arise in which the new and the old intermingle. Marx defined use value as the manifold ways of application, and exchange value as the expression or appearance of a commodity that represents an abstraction from the use value.[80] Therefore in any exchange, the use value is what makes the difference if the exchange value is considered equivalent; the logical third for Marx is the embodied labor-time that goes into creating the use value and the labor that will be extracted in use. The difference between the kind of fetishism that is expressed in collecting and the commodity fetishism lies precisely in the fact that while the collector is anachronistically precapitalist in his assembling of objects and unfolding of their potential interrelations, the latter is the epistemological implication of the process of exchange. But as Werner Hamacher sums up the tradition from Hegel to the present, critiques of fetishism proceed from the assumption that it must be unmasked as a necessary illusion that covers the truth like a screen memory. However, the fetishistic gesture of these theories makes of the critical gaze a substitute for the absence, or insufficient presence, of the object. Thus a critique of fetishism is always a critique of writing as well as of the corruption of spiritual presence through the body.[81] Even and especially the most perceptive theories of fetishism install themselves as the last fetishism of the fetish, unveiling and preserving the veil. Theory must forget what it recollects and retain what it forgets, without knowing it. Yet Hegel would not recognize a limitation of dialectics in this determination of the speculative through the excluded forgetting. For it only remains unsurpassed as long as it is not seen, and is not seen only as long as it is unsurpassed. This implies that even in the most restricted sense of the fetish, nothing will have been free from displacements and reifications of the proper object. That ideal of unveiled transparence and unadulterated objecthood is the ideology of rational self-determination against the pervasive structures of capital. Thus the dissolution of the traditional concept of the fetish requires a reevaluation of the central tropes both of a certain idealism in the wake of Marx and a certain enlightenment in the wake of Freud—which means a redefinition also of the inheritance of Freudo-Marxism in all its international chapters.[82] Still, the fetish is and remains that which doubles over in the new-old mingling of form and content. Whether the new production "cites" old forms in order to ban the uncanny of industrial surroundings and make it seem familiar, as Benjamin observed in his passages on the vernacular of steel and glass architecture, or whether the new is put triumphantly in place of the old cult context, in either case the commodity fetish transforms these spaces into halls of yearning where the consumerist masses learn about exchange values, under the motto "see everything, touch nothing." Thus when Warhol as a producer of exhibition objects states, "I don't like to touch things . . . that's why my work is so distant from myself," his formulation of a radical distance indicates more reflection than his art production is often given credit for.[83] Unlike Narcissus, who is inseparable from himself and thus forever separated from the other,

Warhol is cognizant of the formative rift of both object and subject alike and in their appearance to each other. Benjaminian aura, "the singular apparition of a distance, however close it may be," offers a formulation of the cult value of the work of art in categories of spatiotemporal perception.[84] Aura is sensed only at the appropriate distance by an other; as soon as it is identified, it is lost. Warhol's aura evaporates as soon as it is reproduced, which is to say, produced. But like Benjamin, Warhol was also a theorist of disappearance and aura; he knew about the secularization of auratic art and its irreversible loss of aura in the process:

> Some company recently was interested in buying my "aura." They didn't want my product. They kept saying, "we want your aura." I never figured out what they wanted. But they were willing to pay a lot for it. So then I thought that if somebody was willing to pay that much for it, I should try to figure out what it is. I think "aura" is something that only somebody else can see, and they only see as much of it as they want to. It's all in the other person's eyes. You can only see an aura on people you don't know very well or don't know at all. I was having dinner the other night with everybody from my office. The kids at the office treat me like dirt, because they know me and see me every day. But then there was this nice friend that somebody had brought along who had never met me, and this kid could hardly believe that he was having dinner with me! Everybody else was seeing me, but he was seeing my "aura." When you just see somebody on the street, they can really have an aura.[85]

The crux of the interpretation of aura in Benjamin and Warhol pivots neither on loss of experience under the conditions of technology, nor on the experience of loss in the autonomous work of art, but on the reification of the auratic in kitsch. Arguably, kitsch may be defined as the reification of aura, that which does not oppose technical reproducibility but indeed presupposes it.[86] This is a reason why the question of kitsch is more urgent in modern mass produced art. Arguably, the repetitive, affected artificiality and triviality of Warhol's works squarely inscribes itself as kitsch, but at the same time it also knows something about kitsch; this separates it from the random objects Warhol collected in his home. Where fragments of the past are patched together, Adorno wrote, they exude a mysterious, allegorical sheen; they revive the ruins to a second, ghostly life.[87] Such kitsch no longer appears with the immediacy of art, but as an unreal, lapsed revenant after the world wars.[88] Adorno believed that no disturbance can be caused by such ghosts, since they are not so much presented to the audience as rather "cited from their unconscious memory," as he put it.[89] Yet it is exactly this citation of and from the unconscious memory that continues the weak cultural effect of kitsch as an uncanny repetition.

In the end indignation over kitsch is anger at its shameless revelling in the joy of imitation, now placed under taboo, while the power of works of art still continues to be secretly nourished by imitation.[90]

The crass mass appeal of kitsch in its complete lack of distance exhibits the same logic in nonauratic art that Benjamin had observed in Baudelaire on the destruction of Romantic aura. Moreover, himself collecting the aspects of collecting in the *Arcades Project*, Benjamin expressly aligns it with kitsch. He begins his study of collecting by saying that it is a primal phenomenon of study, since the student collects knowledge. This study, as Benjamin shows and tells, takes up the struggle against dispersion, which is to say against the distancing effects, the losses involved in the passing of time. Thus what Benjamin calls "a sort of productive disorder" exhibits the shared structure between *mémoire involontaire* and collecting. This was, we are led to think, the productive disorder of Andy Warhol. Finally, in a formulation that recurs at various stages of the *Passagenwerk* as Benjamin recollects his collection of insights into collecting, he calls it a "form of practical memory." What is the practical, the productive effect he associates with this activity? "We construct here an alarm clock," Benjamin cites himself, "that rouses the kitsch of the previous century to 'assembly.' This genuine liberation from an epoch has the structure of an awakening."[91] To this extent, it is interesting to note that Ernst Bloch in his work of the 1930s that parallels Benjamin's review of the nineteenth century, also stressed that the aspect that the object turns toward the dream is akin to kitsch. The connection between the aura of kitsch and the trace of what Bloch called the hieroglyphs of the nineteenth century is not a defining difference, but rather corroborates the mutual relation of aura and trace in Benjamin's dialectical image.[92] Thus one might argue that the terms are themselves part of an auratic frame of reference.

As compressed historical index, kitsch is an aestheticizing, mortifying return. Distorted and deformed, it recollects and preserves memories of the past. The same logic applies to the word itself: the acquired meaning of the word kitsch, as Adorno pursued it, is so far removed from its literal sense that the latter, derived from "sketch" or something undeveloped, may explicate the former like a "forgotten secret."[93] Kitsch is a historical screen memory; by getting caught in the same historical dialectics, the discussion of kitsch itself risks becoming kitsch.[94] Once the historical index of kitsch is recovered and decoded, one object is enough to evoke the repressed memory of what had been. Against the horror of an eternal return under industrial conditions of replication that would never emerge from the auratic, Bloch and Benjamin want to awaken you from the dream kitsch through the sudden revelation of the past in an object.[95] Forgotten time and again, the symbols of the past reemerge not as auratic restitution;

they emerge by way of "shock and decomposition." If the same effect continues to haunt the chiastic correlations between proximity and trace, aura and distance in the semantic axes of twentieth-century aesthetics, Warhol's work invites us to test this hypothesis. "This century," as Bloch sums up, "is closer than childhood, farther than China."[96] Thus the collector calls to assembly all the souvenirs and worn objects that evoke the historic as well as the historicity of the present, once they are brought in a quasi-allegoric constellation, as if by déjà vu.[97] The intrusion of technology, then, can be figured as a means of stalking the unrepeatable—capturing, at last, a sense of defamiliarized presence by way of a flash or momentary insight. The overdetermined moment of connection in *a. a novel* is cathected, like a busy signal that arrests the incessant communication of communication:

> I'm sorry baby, listen, I'm sorry but I, I have been calling you since I've arrived and you've been busy; this is the first time you haven't been and there was nobody at the factory and there should have been someone here to receive the uh, the camera. (36)

As the use of tape recorders, video equipment, and answering machines serves to capture the incalculable moment, the impossible goal of total witnessing, total surveillance, total recall becomes contaminated by itself: or by forgetting itself. Forgetting is difficult to circumscribe, since it is never just loss of memory, or the effacement of objective representation. "The curse of total recall," as it is put on the back flap of the 1968 translation of Luria's *The Mind of a Mnemonist*, is that memory is never exhausted in taking in more. In fact, keeping more mnesic representations inevitably entails the contamination of memory with forgetting: a pure remembrance would be nothing but forgetting, detail but no difference, images without categories. If forgetting and memory are not opposites, then we might say that Warhol tried to gain a hold in the moment through the forgetting of forgetting.[98] Of course the apparatus of writing is already a technology. But talk of a "challenge" of the new media abounds, and many commentators share the surmise that "an entire epoch of so-called literature, if not all of it, cannot survive a certain technological regime of telecommunications."[99] It is taken as read that this inability to survive hinges on a supposed loss of the topological anchor, on an alleged dislocation or even loss of body, and of a sense of reality and perception that is bound to the body, and I find this conservative instinct touching.[100] However, it could well be the case that writing has always been touching on the body in this manner, namely on the body lost or estranged, and that writing and other technologies are instants of a certain excarnation. Unaccommodated, unappropriated, unassimilated, estranged, and contaminated, the body touches on the senses of reading; lost on the limits of language it returns as a foreign body within. This sense of loss is restored again and again by dint of a reiteration of the Platonic argument that all new media appear as machines of forgetting from the perspective of the old mediascape.[101] And it is precisely the contemporaneity of the new technology and the old form in which Benjamin recognized the potential for that dialectical image of inversion that we have been calling déjà vu. Benjamin's focus was on the unfolding of a handed-down concept, namely that of the fetish character of commodities.[102] In Warhol's world, what was fetishized, revered, and taxonomized was not the familiar image of Jackie or Marilyn, nor the predictable appearance of the soup can again and again, but the generally affectless, lifeless—but not dead—concept of art as the always already repeated kitsch of technical reproducibility, in all its secretly restored auratic power.

If it is true that society developed the distinction between kitsch and art as a means of defending the realm of the artistic against the hegemony of religious, political, and industrial influences, then it is equally true that there is a long tradition in modernity to undermine and break up that same distinction.[103] More recently, it has even been argued by art critics that "kitsch has become the new avant-garde."[104] This inversion is commonly blamed on or credited to Warhol. When we address kitsch, it is neither to quarantine it nor to embrace it but simply to follow the trajectory of this duplicitous cultural object choice.[105] Along with the discovery of a new capacity for boredom, as Clement Greenberg let it be known in one of his papal decrees, "a new commodity was devised: ersatz culture, kitsch, destined for those who, insensible to the values of genuine culture, are hungry nevertheless for the diversion that only culture of some sort can provide."[106] Although he condemns the poor receptivity of the masses and blames kitsch on their reduced capacity for art, which seems inversely proportional to the increased capacity for boredom, in the end he lets kitsch slip back under the mantle of culture. But it is not the genuine culture anymore: it is ersatz. Both German terms, kitsch and ersatz, play in Greenberg's writing a curiously undialectical role opposite the French term, avant-garde. "If the avant-garde imitates the processes of art, kitsch," he holds, "imitates its effects."[107] Which goes almost so far as to admit that the processes of real art have those effects—but of course they are not the aim of high culture. The "fault" of aberrant imitation is that although it is imitation too, it suffers from a displaced perspective, from a roving eye, from a shifty attention to the "wrong" or "nether" regions of the art world. Greenberg did not update or historicize this strict stance. A quarter century after his article on kitsch appeared in the *Partisan Review*, he was interviewed on kitsch and Warhol, and preferred to refer to pop art as a "period manifestation" rather than serious art.[108]

Before long, this turned into a new paradigm that amounts to averting aesthetics and arguing that "visual culture" finally escapes the regime of criticism and becomes a matter of imitating certain cultural effects, as Greenberg had foreseen. It follows, then, to take him up on another of his imperious hints: "self-evidently, all kitsch is academic," he indicates, "and conversely, all that is academic is kitsch." This codependent character will have become manifest in the academic reception of Warhol. His art, in its reification, is an exact return, by way of apparent parody, of what Greenberg's commodified notion of kitsch vilifies: only here, kitsch is not a truth but a method of production, or more precisely, of marketing. Indeed Warhol's project addresses and performs the imitation of effects. After Warhol, talent that cannot sell itself turns up as a curiosity in the consignment shop, among the formerly coveted melancholic objects that blend into the displays like trees into Echo's forest, silently reflective. For it is exactly the unrepeatability of the Warholian déjà vu effect that makes his career inimitable.[109] It is certainly possible that Warhol's contact with critical discourse was always a calculated case of mistaken identity, as when the famous impersonator Alan Midgette went to the University of Utah to stand in for him. The kitschy silver wig may have been the same, but some students still demanded their money back. They did not understand the switch of values Warhol offered to teach: that in fetishism, the point is to exchange it.[110]

5

UNFORGIVEN: TOWARD AN ETHICS OF FORGETTING

The duel and the gift go until death.
—Jacques Derrida, *Signsponge*

N FILM, according to the influential film theorist Christian Metz, "everything is recorded (as a memory trace which is immediately so, without having been something else before)."[1] What Metz describes as an imaginary relation to time is indeed the structure of déjà vu, recording a past that was never present before it came to consciousness as past.[2] This uncanny repetition exacerbates the already complex dialectics of repetition. We assume that what is repeated has been, or it could not be repeated. Yet that it has been makes repetition something new. So strictly speaking, repetition is impossible; even more so when the repeated did not occur before it returned, for the first time, as repetition. This is déjà vu; even the most realistic representation is a myth since it can never refer directly to an object but must go via another code system, and the optical evidence of the image thus presupposes a déjà vu as its framing gaze.

Pierre Nora deplores "the tremendous dilation of our very mode of historical perception, which, with the help of the media, has substituted for a memory entwined in the intimacy of a collective heritage the ephemeral film of current events."[3] The choice of metaphor is symptomatic for this pessimistic point of view: the fleeting media, with their imperceptible manipulation of the command and control over all forms of transmission, archival access, and cultural cohesion, are producing pure loss. Yet, as Giorgio Agamben counters, it would be hell if memory, whether through technological media or "immediately," could restore to us what was. Instead, memory gives the past its *possibility*. It is therefore a modalization of the real; it can transform the real into the possible and the possible into the real. But what happens when déjà vu is enhanced by media technology? Where photography meets the motor, déjà vu may serve as a definition of cinema, as Giorgio Agamben writes: "one can define déjà vu as the perception of something present as something past, or vice versa—and cinema always performs this transformation, it takes place in this interstice."[4]

Cut and montage are the instances that explicate film's paradox: it seems to conserve the trace and banish forgetting on the one hand, and on the other hand, in the forgetting of forgetting, it forgets even the recollection of memory traces. Film, as the trace of absence, must itself not be absent, but remain actual and available in order to grant access to what passed; as a trace of the trace, film takes the place of the past—in other words, forgets the past.[5] Along common film-theoretical lines, cinema is understood as a projected return to a maternal breast, by way of regression: "Cinema, like dream, would seem to correspond to a temporary form of regression."[6] Yet this does not cover film theory against its own projections. Since Freud's *Totem and Taboo*, psychoanalysis is able to "see through the ghosts and demons flickering on the defensive 'screens' *(Wandschirme)*," and projection has become legible as a form of hostility toward someone close.[7] Not to see past those projections is to return to infancy. But when cinema returns to the infancy of the medium, it is tradecraft, a move that must not be replicated by film criticism. If we take seriously the implications of media as mnemonic technologies, we must not overlook the slips, accidents, and aberrations at their core. By the same token, the politics of memory cannot impose absolute memory—indeed it requires an ethics of forgetting. Therefore, mass media must not be figured as an industry of forgetting, but read with particular attention to their recuperation and manipulation of cultural memory in general, and of the media's own history in particular. It is a characteristic trait of mass media to screen over their own origins in war technology and historical accidents. Where media are self-reflectively presenting their own history and genealogy, they tend to oscillate between two kinds of capturing the impossible: as the imaginary return to a burnished, idealized image of a golden past, or as the painful recollection involved in a haunting confrontation with the irrevocable past. Adorno already recognized the kitsch served up to the masses:

After the catastrophe, the beginning of the film that had been missed returns, just as if nothing had happened, and without anyone's venturing to turn out the patient viewer for whom all the riddles were now resolved. Kitsch contains as much hope as is able to turn the clock back. It is the depraved reflection of that epiphany which is vouchsafed only to the greatest works of art. Kitsch only forfeits its right to exist when it enters into a parasitical relationship to history, mimics it verdict and finds itself forbidden to reverse them.[8]

Although film history can lead the critic back to the interruptions of perception, to the camera's penetrating, intrusive gaze, to the violence of cuts and blackouts, the medium and its genres tend to cover up those fundamental aspects of the medium and serve up the kitsch audiences worldwide associate with going to the movies. Against this trend, one ought to restore a sense of media history, accentuating the other pole of memory on our television and projection screens. Vivian Sobchack diagnoses an undeniably hidden effect of media technology on our culture:

> It is obvious that cinematic and electronic technologies of representation have had enormous impact upon our means of signification during the past century. Less obvious, however, is the similar impact these technologies have had upon the historically particular significance or "sense" we have and make of those temporal and spatial coordinates that radically inform our social, individual, and bodily existences.[9]

This less obvious impact on the conception of cultural time and space is recognizable as the manipulation of memory and forgetting in the mass media of distraction and attention. We are now at the threshold of yet another transition, where the content of electronic media is the message of their predecessors: narration.[10] If there is new potential in pixel photography, digital cinema, Photoshop, and aftereffects software, as Lev Manovich speculates, it may be a return to techniques of painting that virtually took the sidelines with the advent of the first mass media technologies in the late nineteenth century.[11] As the limits and combinations of the new machines were tried and applied, the conventions of time-space perception are challenged and transformed. Film still maintains an affinity to linear narration, it also marks a significant departure from its conventions, by dint of cut and montage, fast-forward and slow motion. In a note for his storyteller essay, Walter Benjamin already articulated the fear that

> it is all repudiated: narration by television, the hero's words by the gramophone, the moral by the next statistics, the storyteller by what one knows about him. . . . *Tant mieux.* Don't cry. The nonsense of critical prognoses. Film instead of narration.[12]

One exemplary path of reconstructing how narration has been transformed in the medium itself is to trace cinematic self-reflectivity. Spielberg's *Minority Report* explores dreamy-state projections and déjà vu, allegorizing the conflict between the system of legal testimony and the structure of cinema, while in *Memento*, the inability to make new memories varies the cinematic stockpile of a protagonist's amnesia, unraveling a complex story of trauma and murder backward until even tattoos, Nietzschean inscriptions of memory on the body, turn out to be unreliable.[13] Film as a medium of aberrations of memory is spoofed in entertainment products such as the science fiction film *Men in Black*—defending earth from outer space, secret agents wield a "memory-messer-upper" that allows them to implant false memories in accidental human witnesses. This exploitation of cinematic déjà vu generated a sequel, *Men in Black II*.[14] And *Star Wars* is not the only cinematic franchise to present the sequel as prequel; the *Terminator* series demonstrated the validity of Bloch's assertion that "popular fiction often depends on false *déjà vu*."[15] Schwarzenegger's *Total Recall* is another commercially successful example of the tendency in science fiction to project inner space into outer space, staging a nightmare of returning to that immemorial place on Mars or in dreams where analysis and solution become possible.[16] *Groundhog Day* dresses déjà vu as a romantic comedy of repetition, but borrows heavily from the Oscar-winning short film *12:01 PM* and its made-for-TV remake by Jack Sholden.[17] Both versions of *12:01* stage the reliving of the same day over and over again, until the consequences of a traumatic trigger-event can be undone by the protagonist. Terry Gilliam's *12 Monkeys* uses the same material, acknowledging that the original idea stems from Chris Marker's *La Jetée*.[18]

Doubling up on itself, *La Jetée* is a recursive narrative of twenty-nine minutes that demonstrates how the time-axis manipulation that is the medium's inherent capacity also becomes a manipulation of memory and desire.[19] Survivors of World War III have gone to live underground. Space has become off limits, so their rescue depends on help from the future, and they begin to devise means of time travel. It is decided that they will first explore travel back in time, and then invert the process to reach out to the future. To return to the time-zone before their immediate past that destroyed their world, a strong memory of a past experience is necessary. They enroll a man who suffers recurrent childhood memories of seeing a man being killed at Orly airport near Paris; but upon his return to the scene, he realizes at the last moment that what he had witnessed as a child was in fact a vision of his own adult death. Proving once again the law of science fiction that outer space is inner space, Marker's *ciné-roman* revolves, in several senses, around just one ambiguous childhood memory. *La Jetée* is exemplary for how *durée* and memory thicken the photographic with the cinematic, as Jameson observed.[20] Although it consists almost exclusively of still photographs, it "projects as a temporal flow," as Vivian Sobchack put it.[21] If this is arguably the very material reality of cinema, "the latent background of every film," then its exposition alone would make Chris Marker's work exemplary, as the radical slow-down and arrest of the materiality of film itself. But what makes this work even more exemplary for our argument is that it serves as a critique of a general trend in the medium, which Jameson called film's "nostalgia for the present."[22] In Marker's vision, film affords an inversion and chiastic intertwining of the axes of time.[23] The future anterior, *ça aura été*, renders visible a loss of orientation in space, a loss felt as the contraction, suspension, and inversion of time.[24] Marked off against the conventions of the moving image, Marker organizes his looping narration around one frozen memory image of a woman on an airport runway. As Barthes wrote, every photograph signals the return of the dead, "it is the living image of a dead thing."[25] Digital film technology opened another way for the dead to return, as visual effects resurrect actresses and actors from the classic age of cinema— casting from Forest Lawn.[26] Arrest and return in the medium of memory become available through technology, and significantly, the only passage in the film that shows movement is the opening of eyes.[27] This entry into the present for one moment breaks away from the sequence of inanimate images and comes alive to the voice-over that doubles as the film's subject.[28]

Cinema, before and beyond taking déjà vu as a device or a theme, guides the investigation of aberrations of cultural memory to a fold. The shared horizon of memory, forgetting, and history constitutes the possibility of forgiveness. Here, we alight on the last term in the constellation we have been tracing throughout, between a memory without memory and a forgetting without forgetting. The pardon is that last form of an uncanny repetition without repetition. Forgiveness, as an ethics of forgetting, is not the mere prescription of amnesty.[29] A general amnesty would allow one to go on "as if nothing had happened," imposing silence about the memory of the unforgettable.[30] Pardon, by contrast, is a modification of forgetting that does not affect the irrevocable, nor repress its memory.[31] In fact, forgiveness requires the exact recall of the injury to be forgiven and reinscribed as modified memory. Again, it is important to distinguish clearly between nostalgia for something irreversibly past— and as we have seen, kitsch is that pathetic aestheticization of the past—versus the recall of the irrevocable.[32] As Vladimir Jankelevitch put it, the irreversible means the past cannot return as past (nor we to it), but the regret felt about this realization is still a mortification of the past, in a Proustian mode. The remorse code that communicates, however obliquely, a revisiting of the unpardonable or irreparable is the inverse impossibility. A pardon either forgives the unpardonable or it is not truly a pardon; it must be unconditional, without exception or restriction.[33]

Arguably, if mass media technology allows the capture of that moment that would otherwise be fleeting, ineffable, or repressed, then the structure of media itself allows us to return to that interruption. And if the genealogy of media is energized by an interruption of our means of perception, then attention to the mechanisms of attention and distraction allows us to recognize the forgotten history of the medium itself. In other words, the historical intervention that mass media represent, above all in their harnessing and generating of effects of repetition and déjà vu, becomes readable only if we reconstruct what the media themselves cover up, for the sake of their effects. This is not to say that we are nostalgic for the nineteenth century, that we want to preserve the moment when such harnessing of repetition becomes available. It is not in the spirit or mortification of media as history, but in the sense of an awareness for the irreversible and traumatic rupture in the fabric of perception, that we recall that moment.

Certain modified forms of recollection or of forgetting come into play in politics: above all, questions of forgiveness and amnesty.[34] Their difference is crucial: the latter, understood as mutual forgetting, stands almost diametrically opposed to the former, insofar as forgiveness in its long monotheistic tradition conjures up the past to the extent of making it present again, repeating the injury, opening the wound, so that its full extent may indeed be forgiven. While amnesty has as its goal an instrumentalized amnesia, forgiveness strives for difference in repetition. The price of forgiving or forgetting is debated not only in the context of recent German or U.S. politics; the representation of a certain split consciousness about the national and individual past is intricately connected with issues of accountability and responsibility above all in matters of a politics of memory. As Margarete Mitscherlich put it, "the repudiation of the past hinders us from learning to distinguish between false values and ideals and those worth remembering, and from being able to recognize clearly their relevance for the present."[35] Consequently, the work that is required will not only make arrangements with a past laid to rest, but will actively recall, or as Mitscherlich writes, "revive" early fantasies and feelings, and this work is the only alternative to a superannuation of the past that foregoes the work of mourning. Forgiveness neither presupposes nor ends in forgetting: on the contrary, it presupposes a lively recollection of the injustice. Just as forgetting is a blockage of reception—one no longer gets it—forgiveness could be described as a stoppage in circulation. Beyond the apparent immediacy and reciprocity of give and take, we encounter the limits of such an economy; we encounter aberrations of mourning that have to do with inhibitions, anxieties, and melancholy. With the consideration of altruism and forgiveness we go to the limits of memory and forgetting. Repetition can push itself to the front as a resistance against remembering; and undoubtedly, such compromising repetition without repetition structures the scene of forgiveness, where an injury is called up again, to its full extent, without being literally repeated.

Mass media focus increasingly on the notion of witnessing events from a distance, and thus on surviving them, be they violent confrontations or meteorological dangers. These events are repeated relentlessly, always presented as news: whenever something happens—a gunfight, a thunderstorm—it simultaneously confirms and disturbs the experience of time. The technically enhanced surveillance of any fleeting, volatile, unrepeatable occurrence in turn gives rise to general coverage: media thrive on the very unrepeatability of that which they strive to repeat. The event would simply disappear if subsumed under a general notion of "violence" or "weather," and thus its singularity is only recognizable when it is split off from the impact or harm by distance. Its singularity is thus the mark of a division, or to put it the other way around, media rely on disappearance as a negative function of repetition in their coverage.[36] The screen memories served up to cover the event as they appear thus cover them up, and this detachment represses all questions of judgment in favor of pure replay. Thus the screening over of morality and justice produces a return of notions that evoke systems of belief—such as finitude of life, transcendence of time, the promise of a future under immemorial threats. On the one hand, ever more refined time-axis manipulation is the technical pivot of modern media, and on the other hand, violence and weather have become two mainstays of media coverage—precisely as a result of their statistical recurrence and recuperation after the fact.

One may wonder whether repetition and novelty, the singular and the serial are mediated differently in art. It is possible to argue that, here, news media diverge from cinema. While one accentuates the transience of the instant, the other stores its moving images for posterity; news loses most of its interest after a short while, movies are supposed to accumulate it—if only because they remain available for comparison and other modes of critical attention. However, both capture our attention by means of difference and repetition.[37] Both uses of the moving image serve our distraction economy by similar technical means, and if we were to insist on a fundamental difference, we might say that the artful use of the medium heightens the traits that characterize all of its forms.[38] That classic among movie genres, the Western, stages the convergence of violence and weather, ending in a hailstorm of bullets. The pleasures of repetition offered by genre film illustrate perhaps better than any other how cinema achieved its considerable cultural effects. And when the Western genre returns from the brink of oblivion, like yesterday's news, in Clint Eastwood's *Unforgiven*, it repeats certain aspects that may have slipped our attention the first time around.

The myth of the American West, the promised land, has found one of its pioneering mediatic representations in the Western, a movie genre that has its roots in the dime novels of the nineteenth century, in the paintings of Frederic Remington, and in countless retellings of legends about the likes of Buffalo Bill, Wild Bill Hickok, Wyatt Earp, and Billy "the Kid" Bonney. Men on their horses, exploring the very edge of civilization, pioneering the way of life that was to become America: this is the formula of Western storytelling. In those outposts, any moral ambiguities had to be reluctantly settled by violence; the revolver is the symbol of the law as well as of the outlaw. Common to both is a code of honor that expressed itself not only in the idealized reluctance to use violence, but above all in the duel: the man-to-man, eye-to-eye combat in the tradition of divine judgment. The gun duel is the most hallowed and clichéd convention of the Western. The settling of accounts may turn into a suicidal last stand, but above all, it is the accepted code of the confrontation and resolution of con-flict—even if it shows the hero as a killer. The gun is not only the symbol of manliness and justice, but also the only means for reconciliation. And while the manly heroics of the lone rider are played out in the foreground, the land-scape of the North American West is playing an equally important role in the background. From the beautiful, inhospitable Monument Valley to the endless barren landscapes of later Westerns, the forces of nature serve as the back-ground to choreographed violence and lawlessness, and directly influence the unlucky inhabitants, threatening their lives, restricting their movement, taking away their courage, driving them to drink and to duel.

Clint Eastwood's movie *Unforgiven* (1992), however, is a Western without a duel, and it offers a radical revaluation of the political economies of the genre. Set in the barren countryside somewhere in the Wyoming of 1880, the timing of its release made it a political film. By coincidence, it was first shown on the big screen the week of the Rodney King beating, which led to riots in Los Ange-les. It not only addresses the brutal beating of an innocent black man, but also deals with such untypical Western material as the predicament of prostitutes, children growing up as virtual orphans, and the pain of dying. In the preced-ing decades, the genre had become unfashionable in the United States—owing to the growing public discussions regarding racial divisions, sexual tensions, Native American sovereignty, and a culture based on greed and violence. The unexpected return of the Western in the early nineties has offered an opportu-nity to examine the legends of how the West was won, the history and morality of the trek to the coast.[39] Only another Western could come to redeem the in-herent racism of the tradition of the Western genre, looking ahead by looking back. In *Unforgiven*, the character of W. W. Beauchamp, scribe and witness, is always at hand to embody the revisionist myth-maker of the nineteenth century, portrayed in the most unflattering light. He is an opportunistic fabricator of lies, a coward who wets himself at the sight of a gun pointed at him, and whenever he sees a chance to attach himself to another potential subject for his hack journalism, he changes allegiance without a second wasted on loyalty and heroism. By the same token, as personification of the media he not only serves as a distorting witness, but also exemplifies a structural separation of morality and justice. This narrator is far removed from Walter Benjamin's storyteller, in whose character the just meets himself.[40] When Beauchamp meets the just, he sees only the personification of the immoral; and since the just has no memory, the scribe must consider his story unreliable—thus the just goes unrecognized until the end.

The town of Big Whiskey has neither courthouse nor church; all interaction converges in Greeley's Saloon, the bar and brothel that serves as Big Whiskey's social hub.[41] Two patrons of Greeley's cause a stir when one attacks a prostitute with his knife in retribution for her naive and careless laughter at the diminutive size of his penis. The cowboy badly scars her face before his companion can intervene. The ugly spectacle of impotent rage is surpassed only by the legal adjudication that follows it. Judging the incident to be little more than a case of damaged property, the corrupt sheriff of Big Whiskey orders the perpetrator to deliver a string of ponies to the owner of the brothel. The outraged prostitutes decide to pool their savings and set a prize of $1,000 on the heads of the two cowboys. Their leader voices their cause: "Just because we let them smelly fools ride us like horses don't mean we got to let them brand us like horses." And so they scorn the young cowboy when he offers a special horse directly to the biblically named Delilah, in excess of the fine imposed that will only benefit the owner of the brothel; they refuse to even consider his apology, as well as his attempt at recompense. Although it seems for a moment as if the scarred Delilah would be prepared to accept the gift, the gesture is scorned by the crowd, and then turned down by the women.

Why would the cowboy offer a horse in excess of the fine imposed, and why is his offer turned down? He seeks to compensate in a way that would not inscribe his guilt, as money does, but transform it, as a gift might. One never gives or takes without regard to forgetting and memory, be it by way of distributing and parceling out, rewarding or repaying, or finally in the form of taking interest. Here, Eastwood stages a labor theory of value: the man who lives by the horse should give a horse. This distinguishes it from the money the women put on the cowboy's head. But these categories are already confounded: the prostitutes sell something that is otherwise only given, or exchanged for like attention; money already contaminates their relationship, so the gift of a horse offered is not seen as qualitatively different from an economic reparation. What the prostitutes want at this point—looking the gift horse in the mouth, as it were—is something above and beyond repayment, since that would only denigrate Delilah again by branding her a commodity. They call for revenge, since in this inverted situation money is the only way they can get what is beyond commerce, what transcends the bond that makes them prostitutes.

In opposing a system of exchange, responsibility, and accountability to an economy of sacrifice, substitution, and debt—lastly, of money—we separate a mode of calculation from what could be subsumed as a monotheistic religious tradition.[42] Some commentators tried to read the film as an allegory of redemption while others presented it as a Calvinist portrait of innate depravity.[43] Unforgiving nature takes the role of condemning, or saving, the people on the frontier; it is the landscape that reminds them of their finitude, the weather announces portentous scenes, and whether they are coming from the mud of a pig farm or falling, shot, into the dirt outside a saloon, their relation to the land is one of antagonism. In Eastwood's film the protagonists of *Unforgiven* are either shown in wide shots as part of endless scenery or in close-up, typically at night, so that in either case, the open land does not represent freedom but imminent danger. Eastwood does not merely point to this in *Unforgiven,* he has it spelled out by English Bob, the first contract killer to arrive in Big Whiskey to collect the reward, who remarks to his fellow travelers on the train across the plains that it was the vastness of America, and the unforgiving climate of the West, that had bad effects on its inhabitants. The gunfighter is driven out of town after a brutal beating by the sheriff, but Beauchamp the scribe stays on. The hack journalist had been writing a hagiography of English Bob as the "Duke of Death" whose gun kept Chinese workers for the railway company at bay.[44] The dangers of exaggerated rumor—and the consequences of overreaction—come to the fore when his boastful attitude earns him scars and scorn. English Bob brings a colonialist view of the settlement in the West to bear on the scene; what gets him kicked out of town is his ridicule of democracy: when the head of state is a royal, he claims, a sense of respect and awe will stay the hands of any potential assassin, but with a president, why not kill him? For blaming violence on democracy, the sheriff decides, he deserves to be on the receiving end of that very violence. Whether as divine mercy or as human capacity, forgiveness is impossible in this old new Western.

Eastwood stages the abyssal division of forgiving versus a calculation of debt, or versus forgetting, or versus the civilized speech acts of excuse, ruefulness, or reparation. What is denied here is not only the *fait social total* sociologists recognize in the structure of the gift and its reception or return, but also the analogous structure of *for*-giving. The three leading men, gunfighters played by Clint Eastwood (William Munny), Gene Hackman (Sheriff Daggett), and Richard Harris (English Bob), slide down the slippery slope to an excess of violence that must cost lives. There is no life on William Munny's farm of dying pigs, dry land, and abandoned children; there are no children to be seen at all in the town of Big Whiskey, just single men and prostitutes. Only violence and death are given in generous quantities.

The three leading actors acquired reputations for portraying explosive violence on screen, and this reputation catches up with them in *Unforgiven*.[45] If Eastwood had become typecast as the self-reliant, brutal, cool, effortlessly superior hero of so many films—Westerns or not—here he spends most of the 132 minutes trying not to become that character. The irony of a self-referential Clint Eastwood playing a decrepit Western legend coming back from retirement led commentators to claim that *Unforgiven* is "a film that deconstructs and then reincarnates Eastwood's 30-year-old persona into a mythic, yet malefic, archangel-antihero."[46] Indeed in this film, the return of the violent persona turns into a moral defeat for the protagonist, but it is a defeat that has, in a sense, always already happened, and Munny has been carrying it around with him, hatching it. It is not only the return of what was believed to be superseded; it is not merely the recall of an old man. Like the unexpected return of the Western genre in the past decade, the return of the superheroic characters Eastwood played in prior roles, ranging from the sardonically brutal to the proto-fascist, is symptomatic. If this is a film about the inability to forgive, about retribution and revenge, its concept of justice is sharply separated from our time-honored moral conventions established in the institutions that administer judgment. Indeed in its portrayal of retribution, it calls to mind the Old Testament and the fact that retribution as such relieves time, or seems supremely indifferent to time: the deadline of the Last Judgment whose instrument Clint Eastwood's protagonist once again plays is that very due-date when all deferrals cease and all debts come due.

The traditional Western is a mythical, metaphorical play of morals; codes of honor prevail, crime does not pay in the end, and the fair-haired hero rides off into the sunset of the frontier landscape, the plains, the desert, the valley, sure of having righted the wrong once more. Most reviews of *Unforgiven* have tended to insist on reading William Munny as the hand of an Old Testament God, and the film as "a morality tale with a strong sense of puritanic gloom."[47] However, it can just as well be construed as an anti-Western in that it shows the complete absence of morality in the lives of the settlers. Moreover, the movie sharply separates justice from morality. As Walter Benjamin and other media theorists have suggested, film is as much about halting, capturing the moment, as it is about animation—and that is how the film is "shot."[48] From the opening scene, Eastwood highlights this by consistent parallel cutting: while the aging ex-killer and inept pig farmer William Munny is in the mud fighting his feverish pigs, the insecure young cowboy is knifing a whore who dared to giggle at his diminutive penis. The dry and barren landscape of the infertile farm is contrasted with the heavy rain that pours down on Big Whiskey. The dovetailed narrative narrows the gap slowly, advancing to the point where Munny reverts to drinking, and to killing, and is eventually in the same room with the remaining cast, blasting them away. The split beginning, the cut from town to country and back, from the sins of the bar and brothel to the attempt at a decent life of hard work and living on the fruit of one's own labor, boils down, very deliberately and menacingly, to a showdown that is also a meltdown of almost every moral or just impulse.

Munny the legend used to consider himself in it only for the money—and at first sight, money seems to be what lures him out of retirement. His opponent is Little Bill, as in the dollar bill; his own daughter, Penny, and his competitor, English Bob, also have names that have a ring of currency. When the rumor reaches Munny, delivered through an aspiring gunslinger, the Schofield Kid, that a violated prostitute in the shantytown of Big Whiskey has been treated like damaged property, this also betrays the mercantilism of the "Western" system of justice. Munny is not interested in avenging the crime committed against the prostitute, nor in any brand of justice, he only wants to save his pigs and kids from illness and starvation by collecting the reward for a double murder contract: Munny needs that money, even if it carries the risks of killing on credit, for the prostitutes do not have that kind of money saved up. He has tried to leave his violent past behind, however; his late wife had helped reform him from a murderous, uncontrollable alcoholic into a temperate pig farmer before she passed away, and his mercenary mind has been repressed. Having stopped drinking, he can hardly mount his horse, but when temptation comes in the shape of the Schofield Kid, a short-sighted boy aspiring to become a feared gunfighter who brings the greatly exaggerated rumor of the slashing of a woman's whole body, and of the reward to be collected by an assassin, Munny cannot hold his old ways in abeyance for long. He abandons his feverish pigs and his small children, seeks out his former partner, Ned Logan (Morgan Freeman), and under portentous dark clouds rides toward Big Whiskey.

By the time Munny reaches the town in heavy rain, he is ill and feverish. Confronted by the sheriff in the saloon where his companions contact the whores to negotiate a contract, he does not defend himself against the vicious beating he receives at the hand of the law. He crawls out of Greeley's onto the muddy street, an innocent old man in the dirt. Lapsing into unconsciousness, he sees the faces of his deceased wife and of the angel of death, but the dream sequence does not bring on a scene of forgiveness. Having killed in a stupor, Munny can only seek redemption in a repetition of his drunken behavior. Delilah's face is the first thing the delirious Munny, persecuted by hallucinations of his past victims, sees when he wakes up from his fever—and he takes her for an angel. Coming alive, he identifies with her scarred appearance and even makes an attempt to console her: "I must look kinda like you now." The exaggerated accounts of her mutilation are in stark contrast to the visual evidence of her beauty, yet the bleeding wounds and scars on both their faces are symbolic of castration, which explains why the prostitute is no longer marketable. As marginal character on the thresholds and in the arcades, the prostitute is the commodity become human, as Benjamin explained. When commodities want to see their own faces, they are personified as whores. They express in displaced and defaced ways the unity of social content and form, seller and commodity at once.[49] Only once, when Delilah is not wearing makeup, can she be recognized as anything other than wares for sale.

It becomes increasingly clear that the entire web of relations in the film is based on exaggerated rumor. The men invent their own nicknames to build fake reputations, the women lie about the money they can pay as reward for a hired killer, the Schofield Kid lies and brags about the many men he supposedly killed, and everyone exaggerates the harm done to the young prostitute. Only Munny resists this general urge to brag. Whenever the Kid tries to elicit more information about who Munny had killed, how, and when, Munny's answer is invariably that he cannot remember, because he had been drunk most of the time: "It ain't like that anymore, Kid. Whiskey done it as much as anything else. I ain't had a drop in ten years. My wife, she cured me of that. Cured me of drink and wickedness." But soon enough, Munny's resolve weakens.

When the three men hoping to collect the reward, Munny, Logan, and the Kid, arrive at the camp of the cowboys, it turns out that the Kid has such bad eyesight that he cannot shoot either perpetrator from the distance. Ned Logan aims his rifle, but finds himself unable to overcome his scruples. In the end, Munny has to wrest the gun from him and shoot. His conscience makes this killing, unlike most such scenes of retribution in a conventional Western, a torture for him. As he peers through the aim, however, he realizes that the cowboy is hit in the stomach and still alive. He allows a companion hidden nearby to bring the suffering victim a drink, but eventually has to shoot a second time to put him out of his misery. Killing has never been this hard in a Western. Ned decides to give up the bounty hunt and rides back, leaving his rifle with Munny. The Kid and Munny follow the group of cowboys to a ranch, where they wait for night to fall. When the second target brazenly goes to the outhouse, the Kid sneaks up on him, opens the door to the toilet, and shoots him point blank. This direct association of the criminal with excrement and money might serve to justify the murder of a defenseless man. The Kid is wracked with guilt afterward, however, and confesses that contrary to his wild claims, he had never killed before. "It's a hell of a thing, killing a man," Munny admits, haltingly, "you take away all he's got and all he's ever gonna have." The Kid sniffles in denial,

"Yeah well, I guess he had it coming . . ."—to which Munny replies laconically, "We all have it coming, Kid." In this certitude, Munny seems to find solace, but the Kid abandons his hopes of becoming a man of the gun and leaves Munny, just as a representative from the brothel arrives to deliver their reward. The prostitutes recoil when they learn about Munny's past and keep their distance; from then on, he is on his own.

Psychoanalytic accounts of the movie assert that it represents "the epic struggle between the Id (violence) and the Superego," the latter personified in Munny's late wife, Claudia, who is responsible for his attempts to sober up and eke out a farmer's life. Yet, this does not allow for an interpretation of the subtle character development over the course of the film, nor does it resonate with the context of the Western as an Eastwood vehicle. Religious interpretations tend toward the view that "to be saved, Munny must become the ultimate sinner," and that his "eschatological control of violence, and his pathological ability not to feel any fear or remorse," are what make him God's instrument of wrath.[50] However, what this interpretation does not account for are the many instances where Munny insists on his newly won virtue, chiding his married partner for considering the services of prostitutes and later turning down a free offer from Delilah, the one whose violation sets off the whole plot. "It ain't right buying flesh," he tells Ned. Long after his wife's death, he keeps his promises to her, the only woman in the movie who is not a prostitute. All other female characters, whatever their differences, are presented as commodities, with crumbling makeup on their harsh, deteriorating faces, their reproductive powers gradually destroyed since only by selling sex do they get money, clothes, food, etc.[51] Munny's asceticism is in stark contrast to the driven nature of most men around him. He not only refrains from sex and alcohol, he also refuses to be drawn into a brawl by the sheriff, who beats him up anyway, to make up for the gun duel that could have ensued. Little Bill Daggett uses his "Ordinance no. 14—no firearms in Big Whiskey" as an excuse to bully any outsiders, but does not enforce it with the townspeople—Skinny Dubois, for one, has a pistol.

The symbolism of America's pervasive gun culture stems largely from the conventions of the Western; the anachronistic continuation has its cause not in the dangers of the frontier life, but in the screen attitude that carries over into the urban sphere.[52] How much the gun equals the phallus in *Unforgiven* becomes even more explicit in the story of how "Two-Gun" Corcoran lost in duel against English Bob: he only had one pistol, but his penis was rumored to be gun-sized. When Beauchamp takes the nickname literally and produces a florid description of a duel, Little Bill has to disabuse him by telling how Corcoran first shot his own foot and then, after his pistol had exploded on the second shot, was killed in cold blood by a drunken English Bob—not at all in the course of a duel, but in the middle of a saloon. In turn, before chasing him out of town in shame, Sheriff Daggett bends the barrel of English Bob's gun, another symbolic insult denoting impotence and self-destruction. The confrontation between the two men who wish to become a legend in their own lifetime is not a stand-off between the law and the criminal, but a media event, a battle of egos where both are motivated by the same seedy aspirations. Little Bill not only chases the competition out of town, he also robs English Bob of his "biographer," thus consigning him to obscurity while trying to secure his own inscription in the myth of the American West. And indeed the film may be seen to oscillate between opposing poles of memory and forgetting, only to converge, finally, on their fold.

As Clint Eastwood says, his approach to *Unforgiven* "was to forget that we're shooting in color. It's as if we're shooting in black and white and getting the kind of look you saw in something like John Ford's *My Darling Clementine* (1947)."[53] This covert operation of shooting in grayscale is also a symptom of the stricture *Unforgiven* must find itself in. Pretending to be in the black-and-white past while nevertheless using muted colors, it screens over the fact that it is informed by, and thus partly detached from and partly indebted to, the films of the past. The screen memory shows itself here as that which leads to a shift in perception; if the spacing out is barred, it yields to a time inversion, to a folding in of past and future: "in remembering the neglected Western, Eastwood presents one that has been deconstructed and reconstituted, dismembered then rebuilt, to express a contemporary understanding of what the West and the Western now mean (and have done) to America."[54] Much the same goes for his character, William Munny, who cannot forget what he will have become once more; he does not come to himself of necessity. But beneath this deflection of his memory, the unavoidable injunction, oscillating between repression and relentless recall, is not to let the forgetting take place, not to let it take hold—and whether by means of censure or erasure, what remains is but a screen memory. And lest we forget, there is an eponymous, older film by John Huston. *The Unforgiven* (1960) is about everything Eastwood's is not: family, inheritance, bringing up children. A girl raised by a white settler family turns out to be a lost American Indian girl, abducted in a raid. She must choose sides and kills one of her Kiawa brothers. This scenario is the inverse of a late John Ford film, *The Searchers* (1956), in which Natalie Wood plays a white girl adopted by Indians. Her uncle, played by John Wayne, goes after her, either to rescue her, or if she is assimilated, to kill her.[55] Unlikely as it seems, none of the secondary sources compare or contrast the eponymous films.

A scrupulous analysis, Freud says, can develop everything that is "forgotten" from screen memories; they represent that which is no longer available as such, "no longer to be had." These previously unconscious imprints would not even have to be true, but on the other hand, they are no mere fantasies either: some memories, as Freud has it, are encountered "in a first phase of repression, so to speak"; a little later, the doubt they produce will have been replaced by forgetting or false memory, and these are the necessary correlatives of the symptoms.[56] This necessity corresponds with an embarrassment, for the manifold manifestations of memory are not just countered by one, monolithic forgetting, which cannot be pluralized. The curse of repetition corrupts it, so that media discourse eventually observes itself as the stuttering repetition of oblivion, a machinery of forgetting; the art of the cover-up on screen follows suit. Moreover, amnesia and memory pathologies are complementary to one another, according to Freud: where we have great gaps of memory, we will find few instances of *fausse mémoire*, and inversely, the latter can cover up the presence of amnesia at first sight.[57] The victorious series of mnemotechnical innovations brought on not only a nearly complete conservation of recent cultural history, but also the concomitant screen memories. The omnipresent reduplication of nearly everything has given rise to a kind of cultural paramnesia, and Eastwood himself, both in the film and in interviews, leaves open the question of whether William Munny has changed or merely reverted to his old wicked ways.[58] Either way, Munny's repressed past sets him up for a dangerous rendezvous with what he cannot entirely forget.

When the townsmen arrest the innocent Ned on his way home, he becomes another victim of the arbitrary "justice" wielded in town. While interrogating Ned about Munny and the Kid, they beat him to death and leave his corpse in a coffin outside the saloon. Munny starts drinking again when he learns of this incident. After finishing a bottle of whiskey, he begins to revert to his old, mean, cold-blooded self. In a rage, he rides back through the bad weather— this time for revenge. By now, he fully remembers what he is. His entry to the saloon is preceded by ominous thunderclaps, and followed by a portentous silence. First, he asks for the owner of the saloon and shoots him without asking any further questions. Then, confronting the sheriff and his henchmen, he admits, "I've killed women and children, killed just about anything that walks or crawls at one time or another. And I'm here to kill you, Little Bill, for what you did to Ned." Yet, when he takes aim—last denouement—his rifle misfires. Swiftly, Munny throws the gun at Sheriff Daggett and draws his pistols, shooting most of the men present without getting hit himself. Here, he is the avenging angel of death, quasi-immortal in his just rage. Neither the hired gun William Munny nor the lawless Sheriff Bill Daggett are expecting or even considering reconciliation. This movie foils any expectation for the sinner-protagonist to be forgiven. No biblically connoted evocation of judgment and atonement through sacrifice intervenes on the scene of rage that ends their opposition. When Munny finally prepares to execute the wounded, pleading sheriff at close range, he shows none of the scruples he had when taking aim at the cowboy earlier. Little Bill swears at him and protests: "I don't deserve this!" But Munny calmly disabuses him of the reference to justice: "Deserve's got nothing to do with it." And with that, he pulls the trigger.

Why would Munny and his associates have gone after other men to take their lives? What economy motivates their transgression of the norms of society and commerce? Surely it is not merely the sum promised, since it is neither guaranteed nor, split among three hired guns, exorbitant. As Freud reports in linking bungled actions and economic problems, an initially insoluble symptom can become accessible to analysis once the immediate interest in repression has subsided.[59] Munny helps the prostitutes but turns down their offers of free sex in order to preserve the memory of his wife.[60] His old associate rides with him out of friendship, despite the protests of his Indian wife. *Unforgiven* intimates the stakes of forgiveness and altruism without making them explicit. Forgiveness and altruism delimit the economy of circulation by going above and beyond reciprocity and exchange. Arguably, the monetary system of capitalist societies invests in a representation of the short-term present that indicates little about future and past and is rarely observed in terms of future or past. By the same token, media entertainment is to transfer loss into the living memory of sequential, ordered recognition that allows one to process the event—that is, to mourn, and to bestow posterity onto the dead instead of anonymous forgetting. While other defensive mechanisms like displacement, denial, or inversion into the opposite affect the dynamics of the drive itself, repression and projection only affect the perception of the drive. Repression sends the unwelcome representation back to the id, but projection sends it to the outside world.[61] In this way, even infants are able to deal with aggressions and desires that threaten to become uncomfortable: they are relegated to the surrounding world and projected onto someone else. Whether or not the gain from social interaction can be said to outweigh the drawbacks of neglecting the pure expedience of self-interest, the question is whether it could ever be rational to act in purely self-regarding ways. The irony of a typecast Eastwood-character playing against stereotype and self-reflectively trying not to become the violent avenger that he usually represents on screen introduces another twist: Munny's motivation is indeed not simply cash, nor the remains of his infamy, nor that he has no alternative. Like his old associate, he exhibits impulses that invite interpretation. One aspect comes out in their attitude toward women, which is a major theme of the movie. The other theme is the difficulty of memory—specifically, throughout the movie, Munny's self-reflection, fraught with notions of a repressed older past and the injunction of a more recent past.

While rationalist interpretations grapple with the possibility of motivated irrationality, for self-helpings of symptom relief, psychoanalysis is already marketed as a user's manual to media effects, as Rickels proposes.[62] The epoch of psychoanalysis promised to redevelop all that is forgotten through thorough analysis—from screen memories representing what is no longer available as such. The corollary of this theory is that unconscious "memories" do not even have to be true, although they cannot be dismissed as pure fantasies either, as exemplified by the vile reputation of the gun-slinging young Munny that in his old age he can neither verify nor falsify while sober. Instead, certain memories are encountered only in a first state of repression, as it were—in the mode of a doubt, only to be replaced a little later by forgetting or false memory. As Eastwood shows, to reduce the effect to one cause denies the structure of the effect itself in its relation to causal thinking. The screen memory eludes premature identifications of Munny's past and present motivations. What Rickels has called the "tragic dimension or blind date of modern neurotic thought: the couplification with an other who keeps always to another time zone" will turn out to be a scene older than memory.[63] For it was always already possible that someone may give too much too soon and then either have to resort to theft or count on the altruism of the other.

Putting someone to death seems to preclude any forgiveness; by the same token, its necessity grows to infinity in the irreparable taking of a human life. Having spared only those who flee or are unarmed, Munny proceeds to scare the greedy, slimy scribe Beauchamp away, who of course immediately sought an interview with his new hero of the moment. Munny preempts any attempt at mythologizing the multiple murders by dismissing it as chance: "I guess I was lucky; but I have always been lucky when it comes to killing folks." Standing alone between the rubble of the saloon and the heavy storm that blows outside, Eastwood's avenging, lucky killer appears to join Walter Benjamin's luckless angel. And here we arrive at an interpretation of the storm that incessantly drives the angel into the future behind his back, while he faces the ruins of the present and the past growing before his eyes—an interpretation that we can corroborate with a note by Benjamin on time in the moral world. In leaving, Munny shouts out into the empty street that he would return to avenge any further harm done to the prostitutes, and that he would not only seek retribution against any perpetrators, but also kill their wives and children. His Old-Testamentary wrath is addressed to the invisible townsfolk, a voice of authority in the storm that howls over Big Whiskey, to be interiorized as the law to replace the regime of corruption. His amnesty of a few witnesses can be seen as a quasi-legal form of the religious principle of forgiveness, but true forgiveness itself would not only suspend any law, it has to supersede it, for it is not of the order of the law. And while the experience of time, that the past is not erased, is pivotal for the scene of forgiveness, the element of retribution is the return of the past in the moment. It suspends the law, and the law of time along with it; for despite the irreversible and irreducible dimension of the crime to be forgiven, any delay of judgment, which would temper justice with mercy, is precisely denied in retribution—significantly, the Last Judgment suspends all time.

This is not the stereotypical quiet before the storm, but rather the cleansing storm that precedes fatal flashes of lightning and claps of thunder. Before we jump to the conclusion that Eastwood, like Benjamin, shows us the medium of cinema itself in those flashes of lightning and claps of thunder, let us dwell on the fact that the entire movie takes place in what precedes and leads up to that final scene. Walter Benjamin's vision of the Last Judgment in a timeless, suspended "world of justice" is not the lonely stillness of fear, but the "loud storm of forgiveness preceding the ever approaching Judgment against which there is no resistance."[64] The true meaning of the day of the Last Judgment, Benjamin argues, can only be disclosed when forgiveness joins retribution. The "storm" of forgiveness that must necessarily recall the past in which a misdeed occurred finds its powerful articulation precisely *in time*. Insofar as, according to Benjamin, this storm is not only the "voice" in which the anxious cry of the criminal is drowned, but also the hand that erases the traces of his misdeed, this is "God's wrath in the storm of forgiveness." Preceding the ever-deferred day of judgment that "flees from the hour of the misdeed relentlessly into the future," the cleansing hurricane of forgiveness comes before the fatal lightning of "divine weather" that would have to annihilate what is left, whatever had not been forgiven. This, according to Benjamin, is the importance of time in the moral world, where it not only erases the traces of the misdeeds, it also offers to attain forgiveness—"beyond all remembering or forgetting"—for their impact: forgiveness, but not atonement.

The temporal fold of the scene of forgiveness and judgment is at once the paradoxical re-presentation of a past misdeed, a hallucination that serves as a screen memory, and the suspension of historicity. *Unforgiven* is framed by a prologue and epilogue, which display a few lines referring to Munny's wife; at the beginning and the end, on the identical background of Munny kneeling before a grave under a tree, it tells of a reformed man of a notoriously vicious temper. It is indicated at the end that in his quest for himself and for money, Munny eventually goes to the California coast and starts a new life there—in business. To do justice to the tensions with which Eastwood charges his movie, both the psychoanalytic approach and a reading informed by the Western religious heritage have to be woven together in a mediation that tries to redeem the Western, tries to preserve the condemned fabrication and mythmaking that are part and saddle bag of the genre. *Unforgiven* takes rigorous stock of the romanticism of the legendary Old West in which it also indulges. The revisionist force and traditional inheritance of Clint Eastwood's old-new Western reside in this fold, and thus Munny becomes the full embodiment of the tensions Nietzsche expressed so pithily: "He forgets most everything in order to do one thing, he is unjust against what is behind him, and knows only one right—the right of that which is to come."[65]

To do justice to the possibility of redemption that Eastwood stages within the medium and for the medium is to recognize the irreducible fold of his simultaneous faithfulness to and forgetting of a genre, a fold that is difficult to indicate without reducing it in turn to a simple editing trick, the effect of a film cut. While it is integral to the logic of the industry and the market of the screen, this fold also exemplifies the logic of cultural paramnesia that will dissimulate and envelop screen memories. *Unforgiven* was only the third Western since 1931 to be nominated and chosen for Best Picture at the Academy Awards; for six decades, there had been no such award for a Western until Kevin Costner's film *Dances with Wolves* won the year before *Unforgiven*. When *Unforgiven* received four Oscars in 1993, there was a general sense that Hollywood was recompensating one of its own for his long career and box office success. At long last, the industry had decided to forgive Eastwood's "spaghetti-Western" past and his infamously violent films under the direction of Sergio Leone and Don Siegel. To award both Best Director and Best Picture to the actor-director whose movie, apart from winning another two Academy Awards (for Best Editing, and for Gene Hackman as Best Supporting Actor), was nominated in no less than nine categories (including Best Actor, Screenplay, Cinematography, Sound, and Art Direction), amounted to a very belated recognition of his screen appeal—and the income generated by it. *Unforgiven*, dedicated to "Sergio and Don," grossed over $100 million in the United States alone, and it won Golden Globes for Best Picture, Best Director, Best Actor, and Best Supporting Actor in 1993. Clint Eastwood directed fifteen films before *Unforgiven*, and acted in many more. Arguably, the regime of judgment the Academy of Motion Picture Arts and Sciences wields year by year is repressing the fact that film is the genre of violence, and trying to rise above that is Hollywood's perennial bad faith. In 1931, *Cimarron* by Wesley Ruggles won an Oscar for Best Picture. Of course, movies such as *Butch Cassidy and the Sundance Kid* (1969) or *McCabe and Ms. Miller* (1971), to name but two that were more interesting than *Dances with Wolves*, successfully continued and transvalued the Western tradition, but were not recognized at the Oscars. Unlike the sentimental *Dances with Wolves*, which offers no critique of the genre and is replete with idealized cultural correctness, in *Unforgiven* Eastwood addresses the weighty heritage of Hollywood's business with the promised land rather directly, and consequently, it appears that what Eastwood had become on the big screen then had to be dissected repeatedly before it could be forgiven by the industry. *Unforgiven* achieves this self-reflection by a complicated folding in on itself, indulging as well as exposing the tall tales that Hollywood sells.

6

SCREEN MEMORIES:
HYPERTEXT

Even the past is no longer safe from the present which consigns
it to oblivion once again in remembering it.
— Theodor Adorno, *Minima Moralia*

NCREASINGLY, READING AND WRITING take place in front of the computer
screen, and the expectations concerning new forms of interaction with data
storage and access are high. Computer mediated communication in particular and screen media in general seem to put into question what older institutions and archives had to offer.[1] The transition from analog to digital media is
perhaps too readily understood as a shift from continuity to fragmentation,
from narration to archaeology. One might view it as a process of translation,
since what is completely untranslatable into new media will disappear as fast
as what is utterly translatable. The shock with which such threats of disappearance are received leads to symptomatic formations in cultural memory. The
implications for learning and pedagogy are the topics of numerous scholarly
efforts.[2] Digital storage and interactivity have become part of many industries,
and the most widely used multimedia systems have even generated what was
hailed as a "new economy." But while the Internet conquers the world, neo-
Luddites form their ambivalent resistance. Their discontent concerns not so

119

much the machine as its purported effect. Both positions pivot on the same unquestioned assumption: that something irreversibly, incontrovertibly new is intruding on the turf of production and perception. Since Hegel, writing and calculating machines have been understood as a threat, because they interrupt and disperse the cultural fabric of sublation, recollection, idealization, and the history of spirit; the mechanical prevents any recuperation into complete and infinite self-presence. Although the authenticity of a paperback book is no greater than that of a screen, neo-Luddites and technophiles share the assumption, apocalyptically or enthusiastically, that machines are omnivores, imploding all referentiality and excluding humans by means of their illegibility. Fredric Jameson worries that no society has ever been as oversaturated with information as ours.[3] On the other hand, qualified net-critique beyond mere consumerism requires new competencies and access for all. "Resistance to the machine" can therefore mean two things: it can induce you to postulate a space beyond all machines, and to strive for utopian imperfection; to do nothing is to give in to consumerism. Our ideas of distance, inherent in all teletechnology, are cathected with forgetting and repression—yet strictly speaking, distance is nothing but the medium of appearing. To see culture under the auspices of the computer does not necessarily mean that the humanities must dissolve, learn to program, and join computer science. One can learn Fortran, C++, Unix, and Java, and will still have to concede that programming is a synthetic group effort, not a critical analysis. And although scores of literary and philosophical computer programs and "hypertexts" have been developed, by themselves they will not liberate textual production or digestion.[4] Nevertheless, new perspectives have been opened for the presentation and production of meaning; if we accept this, then perhaps the assumption that literature is the highest form of human language may become obsolete.

There is no Turing-test for literature.[5] But before we hasten to the conclusion that the introduction of computers turns "even the most intelligent poetry into myth or anecdote," as Friedrich Kittler mockingly writes, the fact remains that the new systems are used not only for the technical documentation of airplane construction and open-heart surgery, but also for the writing of poetry.[6] In 1962, the software "Auto-Beatnik" was introduced by R. M. Worthy in *Horizon Magazine*, "Auto-Poet" and "Scansion Machine" followed, and in 1984, the *Scientific American* reported on "Racter," the first prose generator.[7] It uses a vocabulary database to generate complex, grammatically correct sentences. By now, numerous such programs are available on the Internet; among the best known are "Eliza," imitating a psychiatric conversation, and sentence generators like "Prose."[8] Many commercial Web sites now use customer service bots that interact with visitors handling standard queries and complaints. Search engines parse natural language to better determine the exact nature of your question.

A program, it turns out, is just a text that generates text. With this develop-ment, the task of the critic seems impossible. How can the reader recognize an object as belonging to a class of objects, such as poetry, in such a way that it does not resemble the other members of that class too closely, as in plagiarism or direct imitation? One solution would be to distinguish between dissimula-tion and membership in the class. Twenty years ago, the literary critic Hugh Kenner collaborated in the development of a "travesty generator," a software that would imitate literary texts. He concluded that all texts already followed his travesty principles, and language itself follows the rules of his software.[9] But impossible anteriority leads into paradox. One way to address the issue is to remind ourselves that not every text about literature is literature; not every text generated under the conditions of the machine is machine-generated text. How does technology affect our criteria?

Hypertext is the one popular form of computer-mediated communication that has raised perhaps the highest expectations for a transformation of cul-ture.[10] It has been hailed as a new form of literature, a new encyclopedia, a uni-versal library, and as a meta-medium that would ingest and replace all older media. Theodor Nelson proposed to consider hypertext a "generalized footnote," and other experts like Jacob Nielsen have followed him in this respect.[11] A text that would contain its own exhaustive index would already be nothing but its own index, and thus the end of what it indexes: thus, the computer explodes the boundaries of the book. Hypertext makes relational references within the textual machine available, while their exact manner of connection remains open. Although it seemed as if this structure could solve the most exalted hopes of literature, philosophy, and technicians, writing, as opposed to memory, is not simply a means of data storage. The factors that affect and transform cul-ture are less a matter of the media achievements that challenge the capacity of cultural memory than indeed of the conditions that question the functioning of memory as such.[12] It is feasible that hypermedia are little more than an improved means to an old end, as Thoreau said of the telegraph, but with hind-sight, we know that technologies not only change the institutions of learning, they also transform the juridical and political milieu of culture.[13] At the same time, experts concede that broader acceptance of hypertext in and as culture will only partly be achieved by way of improved technical concepts.[14] Required, therefore, is a careful, attentive reading of all the promises that throw caution to the winds of mass distraction.

To be sure, hypertext can pose significant challenges to the conventions of canon, author, reader, and text. That does not prevent philologists from using hypertext for their analyses.[15] Even the most skeptical media critics demonstrate a degree of technical competence.[16] Lacan called cybernetics and psychoanaly-sis parallel instances of an era of thought experiment.[17] But by far the most

enthusiastic reception of hypertext in all its dimensions was extended by cultural theorists: at long last, all the promises of their approaches seemed to have
come into their own, be they hybridity, nomadism, polyphony, intertextuality,
or discourse analysis. Hypertext was going to prove Umberto Eco, Wolfgang
Iser, or Gilles Deleuze right.[18] But the specific media articulation of each of
these contexts would be lost in the all-encompassing paradigm, and that might
smuggle traditional hermeneutics in through the back door of technological
determinism.[19] Then, every future reading will have been caught; no external,
"extramediatic" observer position would remain.

It is not as if this situation had not been recognized. In fact, it has been claimed
as belated support for a certain deconstructive claim that "there is no transcendental outside-the-text." George Landow was among the first to claim a convergence of hypertext and the theoretical micrologies of the last three decades.[20]
One of the most curious (and curiously one of the most popular) examples for
this thesis is Jacques Derrida's *Glas*.[21] "When designers of computer software
examine the pages of *Glas* or *Of Grammatology*," George Landow believes, "they
encounter a digitalized, hypertextual Derrida."[22] Since its publication in 1974,
Glas has been widely considered both hypertextual and unreadable. As J. Hillis
Miller formulated the comparison:

> *Glas* and the personal computer appeared at more or less the same time.
> Both work self-consciously and deliberately to make obsolete the traditional
> codex linear book and to replace it with the new multilinear multimedia
> hypertext that is rapidly becoming the characteristic mode of expression
> both in culture and in the study of cultural forms. The "triumph of theory"
> in literary studies and their transformation by the digital revolution are
> aspects of the same sweeping change.[23]

Glas is a text typeset in (at least) two columns, shot through with inserts, playing one side against the other. One side grew out of a seminar on Hegel and
the family, the other is a sustained reading of Jean Genet; their balance remains
irreducible to theses or themes. Both columns incorporate a large number of
philosophical and literary texts, but citations are not always marked, and there
are no footnotes. In the three decades after its publication, *Glas* has been called
"Derrida's *chef d'oeuvre*," and "a *Fleurs du Mal* of philosophy," and to be sure,
it still makes the boundaries between philosophy and literature tremble.[24] What
this doubled-over text leads us back to is the question of a clinging relation, a
grip, a suction, of a clamp or a bond, and bind, between its sides. But now it
also makes the boundaries between the book and electronic media tremble,
and is frequently called "Derrida's hypertext." Landow's identification of *Glas*
as hypertext itself exhibits hypertextual drift, if we follow it across the notes:

Landow cites Greg Ulmer, who refers to an interview with Derrida regarding one passage from *Glas*, in which citations from the French *Littré* dictionary are listed. Norbert Bolz agrees—considering both Wittgenstein's *Philosophische Untersuchungen* and Derrida's *Glas* as hypertext *avant la lettre*.[25] Nevertheless, a hypertextual organization or presentation can never simulate reading—too often, *avant la lettre* means *avant la lecture*. Richard Rorty also fell prey to the paramnesia that *Glas* exerts:

> In *Glas*, Derrida has, to be sure, spoken several languages at once, written several texts at once, produced a kind of writing which has no *archai*, no *telos*, and so on. But he is doing brilliantly and at length something most of his readers have been doing spasmodically and awkwardly in their heads. It is no small feat to get this sort of thing down on paper, but what we find in *Glas* is not a new terrain. It is a realistic account of a terrain upon which we have been camping for some time.[26]

As if by way of proof, Hegel returns under the guise of hypertext-enthusiasm and Internet-presentism: "In the twentieth century, the Hegelian concept becomes real in electronic telecommunications," Mark Taylor promises, "the net wires the world for Hegelian Geist."[27] Richard Rorty thinks Hegel "wrote the charter of our modern literary culture" against his intentions, but a kind of déjà vu sneaks in: "It is as if Hegel knew all about this culture before its birth."[28] But under such conditions, how does one arrive at this very observation? And how is a reading of *Glas* possible? Derrida's rigorous thought of the remainder between Hegelian sublation and Genet's excremental output assimilates, stores, but then falls behind the rest, and lets it fall. Once you think you are deciphering, reading, and commenting on it, the remainder observes you from a resistant, secreted space. *Glas* must be read as a singular plural, it is buried in its own ruins.[29] In her "Glaspiece," one of the first commentators, Gayatri Chakravorty Spivak, repeatedly writes, "I can read *Glas*"[30] (as ancestral rite: 22, as counterfiction of cryptonymy: 24, as legend: 25, as folding of the fold: 26, as play of Genet against Hegel: 32, as inclusion of "the early Derrida" in amber: 43). What kind of reading is this if it presents *Glas* as appropriations of the illegible into its various atomic subtexts? The majority of readers present *Glas* either as the ultimate illegible text, or as something we all know already and therefore no longer need to read.

The principal difficulty, as we can read in *Glas* itself, is that despite its apparent fragmentation, if a machine were to select words and themes from *Glas*, they would fit onto three to three and a half pages.[31] Is it then indeed "Derrida's hypercard," a reading machine or automaton that triggers itself without intending meaning?[32] Hypertext cannot guide its reception in the way literary theorists consider intextuality. Where hypertext contexualizes, intertextuality decontextualizes; while intertexts guide interpretations, hypertext disseminates and withdraws. *Glas* goes even beyond that type of intertextuality that would integrate its intertexts partly, to the extent of risking conflicts with them because of stylistic and semantic incompatibility.[33] For its presentation is a matter of a complex and artificial fiction machine that will have been heard—*déjà entendu*—as representational fiction.[34] *Glas* remains split: on the one hand as fiction of the impossibility of any presentation, on the other hand as the necessity to reflect its own fictionality. Thus it is exemplary for a tendency to allegorize itself: as auto-commentary, it becomes the paradigm for a new poetics.[35] Such hydra-poetics is the only sustained reading undertaken: *Glas* as Hegelian hypertext, a book-length talmud on a very short Hegelian dictum, as Riffaterre wrote, or a glossing of its own first sentence, a micrology of the "and" between the "here" and the "now." Indeed most readers tend to make a clear decision that Derrida clearly does not: the decision to read cyclopically either in the Hegel column or in the Genet column.[36] Perhaps neither *Glas* nor any other text of this difficulty will ever have been legible stereoscopically and instantly.

How could such a text have been written? When the magazine *L'Arc* asked Jacques Derrida for a new contribution for a special issue on his work, Derrida was teaching Hegel, but decided in his contribution to focus on Genet's GL effects, in relation to Sartre's text on Genet, and Genet's text on Rembrandt—*Finnegans Wake* always on his mind. In the summer of 1973, then, he wrote four typescripts: one on Hegel, one on Genet, plus annotation to each; subsequently, having calculated (not line by line but page by page) what the "di-rection" should be, he placed text-shards on cardboard with the help of scissors, by hand.[37] (This procedure must have driven the publishers to the brink of ruin.) A few of these proofs are now archived at the University of California at Irvine. Its Critical Theory Archive also holds a set of fifteen seminar sessions on Hegel and the family, typed up with handwritten notes added in the margins, and a few pages on Genet, both of which clearly went into *Glas*. Other files offer information on when these were taught where: Derrida taught Hegel on Religion in Berlin (where he flew every other week in the autumn of 1973) and at Johns Hopkins before the book was published.

Derrida's seminar on Hegel was called "La famille de Hegel." It was offered, ostensibly, as a new introduction, although already within a Hegelian circle of beginnings and "introductory" works. As a guiding concept, strangely necessary though necessarily overdetermined, Derrida chose the family: Hegel's family, the conceptual family, the holy family. Thus the seminar begins with the syllogism of right, morality, and "Sittlichkeit," proceeding from the family to the bourgeois society and to state constitution. Christianity is the speculative religion for Hegel, in its relation between father and son, or the trinity; philosophy is its truth, as speculative dialectics. But if familial love comes to relieve right, it takes its place above or beyond; thus it is the role of the excluded inclusion, the bastard, to marginally mark the Hegelian onto-theology of the family, the familial circle, and the triangulations of trinity. Yet this is not to say anything different, or more, than Hegel; it is unclear whether one reads what Hegel did not read when one says, for instance, that Abraham performed an unfilial rupture with family and tradition in order to be a founder of religion; or when one says that castration, cutting, has to intervene conceptually.[38] The seminar outlines the consumption of the disappearing object in the dialectics of potency, memory, language, tools, property, and family (e.g., language is the product of memory, but it remains evanescent and disappears in the moment it is produced); the double movement of hemming in and potency, repetition and anticipation (e.g., ideality is always the effect of a "Hemmung," repression is essentially idealizing and sublimating, and ideality thus appears already in the structure of the animal desire); gender difference, conscience as medium, monogamous marriage (as the first moment of the family and of the third potency of conscience in which gender difference is sublated), the familial syllogism; questions of cannibalism, anthropophagy, and the Eucharist (as a consummation of difference); the grave, and the functions that relieve the death of death; the sister (Christiane, Nanette, Antigone)—the valor of the family cannot be constituted outside the horizon or without the foundation of theology; the marriage of extreme opposites, in a syllogistic copulation. The infinitely open chain of returns, stone-tomb-erection-death and so on in its disseminative effect threatens to overturn signification at every moment; however, something remains.

In 1982, in his comments on "an absent colossus," John Leavey proposed three preliminary rules for reading *Glas*. First, that deconstruction is not a critical operation, although it is essentially critical to the extent that the critique is its object. Second, that each column must be regarded from the other column, as they sheath each other, control each other, parody each other across the abyss. The insult of one extreme to another, as Hegel had it, is necessary. Third, as corollary to the second rule, Leavey wrote, the obscenity of the colossal stands for excess, the monstrous, the immeasurable—it is almost too big, almost unrepresentable, in an attempt to break out of the Hegelian circles of family, Christianity, spirit with the help of the bastard, the thief, the excremental shred.[39]

Derrida's work on Hegel culminates in *Glas*. But his readings are not to be confused with Hegel exegesis or anti-Hegelianism; rather they insist on the marginal, irreducible remainder.[40] Here, *différance* comes into play, precisely not as dialectical contradiction in the Hegelian sense, but as the critical limitation of the idealized potential of *Aufhebung*.[41] Derrida announced his project of a deconstruction of Hegel's *Aufhebung* early on.[42] But in *Glas*, Hegel is read neither logically nor historically, but systematically.[43] If it is hard to forget Hegel, then it may be even harder to remember him in an un-Hegelian way.[44] But *Glas* resists Hegel when he claims that difference is already contradiction as such. *Aufhebung* is what is sublated and yet remains; Hegel's system lastly rests on the tripartite interpretation of this word: to conserve, to lift up, to dissolve.[45] These mutually exclusive meanings are simultaneous, in a nonparticular and nonuniversal here and now. *Aufhebung* is the condition of time-space, and in the end the only thing that is not sublated. Here, the aspiration to absolute knowledge and the fantasy of perfect self-presence meet. The self-presence (*s'avoir absolu*) of absolute knowledge (*savoir absolu*) knows no forgetting, since spirit keeps "all layers of the past within itself" and thus working on the past is always working on the present, as Hegel argues.[46] In "abstract mnemosyne," what used to be stored without consciousness becomes a linguistic sign of memory; the progress toward the pure thought of the signifier is secured by "mechanical memory," as Hegel assures his audience in the *Encyclopedia*, but only the linguistic sign grants memory its preeminent position of affinity to thought.[47]

Philosophical readers, in turn, tend to encounter *Glas* by way of context or intertexts, approaching its ambience, making it contingent upon a historical moment in academia. And already they take sides: for Hegel, for the system, for family and Christianity, against Genet, excrement, homosexuality, and crime.[48] The only acknowledged function of the Genet column is to offer "heuristic material and patterns of interpretation for the reading of the column dealing with Hegel."[49] This splitting along party lines cannot be disregarded; surely to try to correct Hegel is to celebrate him. Yet Derrida's "démarche bâtarde," a reading of the family from the vantage point of what it excludes, cannot be reduced to any heterosexist, phallocentric position. Can it be enough to exclude Genet, the thief? What would it mean for the reader to be possessive, to claim ownership and defend it? And would speculative dialectics ("mos canis"), as *Glas* asks, have no other place for the homosexual than the prison? It is equally plausible to consider the Hegel column material for interpreting Genet.[50] Geoffrey Hartman, who devoted an entire book to *Glas*, considered it a *Fleurs du Mal* of philosophy, not its end.[51] Nevertheless the bell tolls for the natural father, for Hegel, for Nietzsche, for the book—but not for Genet. *Glas* reconstitutes Hegel's family, his concept of the family, and the family of concepts, and only the Genet column can show what is excluded and included between the columns.

On the other hand, *Glas* reminds some commentators, not just hypertext advocate George Landow, of James Joyce.[52] Instead of rephilosophizing, this path attempts the taming of the fragmentary text by way of comparison with another unreadable text: "contrary to one possible literary model, *Finnegans Wake* by James Joyce, the fragmentary beginnings and endings do not seem to refer to one another or enchain one another," as one critic believes, ignoring the cross-over effects between the two column ends and starts.[53] Geoffrey Hartman admonishes those who would flee before *Glas* as before *Finnegans Wake*, considering the former perhaps less original, but since the latter there had not been such a calculated provocation full of allusions: "There is a real danger of literature getting lost, running amok or running scared after Joyce's *Wake* and Derrida's *Glas*. Everything is infected by equivocations and the repetition of part-objects of language."[54] This stance can also be found in books that advertise an "advanced" introduction into the subject matter: "*Glas* bears to critical discourse a relation like that which *Finnegans Wake* holds with the novel. Excesses of innumerable sorts court unreadability. It is difficult, then, to say we have 'read' *Glas*"—and that is already the end of the advance.[55]

Can we simply resign ourselves to an unreadable *Glas*? The librarians at Konstanz University, an institution familiar with literary theory, were astonished by *Glas* and debated with their dealer whether or not theirs was a complete print, as documented in a correspondence that is glued inside the circulation copy. This supplemental page tries to fix what they perceived as a lack, and thus offers itself as a guide to reading *Glas*. The librarians wrote: "Pages 1–6 and 291–296 are missing" (Nov. 11, 1980). Answer: "Again and again a library complains. I have enumerated the pages that absolutely are not missing" (Feb. 6, 1981). Again, the librarians try: "Unfortunately the missing pages were only noticed when the book came back after being bound." The dealer responds, "Book is complete. Book designer wanted to entertain and began book in mid sentence and ended likewise. I have checked several times and can assure one hundred and fifty percent that THE BOOK IS ABSOLUTELY COMPLETE." Finally the publisher had to mediate, in French: "They look for completion and coherence in a thinking so fundamentally inconsistent and vain as Derrida's! SAD IDIOTS!"[56] The same issue troubled the librarians of another institution that has experience with literary theory, namely Yale. This time, the complaint went directly to Paris, asking for exchange for the supposedly defective copy. Promptly Galilée responded—and this correspondence is also documented inside the library's copy, complete with letterhead stationery—with the reassurance that the copy was not incomplete.[57] The endless loop of beginning and end of the two columns stages a constant rereading of the text that withdraws from any approach: a gallery of texts that read each other, save each other, lose each other.[58]

What would a reading have to be to mediate between the columns and camps? René Wellek thought *Glas* simply annoying: "it sits between three chairs; it offers no aesthetic experience, it is no literary criticism, and it is not good philosophy."[59] In contrast, John Llewelyn claims in deep "Glasnostalgia," there could be no bad reading of *Glas*, for if it was bad in a limited way, it should be considered included in Hegelian absolute knowledge, but if it was infinitely bad, then absolute knowledge would not be absolute knowledge.[60] Consequently, Derrida's own reading in *Glas* can only ever have been too good in its revaluation of *Aufhebung* or "perestroika," as John Llewelyn writes. Hegelian implosions on one side, unreadability on the other: since dialectics only profit from resistances and contradictions, we consider ourselves warned against an opposition of different readings or nonreadings, and against evaluating them. Perhaps a reading of *Glas* as hypertext will be able to acknowledge the resistances and remainders without wanting to nail them by making them either completely immaterial or fully manifest. If we follow the suggestion to read *Glas* as hypertext, the columns clamped together destroy each other in order to preserve their relation. To read hypertextually requires an ethics of decision, for it will always offer at least two paths to the reader. Between arrest and movement, split and self-application, the trace of its message (*carte*) is lost in the interval (*écart*) of texts.[61] Indeed, this might be the proper space of memory, as Renate Lachmann has it.[62] Yet that does not mean that hypertext makes explicit in the network of references whatever linear writing used to make hermeneutics do. Curiously, Norbert Bolz thinks that the differential net of hypertext no longer creates a feeling of delay and deferral, but suggests immersion in a lasting presence of textual motion.[63] Only twenty minutes on the Internet or a short presentation of a CD-ROM can expose how deceptive such fantasies are. The encyclopedic basis for them is the desire for a complete object.[64] But the resistance of the rest, as *Glas* will have demonstrated, remains.[65] Yet media studies can claim *Glas*, Wittgenstein or Hegel, and even the Talmud as proto-hypertexts; as the mishnah is surrounded by the most important references, the Talmudic scholar incorporates the referential structure.[66] "In the heads of philosophers, modern and postmodern literati" there was a "virtual hypertext-machine" long before the invention of the computer, as some enthusiasts claim, again citing *Glas* as preeminent example.[67] "New" media studies participated with glee in the forget-together of the dot-com revolution, and are now often left speechless before its ruins. Just as cultural history has much to learn from the genealogy of media technology, media studies would do well to be grounded in cultural and intellectual history in order to avoid drifting in the fickle winds of *zeitgeist* and hype. Vilém Flusser considered Champollion a computer *avant la lettre,* since he decoded the hieroglyphic code.[68] Friedrich Kittler considers Hegel's notebooks "hypertextual" and calls Babbage a "precursor of the computer," and with Lacan he identifies the "first machine" based on empty placeholders as Pascal's invention of the arithmetic triangle in the year 1654.[69] In short: with hindsight, everybody already knew. What is interesting to the observer of media studies is this split, or doubling, of the perspective on the "new" media: they are either variations of something so old that it is almost forgotten, or so shockingly new that they cannot be understood by anyone just yet. Both defensive gestures, whether by way of a return to before Plato or the promise of an immemorial future, manipulate cultural memory and induce déjà vu.

Recollection becomes oblivion, the interface-principle WYSIWYG becomes WYSIWYF: what you see is what you (for)get. Such parapraxis slips into the discussion of hypertext and the Internet wherever you look. One might say that the symptom of "new" media studies is this screen memory. As long as we remain blind to the texture of this symptom, we seem to get over it simply enough, beheading hypertext and arriving at psycho-biographic significance.[70] But when it becomes evident that *Glas* puts the heads of metalanguage back into the thickets of texts only to pull them out for a short breath, that text therefore constitutes a commentary on what it lacks, what it limits, serves, and encloses, then hypertext will have been nothing but the metalanguage that never presents itself and remains folded in.[71] In the age of digital modification and insufficient version control, the screen is the horizon of memory.[72] Context hides directly beneath the surface, always a click away; there is no world before the machine.

The first words of the much quoted hypertextual short story by Michael Joyce, "Afternoon," are: "I try to recall winter. <As if it were yesterday?> she says, but I do not signify one way or another." This not only allegorizes the process of reading (choosing among five hundred episodes with over nine hundred cross-references), reading can only be rereading in this scenario, just as it was claimed of the more famous Joyce. Indeed Jay David Bolter forces the issue when he asserts: "Reading an electronic text can be both a rereading and a first reading at the same time. . . . An electronic text may never repeat itself in the conventional sense, but we may always read the text as if it were a repetition."[73] There has never been a complete, untouched, and original object, however much we may desire it archaeologically and otherwise. It remains a dream so old that one almost forgets that it is never realized.[74] But if the new turns out to be another form of the old, a screen memory is generated. Digital replication and repeatability, reduplications of reference and perspective undermine not only linear narration, but also linear constructions of recollection; in other words, it is déjà vu, a memory of the present in the rereading of each present as memory.

Intent on establishing the complicity of Derrida's thought and Marxist dialectics in the teeth of all evidence, Michael Ryan cast his net for philosophical terminology inherited from Hegel and Marx. Thus he observes, as is often done, that *Glas* marks a turn in Derrida's published work: "After beginning an intense study of Hegel which culminates in *Glas*, Derrida drops the words 'mediation' and 'negation' from his vocabulary. 'Mediacy' [mediatété] or 'expansive mediacy' appear instead."[75] This philological observation may or may not indicate a modification in Derrida's thinking on Hegel; even an attentive reading of *Glas* will perhaps never solve the debate as to whether or not it marks a significant stylistic, philosophical, conceptual break. Ryan claims that "anyone familiar with Derrida's *Glas* will probably recognize in Adorno's program a version of Derrida's project—to elaborate the origin of literature 'between the two,' that is, between Hegel's seminar of absolute knowledge and Jean Genet's saturnalia of fragmentary dissemination."[76] But what exactly would it mean to be familiar with the unfamiliar, to feel familiarity with this radically antifamilial project? Ryan reduces *Glas* to a self-referential ploy, an implosion of reading: "For Derrida, *Glas* has no meaning apart from the differential shuttling back and forth between columns." Like most commentators on *Glas*, Ryan ignores the Genet column, although he admits it should be part even of the most reduced "meaning" of *Glas*. That the Genet column might at the very least offer clues, interruptions, interceptions integral to the reading of Hegel with and against himself in *Glas*, or indeed that the Hegel column might serve a similar function for the readability of the Genet column, not to speak of the many Judases, is only alluded to. The typographic peculiarity of *Glas* is imitated toward the end of Ryan's book, where he makes light of Derrida's "use of the double column in *Glas*" that, he writes, "emphasizes relations between the sides and thereby undermines the rationalist focus on a nonrelational, single discursive line" by then offering a paragraph on race and gender difference set as a double column.[77] But typographic imitation can neither reproduce the tensions between the interwoven discourses of *Glas*, nor direct the same intense focus onto the balance and relationality, hierarchy and undermining, of Derrida's strategy in the experiment of *Glas* that predated desktop publishing by a number of years.[78]

Derrida's thought experiment brackets past and future in a Hegelian embrace of the *Dreckerinnerung* of the remainder. *Glas* listens to the sound of words—such as *glas*. "Words such as *fouet* and *glas*," wrote Ferdinand de Saussure, "may strike some ears as having a certain sonority," but then he argued that any knowledge of their Latin origins would debunk all pretensions of onomatopoeia.[79] Yet the whip and the knell "can strike" (*peuvent frapper*), as Saussure himself puns. If, therefore, we suspect etymological play of being "logocentric," the fact remains, after Saussure, that such friction between signifier and signified can produce effects—and that Derrida's *Glas* is full of them.[80] Linguists speak of arbitrary sliding, and it is the first hurdle to any reader of *Glas* that Derrida consciously, calculatedly, slides along the fault lines of sub- and trans-linguistic shifts that turn sense and certainty inside out. *Glas*, the French death knell, is also a Slavic word denoting "voice," and indeed in *Glas*, Derrida plays the "living voices" off against their "death by writing." Voices from so many other works make this book so encyclopedic and unreadable; it swallows its reading and coughs up morsels. Although *Glas* itself has no footnotes, references to *Glas* permeate most later texts by Derrida.[81] It enters into a relation to the absolute past, "to an always already-there that no reactivation of the origin could fully master and awaken to presence."[82] That absolute past, while perhaps no longer deserving of the name, can never be excavated—it begins by coming back. To read *Glas* therefore promises to trace Derrida's work back to a moment of originary insight about the nonoriginality of origins and originary insights, about an irreducible originary complexity.[83] At the same time Derrida calls *Glas* "my apocalypse" and "a sort of wake."[84] What he tried to describe, he says, was a nonsubjective experience of mourning.[85] *Glas* clings, among other things, to the de-clinging, to the *dé-cramponnement* of a certain filial structure. A reading of that clamp will have to cling to and push against Derrida's clinging to the clamp. *Glas* writes a "theory of the clutching hook, of clutching in general," Derrida said in an interview.[86] That clutch or clamp is nothing more or less than the "siglum or acronym of the book."[87] An acronym may be our masterkey, anagrammatically at play, *toujours déjà*. In *Glas*, we read that this "text only 'exists,' consists, represses, only lets itself be read or written by being acted upon by the unreadability of a proper name." And that proper name, we will be forgiven for thinking, might as well be *De, Ja*. For arguably, Jacques Derrida plays on the *derrière*, the logic of the *a tergo* in Genet and in dialectics ("mos canis"), extending all the way to the acronym of Hegelian circularity, SA (for *savoir absolu*). Mixing the voices on parallel tracks, *Glas* is the score and the machine by the same token: produced by DJ Vu.[88] The machine is the hidden and the means of hiding, and this goes for technicity from writing to the computer— "that machine is already in place, it is the 'already' itself."[89] Is it possible, after all the above, to consider the Internet an archive where cultural memory and its necessary overwriting are accessible?

A century ago, Wilhelm Dilthey urged the collection of philosophical papers and literary scripts of "persons of intellectual distinction" whose heritage he considered in peril of disappearance. With envy he noted the rich archives of history, even of contemporary political studies, and called for comprehensive means of collection and preservation for the sake of those studying "poetry and philosophy, history and science" in context. To this end, Dilthey propagated a return to two virtues he saw as dating from the latter half of the eighteenth century: philology in its methodological aspect on one hand, and on the other, a Hegelian history of humanity culminating in philosophy. To recognize the historicity of human nature through the eighty-four generations since Thales required an archive, Dilthey argued, of philosophy and its exegesis according to philological strictures. Presupposing an already constituted objective spirit, Dilthey wished for the significations and values of this objective milieu to be interiorized and assumed as such. He concluded, "the collation of manuscripts somewhere in a state archive of literature has to begin as soon as possible," expressing his confidence that "in the rooms of such an archive, a spirit of the house will appear that watches over these papers, at once opening and preserving, tending and communicating them."[90]

As of spring 1996, the University of California at Irvine hosts an archive that has begun to collect Critical Theory (including the remains, as it were, of Derrida), while at the same time qualifying its relation to Dilthey's parameters.[91] There is little doubt that in Derrida's work, one finds considerable resistance against appropriations of any kind, a distrust of "state archives" and institutions, a suspicion against notions of continuity and method, and an uneasy relation, at best, to the history of philosophy. What spirit would be needed or able to tend and open, today and tomorrow, the texts signed "Jacques Derrida," in order to prevent their disappearance? As of late, computers appear to promise an open archive, but the relationship of deconstruction to computer writing, and to hypertext in particular, needs yet to be determined: does deconstruction somehow "theorize" hypertext, or hypertext "literalize" deconstruction? While Gregory Ulmer thinks that Derrida's texts "already reflect an internalization of the electronic media," Mark Poster holds that "computer writing instantiates the play that deconstruction raises only as a corrective."[92] Thus two different ways of preempting the computer age are ascribed to Derrida: he incorporated its future potential, or at least raised expectations that were then met by computer writing. According to Mark Taylor, "Deconstruction theorizes writerly practices that anticipate hypertexts."[93] Yet, as demonstrated above, the repeated, widespread attempts to render the columns clamped together in *Glas* readable as hypertext *avant la lettre* more often than not tend to preempt reading and dismiss the commentary found in *Glas* on the Hegelian bias against the machine; it would then only be hypertext *avant la lecture*.[94]

Nevertheless, if in the "nonspaced space or spaced-out space of the internet, everything is in a sense everywhere at all times," as J. Hillis Miller tried to understand it, "and everything is juxtaposed to everything else," then it ought to be possible for theoretical work, prescient or not, to be collected, opened, tended to, and communicated via the Internet, allowing an almost instantaneous access to any page or work or mark in store—while at the same time remaining open to a logic of the unforeseeable.[95] Yet until recently, theorists made comparatively little use of the abilities to combine text, image, sound, and animation on the basis of hypertext markup language on the World Wide Web. At a time when many interface-metaphors on "the net" turn out to be merely empty thoroughfares, it seems necessary to summon resistance to endless streams of telephatic chatter.[96] Suspended between the old-fashioned desire for an encyclopedic grasp of "Derrida," and the surmise that such a project must appear to go diametrically against the claims of deconstruction, we encounter in Derrida's texts a strong concern with the archive, with memory and dispersion in relation to the reception or nonreception, assimilation or rejection, digestion or exclusion, absorption or expulsion, incorporation or foreclosure, of issues of hypomnesis and forgetting. However, in order to find out what such an archive could be, we must try not to know always already, but pay heed to the teletechnological deferrals of information and communication.[97] It is perhaps less a matter of archeology than of that which is yet to come.[98]

These questions in their relation to computerized textuality are addressed in Geoffrey Bennington's *Derridabase*—the linear version, as he put it, of a book without prescribed order of reading, written in hypertext, to appear subsequently in electronic form. Claiming that if writing had for Derrida a privileged empirical version, it would be the computer, Bennington set out to "systematise J.D.'s thought to the point of turning it into an interactive program which, in spite of its difficulty, would in principle be accessible to any user."[99] It would appear, then, that Bennington's "discontinuous jumps establishing quasi-instantaneous links" attempt to make manifest what other ways of presentation must fail to do, having "absorbed Derrida, his singularity and his signature, the event we were so keen to tell you about, into a textuality in which he may well have quite simply disappeared." However, we do not subscribe to Bennington's apparent suggestion that one day it will no longer be necessary to cite Derrida, because he will have passed into the language. On the contrary, it seems necessary to cite his texts, and cite again, and to keep the citations circulating; thus, the archive will have to be an open one, facilitating access and storage: a Web site, for instance.[100]

At first, to represent Derrida online must appear preposterous. How to "collect Derrida," how to consign deconstruction to an Internet archive? The Net, as master trope of computer-mediated communication, holds the promise of storage and access; the same goes for the conglomeration of representation that digital multimedia may broadcast, in theaters, to your television, or to any mobile device. It comes as no surprise, however, that disgruntled talk abounds of a challenge to literature and culture, fulfilling, perhaps, Derrida's surmise that "an entire epoch of so-called literature, if not all of it, cannot survive a certain technological regime of telecommunications."[101] In all reiterations of the Platonic suspicion of writing, new media are perceived as apparatuses of forgetting from the perspective of the old mediascape. But the uncannily prescient writer of the *Post Card* could not be said to be a technophobe; as Derrida admits a decade before the invention of the World Wide Web, he would

> want to write and first to reassemble an enormous library on the courier, the postal institutions, the techniques and mores of telecommunication, the networks and epochs of telecommunication throughout history—but the "library" and the "history" themselves are precisely but *posts*, sites of passage or of relay among others, stases, moments or effects of *restance*, and also

particular representations, narrower and narrower, shorter and shorter
sequences, proportionally, of the Great Telematic Network, the "worldwide
connection." What would our correspondence be, and its secret, the
indecipherable, in this terrifying archive?[102]

The archive is terrifying because it is irresistible: indeed, to summon the force
of that which is "off the record" will be the impossible task of deconstruction.[103]
Hence, emphasis lies on the "effects of *restance.*" At stake is not a simple opposition between interiorization and technical-mechanical hypomnesis; rather,
one comes to haunt the other in a nondialectical movement of what remains.[104]
Web sites might be among those "sites of passage or of relay among others."
What Derrida offers is not a techno-positivism that argues in favor of a radical presentism in the absolute archive, believing with Nietzsche in the forgetting of history.[105] Nevertheless, Derrida has affirmed that what concerns him is
something "homogeneous with a development of the techno-mathematical kind
that no longer allows one to treat the techno-scientific as Heidegger does."[106]
Navigating thus between Heideggerian nostalgia and Nietzschean force, he proposes a consideration of the archive inasmuch as it would not exist without a
place of consignment, a technique of repetition, and a certain exteriority. What
is more, the archive is not just a prosthesis or stockroom, it contains its own
principle of selection so that "there is no meta-archive"; thus the question of
the archivable concept of the archive becomes "a question of the future."[107]
No mere Derridean philology or philography for us, then—although it is not
entirely without interest if the archive informs us that a passage from "Archive
Fever" echoes another in "The Gift of Death," that the Marx passage in the *Post
Card* (taken up again in *Specters of Marx*) was already developed in an interview from 1977, or that another passage of "Archive Fever" takes up a morsel
from *Glas*, and so forth.[108] This kind of dynamic archiving puts on the line the
most pivotal concern. Derrida sketches his work as follows:

> As for a book project, I have only one, the one I will not write, but that
> guides, attracts, seduces everything I read. Everything I read is either forgotten
> or else stored up in view of this book. . . . It would be at least a crossing of
> multiple genres. I am looking for a form that would not be a genre and that
> would permit me to accumulate and to mobilize a very large number of
> styles, genres, languages, levels . . . That's why it is not getting written.[109]

If all of Derrida's efforts go into that one, unwritten book, and each new publication inscribes itself in it as if by déjà vu (as becomes evident when *Specters
of Marx* appears as if by self-citation from *The Post Card*), then perhaps his
oeuvre is the ghostly correspondence between the not-quite-forgotten project
and its published discards. In their sustained interest in Hamlet, Shakespeare's

contexts, and the actuality of Marx, Heiner Müller and Derrida were surprisingly close.[110] They never met, but they knew of each other's work. Until March 1995, Müller was repeatedly in California as a guest of the Feuchtwanger Villa and the Getty Institute. There, within close range of the Riverside campus that had hosted a conference on "Whither Marxism? Global Crises in International Perspective" in April 1993, Müller wrote *Germania 3 Gespenster am toten Mann*, which some celebrate as evidence that Müller had preempted Derrida's turn to the theatrical specters of Marx.[111] One might even suspect that Derrida's book on the *Specters of Marx* may have been ghost-written by Müller.[112] The issue is not one of anxiety of influence; our interest is not to establish precedence but to reflect on the potential meaning of such a cross-pollination, which Hans-Thies Lehmann had already pointed to many years earlier.[113] In a recent text, Derrida goes on record about his failed encounter with Müller in Berlin that had been arranged after the publication of *Spectres de Marx*.[114] After many deferrals came a phone call one night: Müller is dead. Derrida, in Italy at the time, is told that Müller had wanted him to speak at his grave. Derrida declines. His apparent betrayal of the unknown, great friend, of the kindred thinker, then produced the short text to which Derrida consigns his memory. It is the memory of a kind of treason that he hopes Müller would have understood: not because of any number of—unspoken—reasons for remaining silent at this moment, since they had not yet met, but because the respect they felt for each other and the study of each other's texts made it more appropriate, indeed more faithful, not to participate in a public rite of mourning in Berlin, and instead to refer mutual friends to that public space of labor that is the published text, the image, and the theater.

The discussions of faithful treason and treacherous faith around Marx and his specters raise another concern that Derrida and Müller share. Face to face with a troubling history written by winners, by men, by those who did not die and did not labor in order for it to become what it will have been, both Müller and Derrida resort to an image—that of déjà vu, of a troubled sense of recollection whose time has not yet come. Both Müller and Derrida ascribe to the kind of treason staged in *Hamlet* a productive and indeed theatrical force that sets the plot in motion. Without this force, there would be no future, no decision, no resolution. We have seen Müller's déjà vu as the conscientious awareness that the historical meaning of a given experience may be barred but will become evident with hindsight, and Derrida's text adds a dimension of tragic and farcical repetition in history. Derrida speaks explicitly, at the outset of *Spectres de Marx*, of a troubling sense of déjà vu. Having announced that he would resist the temptation of memory—resist the insistence of a paternal agency of Marxist thought that accompanied theory in the twentieth century—Derrida soon shows characteristic symptoms: "I am speaking of a troubling effect of

'*déjà vu*,' and even of a certain '*toujours déjà vu*.' I recall this malaise of perception, hallucination, and time"; and the paradox, here, is less that he is able to
recall it, but that a certain end of communist Marxism had already come at the
beginning of the 1950s.[115] This end, with which Derrida is evidently not finished, had not awaited the excesses of communism after World War II, nor the
end of the cold war, nor the fall of the Berlin Wall, nor the collapse of Soviet-
style regimes elsewhere. This unfinished end, in short, is what returns at the
opening of the conference where the first part of Derrida's remarks on the
specters of Marx were pronounced. This return, then, had seemed, to Derrida,
"like an old repetition" from the time he was young: "All that started—all that
was even *déjà vu*, indubitably—at the beginning of the '50s" (12). Not only,
then, a déjà vu, but of course already a déjà vu of a déjà vu. The return of an
old repetition that would seem to open, now, in unfamiliar and certainly multiply distorted ways, a sense of the future. Surely this opening, this release,
stems partly from an explicit "resistance to memory"—neither an active forgetting nor an anamnetic interiorizing of recollection, but something altogether
more complex. In Derrida's sense of déjà vu we can recognize both senses of the
already doubled déjà vu—a boring return to an old repetition of the old, and
an entirely new sense of something troubling. Déjà vu is the opposite of the
"end of history."

While Müller held that everything new is a treason of the old, but at the
same time a necessary and revolutionary force, and that revolution is in fact
only conceivable as treason of revolution, Derrida proposes, and proceeds, to
bracket off certain recollections and repetitions, in favor of "another reading
of the media's anachronism and of good conscience"—precisely "so that one
might better appreciate the discouraging impression of *déjà vu*" (13). Between
redundancy and utopian hope, between historicist tautology and a nostalgia for
the future, he presents a vision past the future: a politics of reading that would
always remain mindful of, if never absolutely faithful to, the dead. The spectacle of the specter may confirm—whether in terms of repression and the fetish,
memory and forgetting, hope and hiding, monuments and their toppling, repetition and technology, or the relation to the feminine in its different guises—
what the entire work of Müller and Derrida surmised even where they did not
directly address Marx and Shakespeare.[116] If both theory and déjà vu double
up a vision past the future, then etymology alone, as Nicholas Royle has suggested, indicates a relation between structure and vision that leads to their necessary juncture in the spectacle of the spectral.[117] Therefore, if only by way of
an appendix, one might supplement Müller's theater with Derrida's specters
of theory. Continuing to make the same vanishing point, they turn us on to a
politics of reading. This supplement always already accompanied their projects,
in the double sense of the déjà vu as both the distortingly unfamiliar and the

boringly repetitive. Both writers, both thinkers, labored to fend off the closure of the latter, and to provide the former. This will have been their communal work.

In openly acknowledged contradiction to the fantasy of the one, all-encompassing book project, in *Glas* Derrida confesses, not unlike Müller, to a certain oblivion: "I forget, in a certain way, everything I write, doubtless also, in another way, what I read."[118] And in an interview, Derrida remembers that "a certain amnesia has given me this taste, which one may consider a force or a weakness. I do not say that I know how to forget, but I know that I forget, and that is not only, nor always, a bad thing."[119] Forgetting, amnesia, false memories are subjected to the steady undertow of something that operates on them, beneath them, in secret. If one were to collate a Derrida CD-ROM, as both Geoffrey Bennington and David Wills suggested, or a Derrida Web site, as I have done, how will such archival projects respond to search queries? They might allow various means of access to the published work, quickly and automatically pulled up. Wills hastens to promise, "if there is a deconstructionist mnemo-technology, as I am about to affirm, it would above all depend on a certain rapidity of response, the capacity of having information available a finger's click away."[120] Such storage would circulate certain correspondences and continui-ties in our attention economy, aligning each query with a déjà vu effect that is deeply complicit with archival technology. What would this procedure yield concerning the secret cohesion of an oeuvre, how would it respond to such questions of disclosure? Such an archive would seek to install itself as the for-gotten metaproject, the machine that would program the unwritten book. The mnemotechnological crutch would have to be devoted to forgetting. Thus the very old can seep into the most innovative achievements, and effectively make the present a form of unconscious recollection or symptomatic embodiment: "cyberspace is a gigantic machine of unrecognized forgetting or unconscious remembering."[121] Of course, to be unable to forget is the ultimate semiotic mis-hap. But a sense of dislocation and of the problematics of memory would seem to suit the desire "to make enigmatic what one thinks one understands by the words 'proximity,' 'immediacy,' 'presence' (the proximate, the own, and the pre-of presence)" that Derrida proposed, early on, as his "final intention."[122] In this sense, the Internet may indeed fill the need for machines of forgetting, as the Web designer Florian Brody requested: "Today, we have a wide range of machines that help us remember, but only a few contraptions that help us forget. Perhaps we need to focus on forgetting."[123] In this light, the site of the Internet archive is itself displaced to the extent of turning into a *para-site*.

Although he is a savvy critic of mediatic "actuvirtuality," Derrida has made ample use of television, radio, telephones, and the computer in interviews and publications.[124] The accelerated development of teletechnologies, of cyberspace, of virtuality questions and dislocates the traditionally dominant concepts of state or citizen in their relation to the actuality of a territory—a "practical deconstruction," as Derrida says, of the process of the political.[125] This taking place of the event affects the experience of place itself. After Derrida, one can make this promise only in terms of erasure: in the archive, "deconstruction" (that surprisingly successful word) will have been erased in many ways.[126] Electronic media always harbor that potential, as is illustrated by the following example. A short interview with Elisabeth Weber on German radio was broadcast and subsequently published in a transcription.[127] The notes to that first transcription state that the reader is presented with the "completed text" of an introduction and conversation that took place on May 22, 1990. However, the English translation, published in 1995, contains a passage that was not included in the "completed" German version—and when quizzed about this, neither the interviewer, nor Derrida, nor the translator, Peggy Kamuf, could tell whence it came.[128] It is a double betrayal of the original, a forgetful and strange growth in translation that seems to know of its own uncanny intervention:

Yes, if there is anamnesis, it is not just a movement of memory to find again finally what has been forgotten, to restore finally an origin, a moment or a past that will have been present. One would naturally have to distinguish between several kinds of anamnesis. And every philosophy in history has been an interpretation of anamnesis. The Platonic discourse is essentially anabasis or anamnesis, that is, a going back toward the intelligible place of ideas. The conversion in speleology, the Platonic cave, is an anamnesis. The Hegelian discourse is an anamnesis. The Nietzschean genealogy is an anamnesis. Repetition in the Heideggerian style is an anamnesis. Today, to want to remember philosophy is already to enter into an interpretive memory of all that has happened to memory, of all that has happened to anamnesis, of all the anamnesiac temptations of philosophy. It is naturally a very complicated operation since these anamneses are enveloped in each other. But it is also an interminable operation—there is precisely one of the motifs of deconstruction, let us say to go quickly—for if there is anamnesis, it is because the memory in question is not turned toward the past, so to speak, it is not a memory that, at the end of a return across all the other anamneses, would finally reach an originary place of philosophy that would have been forgotten. The relation between forgetting and memory is much more disturbing. Memory is not just the opposite of forgetting. And therefore the anamnesis of the anamneses I just mentioned will never be able to lift an origin out of oblivion. That is not at all its movement. To think memory or to think anamnesis, here, is to think things as paradoxical as the memory of a past that has not been present, the memory of the future—the movement of memory turned toward the promise, toward what is coming, what is arriving, what is happening tomorrow. Consequently, I would not feel, let's say, at ease in a philosophical experience that would simply consist in practising anamnesis as remembering. It is not just a matter of remembering but also of something altogether other.[129]

An Internet "archive" might be an attempt at a memory of such forgetting, offering an uncanny place for such strange growth in translation. But a memory of forgetfulness remains a paradoxical recuperation. Forgetting is precisely not just the other of memory, because a forgetting as forgetting would already turn forgetting into something phenomenal and thus deny it. It would seem that the movement is not merely one of growth in translation, but at the same time one of loss. Thus when Derrida remarks in recent texts on saving texts on his "bloc de macintosh," one may think not only of disk drives, but also of the death drive.[130] In "Archive Fever," Derrida talks of the peculiar "retrospective science fiction" of what might have happened to the psychoanalytic archive, had technological gadgets such as telephonic credit cards, portable tape recorders, computers, printers, faxes, televisions, and computer-mediated communication interfaces existed earlier.[131] "Plus de dehors"—the boundary violently inscribed between living and nonliving, inside and outside, extant and extinct separates, as Derrida writes, "not only speech from writing, but also memory as an unveiling (re-) producing a presence from re-memoration as the mere repetition of a monument." The folding in of a resistance, then, is possible only in repetition, deferral, trace—which is to say in a double gesture of preserving life, and death at the origin of life.[132] Here, the line is more than subtle: "On both sides of that line, it is a question of repetition."[133] To this extent, the archive is a transgression in and of itself; saving the text, it eats itself and repeats itself. But at the same time, it also gestures toward itself as an opening to the future. In its complicity with and complication of such divisions, the archive must be a memory of the future so as not to cancel itself out.

If the archive is intricately linked to the institution, to that which authorizes it, then the law of selection, inclusion or exclusion, would appear to be a quasi-transcendental, dark "outside." Although this law is itself implied in the archive, it decides what is represented in it, and what is not. Yet hypertext, it is claimed by its champions, accomplishes a virtually universal memory as envisioned by Vannevar Bush and Theodor Holm Nelson.[134] Claiming to have foreseen in 1960 the development of personal computing, word-processing, hypermedia, and populist network publishing, Nelson to this day protests that nobody has yet understood how this structure can organize every connection and use of information, beyond inclusion or exclusion: hence his neologism, transclusion.[135]

Transclusion would enable one to reuse information with its identity and context intact, although everything about them changes all the time.[136] However, just what the identity of context would be is the question: arguably, such a limitless memory would not be a memory at all, but infinite self-presence. Memory constantly revives the aposemiological corpse of the sign in referential paraphrases to recall the nonpresent with which it is necessarily in relation.

Any claims that hypertextuality somehow realized the supposed aims of deconstruction must be mistaken, for "hypertexts can just as well be presented as a fulfillment of a metaphysical view of writing."[137] Indeed, hypertextual structures make the limitations of writing only more tangible—and anyway, dispersive reading would not depend on textual design: "the 'hypertext' aspect of *Derridabase*, which is constantly sending the reader forward to further forward references, many of which go nowhere," as Bennington says, "tries to dramatise that fact." It is important to observe the clear distinction between Derrida's and de Man's writing on this subject: only a detautologized de Man would allow us to avoid the sterility of what Jürgen Fohrmann rightly calls "the boring *déjà vu*-effect" of a recurrent affirmation of a transcendental signified.[138] In a recent interview, Derrida delineates the evolution of calculating machines, thought machines, translation machines, and formalization in general—up to a culture dominated by technical apparatuses of inscription and archiving. Surely it would be unthinking to interpolate such machinations back onto the history of reading.[139] And thus Derrida doubts that deconstruction is always already at work in literature, for instance in Rousseau, as de Man claimed:

> I remember having put this question to Paul de Man in the form of a virtual objection: if this be so, then there would be nothing left to do; yet how would we interpret the fact that deconstruction, in spite of all this, constitutes a topic, that it influences certain events and something happens? . . . Deconstruction is not a memory which simply recalls what is already there. The memory work is also an unforeseeable event, an event that demands a responsibility and gestures, deeds. This act is caught, however, in a double bind: the more you remember, the more you are in danger of effacing, and vice versa. Deconstruction cannot step out of this aporia, of this double-bind, without diffidence.[140]

As Derrida warns against the mechanism of the de Manian "always already," so he warns against the Heideggerian attempt to sanitize and keep separate an essence of technology from technology itself, recognizing this traditional gesture as a protection against the risk of parasitical contamination or an oppositional *différance*.[141] Likewise, the inscription of deconstruction into a world-wide net of computer-mediated communication will not simply always already have taken place; it remains unforeseeable, its technicality must be interrogated without reducing such an interrogation to a participation in the same order.[142]

Nelson claims that "the transclusion paradigm is a fundamentally different way of thinking about almost all computer issues. If we use more conventional terminology, it will anchor our thinking in a different system of conventions, and it will be harder to understand this fundamentally different paradigm." Nelson's penchant for neologisms like "structangle," "docuverse," "teachotechnics," or "showmanshipnogogy" illustrates this attitude.[143] Derrida, by contrast, argues in favor of something he calls paleonymy: keeping the old name, despite all radical displacement and grafting of its connotations. Remonstrating the fundamental impossibility of the transparent immediacy that McLuhan and Nelson believe in, Derrida advocates a powerful historical expansion of general writing: "To leave to this new concept the old name of writing is tantamount to maintaining the structure of the graft, the transition and indispensable adherence to an effective intervention in the constituted historical field. It is to give everything at stake in the operations of deconstruction the chance and the force, the power of communication."[144] The difference between the two approaches lies not just in the strategies of naming them. To Derrida, communication, "if we want to retain that word," is not transference of meaning but inscription or grafting, and its effect a dissemination that is irreducible to the mere polysemy hypertext supposedly embodies, according to Nelson.

Hypertext is not the sublation of a system of traces and marks into fully manifest context, but rather an extension of the same structure. Writing, therefore, is not dead. If death, as radical absence, constitutes the condition of media, but is not represented by them, it will sneak back in as catastrophic spectrality. What, however, happens to media that are diagnosed as dead? They too will return. The Internet began as a text-based environment, and its workings are still based on code, not on sound or images. Thus hypertext and code as condition of possibility for hypermedia announce the ironic return of the purported "metamedium" of writing, which had already been declared obsolete for our iconic global village. Since the inauguration of the World Wide Web in 1992, hypertext markup language (HTML) has given a new lease of spectral life to that paleonym, "writing." Looking back on the technology of the book, the Internet comes to be seen as an extended book review. The law of its composition may not be harbored in the inaccessibility of a secret, but neither can it be booked into a presence.[145] If it seems that hypertext can allow for survival by dint of decentered, dispersive storage on the Internet, then it is due to its textual codes, not due to its commingling with audiovisual codes. Images for some, text for all is now the inverted formula, and its dispersion does not entail complete disappearance. Rather, as Nicholas Royle put it, "to talk about writing in reserve is to engage with the thought of a critical glossolalia, a poetico-telephony or computer network operating multiple channels simultaneously. A sort of hydrapoetics, in effect."[146] Arguably, in the name of such monstrous *écriture*, Derrida online may be presented as a structure of many heads, the totality of which cannot be retrieved and is perhaps indeed saved by its irretrievability.

7

WRAPPING IT UP: MUMMY EFFECTS

> To repeat what one has not heard and what has not been said:
> to repeat this also—and to stop suddenly, pretending to see in
> this the essence of repetition.
>   —Maurice Blanchot, *The Step Not Beyond*

I F DÉJÀ VU IS NEITHER FORGETTING NOR MEMORY, if both are already caught up in its logic of the cover, one ought to recapture a sense that the déjà vu is impossible to recapture. In addition to the turn, around mid-century, that adds a second and pejorative meaning to the formerly haunting, uncanny experience, there is now, at the turn of another century, a renewed onslaught of wordplay and nonce words based on déjà vu. Some are analogous to the tedium of repetition—after Warhol, we are not surprised by "Degas vu" (so familiar that his originality repeats itself) or "Dijon vu" (I think I had this mustard before). Advertising and entertainment have successfully repackaged a term that originally expressed a sense of unease with just such packaging. Pushing the envelope of the concept and the phrase, there has also been the attempt to coin a phrase that would be an antonym to repetition: "vu ja de," or the eerie sense that you never want to be in the same place again.[1] Yet as we saw, the pleasantly diminished returns (in the modes of distraction and entertainment) that serve to screen over certain unpleasant returns (such as the involuntary one

143

to the caesura of memory that is trauma, or the intentional invocation of a painful memory in the scene of forgiveness) are not, properly speaking, ways to move on. Nor can the dialectics of forgetting and memory be sidestepped in the gratuitous returns of popular culture. While communication serves to bridge and shrink time and space, entertainment distracts us from time and place. In either mode, the value of information still depends on its time and place, and media studies must address these layers of experience and processing. Prominent reminders of this ineluctable constant in a global mass media society are interruptions by war, sometimes considered the father of media technology.

Pushing the envelope, an idiom often used for stretching the boundaries of a notion, has its origin in flight and rocket technology as it attempts escape from gravity and the grave, and distorts perceptions of time and space. This is brought home time and again by mass media coverage of war:

> To know what war is, we no longer need to read the *Ilias* or Jünger, and not even the newspaper any more. In technical zero-gravity, we can experience it in real time from Hertz's tele-distance.[2]

Time in the age of the media is what Elisabeth Lenk has called "Achronie," a sense of the contemporaneity of all times beyond all historic sequence: achronic unity would be the equivalent of the reductive reach of media technology across space.[3] Once we can witness the incessant series of destructive, traumatic moments from afar, nothing is older than yesterday's news. For the sake of dominating space, the media industry has sacrificed the depth of time.[4] This is the irreconcilable difference between literature and mass media: for literature, all past is present. By extension, its futurity is laid in reserve, not exposed or endangered by the acceleration of technology. Each time we read, two experiences of time will be juxtaposed and intermingled in the time of reading: the timeless age of technology, and the ageless time of literature. Literature, nowadays, is extant as the expression of that which has been excluded from (scientific) time since the beginning of mechanical time-telling.[5] But once the experience of war is as free from the delays of reporting, filtering, and analysis as it is free from gravity for the bomber pilot and the remote-controlled rocket, its time and space are redefined. For pilots, as Joseph Heller's novel *Catch-22* shows in ample detail, life does not "flow in a regular, unfolding ribbon."[6] Over several chapters, the law of catch-22 is referred to as if the reader already knew about it; one comes away only with vague ideas about censorship, a double bind arising from interdiction or inhibition.[7] Only in chapter five is the logic of catch-22 explained further: "There was only one catch and that was Catch-22, which specified that a concern for one's safety in the face of dangers that were real and immediate was the process of a rational mind." What this association of self-interest and rationality means for the pilot becomes clear a few lines later: "If he flew then he was crazy and didn't have to; but if he didn't want to he was sane and had to." Momentarily, Yossarian understands this absurd law "clearly in all its spinning reasonableness," as if he had always already known about its "elliptical precision," but soon he loses his grasp on it and can no longer recall his full understanding of it. Searching for an explanation for his déjà vu, Yossarian seeks the advice of a chaplain, who asks him whether he has ever "been in a situation which you felt you had been in before, even though you knew you were experiencing it for the first time."[8] Speculating on a lagging nervous system as well as on Augustine's ideas on rebirth, the chaplain himself struggles with experiences of déjà vu; for a few "precarious seconds," Heller writes,

> he tingled with a weird occult sensation of having experienced the same situation before in some prior time or existence. He endeavored to trap and nourish the impression in order to predict, and perhaps even control, what incident would occur next, but the afflatus melted away unproductively, as he had known beforehand it would. *Déjà vu.*

The chaplain's flashbacks are interspersed with speculations on hallucination and déjà vu, and he is haunted by the persistent "feeling that he had met Yossarian somewhere before the first time he *had* met Yossarian."[9] Often as premonitions or dreams, other instances of déjà vu are interspersed throughout *Catch-22,* culminating in a death that appears bleakly comic because of how it is foreshadowed: Hungry Joe suffers nightmares in chapter three, dreams of a cat sitting on his face in chapter six, and then in chapter twelve goes to bed after fighting a cat, dreaming once again that a cat is sitting on his face, suffocating him. Sure enough, in chapter forty-one he "died in his sleep while having a dream. They found a cat on his face." Heller's compulsive obsessionals demonstrate how little disturbances that enter memory can have a devastating effect.[10] In ways that undermine attention and analysis, war is everywhere in culture, dissolved into a status of latency, repressed into deeper strata, and comes forth from under the thin veil of altruistic acts and a certain state-administered violence with the force of unbridled primal aggression. Culture, in this sense, is the hypocritical repression of drives at extremely high costs in terms of neurotic compensation. These pathogenic mechanisms are at every moment threatened by a falling back into "earlier states of affectual life."[11] The outbreak of war takes the later cultural layers off and allows earlier stages of development to return, in an exorcism of modernism that has pathogenic effects. Socialization costs the group an arm and a leg, and subsequently leads to compensating defensive formations.[12] The experience of the first total war was understood as the sublation of the individual and of individualism in the group, the mass, as member of a collective.[13] As Andreas Huyssen writes,

we know how slippery and unreliable personal memory can be; always
affected by forgetting and denial, repression and trauma, it, more often than
not, serves as a need to rationalize and maintain power. But a society's
collective memory is no less contingent, no less unstable, its shape by no
means permanent.[14]

In 1944, Adorno surmised that the fate of the future might soon be unthinkable, not because it harbors the absolute danger of what is to come, but inversely because nothing might be able to come any more—or at least, that soon
nobody would be able even to think of it, since each shock and each trauma
serves as ferment for coming destruction.[15] If it was true in 1944 that war is
completely covered over by information, propaganda, commentary, film footage,
and generalization, it will have become "more true," as it were, since then; the
future peril appears as a peril to the future, and "war coverage" can entail the
forgetting of war. Yet the possibility and stability of such memories depends
on the extent to which mediatized distraction warps what we consider witnessing.[16] While the speed of news transmission and transport in space has constantly accelerated throughout the last centuries, the speed of our movement
through time has been reduced. In this light, it is not always obvious why we
call the slow countdown of mechanical time to the next media event "progress."
Don Delillo's *White Noise* demonstrates the intricacy of media effects and affec-
tive stages of emergency.[17] The "airborne toxic event" that disrupts the college-
town setting of this novel causes "heart palpitations and a sense of déjà vu" (116).
At first a suggestion over the radio waves (125), déjà vu soon becomes the only
way out of a media sensurround of unexplained and incomprehensible threats—
it is the defensive formation that doubles back on itself: talking about déjà vu
is itself a déjà vu when the parents debate whether to tell the children what
déjà vu means (126) and puzzle over the difference between true and false déjà
vu (133). The theory a precocious student offers to explain déjà vu is a curious combination of Freud's assumption about repression and death with Benjamin's extension of the argument to precognition or premonition (151). In the
end, although déjà vu is "still a problem in the area," the immediate paradox
gradually recedes, and "over a period of time it became possible to interpret
such things as signs of a deep-reaching isolation we are beginning to feel" (176).
The rupture in time is associated with an event, but its redoubling effects can
only be processed as hearsay and with hindsight.

Whether we consider déjà vu or its attempted inversion to the eerie sense that
you never want to be in the same place again, it is intricately related to a sense
of being slightly out of place. The administration of our fragmented space is
the domain of architecture, as the first and last medium of memory. What

architecture contributes to a transformation of our space of common sense, knowledge, and social practice is enshrined in everyday discourse, in abstract thought, in communication systems.[18] For Benjamin, observing the turn of the century was to observe how the transformation of individual and collective experience impinged on cultural memory.[19] As the cohesion of the old structures unravels, new artistic statements capture the imagination—and with them, new theoretical and practical knowledge of social life. What had seemed solid, a cube or volume, framing and safely containing all interactions, was suddenly broken, dissolved in telescoped inclusions and exclusions. At this point, where the architecture of architecture, as it were, comes to the foreground, space is no longer imaginable as ineffable yet solid matter. In Sigfried Giedeon's tripartite history of space, architectural volumes were first conceived from without, as in Egyptian and Greek buildings, while the Romans shifted the focus to interior space; the third phase would come to negotiate the dichotomy of inside and outside. "Architecture is bound up with the notion of 'monumentality,'" as Giedeon pointed out—and the uncanny effects of a certain "mummy effect" come to haunt all media, not only architectonic geometry.[20] Henri Lefebvre inverts this argument, whereby the Greek and Egyptian structures enclose sacred space, whereas the Roman Pantheon opens to light and exteriority. Either way, since the concept of space itself cannot be a space, it gives itself to think as barred or traversed obliquely by displacements, condensations, and irremediable obstacles to pure abstraction and sublation in synthesis. This sense of blockage that comes to break up the unified sense of space forces us to narrativize and temporalize.[21]

The ancient spatial metaphors of the art of memory directly link forgetting and anamnetic solidarity, survival and death with memorial architecture. Thus Quintilian and Cicero both offer the canonical anecdote that ascribes the invention of mnemotechnics to the rhetorical skills of Simonides of Keos.[22] When Simonides, suffering a temporary lapse of memory, inserts a few staple verses dedicated to Castor and Pollux in a paid tribute to the boxing skills of his host, he is denied full payment for his poem. The justification—that he had only partly praised the host, and should receive the remainder of his reward from the twin dioscures—proves to be informative for the history of memory. Simonides is called away from the pugilist's feast, because two young men are waiting for him outside. As soon as Simonides crosses the threshold, the house collapses and buries all guests in its rubble, sparing nobody except the poet, who is thus rewarded by the twin demigods. Since the victims are unrecognizable among the rubble, only Simonides, as surviving witness, can inform the relatives who was sitting where, so they can receive their proper burial. In this manner, the artificial support of the poet's oral delivery, the mnemotechnical loci or topoi that aid the delivery of a performance, literally carve out memorial space for the dead.

While antique sources are divided on who the ill-fated host was, we do know some things about Simonides. The historical Simonides (557–467 BC) had a reputation for being greedy, and he indeed composed a poem in honor of a pugilist in which he praises Castor and Pollux, as was the tradition.[23] For the twins are associated with thresholds, but also patrons of boxing, and so their aid to Simonides is not only to reward him, it is also to avenge and compensate for another injustice—since the pugilist should have acknowledged their role in his success. But the host honors neither past nor future, neither the demigods in whose name the art of boxing is cultivated, nor the poet in whose words his memory was to live on; thus he brings down the death of his house. As the newly instituted medium of memory, Simonides was the first to benefit from the distance that makes witnessing possible, inscribed for posterity as the inventor of posterity, as the pivotal figure in an anecdote that combines deception and restitution, payments due, burial, and recognition in death. As Stefan Goldmann has pointed out, the majority of classicists and historians ignored the role of Castor and Pollux in the story, reducing the twins to an ornamental side plot. Thus their role lost both its historical and metaphorical meaning. However, as Goldmann shows, this is a "historical screen memory."[24] That is to say, something is covered over, not only in regard to a historical event, but in regard to repeated conflicts that lead to the formation of this structure. The underlying historical material is displaced, condensed, and inverted; indeed it emerges not as a recollection from the past, but as a false memory of indirect and inflected witnessing and passing on. In other words, this handing down of a single inaugural event, the invention of mnemotechnics, is the dense literary inscription of a multitude of associations and connections assembled over time. Yet to dismiss the anecdote as not true but well invented would risk covering over interesting cracks between various building blocks of such superficial reading.

Some aspects of this historical screen memory are instructive for our project. First, the twin mediators appear in their role as *mnemones*, as patrons of poesy and "living archives." Watching at the threshold of human and divine interaction over sacrificial offerings and gifts, they also survey the just distribution and attribution of praise and dues.[25] Thus when the greed of the poet clashes with the stinginess of his client and host, their role is not to protect but to destroy the household.[26] This aspect of their appearance in the anecdote, which firmly connects the accounting for goods and memory with potential erasure of life and goods, is forgotten in most interpretations of the myth. Thus the maiming of the host and all his guests except one is a punishment for hubris; because they refuse recognition, they are themselves rendered unrecognizable. However, this *damnatio memoriae* is lifted and inverted by allowing the slighted witness to reconstruct for posterity both their punishment and their memory. Thus the story of Simonides offers a definition of witnessing in all media: survival owed to a minimal distance, plus spatial attention and recollection owed to a temporary distraction. In this mode of partial distraction, one can detect another twist in the story.

Arguably, the entire anecdote pivots not around the strength of memory, but around the momentary lapse: the poet slips and blanks out and, to find his footing, extemporizes about staple addressees of honorific poesy—Castor and Pollux and the emblems of brotherly love—before remembering, and returning to, the occasional poem he was to deliver for the festive event. Indeed, the lapse of mnemotechnics and the collapse of the building are instituted as the foundation in ruins of an architecture of memory. In a time when the twin towers of the World Trade Center in Manhattan are memorialized in kitschy snow globes, and the proposals for what should take their place energize political and cultural debates fanned by mass media attention, it is important to remind ourselves of this basic fact: every monument is always already building on death as the complex juxtaposition of forgetting and posterity, erasure and inscription, recollection and covering over. And it is just such a covering over that anoints Simonides the inventor of mnemotechnics, an anecdote that is based only partially on historical accounts of his life and times, and partially on the projection of a later problem onto the memorialization of Simonides. Thus it is clear that the myth of Simonides also marks a central "historical" reference of the screen memory. If there was a proper place where the puzzling experience of déjà vu can "take place," it would not be in the dictionary, as we have seen, but perhaps in architecture.[27]

Why does that partial lapse of memory, that partial failure of correct attribution that constitutes déjà vu, occur at a given moment? Even explanations offered by neuroscientists tend to assume that "it comes mostly at moments of anxiety"—for instance when one finds oneself "in an unfamiliar situation where it serves to reassure" one that one has already been there before and got through it.[28] This defense against finding oneself in an unfamiliar, uncomfortable space is worth a closer look. What constitutes the familiar, what offers the comfort that one lacks at this juncture? What administration of space, and what time management, explain the phenomena? The architectural critic Anthony Vidler suggests that it be understood as "a significant psychoanalytic and aesthetic response to the real shock of the modern."[29] Neurotic anxiety in modern architecture is discussed at length by Vidler in a book that aligns the uncanny, as weak Freudian force, with the cultural effects of déjà vu. Down to its very organization, Vidler's book enacts a dispersal: as his chapters grow shorter and more fragmentary towards the end, *The Architecture of the Uncanny: Essays in the Modern Unhomely* stages the threats of repetition, doubling, and existential strangeness.

Unhomely cannot be found in any dictionary. As transliteration of a German thought, it tries an alternate translation for *unheimlich*. Vidler, it seems, wanted to avoid the repetition of the word "uncanny" in the title. From the start, the uncanny is doubled over and spliced into two words. "Homely," however, has four entries in *Webster's Ninth New Collegiate* dictionary. "1: suggestive or characteristic of a home; 2: being something familiar with which one is at home . . .; 3a: unaffectedly natural: SIMPLE; 3b: not elaborate or complex . . . 4: plain or unattractive in appearance—homeliness." What would the inverse be, then? Not suggestive of a home, uncharacteristic of a home, unfamiliar, affectedly unnatural, elaborate, complex, and attractive in appearance. In other words, Vidler seems to ask, *modern architecture?* If it were a matter of simple opposition, this could be the gist of Vidler's polemic. But the prefix *un*, as Vidler cites Freud, is the "token of repression" (55). The uncanny is not only the negation of an ability, a knack or knickknack, but also an entry in the lexicon of psychoanalysis, referring to Freud's essay that traces *unheimlich* to various doublings and distancings, to sexual fears, primarily of female genitalia, and by extension, to the fear of lack, absence, loss of center, and death. Under the line, in the secreted space of the footnote, Freud cites Schelling's twenty-eighth lecture on the mythology of Homeric polytheism, which "encrypts a mystery, is built upon an abyss," as it is based on a forgetting of the mystical. Schelling writes of "the dark and darkening force of that uncanny principle (uncanny one calls everything which should have remained secret, in hiding, in latency and has come forth)."[30] That force cannot shake the duplicity of what it only brackets, as included exclusion: the effect of a forgetting of the origin, of a decentering of the center. It disturbs any safety, any distinction, any line. If it "has, not unnaturally, found its metaphorical home in architecture," as Vidler posits, this need not mean only buildings—writings and drawings are part of architectural practice, folded in and doubled over without always resulting in buildings. Such architecture must be at home with itself as strange, familiar with its own unfamiliarity. For Freud, negation is not an operative principle of the unconscious: the repressed makes its way into consciousness precisely *on condition that it is denied*. The ambivalent meaning of the word *heimlich* develops until it coincides with its opposite, *unheimlich*. In this fold, negation of the past touches affirmation of the past in repetition compulsion. Vidler's splicing it up to avoid repetition yields two directions of inquiry. On the one hand, it is only in the duplicity of the exterior/interior that space becomes "palpable" (167); but if architecture merely doubles space, the uncanny would be everything, everywhere. On the other hand, if, as Vidler posits with reference to anxiety, space is administered *by the architect*, then there is no uncanniness in space management (221–25). This is not to pretend that the question of anxiety can simply be reduced to uneasiness about interior and exterior space, nor to conflate the uncanny and déjà vu.

Rather, déjà vu is a weak force like the uncanny, and combines moments of anxiety management and spatiotemporal disorientation.

Vidler's research warrant for contemporary dwellings is flashed only briefly as he enters a maze of splintered descriptions of what is repressed in all too familiar architecture. If "architecture finds itself 'repeating' history, whether in traditional or avant-garde guise" (13), then why put the repetition in quotation marks, scarecrows, irony font? And if this happens, as Vidler continues, "in a way that gives rise to an uncanny sense of *déjà vu* that parallels Freud's own description of the uncanny as linked to the 'compulsion to repeat,'" then what separates Vidler's sense of déjà vu from Freud's "parallel" description of repetition compulsion? If indeed it is *only in the duplicity* of exterior/interior distinctions that space becomes palpable, and yet architecture simply *doubles* space, then everything would be uncanny. However, it is only a specific spatial envelope that gives rise to anxiety, to claustrophobia: to the feeling of being surrounded by shelter and prison, house and grave. The question whether there is indeed a difference between the uncanny and déjà vu must be discussed separately from the question whether either of them parallel Freud's own description of the repetition compulsion. But Vidler wants to historicize the uncanny only to make it his own gadget of eternal return. Such returns can be anything, as the architectural critic Paolo Portoghesi states: "The world now emerging is searching freely in memory, because it knows how to find its own 'difference' in the removed repetitions and utilizations of the entire past."[31] That difference is set up in Vidler's book as the "apparently irreconcilable demands for the absolute negation of the past and full 'restoration' of the past" that meet in architectural forms that "seem, on the surface at least, to echo already used-up motifs *en abyme*" (55). And yet, in the canonical geometry ascribed to modernist aesthetics, postmodern architecture cannot simply be conceived as an extension wing, nor a literalization of the screen of historical projections and repressions. Nevertheless, some claim that "the most appropriate architecture for this vision of our world would be a simple cube whose surfaces, inside and out, provided screens for projections that would change the building into any and every style."[32] But if the threshold between modern and postmodern would consist in nothing more than a white cube, and if architecture could be reduced to an arbitrary decision on style, then the alleged historical step is not a step in the history of architecture. It would, in fact, represent a regression to a Platonic cave, without any reflection on the materiality that allows for projection. If architecture doubles for, reframes, and represents space, covering for mourning, defensively screening over our mortality that forever perforates the divisions we erect, then the screen memory that architecture keeps returning to is nothing but the effect of a constant yoking and splicing up of time and space, or the material of architecture itself.

If architecture were placed under analysis, to vary a phrase by Bazin, its practice of entombing would reveal the mummy complex at the origins of memory
and building.[33] The secret of the pyramids was that apart from food for the
dead, one placed terra cotta statues next to the corpses—preservation of life by
representation of life. Over the course of history, the arts panned out in two
dimensions, and sculpture flatlined in the portrait, which is less messy than
embalming, and more effective in screening the loss. Architecture still covers
the originary memory lapse of Simonides: when his sponsor called breach of
contract and asked for the bill to be split, the twin Gods of the Threshold paid
up by saving his life and by securing his name in eternity, since his identification of the corpses earned him the honorary title of the inventor of mnemonics. But to take architecture as the art of building is to take the effect for the
cause—a literal inversion that it is our task to turn around and reinscribe. If
architecture on the other hand came to stand merely for any and every organization of space, then a total dematerialization of architecture would raise the
question of what distinguishes it from any other human activity, from any other
space of representation. Thus between an inflationary concept of architecture
as social theory and the specificity of given building practices, one may situate
architecture as an organization of human space, bringing it up to speed with
media technology and its effects. Fragmented space holds surprises, allows
glimpses into folds and recesses where something secret may hide.[34] Phenomenon of a distance, but tied to presence, the aura of the aesthetic object and its
disappearing act cannot be copied. As we saw in Walter Benjamin's inversion
of uncanny space, in the *Berlin Childhood* the pockets and envelopes of psychic
space articulate the experience of space itself.[35] "Architecture," Benjamin wrote,
"has always represented the prototype of a work of art the reception of which
is consummated by a collectivity in a state of distraction."[36] Here, architecture
offers the dialectical image of space and time.[37] Since it is always necessary, it
is older than other arts; its distracted reception is both tactile and optical.[38] The
tactile mode of experience is based on our habits, which in turn also determine
optical perceptions of architecture. In his logic of the either-aura, Benjamin
proceeds to include film in the same mode. To the distracted but augmented
eye, cinema renders visible what the unarmed eye would not catch even with
the greatest attention.

Silent film, Virilio has argued, made the screen speak like the mnemo-
technician makes his room or the stage speak—namely in retrospect. To this
extent, cinema began in the tradition of revisualizing childhood.[39] When the
voice-over of the narrator in Chris Marker's *La Jetée* fades out toward the end,
it is hard to catch the last words it whispers, just one word, repeated several
time, in German: *Gedächtnis*, memory. Only a firm belief in the law of entropy
can anchor the conception of a linear time and clarify whether a film runs

forward or backward.[40] But even the most clever time-axis manipulation cannot defuse the incontrovertible fact that as actors, we are already our own doubles; as Adorno diagnosed, "the empire of déjà vu is inhabited by doubles."[41] Film audiences see double in every sense: the general duplicity of the medium creates a playful reflexivity that seeks outlets in movies on twins, shadows, doubles, or invisible men, and of course the industry would be unthinkable without extras, stunt people, body doubles, and cameos. No star would be recognizable without this doubling over. Popular culture now offers reflections of déjà vu, television especially: the barrage of reruns, second chances, and familiar faces is now presented self-consciously, tongue-in-cheek. Whether they exploit nostalgia for an earlier, more innocent era or poke fun at clumsy attempts to shock the audience, entertainment media now primarily take themselves as their content or message.

The theory of intellectual doubt, of critical distance and approximation, developed by Freud and after him could be said to culminate in virtual memory. To speak of a culture of déjà vu is to analyze virtual memory—not just as optical stimulation, or as a question of time and its passing, but in terms of an acceleration of all media technologies. The anamnesis at stake must confront the doubling repetition of representation, without recurring to the comforting rhetoric of origins. If truth, classically, would not be truth without appearing, then in the logic of screen memories, there is only the duplicitous effect of a cover-up: the origin is already an effect. The origin as origin will have been irrecuperable, because it is folded into the dialectics of secret correspondence between idea and materiality, memory and history, apperception and object. The search for true representation would have to recall, anamnetically, the originary face-to-face with the ideas; such representation of truth itself must be excluded as false, since anamnesis cannot show the truth but only the means to remember it after its disappearance—in Plato's words, after one has drunk from the waters of Lethe. This performative contradiction, inherent in every attempt to use language in order to represent thought (understood as something that is outside and above language) is above all a problem of metaphor.[42] Nevertheless, the idea of originary concealment has haunted cultural history since Hesiod. If reading is to recollect a past that never was, how do we grasp the specificity of the technological conditions of reading and of cultural history? Is the effect of technology itself complicit with the structure of déjà vu, to the extent of making all accounts of déjà vu tautological? The generalizability of such a concept may go too far: "Perhaps the covert goal," as we quoted Adorno's criticism of techno-modernity, "is the availability, technification, collectivization of déjà vu in general."[43] The paradoxical recollection of a future that never will be past reinforces the assumption that déjà vu must remain irreducible to the familiar. Instead, it appears as virtuality: its structural determination of indeterminacy is an anticipated deferral of closure. The history of déjà vu is nothing but the demonstration of its effects; it may seem, therefore, as if there had never been anything before déjà vu. From false memory to uncanny repetition, from trauma to premonition, and from mere trick to deep insight, déjà vu in all its recent popularity may simply be the latest guise of metaphysical thought: "obviously, the metaphysics in question is not of the highest order, but the moment of revelation, with its reawakening of the immediate orientational act itself, always packs a devastating punch."[44] This insight, which comes with hindsight, corresponds to the classical determination of truth as that which resembles being so closely that it becomes its double. Such hindsight flips forward as the recollection of the present, and remarks the experience of the present as a memory.[45] Whenever we try to distinguish between the truth of utterances and that of facts, the mimetic arts are demoted—they show only doubles and thus are doubly removed from the truth. Wherever our perception is disjunctive, we fall into a paradox and say that the "historical root" of the problem is a forgetting of simple origins in the double. The originary double, then, has already covered itself. The past is yet to come:

> The originary is never recognized in nakedly obvious statements of facticity, its rhythm is open only to a double vision. On the one hand it wants to be seen as restoration, as repetition, on the other hand and by the same token it wants to be recognized as incomplete, unfinished.[46]

NOTES

The following abbreviations are used in the Notes:

GS = Walter Benjamin, *Gesammelte Schriften*, 7 vols. (Frankfurt: Suhrkamp, 1991). All translations from this work are mine unless otherwise indicated.

GW = Sigmund Freud, *Gesammelte Werke* (London: Imago, 1941–50).

SE = Sigmund Freud, *Standard Edition of the Complete Psychological Works*, 24 vols. (London: Hogarth Press, 1955–64).

BEEN THERE, DONE THAT

1. Excluded from this investigation of the cultural logic of déjà vu is the latest neuroscientific take on memory. While the explanations of paramnesia offered there are of related interest, they do not account for its cultural effects and their exploitation (the focus of this study). See above all the work of Daniel Schacter, "The Cognitive Neuroscience of False Memories," *Psychiatric Annals* 25 (1995): 426–30 (with Tim Curran); Daniel Schacter et al., "False Recognition and the Right Frontal Lobe: A Case Study," *Neuropsychologica* 34, no. 8 (1996): 793–808; and Daniel Schacter, *The Seven Sins of Memory* (Boston: Houghton Mifflin, 2001). See also Sharon Begley, "Memory's Mind Games," *Newsweek*, 16 July 2001, 52–54, as well as Dietrich Blumer and A. Earl Walker, "Memory in Temporal Lobe Epileptics," in *The Pathology of Memory*, ed. George A. Talland and Nancy C. Waugh (San Francisco: Academic Press, 1969), 65–73, and Naoto Adachi et al., "Interictal 18FDG PET Findings in Temporal Lobe Epilepsy with Déjà Vu," *Journal of Neuropsychiatry and Clinical Neuroscience* 11 (August 1999): 380–86.

2. Barbara Lazerson Hunt, "Déjà Vu," *American Speech* 69, no. 3 (1994): 285–93, cites evidence from the *Barnhart Dictionary of Etymology* that the first mention in English occurred in 1903 and that the phrase acquires a second, pejorative meaning in the early 1950s. The *Oxford English Dictionary* records the "illusory feeling" of paramnesia as the first use in 1903 and the "correct impression" of tedious familiarity in 1960.

3. Daniel Dennett, "Are Dreams Experiences?" *The Philosophical Review* (1976), 159, n. 13. As Dennett argues, challenging the received view on memory "would be rather like learning that dream-recall was like déjà vu—it only *seemed* that you had experienced it before—and once you believed *that*, it would no longer seem (as strongly) that you were recalling." See also H. N. Sno, D. H. Linszen, and F. de Jonghe, "The Déjà Vu Experience: Remembrance of Things Past?" *American Journal of Psychiatry* 147, no. 12 (1990): 1587–95.

4. Hillel Schwartz, *The Culture of the Copy* (New York: Zone, 1996), 300; Theodor W. Adorno, "Notes on Kafka," in *Prisms* (Boston: MIT Press, 1981), 246 and 252 ff. ("Aufzeichungen zu Kafka," in *Versuch das Endspiel zu verstehen* [Frankfurt: Suhrkamp, 1973], 138 ff.).

5. Freud's positions are covered in Nicholas Royle, "Déjà Vu," in *Post-Theory: New Directions in Criticism,* ed. Martin McQuillan (Edinburgh: Edinburgh University Press, 1999), 3–20.

6. "One can observe very elaborate forms of resentment in the philologies: instead of talking about 'poetic communication,' poetry is still comprehended as the opposite of communication; instead of observing literary forms as forms of media, one prefers to describe literature in contrast to 'the media'": Georg Stanitzek, "Fama/Chain of Muses: Two Classic Problems of Literary Studies with 'the Media,'" in *Medium Cool* (*South Atlantic Quarterly* 101, no. 3), ed. Andrew McNamara and Peter Krapp (Durham: Duke University Press, 2002), 609.

7. Andreas Huyssen, *Twilight Memories* (New York: Routledge, 1995), 249. See also Huyssen, *Present Pasts* (Stanford: Stanford University Press, 2003).

8. "Armed with a good conscience that is imperturbable because often enveloped in ignorance or obscurantism," Derrida warns, "there are those who are not content to profit from the ghosts that haunt our most painful memory. They also authorize themselves thereby, in the same élan, to *manipulate* with impunity, without any scruple, the very word *revisionism*. They are prepared to use it to accuse anyone who poses critical, methodological, epistemological, philosophical questions about history, about the way it is thought, written, or established": Jacques Derrida, *Specters of Marx: The State of the Debt, the Work of Mourning, and the New International* (London: Routledge, 1994), 185–86.

9. Compare Umberto Eco, "An Ars Oblivionalis? Forget It," *PMLA* 103 (1988): 254–61, and Helmut Lethen, "Damnatio Memoriae und die Rhetorik des Vergessens," in *Schweigen: Unterbrechung und Grenze der menschlichen Wirklichkeit,* ed. Dietmar Kamper and Christoph Wulf (Berlin: Reimer, 1992), 159–68.

10. "Hegel, who is often said to have 'forgotten' about writing, is unsurpassed in his ability to remember that one should never forget to forget": Paul de Man, "Hypogram and Inscription," in *The Resistance to Theory* (Minneapolis: University of Minnesota Press, 1987), 42.

11. The "prevalent notion of forgetting as a form of illness, a loss of self, and a threat to subjectivity," as Marita Sturken admonishes, is "perhaps the most powerful cultural defense" that stymies debates over memory and culture. Inversely, "remembering becomes a process of achieving closer proximity to wholeness, of erasing forgetting: that is why I am so unhappy, that explains everything": Marita Sturken, "Narratives of Recovery: Repressed Memory as Cultural Memory," in *Acts of Memory: Cultural Recall in the Present,* ed. Mieke Bal, Jonathan Crewe, and Leo Spitzer (Hanover: University Press of New England, 2001), 243.

12. "Repetition and recollection are the same movement, except in opposite directions, for what is recollected has been, is repeated backwards, whereas genuine repetition is recollected forward. Repetition, therefore, if it is possible, makes a person happy, whereas

recollection makes him unhappy—assuming, of course, that he gives himself time to live and does not promptly at birth find an excuse to sneak out of life again, for example, that he has forgotten something": Søren Kierkegaard, *Repetition* (Princeton: Princeton University Press, 1941), 131.

13. Kierkegaard's overweaning concern with stillborn babies, associating forgetting with original sin, raises the question whether those who are never born—let alone twice, coming to themselves in thought—are free from original sin. Sneaking out of life before it begins parallels suicide; the hastily rewritten end of his treatise on repetition places marriage and suicide into a curious equivalence. See the symptomatic novel by Gert Hofmann, *Unsre Vergeßlichkeit* (Darmstadt: Luchterhand, 1987) and Sigrid Weigel's commentary, "Pathologie und Normalisierung," in *Vom Nutzen des Vergessens*, ed. Gary Smith and Hinderk Emrich (Leipzig: Akademie Verlag, 1996), 241–63.

14. See Michel Foucault's gesture at the end of his introduction to *L'archéologie du savoir* (Paris: Gallimard, 1984).

15. Alfred Andersch already pointed to the instability of the "theme of memory and its split into recollection and forgetting": Alfred Andersch, "Alles Gedächtnis der Welt," in *Die Blindheit des Kunstwerks und andere Aufsätze* (Frankfurt: Suhrkamp, 1965), 95.

16. Friedrich Kittler, "Forgetting," *Discourse: Berkeley Journal for Theoretical Studies in Media and Culture* 3 (1981): 89 ("Vergessen," in *Texthermeneutik: Aktualität, Geschichte, Kritik*, ed. Ulrich Nassen [Paderborn: UTB, 1979], 196).

17. Harald Weinrich, *Lethe: Kunst und Kritik des Vergessens* (Munich: C. H. Beck, 1997), 11.

18. Further reading on forgetting: for the continental philosophical tradition, David Farrell Krell, *Of Memory, Reminiscence, and Writing* (Bloomington: Indiana University Press, 1990); for psychoanalysis and Holocaust studies, G. C. Tholen and E. Weber, eds., *Das Vergessene: Anamnesen des Undarstellbaren* (Vienna: Turia & Kant, 1997); for intellectual history, Smith and Emrich, eds., *Vom Nutzen des Vergessens*, and Gerburg Treusch-Dieter, *Denkzettel Antike: Texte zum kulturellen Vergessen* (Berlin: Reimer, 1989). Regrettably, Aleida Assmann, *Erinnerungsräume: Formen und Wandlungen des kulturellen Gedächtnisses* (Munich: C. H. Beck, 1999), addresses the recent false memory debates without reference to paramnesia from Aristotle to the present. For persuasive efforts to debunk the "recovered memory" fad, see Sturken, "Narratives of Recovery," and Elaine Showalter, *Hystories: Hysterical Epidemics and Modern Media* (New York: Columbia University Press, 1997).

19. "On dirait que, dans notre monde mediatisée, rien ne peut plus 'vieillir,' on ne peut prendre distance à l'égard du 'passé.' Le passé revient continuellement": Gianni Vattimo, "L'impossible oubli," in *Usages de l'Oubli: Colloque de Royaumont* (Paris: Seuil, 1988), 79.

20. To credit Nietzsche with the "discovery" of repression requires at least one citation: "'Das habe ich gethan,' sagt mein Gedächtniss. Das kann ich nicht gethan haben—sagt mein Stolz und bleibt underbittlich. Endlich—giebt das Gedächtniss nach": Friedrich Nietzsche, *Kritische Studienausgabe*, ed. Giorgio Colli and Mazzino Montinari (Munich: DTV, 1988, 5:86 ("'I did this,' my memory says. I cannot have done this—says my pride and remains adamant. Finally—the memory yields"). In my simplified account, I am indebted to Berel Lang, *Mind's Bodies: Thought in the Act* (Albany: SUNY Press, 1995).

21. "Es ist möglich fast ohne Erinnerungen zu leben, ja glücklich zu leben, wie das Thier zeigt; es ist aber ganz und gar unmöglich, ohne Vergessen überhaupt zu leben. Oder, um mich noch einfacher über mein Thema zu erklären: *es giebt einen Grad von Schlaflosigkeit, von Wiederkäuen, von historischem Sinne, bei dem das Lebendige selbst zu Schaden kommt, und zuletzt zu Grunde geht, sei es nun ein Mensch oder ein Volk oder eine Cultur*": Friedrich Nietzsche, "Vom Nutzen und Nachtheil der Historie für das Leben," *Kritische Studienausgabe*, 2:250 (emphasis in the original).

22. Ludwig Klages, *Die psychologischen Errungenschaften Nietzsches* (Leipzig: J. A. Barth, 1930); see also Ludwig Klages, *Der Geist als Widersacher der Seele* (Bonn: Bouvier, 1960).

23. Heidegger sees the doctrine of eternal return as pervasive in Western philosophy, "a thought that remains concealed but is its genuine driving force" and reverts the entire tradition to origins: Martin Heidegger, *Nietzsche I* (San Francisco: Harper and Row, 1982), 19. "The thought of the eternal return," as Nancy believes, "is the inaugural thought of our contemporary history": Jean-Luc Nancy, *Être singulier pluriel* (Paris: Galilée, 1996), 22. A decade earlier, Nancy closed his book *L'oubli de la philosophie* (Paris: Galilée, 1986) leaving undecided whether that is a subjective or objective genitive: the representation of philosophy can be figured either as the imaginary disparition of an anterior signification, or as that withdrawal that is an arrival. See also David Farrell Krell, "Phenomenology of Memory from Husserl to Merleau-Ponty," *Philosophy and Phenomenological Research* 42, no. 4 (1982): 492–505, esp. 503–04.

24. Friedrich Nietzsche, "Wendepunkt," *Kritische Studienausgabe*, 10:515.

25. We decide selectively against Deleuze's and Kofman's allegation of Nietzsche's quasi-Darwinist principle of selection behind the doctrine of eternal return. Gilles Deleuze, *Nietzsche and Philosophy* (New York: Columbia University Press, 1983), 68ff.; Sarah Kofman, "A Fantastical Genealogy: Nietzsche's Family Romance," in *Nietzsche and the Feminine*, ed. Peter Burgard (Charlottesville: University of Virginia, 1994), 32–52. See also Pierre Klossowski, *Nietzsche et le cercle vicieux* (Paris: Mercure de France, 1975).

26. Klages, *Die psychologischen Errungenschaften Nietzsches*, 214–15; compare also 29ff. (section III) and *Der Geist als Widersacher der Seele*, 354ff.

27. Ned Lukacher, *Time Fetishes: The Secret History of Eternal Recurrence* (Durham: Duke University Press, 1998), 105. Lukacher seems to perpetuate the belief in a select group of initiates who can observe what must remain veiled to others (x). Yet he confounds Nietzsche's forgotten "Regenschirm" (an umbrella to protect from the rain) with what would surely be a "Sonnenschirm" (protection from Nietzschean noon sun), and treats Nietzsche's attempts to furnish mathematical and physical proofs for his doctrine as a decade of desperate make-believe, ignoring Oskar Becker's important analysis. See Oskar Becker, *Dasein und Dawesen* (Pfullingen: Neske, 1963).

28. This example by Ferenczi (from an article in the *Internationale Zeitschrift für Psychoanalyse* 3, 1915) is discussed by Freud in *The Psychopathology of Everyday Life*, SE, 6, chapter 12, section D.

29. Without knowing of Nietzsche's notorious note, psychoanalysis received its unforgettably false recollection of the forgotten umbrella long before Martin Heidegger, Hans-Georg Gadamer, or Jacques Derrida tried to pick it up. See Jacques Derrida, *Spurs:*

Nietzsche Styles (Chicago: University of Chicago, 1979), 77. Like Sartre, Derrida seems to believe that Nietzsche had only pretended to believe in the doctrine of the eternal recurrence. Compare Jean-Paul Sartre, *Saint Genet* (New York: Mentor, 1964), 378–80.

30. E. Boirac, "Correspondance," *Revue philosophique* 1 (1876): 430–31; Henry F. Osborn, "Illusions of Memory," *North American Review* 138 (1884): 476; see also James Sully, *Illusions: A Psychological Study* (New York: Appleton, 1881).

31. Emil Kraepelin, "Über Erinnerungstäuschungen," *Archiv für Psychiatrie der Nervenkrankheiten* 4 (1874): 244. According to the *Larousse* dictionary, the first recorded use of *amnesie* was 1803. See also Emil Kraepelin, "Über Erinnerungsfälschungen," *Archiv für Psychiatrie der Nervenkrankheiten* 17 (1887): 830–43, and 18 (1888): 199–239, 395–436, as well as Ludovic Dugas, "Sur la fausse mémoire," *Revue philosophique* 37 (1894): 34–35, and A. Pick, "On Reduplicative Paramnesia," *Brain* 26 (1903): 260–67.

32. John Hughlings Jackson, "On a Particular Variety of Epilepsy (Intellectual Aura)," *Brain* 11 (1888): 179–207; repr. in *Selected Writings of John Hughlings Jackson*, vol. 1 (London: Houghton and Stodder, 1931). Jackson cites Charles Dickens's *David Copperfield* as an early instance of déjà vu, but also mentions Tennyson and Coleridge. See also T. F. Richardson et al., "Déjà Vu in Psychiatric and Neurological Patients," *Archives of General Psychiatry* 17 (November 1967): 622–25, and G. E. Berrios, "Déjà Vu in France during the 19th Century: A Conceptual History," *Comprehensive Psychiatry* 36, no. 2 (1995): 123–29, as well as the early discussions by A. L. Wigan, *The Duality of the Mind* (London: Longman, 1844), 84–85, and W. Sander, "Über Erinnerungstäuschungen," *Archiv für die Psychiatrie der Nervenkrankheiten* 4 (1874): 244–53.

33. Théodul Ribot, *Les Maladies de la mémoire* (Paris, 1881), translated as *Diseases of Memory* (New York: Appleton, 1890). See also Hermann Ebbinghaus, *Memory: A Contribution to Experimental Psychology* (New York: Dover, 1885), and Albert Guillon, *Les Maladies de la mémoire: Essai sur les hypermnésies* (Paris: Bailliére & Fils, 1897).

34. ". . . car sans angoisse, le phénomène n'existe pas, l'angoisse en fait partie integrante et nécessaire": Jean Grasset, "La sénsation du déjà vu," *Journal de psychologie* 1 (1904): 17.

35. Here may lie one potential reason for a historical "lettre volée": Sigmund Freud, who would at first deny and then admit knowledge of Grasset's essay, also incorporates a letter from a reader into a text on déjà vu. In Grasset's case, it is a letter from novelist Paul Bourget, 10 July 1903. In the next chapter, we will return to the possibilities of *déjà lu* in the collapse of critical distance.

36. "ce caractère singulier d'une pretendue reconnaissance qui tient à la fois du souvenir et de la prévision": André Dromard, "Essai théorique sur l'illusion dite de fausse reconnaissance," *Journal de psychologie normale et pathologique* 19 (1905): 228.

37. Indeed, Pierre Janet held decidedly pragmatic views on accurate recall: he would replace traumatic memories with screen memories under hypnosis if he thought this would serve his patients better. As Ian Hacking put it, "he helped his patients by lying to them, and did not fool himself that he was doing anything else": Ian Hacking, *Rewriting the Soul: Multiple Personalities and the Sciences of Memory* (Princeton: Princeton University Press, 1995), 197. Verlaine's poem "Kaleidoscope," written in October of 1873, construes and questions the experience of déjà vu as a moment that is perceived

as simultaneously vague and acute, comparing it to the interruption of waking from a dream only to fall asleep and dream the same dream again. "Dans une rue, au coeur d'une ville de rêve / Ce sera comme quand on a déjà vecu: / Un instant à la fois trés vague et trés aigu . . . / O ce soleil pami la brune qui se lève! . . . Ce sera comme quand on rêve et qu'on s'éveille / Et que l'on se rendort et que l'on rêve encore / De la meme féerie et du même décor / L'été, dans l'herbe, au bruit moiré d'un vol d'abeille": Paul Verlaine, *Oeuvres complètes* (Paris: Gallimard, 1951), 201–2.

38. F.-L. Arnaud, "Un cas d'illusion du 'déjà vu' ou de fausse mémoire," *Annales médico-psychologiques* 5–6 (1896), as discussed in Pierre Janet, "A propos du 'déjà vu,'" *Journal de psychologie normale et pathologique* 19 (1905): 283. See also Ruth Leys, "Traumatic Cures: Shell Shock, Janet, and the Question of Memory," *Critical Inquiry* 20 (1994): 623–62.

39. See Henri Bergson's letter to William James, cited in Ralph Barton Perry, *The Thought and Character of William James* (Boston: Little, 1935), 2:623.

40. Henri Bergson, *Matière et mémoire* (Paris, 1896), 36. See also Philip Merlan, "A Certain Aspect of Bergson's Philosophy," *Philosophy and Phenomenological Research* 2, no. 4 (1942): 529–45, esp. 535: "inattention to life, possibility of a disinterested knowledge."

41. Henri Bergson, "Le Souvenir du présent et la fausse reconnaissance," *Revue philosophique* 66 (1908): 561–93, repr. in Henri Bergson, *Oeuvres* (Paris: Presses Universitaires Françaises, 1959), 897–930; Deleuze referred to this Bergsonian memory as "virtual coexistence." See chapter 3 of Gilles Deleuze, *Bergsonisme* (Paris: Presses Universitaires Françaises, 1966).

42. "Philosopher consiste à inventir la direction habituelle de la pensée": Bergson, *Matière et mémoire*, 214. See also Bruce M. Ross, *Remembering the Personal Past: Descriptions of Autobiographical Memory* (Oxford: Oxford University Press, 1991), 28–29, on James and Bergson.

43. For the ancient Greeks, Mnemosyne, the mother of the Muses, knows everything, past, present, and future, and is the basis of all life and creativity. Forgetting the true order and origin of things is lethal, from Lethe, the river of death in Greek mythology, which destroys memory.

44. Michael Roth, "Remembering Forgetting: *Maladies de Mémoire* in Nineteenth-Century France," *Representations* 26 (spring 1989): 49. Compare also Berrios, "Déjà vu in France during the 19th Century," 123–29, and Richard Terdiman, *Present Past: Modernity and the Memory Crisis* (Ithaca: Cornell University Press, 1993).

45. See Hannes Böhringer, "Goldstücke," in *Metamorphosen: Gedächtnismedien im Computerzeitalter*, ed. Götz-Lothar Darsow (Stuttgart: Frommann-Holzboog, 2000), 51: "Vor allem aber muß das Gedächtnis Lücken lassen, damit das *Déjà vu* des Historikers nicht alles lähmt, damit noch Neues entstehen kann."

46. Aristotle, *Ethics* 1152a. 25–27. This is an argument against Socrates, who held, according to Plato, that no one can willingly act counter to what one knows to be right, and therefore only ignorance can explain foolishness and evil acts.

47. Immanuel Kant, "On a Supposed Right to Lie Because of Philanthropic Concerns," in *Grounding for the Metaphysics of Morals*, trans. James Ellington (Indianapolis: Hackett Publishing Co., 1993), 64–65.

48. Rationalism seeks to eradicate anything that can jeopardize the unified operation of a strict rationality that will correct beliefs in the light of available evidence; yet adaptivity asks that one not undermine tacit beliefs unless absolutely necessary. See Amelie Oksenberg Rorty, "Belief and Self-Deception," *Inquiry* 15 (1972): 401–2.

49. Rorty, "Belief and Self-Deception," 388; like Rousseau, Freud discusses social relations on the assumption that the same mechanisms internally divide a person, while strict rationality seeks to avoid the internal rift that would cause fundamental insecurities.

50. This is why Aristotle considered *akrasia* useful for self-reform, and self-deception poses more "danger," as Amelie Oksenberg Rorty points out in her follow-up study, "Self-deception, Akrasia and Irrationality," *Social Science Information* 19, no. 6 (1980): 905–22.

51. Even Habermasian intersubjectivity remains subjectivist when he claims, "an assertion can be called rational only if the speaker satisfies the conditions necessary to achieve the illocutionary goal of reaching an understanding about something in the world with at least one other participant in communication": Jürgen Habermas, *Theory of Communicative Action*, vol. 1 (Boston: Beacon Press, 1987), 11 (*Theorie des kommunikativen Handelns*, vol. 1 [Frankfurt: Suhrkamp, 1981], 29).

52. Donald Davidson, "Paradoxes of Irrationality," in *Philosophical Essays on Freud*, ed. Richard Wollheim (Cambridge: Cambridge University Press, 1982), 289–305; Donald Davidson, "How Is Weakness of the Will Possible?" in *Essays on Actions and Events* (Oxford: Oxford University Press, 1980).

53. See Rorty, "Self-deception, Akrasia and Irrationality," 913.

54. Maurice Halbwachs, *Les cadres sociaux de la mémoire* (Paris: Albin Michel, 1994), and *La Mémoire collective* (Paris: Presses Universitaires Françaises, 1950).

55. Halbwachs, *Les Cadres sociaux de la mémoire*, 57–59.

56. "It is impossible to remember the future," Aristotle admonishes, "which is an object of conjecture or expectation" (449b10–11), yet he admits that "there might be a science of expectation as some say there is of divination" (449b12): Aristotle, "Of Memory and Recollection," in *Parva Naturalia*, trans. W. S. Hett, Loeb Classical Library 8 (Cambridge: Harvard University Press, 1975), 285–313. This reverberates in Lacan's commentary on Freud, characterizing the "question of recollection" as one "in which conjectures about the past are balanced against promises of the future": Jacques Lacan, *Ecrits*, ed. and trans. Alan Sheridan (New York: Norton, 1977), 48.

57. Halbwachs, *Les Cadres sociaux de la mémoire*, 131–33.

58. Halbwachs, *Les Cadres sociaux de la mémoire*, 163–70. For Freud, there is never any ambiguity about the fact that repetition cannot reproduce the past. See Jacques Lacan, *The Four Fundamental Concepts of Psychoanalysis* (New York: Norton, 1978), 50.

59. Halbwachs, *Les Cadres sociaux de la mémoire*, 368 and passim.

60. Halbwachs, *La Mémoire collective*, 7, 63, and passim.

61. Jean Pouillon's *Temps et Roman* (Paris: Gallimard, 1946) proposed to formulate the imagination of time, but after a lengthy consideration of the philosophical and psychological status of imagination only got to contingency and destiny. Georges Poulet attempted a study of the human experience of time in two volumes, *Études sur le temps humain* (Paris: Plon 1950) and *La Distance intérieure* (Paris: Plon 1952). In portraits of

writers from Montaigne to Valéry, he offers a history of time consciousness in literature, but makes no mention of paramnesia. In 1928, Wyndham Lewis points out in *Time and Western Man* that although the nineteenth century saw a shift towards sequential scientific models such as evolution and historical hermeneutics, time becomes a predominant literary topic only in the twentieth century.

62. Sabina Spielrein, "Die Zeit im unterschwelligen Seelenleben," *Imago* 9 (1923); Paul Schilder, "Psychopathologie der Zeit," *Imago* 21 (1935); Thomas Mann, *Freud und die Zukunft* (Vienna: Bermann-Fischer, 1936); Marie Bonaparte, "Time and the Unconscious," *International Journal of Psychoanalysis* 21 (October 1940): 427–68; Lionel Trilling, "Psychoanalysis and Literature," *Horizon* 9 (1947).

63. See for instance Madeleine B. Stern, "Counterclockwise: Flux in Time in Literature," *Sewanee Review* 44 (1936): 338–65.

64. Aleida Assmann and Jan Assmann, "Schrift und Gedächtnis," in *Schrift und Gedächtnis*, ed. Aleida Assmann, Jan Assmann, and C. Hardmeier (Munich: Fink, 1983), 277 and 281.

65. I. A. Richards, *Principles of Literary Criticism* (London: Kegan Paul, 1924), 105; see also 40–41.

66. I. A. Richards, *Principles of Literary Criticism*, 104.

67. Percy B. Shelley, "Catalogue of the Phenomena of Dreams, as Connecting Sleeping and Waking," in *Shelley's Prose or The Trumpet of a Prophecy*, ed. David Lee Clark (London: Fourth Estate, 1988), 193–94. Compare Sir Walter Scott's ideas on the "sentiment of pre-existence" in *Guy Mannering* (London: Dent; New York: Dutton, 1906). According to Daniel Schacter, one may recognize déjà vu in Dante Gabriel Rossetti's poem "Sudden Light" from 1854 (Schacter, *The Seven Sins of Memory*, 89). See also Walter Scott, *The Journal of Sir Walter Scott*, vol. 2 (Edinburgh: D. Douglas, 1890), 124.

68. Charles Dickens, *David Copperfield* (Oxford: Clarendon Press, 1981), 483. Lukacher astutely observes how "in the culture of psychoanalysis, Dickens has always been the figure of both its prehistory and its future": Ned Lukacher, *Primal Scenes: Literature, Philosophy, Psychoanalysis* (Ithaca: Cornell University Press, 1986), 336. Compare the use of paramnesia in Leo Tolstoy, *War and Peace* (New York: Random House, 1992).

69. See for instance Martin Heusser, "*Déjà Vu* with a Difference: Repetition and the Tragic in Thomas Hardy's Novels," in *Repetition*, ed. Andreas Fischer (Tübingen: Narr, 1994), 171–87. Dickens described another false déjà vu in which Venice, seen for the first time on a trip taken in 1844 and written up in 1846, seems to him like London in a dream. Charles Dickens, *Pictures from Italy* (Edinburgh: University Union, 1898), 392–401, 435, 487. This is a little known passage—the pages of the two editions I consulted, at Konstanz and Los Angeles, were still uncut: the book had remained unread for the entire time-span we discuss here.

70. John Hagan, "Déjà Vu and the Effect of Timelessness in Faulkner's *Absalom, Absalom!*," *Bucknell Review* 11, no. 2 (1963): 31–52; William E. Buckler, "Déjà Vu Inverted: The Imminent Future in Walter Pater's 'Marius the Epicurean,'" *The Victorian Newsletter* 55 (spring 1979): 1–4; Regina Weinreich, "The Dynamic Déjà Vu of William Burroughs," *Review of Contemporary Fiction* 4, no. 1 (1984): 55–58; Nancy Blake, "Fiction as Screen Memory," *Delta* 21 (October 1985): 95–104. Compare Ludwig Tieck, *Der Blonde Eckbert*

(Stuttgart: Reclam, 1986). See also H. N. Sno, D. H. Linszen, and F. de Jonghe, "Art Imitates Life: Déjà vu Experiences in Prose and Poetry," *The British Journal of Psychiatry* 160 (1992): 511–18.

71. Nathaniel Hawthorne, *The Letters 1853–1856*, ed. Thomas Woodson (Columbus: Ohio University Press, 1987), 537. The opposite case, a fatal premonition in a poem by Friedrich Hebbel, is also no true déjà vu, as discussed by Sandor Ferenczi, "Friedrich Hebbel's Explanation of Déjà Vu," in *Further Contributions to the Theory and Technique of Psychoanalysis* (New York: Boni and Liveright, 1927), 422.

72. Nathaniel Hawthorne, "Near Oxford," in *Our Old Home*, in *The Centenary Edition of the Works of Nathaniel Hawthorne*, ed. Fredson Bowers (Columbus: Ohio University Press, 1970), 5: 183–84. See also the use of paramnesia in Ivan Gontcharov, *Oblomov* (New York: New American Library, 1963).

73. See Edwin H. Miller, *Salem Is My Dwelling Place: A Life of Nathaniel Hawthorne* (Iowa City: Iowa University Press, 1991), 338 and 408.

74. James Joyce, *Ulysses* (New York: Garland, 1984), 506. See Shari Benstock, "Through a Glass Darkly," *James Joyce Quarterly* (summer 1976): 473–76. Also Chester G. Anderson, "Leopold Bloom as Dr. Sigmund Freud," *Mosaic* 6 (fall 1972): 23–43; Sheldon Brivic, "James Joyce: From Stephen to Bloom," in *Psychoanalysis and Literary Process*, ed. Frederick Crews (Cambridge: Winthrop, 1970), 118–62.

75. James Joyce, *A Portrait of the Artist as a Young Man* (New York: Penguin, 1977), 51, 53, 41, and 50, respectively. See also Walker Percy, *The Last Gentleman* (New York: Farrar, Straus & Giroux, 1966), 10 and 66.

76. Benstock ("Through a Glass Darkly") shows that at the time, Joyce himself was no longer wearing glasses, which vindicates her reading of the Circe chapter based on autobiographical information about Joyce.

77. As W. J. Harvey writes on occasion of telepathy and foreboding in George Eliot's novel *The Lifted Veil*, the idea of narrative structure is "complicated by the fact that most of our readings are actually re-readings": W. J. Harvey, *The Art of George Eliot* (London: Chatto & Windus, 1961), 95 and 100; cited after Charles Swann, "Déjà Vu: Déjà Lu: *The Lifted Veil* as an Experiment in Art," *Literature and History* 5 (1979): 40–57. Harvey is taken in by Eliot's suggestion that one will not have read any novel without already having preconceived notions about its text. Again, this effect is harnessed, of course, in advertising and marketing.

78. Roland Barthes, *S/Z* (Paris: Editions du Seuil, 1970), 9–28, sections iv, v, ix.

79. "I frequently read a new poem with a vague sense of familiarity . . . and I quickly realize that it is explainable by the fact that the writer has fallen under the influence of Heine, or Tennyson, or Rosetti, as the case may be. One may have similar experiences with regard to new psychological theories": Havelock Ellis, "A Note on Hypnagogic Paramnesia," *Mind* (April 1897), 285. Ellis, like Freud, offers a visit to a ruin as his only autobiographical substantiation. The remark on recollections of theories is cut from the extended version in Havelock Ellis, *The World of Dreams* (London: Constable, 1911), chapter 9 (212ff., especially 230–60).

80. "When Freud refers to interpretations of déjà vu which preceded his own he always takes cognizance of the 'mystical' and 'vague' conviction that this double take refers

to experiences from another life": Laurence Rickels, *Aberrations of Mourning: Writing on German Crypts* (Detroit: Wayne State University Press, 1988), 253.

81. "in frühen Jahren leistungsfähiger, weil weniger überladen als in späteren": Sigmund Freud, "Vorlesungen zur Einführung in die Psychoanalyse," GW, 11:204.

82. Sigmund Freud, SE, 5:539 and 540n (1925). See also "Note upon the 'Mystic Writing-Pad,'" SE, 19: 227–32, and chapter 4 of *Beyond the Pleasure Principle*, SE, 18.

83. Sigmund Freud, SE, 2:7. See Lacan, *Ecrits*, 52.

84. Jacques Lacan, *L'éthique de la psychanalyse: Le Séminaire VI* (Paris: Seuil, 1986), 272.

85. With Ricoeur or Hegel, some may prefer the term "lethopathology"; see Paul Ricoeur, *La Mémoire, l'histoire, l'oubli* (Paris: Seuil, 2000).

86. As rumors about the inversion of psychoanalysis have it, the culture industry or National Socialism is "psychoanalysis in reverse." Andreas Huyssen, "Adorno in Reverse," *New German Critique* 29 (1983): 15; Laurence Rickels, *The Case of California* (Baltimore: The Johns Hopkins University Press, 1991), 1. Skirting the tedious repetition of such rumors, we point to the three volumes of Laurence Rickels, *Nazi Psychoanalysis* (Minneapolis: University of Minnesota Press, 2002). While Frankfurt School Marxism wanted to distance itself from the way psychoanalysis clicked for the Nazis, the Nazis tried perhaps even harder than Sartre to reprogram psychoanalysis in order to make it compatible with a melancholic, future-driven mindset.

87. See Anna Stüssi, *Erinnerungen an die Zukunft* (Göttingen: Minerva, 1977).

88. This criticism must also be directed against Paul Virilio's *The Vision Machine* (Bloomington: Indiana University Press, 1994), where the motto from Norman E. Spear stakes an impossible claim: "Memory content is a function of the rate of forgetting." Someone dedicating an entire chapter to topographical amnesia should cite such a positivist formula only ironically. See Norman E. Spear, *The Processing of Memories: Forgetting and Retention* (New York: Halstead-Wiley, 1978).

89. Ernst Bloch, "Tübinger Einleitung in die Philosophie," in *Werkausgabe*, vol. 13 (Frankfurt: Suhrkamp, 1970), 282.

90. Walter Benjamin, "Das Kunstwerk im Zeitalter seiner technischen Reproduzierbarkeit," GS, 1.2:449–51 (this is the first version; compare the second version, 7.1:369f., and the third version, 1.2:488–89).

91. Benjamin, GS, 7.1:369–71. See 1.2:454f. and 488f.

92. "Jeder heutige Mensch hat einen Anspruch, gefilmt zu werden": Benjamin, GS, 1.2:455. See 7.1:371.

93. Vladimir Jankelevitch, *L'irreversible et la nostalgie* (Paris: Flammarion, 1974), esp. chapter 4.

94. For the politics of pardon, see Natalie Zemon Davis, *Fiction in the Archives: Pardon Tales and Their Tellers in Sixteenth-Century France* (Stanford: Stanford University Press, 1987), and Nicole Loraux, *La Cité divisée: L'oubli dans la mémoire d'Athènes* (Paris: Payot, 1997). For further reading, see Jacques Derrida, *On Cosmopolitanism and Forgiveness* (London: Routledge, 2001), 27–60, and Ricoeur, *La Mémoire, l'histoire, l'oubli*, which culminates in an "epilogue" on pardon, 593–656.

95. Stanley Cavell, *Pursuits of Happiness: The Hollywood Comedy of Marriage* (Cambridge: Harvard, 1981), 386. See also Janice Galloway's novel of déjà vu, *The Trick Is to Keep Breathing* (Edinburgh: Polygon, 1989), especially 64, 110, 174, 194, and passim.

96. Laurence A. Rickels, "Psychoanalysis and the Two Orifices of Film," *American Journal of Semiotics* 5, nos. 3–4 (1987): 419–45. See Rickels, *Aberrations of Mourning,* 135–56.

97. Extreme forms of distraction or self-deception are not identical with lying to one-self, although their proximity would have to be discussed in detail; arguably, the person who lies to himself believes both p and not-p, and is capable of doing so because he is distracted from the former.

98. Walter Benjamin, "The Work of Art in the Age of Mechanical Reproduction," in *Illuminations* (New York: Schocken Books, 1969), 240. (GS, 7.1:369–71. See 1.2:454f. and 488f.)

99. Henning Ritter, "Thinking Incognito," *New Literary History* 27 (1996): 603.

1. SECRET AGENTS

1. Cited, as unremarked irony, after Nicholas Royle, "Déjà vu," in *Post-Theory: New Directions in Criticism,* ed. Martin McQuillan (Edinburgh: Edinburgh University Press, 1999), 3–20.

2. Royle, "Déjà vu," 8–9. Royle points out that in February 1914, Freud dismissed his take on déjà vu in a letter to Ferenczi as "a piece of junk": *The Correspondence of Sigmund Freud and Sándor Ferenczi,* vol. 1: *1908–1914* (Cambridge: Belknap, 1993), 540. Ultimately, Royle aligns the experience of the déjà vu with the uncanny—recycling once again the weak Freudian force par excellence, and putting all specificity of the particular mass media effect of déjà vu in peril, though Royle seeks to recuperate it by invoking the logic of the supplement and the ghost.

3. Sigmund Freud, *The Psychopathology of Everyday Life,* SE, 6:266; "*Fausse Reconnaissance ('déjà raconté')* in Psychoanalytic Treatment," SE, 13:207; "The Uncanny," SE, 18:245–48; "A Disturbance of Memory on the Acropolis," SE, 22:245. For the German, see "Psychopathologie des Alltagslebens," GW, 4; "*Über fausse reconnaissance ('déjà raconté')* während der psychoanalytischen Arbeit," GW, 10:116–23; "Das Unheimliche," GW, 12:229–68; "Brief an Romain Rolland (Eine Erinnerungsstörung auf der Acropolis)," GW, 16:250–57.

4. Sigmund Freud, "The Psychical Mechanism of Forgetfulness," SE, 3:289–97; compare *The Psychopathology of Everyday Life,* SE, 6, passim.

5. Sigmund Freud, "Recommendations to Physicians Practising Psycho-Analysis," SE, 13:111–20.

6. Ibid., 297

7. Sigmund Freud, "Screen Memories," SE, 3:303–22.

8. Josef Breuer and Sigmund Freud, *Studies on Hysteria* (New York: Basic Books, 1978), 117 n. 1. Compare SE, 2, passim.

9. Sigmund Freud, "Remembering, Repeating and Working-Through," SE, 13:148.

10. Sandor Ferenczi, "Über vermeintliche Fehlhandlungen," *Schriften zur Psychoanalyse* 1 (1966): 221–26.

11. Samuel M. Weber, *Institution and Interpretation* (Minneapolis: University of Minnesota Press, 1987), 74–75.

12. Posttheoretical: the end of theory that has persistently been announced over the past decades may eventually catch up with its fama when the structure of spatiotemporal

certainty is questi ned and "theories" undergo scrutiny, in the mode of self-application or otherwise. After theory hit the post, a post-theory perspective would still be looking after theory.

13. Freud, "Screen Memories," SE, 3:312.

14. Ibid., 318.

15. Ibid., 320.

16. In *The Interpretation of Dreams*, chapter 6E, Freud offers an account of the déjà vu as it occurs in dreams, but he will apparently discard it later; see SE, 5:399.

17. Freud, *"Fausse Reconnaissance,"* SE, 13:201–07 ("Über *fausse reconnaissance ('déjà raconté')* während der psychoanalytischen Arbeit," GW, 10:116–23). See Dale Boesky, "The Reversal of Déjà Raconté," *Journal of the American Psychoanalytic Association* 17 (1969): 1114–41.

18. Freud, *The Interpretation of Dreams*, SE, 5:447 (see also 399 and 478).

19. Freud, *"Fausse Reconnaissance,"* SE, 13:203; compare *The Psychopathology of Everyday Life*, SE, 6, chapter 12, section D.

20. Resistance is quintessential for critical reading. See Paul de Man, *The Resistance to Theory* (Minneapolis: University of Minnesota Press, 1987), which despite its own tacit resistance to psychoanalysis formulates a structure that is operative here.

21. Freud, "A Disturbance of Memory," SE, 22:239–50; "Brief an Romain Rolland," GW, 16:250–57.

22. Sigmund Freud, "The Future of an Illusion" (1927), chapter 5, SE, 21:25. There, Freud writes of an apparition I feel more familiar with—the city of Konstanz on the Bodensee: "and I am now completely convinced of the correctness of this geographical assertion."

23. Freud, "A Disturbance of Memory," SE, 22:245; "Brief an Romain Rolland," GW, 16:255: "Das alles ist noch so dunkel, so wenig wissenschaftlich bezwungen, daß ich mir verbieten muß, es vor Ihnen weiter zu erörtern."

24. The editors of the *Standard Edition* provide title and year (Anna Freud, *The Ego and the Mechanisms of Defense*, 1936); the German edition does not.

25. See Harry Slochower, "Freud's Déjà Vu on the Acropolis: A Symbolic Relic of 'Mater Nuda,'" *Psychoanalytic Quarterly* 39 (1970): 90–102.

26. Whether one reads this literally as scaling the mons pubis or more figuratively as the return to the womb (as Freud himself has it in his essay on the uncanny), the effect remains the same. See also Eli Marcovitz, "The Meaning of Déjà Vu," *Psychoanalytic Quarterly* 21 (1952): 481–89.

27. Otto Fenichel, *The Psychoanalytic Theory of Neuroses* (New York: W. W. Norton, 1945), 146.

28. Most commentators assume that self-deception is analogous in structure to the deception of another person; see John King-Farlow, "Self-Deceivers and Sartrian Seducers," *Analysis* 23 (1963): 131–36, referring to John V. Canfield and Don F. Gustavson, "Self-Deception," ibid., 32–36.

29. Compare the "sincere" deconstructive claim that is, as Geoffrey Bennington put it, an "originary and irreducible quasi-transcendental dehiscence constitutive of anything like meaning such that any speech-act at all is caught up in something that looks like

performative contradiction when seen from a metaphysical vantage-point," such as the one put forth by Jürgen Habermas. Geoffrey Bennington, "Ex-Communication" (Paper delivered to the Social and Political Thought Seminar, University of Sussex, 4 March 1996: round table with Peter Dews and William Outhwaite), *Foreign Body* 6 (1997), www.hydra.umn.edu/fobo/harras.html.

30. An elaborate account of self-deception and sincerity in cases where someone "knew all along" is found in F. A. Siegler, "Demos on Lying to Oneself," *Journal of Philosophy* 59 (1962): 469–75, referring to Raphael Demos, "Lying to Oneself," *Journal of Philosophy* 57 (1960): 588–95.

31. An important debate is found in Jacques Derrida, *Limited Inc.* (Evanston: Northwestern University Press, 1988); see J. L. Austin, *How to Do Things with Words* (Cambridge: Harvard University Press, 1962), in particular the twelfth lecture, 150f.

32. André Gide, *The Counterfeiters* (New York: Modern Library, 1955), 394.

33. For further reading, see Jacques Derrida, "History of the Lie: Prolegomena," *Graduate Faculty Philosophy Journal* 20, no. 1 (1997): 129–61.

34. Perez Zagorin, *Ways of Lying: Dissimulation, Persecution and Conformity in Early Modern Europe* (Cambridge: Harvard University Press, 1990), 3: "Dissimulatio signified dissembling, feigning, concealing or keeping secret. Simulatio also meant feigning or a falsely assumed appearance, deceit, hypocrisy, pretense or insincerity. . . . For precision's sake, however, we can also say that in a strict sense dissimulation is pretending not to be what one actually is, whereas simulatio is pretending to be what one actually is not."

35. In ancient Greek, *pseudos* meant lie as well as falsehood, cunning, or mistake, and deception or fraud as well as poetic invention, multiplying the potential for misunderstanding what is meant by misunderstanding. Fable and phantasm are neither errors nor deceptions, false witnesses nor perjuries; to speak about them is not a question of veracity or mendacity. Therefore, any history of the lie—if possible—must be told as confabulation.

36. Augustine, "On Lying," in *Treatises on Various Subjects*, chapter 3, ed. Roy J. Deferrari, vol. 16 of *The Fathers of the Church* (Washington: Catholic University of America Press, 1952), 54–55: "Sometimes, he who believes realizes that he does not understand that which he believes, although if he believes it very firmly he does not doubt at all about the matter which he realizes he does not understand. On the other hand, he who holds an opinion thinks that he knows what he does not know. Whoever gives expression to that which he holds either through belief or opinion does not lie even though the statement itself may be false."

37. For two pithy historicizations of a modern political culture of the lie, see Hannah Arendt, "Truth and Politics," in *Between Past and Future: Eight Exercises in Political Thought* (New York: Viking Press, 1961), 227–52, and "Lying in Politics: Reflections on the Pentagon Papers," in *Crises of the Republic* (New York: Harcourt, Brace, Jovanovich, 1972), 3ff.

38. At times it is suggested that Freud was hostile to philosophy, although he went on record, in a remark to Wilhelm Fliess about the latter's circuitous medical route of inquiry, as secretly nursing the hope of arriving "by the same route at my original objective, philosophy. For that was my original ambition"—an ambition to which Lacan would have returned his Freud. Sigmund Freud, "Letter 39 of January 1st, 1896," in *The Origins*

of Psychoanalysis (New York: Basic Books, 1954), 141. Surely the introduction of psycho-analysis into the field of inquiry is not a displacement of philosophy, nor a reduction of irrational conflicts to desire.

39. Theodor W. Adorno, *Minima Moralia* (London: Verso, 1978), 108: *Pseudomenos.*

40. Demos, "Lying to Oneself"; of course Augustine had already stressed intention: "fallendi cupiditas, voluntas fallendi" (see n. 36 above).

41. T. Penelhum, "Pleasure and Falsity," in *Philosophy of Mind,* ed. Stuart Hampshire (New York: Harper & Row, 1966), 242–66.

42. In Plato's distinction between lying in words or in the soul (*Republic* 382a), self-deception is a terrible evil that makes man his own prisoner (*Cratylos* 428d). Our brief gist of ordinary language philosophy owes to the concise, if partial and somewhat dated, discussions in Sissela Bok, *Secrets: On the Ethics of Concealment and Revelation* (New York: Pantheon, 1983), and *Lying: Moral Choice in Public and Private Life* (New York: Pantheon, 1978).

43. For Lacan's "return" or "update" and his grammar of the future anterior, see Jacques Derrida, "Pour l'amour de Lacan," in *Lacan avec les philosophes* (Paris: Albin Michel, 1996), 397–420; and Derrida, "For the Love of Lacan," in *Resistances of Psychoanalysis* (Stanford: Stanford University Press, 1998), 39–69.

44. In chapter four of the *Psychopathology of Everyday Life* (SE, vol. 6), the process of displacement of childhood memories is taken as revelation of how certain other, perhaps more significant impressions are not reproduced due to resistance; thus many seemingly insignificant childhood recollections are what Freud calls "concealing memories."

45. It is important to note that Freud would opt for a coherent theory over pragmatic flexibility. Ian Hacking argues that Freud "lived for Truth, and quite possibly deluded himself a good deal of the time and even knew he was being deluded": Ian Hacking, *Rewriting the Soul: Multiple Personalities and the Sciences of Memory* (Princeton: Princeton University Press, 1995), 195. See Elizabeth Loftus, "When a Lie Becomes Memory's Truth: Memory Distortion After Exposure to Misinformation," *Current Directions in Psychological Science* 1, no. 4 (1992), 120–23.

46. Jean-Paul Sartre, *Being and Nothingness,* trans. Hazel Barnes (New York: Philosophical Library, 1956), 48 ff.

47. Sartre, *Being and Nothingness,* 45.

48. Sartre, *Being and Nothingness,* 68.

49. Sartre, *Being and Nothingness,* 70.

50. Sissela Bok, "The Self Deceived," *Social Science Information* 19, no. 6 (1980): 923–35, illustrates the condescending flip side to such a coercive imposition with a citation from Dostoyevsky's *Brothers Karamazov,* where the Grand Inquisitor maintains that he lied *out of his own altruism* to the people who, he assumes, can only thrive in enslavement, "so that the poor blind creatures may at least on the way think themselves happy." Both the coercive interventionism and the condescending fraud, she concludes, derive an aura of altruism from this concept of self-deception that they would not otherwise deserve.

51. Sartre, *Being and Nothingness,* 47–70; as Rorty puts it, "Sartre makes self-deception endemic to the human condition, the plight of a consciousness that cannot grasp itself as the nothing it is. . . . All self-predication is self-deceptive, masking a purely arbitrary

choice as an explicable discovery": Amelie Oksenberg Rorty, "Belief and Self-Deception," *Inquiry* 15 (1972): 398.

52. Sartre, *Being and Nothingness*, 56 and 49.

53. Sartre's inversion of Freudian notions with regard to past and future will be taken up again in the context of gadget love (chapter 5).

54. See Mary Warnock, *The Philosophy of Sartre* (London: Hutchinson, 1965), 50–60.

55. For Adorno and Horkheimer reification is forgetting: "alle Verdinglichung ist ein Vergessen." Theodor W. Adorno and Max Horkheimer, *Dialektik der Aufklärung* (Leipzig: Reclam, 1989), 255.

56. Sartre, *Being and Nothingness*, 67.

57. Friedrich Nietzsche, *Kritische Studienausgabe*, ed. Giorgio Colli and Mazzino Montinari (Munich/Berlin: DTV/de Gruyter, 1988), 13:144.

58. Royle, "Déjà Vu", 10. See Jacques Derrida, *The Post Card: From Socrates to Freud and Beyond* (Chicago: Chicago University Press, 1987), 379.

59. Herbert Fingarette, *Self-Deception* (London: Routledge, 1969), 114 and 49, respectively.

60. Sigmund Freud, "Fragment of an Analysis of a Case of Hysteria," SE, 7:3f.; "Bruchstück einer Hysterie-Analyse", GW, 19:175.

61. J. P. Vernant, "Arbeit und Natur in der griechischen Antike," in *Die Entstehung von Klassengesellschaften,* ed. K. Eder (Frankfurt: Suhrkamp, 1973): 268.

62. Karl Marx, *Das Kapital,* vol.1 (Berlin: MEW, 1979), 386–89; compare Plato, *Politeia* 369b–f. The ancients focused not on speculative exchange value but on use value: in service to the gods, to gain favor in court, in the care of animals, or in tending to the sick, in the sense of medical treatment or cure. See Plato, *Republic* 427b, and *Protagoras* 345a, 354a; Aristotle, *Historia Animalium* 578a7 (*Liddell-Scott-Jones Lexikon of Classical Greek*, www.perseus.tufts.edu).

63. Sigmund Freud, "On Beginning the Treatment," SE, 12:126.

64. Sigmund Freud, "The Future Prospects of Psycho-Analytic Therapy," SE, 11:141–51.

65. Freud, "Future Prospects," SE, 11:142.

66. Cited after Avital Ronell, *Dictations: On Haunted Writing* (Lincoln: University of Nebraska Press, 1986), 42–43.

67. Freud, "Future Prospects," SE, 11:145.

68. Freud, "Future Prospects," SE, 11:148.

69. Freud, "On Beginning the Treatment," SE, 12:141.

70. See Samuel Weber's new introduction to the second edition of his *Legend of Freud* (Stanford: Stanford University Press, 1998); first published as *Freud-Legende: Drei Studien zum psychoanalytischen Denken* (Freiburg: Olten, 1979); extended and revised as *Freud-Legende: Vier Studien zum psychoanalytischen Denken* (Vienna: Passagen, 1989); first published in English as *Legend of Freud* (Minneapolis: University of Minnesota Press, 1982).

71. Breuer and Freud, *Studies on Hysteria*, 117 n. 1. Compare SE, 2:passim.

72. Freud, "Future Prospects," SE, 11:148. The question of illusory gains from the dynamics of the secret brings mass media technology into focus for our investigation of cultural déjà vu effects such as the inversion of the envelope of time.

73. All citations from Sigmund Freud, "The Unconscious," SE, 14:166–204.

74. Vincent Descombes, *L'inconscient malgré lui* (Paris: Gallimard, 1978), 32.

75. Régis Durand, "The Anxiety of Performance," *New Literary History* 12:1 (1980): 167–76. See Descombes, *L'inconscient malgré lui*, 35.

76. Freud, "On Beginning the Treatment," SE, 12:137.

77. Freud, "On Beginning the Treatment," SE, 12:136f.

78. Carl Fulton Sulzberger, "Why Is It Hard to Keep Secrets," *Psychoanalysis* 2 (1953): 39 and 37.

79. Theodor Reik, *The Secret Self* (New York: Grove, 1952); the compulsion to confess can be related to the wish to "return" to an imaginary state without separation.

80. More often than not, this pretense goes along with a preference for personal myth or autobiographical memory, which serves as a protective screen against any analysis of resistance, by replacing the neurotic secret with a more adaptive, but no less self-deceived myth.

81. Distinguishing memory from recollection, Aristotle associated the latter with good learners and knowledge ("Those who learn more easily are better at recollecting"), whereas the former characterizes the slow-witted ("the slow-witted have better memories"): Aristotle, "Of Memory and Recollection," 449b7–8 in *Parva Naturalia*, ed. W. S. Hett, Loeb Classical Library 8 (Cambridge: Harvard University Press, 1975), 285–313.

82. Rudolf Ekstein and Elaine Caruth, "Keeping Secrets," in *Tactics and Techniques in Psychoanalytic Therapy*, ed. Peter Giovacchini (New York: Science House, 1972), 210.

83. Ekstein and Caruth, "Keeping Secrets," 201 (emphasis in original).

84. Sigmund Freud, "The Splitting of the Ego in the Process of Defence," SE, 23:275.

85. Michel Foucault, *Raymond Roussel* (Paris: Gallimard, 1963), 10; Michel Foucault, *Death in the Labyrinth: The World of Raymond Roussel* (New York: Doubleday, 1986), 3.

86. A third type of constructing the secret is neither neurotic nor psychotic, but an extreme narcissistic disturbance, as analyzed below, in the case of Andy Warhol. It consists in falling for the seduction of pure surface, where the secret is not what is hidden inside—rather, it is an excess on the surface. In such regression, you are not libidinally connected to anything but your own self. Consequently, any stimulation, whether in the form of a demand from another person or an impulse from within oneself, is inevitably perceived as technological. This may be the inverse of paranoia; unlike Daniel Paul Schreber, Warhol in his gadget love is not into paranoid overinterpretation—he never interprets anything: everything is plain, on the surface.

87. Friedrich Kainz, "Arthur Schnitzler und Karl Schönherr," in *Deutsch-Österreichische Literaturgeschichte*, ed. Johann Nagl, Jakob Zeidler, and Eduard Castle (Vienna: Literaturverlag, 1937), 1759 (my translation).

88. This citation and the next from Freud, "The Unconscious," SE, 14:169 and 170.

89. Laurence Rickels, "ZAP: Depersonalized," in *The Case of California* (Baltimore: Johns Hopkins University Press, 1991), 267–69; referring to Owen Renick, "The Role of Attention in Depersonalization," *Psychoanalytic Quarterly* 47 (1978): 588–605.

90. Otto Pötzl, "Zur Metapsychology des *déjà vu*," *Imago* 12 (1926): 393–402.

2. Future Interior

1. Walter Benjamin, "Berliner Kindheit um Neunzehnhundert," GS, 4.1:251–52. Compare Benjamin's "Eine Todesnachricht," GS, 7.1, 410–11.

2. Peter Szondi, "Hoffnung im Vergangenen: Über Walter Benjamin," in *Satz und Gegensatz* (Frankfurt: Suhrkamp, 1964), 79–97. Peter Szondi, "Hope in the Past," *Critical Inquiry* 4 (1978): 491–506.

3. The proliferating idea of Benjamin's Proust-addiction is usually based on Adorno's account: "[Er] wolle nicht ein Wort mehr von Proust lesen, als er jeweils zu übersetzen habe, weil er sonst in süchtige Abhängigkeit gerate, die ihn an der eigenen Produktion . . . hindere": Theodor W. Adorno, "Im Schatten junger Mädchenblüte," in *Dichten und Trachten: Jahresschau des Suhrkamp Verlags*, vol. 4 (Frankfurt: Suhrkamp, 1954), 74. Compare Walter Benjamin and Gershom Scholem, *Briefwechsel 1933–1940* (Frankfurt: Suhrkamp, 1985), 20.

4. According to Jewish tradition, investigation into the future is forbidden; learning about the Torah will direct the scholar in remembrance of the past, as Benjamin paraphrases. GS, 1:704. See also 5:599f., and Gershom Scholem, "Zum Verständnis der messianischen Idee im Judentum," *Judaica*, vol. 1 (Frankfurt: Suhrkamp, 1986), 7–74. Compare Benjamin, *Illuminations* (New York: Schocken, 1969), 264, and GS, 1.3:1252.

5. Howard Stern, "Umkehrung des déjà vu: Zu einem Text der 'Berliner Kindheit,'" *Text und Kritik* 31 (1979): 91–93.

6. Christiaan Hart Nibbrig, "Das déjà vu des ersten Blicks: Zu Walter Benjamins *Berliner Kindheit um Neunzehnhundert*," *Deutsche Vierteljahresschrift für Geistesgeschichte* 47, no. 4 (1973): 723: "Das déjà vu ist in der *Berliner Kindheit* methodisches Prinzip." "In the *Berlin Childhood*, déjà vu is not a methodical principle."

7. "Der Form des neuen Produktmittels, die im Anfang noch von der des alten beherrscht wird (Marx), entsprechen im Kollektivbewußtsein Bilder, in denen das Neue sich mit dem Alten durchdringt. Diese Bilder sind Wunschbilder und in ihnen sucht das Kollektiv die Unfertigkeit des gesellschaftlichen Produkts sowie die Mängel der gesellschaftlichen Produktionsordnung sowohl aufzuheben wie zu verklären. Daneben tritt in diesen Wunschbildern das nachdrückliche Streben hervor, sich gegen das Veraltete—das heißt aber: gegen das Jüngstvergangene—abzusetzen": Walter Benjamin, GS, 5:46.

8. Walter Benjamin, "Über den Begriff der Geschichte," GS, 1.2:691–704.

9. Jack Zipes, "Kinderliteratur und Kinder-Öffentlichkeit in Walter Benjamins Schriften," in *Walter Benjamin und die Kinderliteratur*, ed. Klaus Doderer (Weinheim: Juventa, 1988), 188–95. See already Carol Jacobs, "Walter Benjamin: Image of Proust," *Modern Language Notes*, 86, no. 6 (1971): 910–32.

10. "Es gibt Noch-nicht-bewußtes-Wissen vom Gewesenen, dessen Förderung die Struktur des Erwachens hat": Benjamin, GS, 5:490. Further notes on a psychoanalytic excavation of awakening can be found on pp. 140 (the dream as access to the prehistory of the nineteenth century), 492 (collective consciousness between sleep and wakefulness), 580 (interpretation of dreams as dialectical image), and 1012 (a variety of states of consciousness between being awake and asleep).

11. This turn toward Freud occurred under the friendly pressure of Adorno, as a more

manifestly materialist critique. In 1918, Benjamin's reading of Freud for his doctoral exams had been decidely negative. Less than two decades later (10 June 1935) he writes to Adorno, "Ich werde Freud demnächst vornehmen. Ist Ihnen übrigens aus der Erinnerung bei ihm selbst oder in seiner Schule eine Psychoanalyse des Erwachens gegenwärtig? oder Studien dazu?": Walter Benjamin, *Gesammelte Briefe*, vol. 5: *1935–1937*, ed. Christoph Gödde and Henri Lutz (Frankfurt: Suhrkamp, 1999), 110 ("Soon I will tackle Freud. By the way, do you remember a psychoanalysis of awakening in his works or those of his school? Or studies of it?"). Compare Szondi, "Hoffnung im Vergangenen," 91. Other traces of reading Freud are two enthusiastic comments on the essay on telepathy, and occasional allusions in book reviews Benjamin wrote and published during the 1930s.

12. Gershom Scholem, "Ahnen und Verwandte Walter Benjamins," in *Walter Benjamin und sein Engel: Vierzehn Aufsätze und kleine Beiträg* (Frankfurt: Suhrkamp, 1983), 128–57.

13. Benjamin, "Berliner Kindheit um Neunzehnhundert," GS, 4.1:294.

14. "Wie Proust seine Lebensgeschichte mit dem Erwachen beginnt, so muß jede Geschichtsdarstellung mit dem Erwachen beginnen, ja sie darf eigentlich von nichts anderm handeln": Benjamin, GS, 5:580 ("As Proust begins his life's story with awakening, any historical account must begin with awakening, indeed must not treat of anything else"). Compare also 491, 1006, and 1058: "Erinnerung und Erwachen sind aufs Engste verwandt. Erwachen ist nämlich die dialektische, kopernikanische Wendung des Eingedenkens" ("Recollection and awakening are most intimately related. For awakening is the dialectical, Copernican turn of memorialization"). (For English translations, see Benjamin, *The Arcades Project* [Cambridge: Harvard University Press, 1999], 388f., 463f., 883, and passim.) Compare Horst Folkers, "Die gerettete Geschichte: Ein Hinweis auf Walter Benjamins Begriff der Erinnerung," *Mnemosyne* (1991): 363–77.

15. "[D]ie Anekdote darf wohl unkommentiert bleiben": Stern, "Umkehrung des déjà vu," 91–93 ("The anecdote can probably remain unannotated"). Compare Benjamin, "Fassung letzter Hand," GS, 7.1:410–11.

16. While the majority of these short pieces appeared during Benjamin's life, there is no reliable edition; three early pieces about childhood are not included in the *Gesammelte Schriften*. See Benjamin, "Kinder," *Die literarische Welt* 2, no. 49 (1926). Adorno's 1950 edition was included in vol. 4 of the *Gesammelte Schriften*, but after a typescript from 1938 had turned up in Paris in 1981, it was reproduced in vol. 7. Yet scholars cast doubt also on the status of this version, and point to an unpublished 1933 manuscript at the University of Gießen; see Detlev Schöttker, *Konstruktiver Fragmentarismus* (Frankfurt: Suhrkamp, 1999), 230.

17. Walter Benjamin, "The Work of Art in the Age of Mechanical Reproduction," in *Illuminations*, 240. Compare GS, 7.1:350–84.

18. Benjamin, "Zu Grenzgebieten: Einiges zur Volkskunst," GS, 6:186.

19. Fredric Jameson, *Postmodernism, or the Cultural Logic of Late Capitalism* (Durham: Duke University Press, 1991), 101–4.

20. Walter Benjamin, "Traumkitsch," GS, 2.2:620–22.

21. While Benjamin's *Theses on the Philosophy of History* make do without the concept of aura, he cast the forces of habit in terms of an aura without aura: it is formed not in

the aura of novelty but in that of habit, in recollection, childhood, and dream ("nicht in der Aura der Neuheit sondern in der der Gewöhnung. In Erninnerung, Kindheit und Traum": GS, 6.1:576).

22. Walter Benjamin, "Vergiß das Beste nicht," GS, 4.1:407.

23. Walter Benjamin, "Gewohnheit und Aufmerksamkeit," GS, 4.1:407–8.

24. In part, *The World of Dreams* by Havelock Ellis was popularizing, for the English-speaking world, an early reception of Freud's *Interpretation of Dreams*, but partly it went back to pre-Freudian modes of interpretation.

25. "Die Sprache des Traums liegt nicht in ihren Worten, sondern unter ihnen. Die Worte sind im Traum Zufallsprodukt des Sinns, welcher in der wortlosen Kontinuität eines Flusses liegt. Der Sinn ist in der Traumsprache versteckt nach Art einer Figur in einem Vexierbild. Es ist sogar möglich, daß der Ursprung der Vexierbilder in solcher Richtung zu suchen ist, sozusagen als Traumstenogramm": Benjamin, GS, 6:601.

26. "Sollte Erwachen die Synthesis sein aus der Thesis des Traumbewußtseins und der Antithesis des Wachbewußtseins? Dann wäre der Moment des Erwachens identisch mit dem Jetzt der Erkennbarkeit, in dem die Dinge ihre wahre Miene aufsetzen": Benjamin, GS, 5:579.

27. "Denn wer vermöchte mit einem Griff das Futter der Zeit nach außen zu kehren? Und doch heißt Träumeerzählen nichts anderes": Benjamin, GS, 4:991; compare *Gesammelte Briefe*, 1:336.

28. Sigmund Freud, "Psychopathologie des Alltagslebens", GW, 4:49; see Jacques Lacan, *Seminar I* (New York: Norton, 1988), 196f.

29. Benjamin, GS, 4:422.

30. "Zur Kenntnis der *mémoire involontaire:* ihre Bilder kommen nicht allein ungerufen, es handelt sich vielmehr in ihr um Bilder, die wir nie sahen, ehe wir uns ihrer erinnerten. Am deutlichsten ist das bei jenen Bildern, auf denen wir—genau wie in manchen Träumen—selber zu sehen sind. Wir stehen vor uns, wie wir wohl in Urvergangenheit einst irgendwo, doch nie vor unserem Blick, gestanden haben": Benjamin, GS, 2:1064.

31. Walter Killy, *Deutscher Kitsch* (Göttingen: Vandenhook & Ruprecht, 1964).

32. Jochen Schulte-Sasse, *Die Kritik an der Trivialliteratur seit der Aufklärung: Studien zur Geschichte des modernen Kitsch-Begriffs* (Munich: Fink, 1971); J. Schulte-Sasse, ed., *Literarischer Kitsch* (Tübingen: Niemeyer, 1979).

33. The majority of publications on kitsch in the twentieth century are polemically dismissive of it as an aberration of taste. See J. Schulte-Sasse, "Kitsch," *Historisches Wörterbuch der Philosophie* 4 (1976): 844–45. However, such certainty of taste leads into infinite reflection: if the rules define the example as aberration, who makes the rules?

34. Benjamin, "Zu Grenzgebieten," GS, 6:187.

35. Benjamin, "Traumkitsch," GS, 2.2:621.

36. Theodor Adorno, "Charakteristik Walter Benjamins," in *Prismen* (Frankfurt: Suhrkamp, 1955), 289.

37. "Wirkung des Moments": Killy, *Deutscher Kitsch*, 14.

38. Ludwig Giesz, *Phänomenologie des Kitsches* (Munich: Fink, 1971).

39. Compare Benjamin, GS, 2.1:217–18 and "Hochherrschaftlich möblierte Zehnzimmerwohnung," GS, 4.1:88–89. See Benjamin, *One-Way Street* (London: New Left Books,

1979), 158. The trace is the inverse of the aura: "In der Spur werden wir der Sache habhaft; in der Aura bemächtigt sie sich unser" (GS, 5.1:560).

40. "Etui": Walter Benjamin, "Zentralpark," GS, 1.2:671. Compare also 5.1:1054.

41. Walter Benjamin, "Der enhüllte Osterhase oder Kleine Verstecklehre," GS, 4.1:398–99.

42. Ernst Bloch, "Schreibender Kitsch," in *Erbschaft dieser Zeit* (Frankfurt: Suhrkamp, 1962), 28; Ernst Bloch, "Kitsch that Writes," in *Heritage of Our Times* (Berkeley: University of California Press, 1991). See Benjamin, GS, 2.2:622, as well as 5.1:500, and 5.2:1058.

43. Ernst Bloch, "Rettung Wagners durch surrealistische Kolportage," *Frankfurter Opernhefte* 4 (1975): 29ff.; Bloch concurs with Giesz in positing that Nietzsche on Wagner may be read as an early phenomenological analysis of kitsch. To be sure, the academic Benjamin-industry in turn generates Benjamin-kitsch.

44. Ernst Bloch, "Bilder des Déjà Vu," *Literarische Aufsätze*, in *Werkausgabe*, vol. 9 (Frankfurt: Suhrkamp, 1965), 232–42; now available in an unreliable translation: Ernst Bloch, "Images of Déjà Vu," in *Literary Essays* (Stanford: Stanford University Press, 1998), 200–9. In an important passage about extant superstitious ideas about déjà vu, the translation not only misrepresents Bloch's contempt for Jungian views on soul transmigration and ancestral memories; it also distorts Bloch's metaphor for how such views can persevere "in a vegetative mode," by ascribing it to "vegetarians" (203; compare the original, 235).

45. Gunter Krause, "Das Theater gegen die Schrift: The Enormous Room," *Cahiersd'Etudes-Germaniques* 20 (1991): 177–89.

46. Benjamin, GS, 5.1:280.

47. For further reading on what is hidden in technology, see Friedrich Kittler, *Grammophon Film Typewriter* (Berlin: Brinkmann und Bose, 1986). Translated as Friedrich Kittler, *Gramophone, Film, Typewriter* (Stanford: Stanford University Press, 1999).

48. But note that in his last version of the *Berlin Childhood*, Benjamin erased his discussion of déjà vu altogether. See "Fassung letzter Hand," GS, 7.1:410–11.

49. Here I disagree with Andrew Benjamin's reading in *Present Hope: Philosophy, Architecture, Judaism* (London: Routledge, 1997), 63–64.

50. Walter Benjamin, "Verstecktes Kind," GS, 4.1:115–16.

51. Walter Benjamin, "Verstecke," GS, 4.1:253–54.

52. Benjamin, "Über den Begriff der Geschichte," GS, 1.2:691–704.

53. Walter Benjamin, "Franz Kafka: Zur zehnten Wiederkehr seines Todestages," GS, 4.1:409–38, esp. 425–32; Walter Benjamin, "Franz Kafka: Beim Bau der Chinesischen Mauer," GS, 4.1:676–83.

54. Walter Benjamin, "Das bucklichte Männlein," GS, 2.2:425f.; see Rebecca Comay, "Benjamin's Endgame," in *Walter Benjamin's Philosophy: Destruction and Experience*, ed. Andrew Benjamin and Peter Osborne (London: Routledge, 1994), 258.

55. Irving Wohlfahrt, "Märchen für Dialektiker," in *Walter Benjamin und die Kinderliteratur*, ed. Doderer, 126; for déjà vu, see 145. Also Burkhardt Lindner, "Benjamins 'Bucklichtes Männlein': Zu einem Prosastück der 'Berliner Kindheit um neunzehnhundert,'" *Die Neue Gesellschaft: Frankfurter Hefte* 36 (1989): 445–50, and Burkhardt Lindner, "Zwerg und Engel: Benjamins geschichtsphilosophische Rätselfiguren und die Herausforderung des Mythos," in *Was nie geschrieben wurde, lessen: Frankfurter Benjamin-Vorträge*, ed. Lorenz Jäger and Thomas Regehly (Bielefeld: Aisthesis, 1992), 235–65.

56. For further reading, see Catherine Liu, *Copying Machines: Taking Notes for the Automaton* (Minneapolis: University of Minnesota Press, 2000).

57. Walter Benjamin, "Die Aufgabe des Übersetzers," GS, 4.1:9–10f.

58. Gershom Scholem, *Walter Benjamin und sein Engel* (Frankfurt: Suhrkamp, 1983), 22–37; Hanns Zischler, *Kafka Goes to the Movies* (Chicago: University of Chicago Press, 2003), 98–99.

59. "Das ist auch so ein Vergessenes, das bucklige Männlein, das wir einmal gewußt haben, und da hatte es seinen Frieden, nun aber vertritt es den Weg in die Zukunft": Benjamin, "Franz Kafka: Beim Bau der Chinesischen Mauer," GS, 4.1:682.

60. Theodor W. Adorno, *Aesthetic Theory* (Minneapolis: University of Minnesota Press, 1997), 239. Adorno, *Ästhetische Theorie* (Frankfurt: Suhrkamp, 1970), 355: "Kitsch ist nicht, wie der Bildungsglaube es möchte, bloßes Abfallprodukt der Kunst, entstanden durch treulose Akkomodation, sondern lauert in ihr auf die stets wiederkehrenden Gelegenheiten, aus der Kunst hervorzuspringen."

61. See Hannah Arendt, *Benjamin. Brecht. Zwei Essays* (Munich: Piper, 1971).

62. To see how Benjamin aligns aura and *mémoire involontaire*, compare GS, 1.2:637–48. We will return to this in discussing Andy Warhol on kitsch and aura.

63. See Galen Johnson, "Generosity and Forgetting in the History of Being," in *Continental Philosophy, vol. 5: Questioning Foundations*, ed. Hugh Silverman (London: Routledge, 1993), 196–212: "What would it mean to say that vision is similarly reversible? It does not mean that absurdity, that the trees and things I see also see me in return. Rather, in seeing objects, they reflect back to me an image of myself. Inanimate things do so only feebly." Compare also Maurice Merleau-Ponty: "There is no coinciding of the seer with the visible. But each borrows from the other" (*The Visible and the Invisible* [Evanston: Northwestern University Press, 1969], 261; *Le visible et l'invisible* [Paris: Gallimard, 1966], 314).

64. Walter Benjamin, GS, 3:194.

65. Walter Benjamin, "Metaphysik der Jugend: Das Gespräch," GS, 2.1:93; see Sigrid Weigel, *Entstellte Ähnlichkeit: Walter Benjamins theoretische Schreibweise* (Munich: Fischer, 1997), 139f.

66. Benjamin, GS, 2.1:95. See also 6:523 (letter to A. Lacis): "Denn jede Frau hat die Vergangenheit und jedenfalls keine Gegenwart" ("for every woman has the past and at any rate no present").

67. "Die Zeit des Schicksals ist die Zeit, die jederzeit gleichzeitig (nicht gegenwärtig) gemacht werden kann": Benjamin, GS, 6:91 ("The time of fate is the time that can be made synchronous at any time, but never present"); "Die Essenz des mythischen Geschehens ist Wiederkehr": GS, 5.1:178 ("The essence of mythic plot is return"); "Die 'ewige Wiederkunft alles Gleichen' ist das Zeichen des Schicksals": GS, 1.1:137 ("The 'eternal return of all the same' is the sign of fate"). See also Wilfried Menninghaus, *Schwellenkunde: Walter Benjamins Passage des Mythos* (Frankfurt: Suhrkamp, 1986).

68. Benjamin, GS, 1.2:663, 680, and passim.

69. Benjamin, "Das bucklichte Männlein," GS, 4.1:302–04.

70. Clemens Brentano, "Des Knaben Wunderhorn," in *Sämtliche Werke und Briefe*, vol. 9.3, ed. Heinz Rölleke (Stuttgart/Berlin/Cologne: Kohlhammer, 1978).

71. Comay, "Benjamin's Endgame," 258; also Scholem, *Walter Benjamin und sein Engel,* 22–37.

72. Walter Benjamin, "Das Kunstwerk im Zeitalter seiner technischen Reproduzierbarkeit," GS, 1.2:500.

73. See Benjamin, GS, 2.3:1064; compare 1.2:646. The significance of Venice for the provocation of déjà vu was marked in chapter 1, above.

74. Bettine Menke, "Das Nach-Leben im Zitat: Benjamins Gedächtnis der Texte," in *Gedächtniskunst: Raum–Bild–Schrift. Studien zur Mnemotechnik,* ed. Anselm Haverkamp and Renate Lachmann (Frankfurt: Suhrkamp, 1991), 74–110; compare Bettine Menke, *Sprachfiguren: Name–Allegorie–Bild nach Walter Benjamin* (Munich: Fink, 1991).

75. "Ein neues Manuskript, ein, winziges, Buch bringe ich mit, das Sie wundern wird": Benjamin in a letter to Adorno, 10 November 1932. Note that Edgar Allan Poe's article on Maelzel's Chess Player already mentioned "a remarkable stoop in the shoulders" of the dwarf.

76. Benjamin, "Berliner Kindheit um Neunzehnhundert," GS, 4.1:303.

77. "Daß diese Stufe vergessen ist, besagt nicht, daß sie in die Gegenwart nicht hineinragt. Vielmehr: gegenwärtig ist sie durch diese Vergessenheit": Benjamin, GS, 2.2:428 ("That this stage is forgotten does not imply that it does not reach into the present. Rather, it is present by way of that past"). Compare 2.3:1064: "Ihre Bilder kommen nicht allein ungerufen, es handelt sich vielmehr um Bilder, die wir nie sahen, ehe wir uns ihrer erinnerten" ("Its images not only arrive uncalled for, it is rather a matter of images that we never saw before we remembered them").

78. Benjamin, GS, 2.3:1236.

79. Walter Benjamin, "Zum Bilde Prousts," GS, 2.1:311: "Steht nicht das ungewollte Eingedenken, Prousts *mémoire involontaire* dem Vergessen viel näher als dem, was meist Erinnerung genannt wird?" ("Does not involuntary memorialization, Proust's *mémoire involontaire* come much closer to forgetting than to what is commonly called recollection?").

80. "die Tilgung von Erinnerung eine Leistung des allzu wachen Bewußtseins": Theodor W. Adorno, "Was bedeutet Aufarbeitung der Vergangenheit," in *Schriften,* vol. 10, pt. 2, ed. Rolf Tiedemann (Frankfurt: Suhrkamp, 1973), 558.

81. For Benjamin, the unique quality of the anachronistic images of *mémoire involontaire* in Proust is "that they have an aura": (GS, 1.2:646). In order for involuntary memory to recollect lost time in an instant, its images can never before have been conscious, but become memory by returning as such, for the first time.

3. POSTHISTOIRE IN RUINS

1. Heiner Müller, *Jenseits der Nation: Heiner Müller im Gespräch mit Frank M. Raddatz* (Berlin: Rotbuch, 1991), 23. All translations from the German are mine, unless otherwise marked. If I quote the original, it will be in the notes.

2. "Die großen Texte kennt man am *déjà vu.* Sie sagen was man weiß und verdrängen oder vergessen wollte": Heiner Müller, "Beschreibung einer Lektüre," *Theater der Zeit* 1/2 (1993): 42.

3. Forgetting and historical error, as Ernest Renan speculated at the end of the nineteenth century, can play a significant role in creating a nation, and advances in historiography might pose dangers to politics. See Ernest Renan, "Das Plebiszit des Vergeßlichen,"

Frankfurter Allgemeine Zeitung, 27 March 1993. Serious inquiries into the politics of memory in Germany include *Amnestie oder Die Politik der Erinnerung,* ed. Gary Smith and Avishai Margalit (Frankfurt: Suhrkamp, 1997) and the broad public debate after the (re)unification of Germany.

4. Müller, *Jenseits der Nation,* 31 and 71, respectively.

5. Paul-Gerhard Klussmann, "Deutschland-Denkmale: Umgestürzt: Zu Heiner Müllers Germania Tod in Berlin," in *Deutsche Misere einst und jetzt: Die deutsche Misere als Thema der Gegenwartsliteratur: Das Preussensyndrom in der Literatur der DDR,* ed. Paul-Gerhard Klussmann and Heinrich Mohr (Bonn: Bouvier, 1982), 159–76.

6. Pierre Nora, *Les Lieux de Mémoire* (Paris: Gallimard, 1982–92), vol. 1, *La République,* vol. 2, *La Nation,* vol. 3, *Les France.* Compare Pierre Nora, "Between Memory and History: Les Lieux de Mémoire," *Representations* 26 (1989): 7–24.

7. "On ne parle tant de mémoire que parce qu'il n'y en a plus": Nora, *Les Lieux de Mémoire,* 1: xvii ("One only talks so much of memory because it no longer exists"). See also Lutz Niethammer, *Posthistoire: ist die Geschichte zu Ende?* (Hamburg: Rowohlt, 1989), esp. 151 f. (on Heiner Müller).

8. Karlheinz Barck, "Passé vecu / mémoire absente: Gedächtnis und ästhetische Reflexion," in *Metamorphosen: Gedächtnismedien im Computerzeitalter,* ed. Götz-Lothar Darsow (Stuttgart: Frommann-Holzboog, 2000), 64.

9. "Die Handlung ist beliebig, da die Folgen Vergangenheit sind, Explosion einer Erinnerung in einer abgestorbenen Struktur": Heiner Müller, "Bildbeschreibung," in *Heiner Müller Material: Texte und Kommentare,* ed. Frank Hörnigk (Göttingen: Steidl, 1989), 14 ("The action is random, since the consequences are past, explosion of a memory in a mortified structure").

10. Heiner Müller, "*Der glücklose Engel*" (1958), in *Rotwelsch* (Berlin: Merve, 1982), 87; translated as "The Luckless Angel," in *Germania,* ed. Sylvère Lotringer (New York: Semiotexte, 1990), 99. Compare Heiner Müller, *Tractor,* in *Plays, Prose, Poems* (New York: PAJ Publications, 1989). Heiner Müller, *Theatremachine* (London: Faber & Faber, 1995). Heiner Müller, *Hamletmachine,* in *The Task, Hamletmachine and Other Texts for the Stage,* ed. and trans. Carl Weber (New York: PAJ Publications, 1984).

11. Heiner Müller, "Herakles 2 oder Die Hydra," in *Heiner Müller Material,* ed. Hörnigk, 74–77.

12. Arlene Akiko Teraoka attempts a "postmodernist" reading in "Writing and Violence in Heiner Müller's 'Bildbeschreibung,'" in *Vom Wort zum Bild: Das neue Theater in Deutschland und den USA,* ed. Sigrid Bauschinger and Susan Cocalis (Bern: Peter Lang, 1992), 179–98.

13. "Dichtung in einer Erfahrung fundiert . . . , der das Chokerlebnis zur Norm geworden ist": Walter Benjamin, "Über einige Motive bei Baudelaire," GS, 1.2: 614 ("Literature is founded on an experience which has normalized shocks"); compare 632, 636, and 652. War experience increases the perception of shock and leads to a loss of storytelling, since people returned from the war poorer in experience, not richer.

14. Heiner Müller, "Der Schrecken ist die erste Erscheinung," in *Rotwelsch;* see Bertolt Brecht, "Dialog über Schauspielkunst" (1929), in *Werke,* vol. 21 (Berlin: Aufbau, 1992).

15. "Ich fange an, meinen Text zu vergessen. Ich bin ein Sieb. Immer mehr Worte fallen

hindurch. Bald werde ich keine andere Stimme mehr hören als meine Stimme, die nach vergessenen Worten fragt": Heiner Müller, *Herzstück* (Berlin: Rotbuch, 1983), 35.

16. Bertolt Brecht, "Kleines Organon für das Theater," in *Werke*, vol. 23 (Berlin: Aufbau, 1993).

17. Paul Virilio, *War and Cinema: The Logistics of Perception* (London: Verso, 1989).

18. Theodor W. Adorno, "Out of the Firing Line," in *Minima Moralia* (London: Verso, 1978), 54. Adorno, "Weit vom Schuß," in *Minima Moralia* (Frankfurt: Suhrkamp, 1973), 59–61: ". . . mit jeder Explosion hat er den Reizschutz durchbrochen, unter dem Erfahrung, die Dauer zwischen heilsamem Vergessen und heilsamem Erinnern sich bildet."

19. Theodor W. Adorno, "To Them Shall No Thoughts Be Turned," *Minima Moralia* (London), 47. Adorno, "Nicht gedacht soll ihrer werden," in *Minima Moralia* (Frankfurt), 52: ". . . selbst das Vergangene ist nicht mehr sicher vor der Gegenwart, die es nochmals dem Vergessen weiht, indem sie es erinnert."

20. Michael Opitz and Erdmut Wizisla, "Jetzt sind eher die infernalischen Aspekte bei Benjamin wichtig: Gespräch mit Heiner Müller," in *Aber ein Sturm weht vom Paradiese her: Texte zu Walter Benjamin*, ed. Michael Opitz and Erdmut Wizisla (Leipzig: Reclam, 1992), 348–62.

21. "Den Pessimismus organisieren: Heiner Müller liest Walter Benjamin. Aufzeichnung einer Lesung in den Hamburger Kammerspielen vom 4. 11. 1990." Audiocassette: 52 minutes (Berlin: Alexander Verlag, 1998).

22. See Müller, "Der glücklose Engel," 87; "The Luckless Angel," 99. See Francine Maier-Schaeffer, "Utopie und Fragment: Heiner Müller und Walter Benjamin," in *Heiner Müller: Rückblicke, Perspektiven. Vorträge des Pariser Kolloquiums 1993*, ed. Theo Buck and Jean-Marie Valentin (Frankfurt-New York: Peter Lang, 1995).

23. See Thomas Weber, "Glücklose Engel: Über ein Motiv bei Heiner Müller und Walter Benjamin," *Das Argument* 35, no. 198 (1993): 241–53; Helen Fehervary, "Enlightenment or Entanglement: History and Aesthetics in Bertolt Brecht and Heiner Müller," *New German Critique* 8 (1976): 93. See also Jost Hermand and Helen Fehervary, *Mit den Toten Reden: Fragen an Heiner Müller* (Cologne: Böhlau, 1999).

24. Cited after Opitz and Wizisla, "Jetzt sind eher die infernalischen Aspekte bei Benjamin wichtig," 348–62. There, we also find another literary echo of Müller's impact on German writing: "Der Heinermüller ist aus dem Holz jener Schamanen geschnitzt, die auf den 'Brettern, die die Welt bedeuten,' die Asche der Visionen säen. Bitternis und Trauer haben ihm einst schmerzbetäubende Flügel verliehen, von denen ihm aber der Rechte immer wieder unter die Räder des Weltgeschehens gerät, woraufhin er immer wieder mit der Linken in 'Richtung Deutschland' abwinkt" (Andreas Koziol) ("The Heinermüller is cut from the wood of those shamans who sow the ashes of visions on the theater planks that mean the world. Bitterness and mourning had once given him numbing wings, but the right one of them always gets under the wheels of world events, which makes him wave the left one towards Germany").

25. Müller, *The Task, Hamletmachine and Other Texts for the Stage*, 87.

26. Heiner Müller, *Gesammelte Irrtümer 2* (Frankfurt: Verlag der Autoren, 1990), 63.

27. "Reise aus der Vergangenheit rückwärts in die Gegenwart, denn die Vergangenheit liegt vor uns und die Zukunft, die in der Gegenwart eingeschlossen war, hinter uns": Heiner Müller, *Gesammelte Irrtümer 3* (Frankfurt: Verlag der Autoren, 1994), 123.

28. Müller, *Gesammelte Irrtümer 2*, 148.

29. "Die ganze Technik drängt auf Auslöschung von Erinnerung": Müller, *Jenseits der Nation*, 70–71.

30. For this reading of Baudelaire, compare Hans Jost Frey, "Über die Erinnerung bei Baudelaire," *Symposion* 33, no. 4 (1979): 312–30, and Manfred Koch, *Mnemotechnik des Schönen: Studien zur poetischen Erinnerung in Romantik und Symbolismus* (Tübingen: Narr, 1988), 103–50.

31. "wirkliche Erinnerung ein Bild zugleich von dem der sich erinnert": Walter Benjamin, "Ausgraben und Erinnern," GS, 4.1:400–401.

32. Walter Benjamin, "Zum Bilde Prousts," GS, 2.1:311. Also see Carol Jacobs, "Walter Benjamin: Image of Proust," *MLN* 86, no. 6 (1971): 910–32.

33. "Wie früher Geister kamen aus Vergangenheit / so jetzt aus Zukunft ebenso": Heiner Müller, *Krieg ohne Schlacht. Leben in zwei Diktaturen* (Cologne: Böhlau, 1992), 361. This favored citation from Bertolt Brecht, *Der Untergang des Egoisten Johann Fatzer. Bühnenfassung von Heiner Müller* (Frankfurt: Suhrkamp, 1994), 73, is also found in Müller, *Jenseits der Nation*, 62, and Alexander Kluge and Heiner Müller, *"Ich bin ein Landvermesser": Gespräche. Neue Folge* (Hamburg: Rowohlt, 1996), 135. See also Uwe Wittstock, "Die schnellen Wirkungen sind nicht die neuen: Ein Porträt des Dramatikers Heiner Müller," *Text und Kritik* 73 (January 1982): 10–19.

34. Gerhart Pickerodt, "Zwischen Erinnern und Verdrängen: Heiner Müllers Autobiographie 'Krieg ohne Schlacht. Leben in zwei Diktaturen,'" *Cahiers-d'Etudes-Germaniques* 29 (1995): 63–71.

35. Müller, *Krieg ohne Schlacht*, 299: "einzige Möglichkeit, meine Texte zu vergessen, ein Befreiungsakt, eine Therapie."

36. One of the very last interviews with Heiner Müller before his death was conducted by my colleague at Konstanz, Hendrik Werner, and recorded as "Krapp's tape" with my dictaphone; the transcript is published on my Heiner Müller Web site, work on which ceased after Müller's death that same year: I have not touched it since (see http://www.hydra.umn.edu/mueller/ for an index to my pages under the sign of Müller's "Herakles 2 oder Die Hydra"). This chapter closely follows that historic interview, subsequently published (or buried in the archive) as "'Verwaltungsakte produzieren keine Erfahrungen': Zum Supergedenkjahr: Heiner Müller im Gespräch mit Hendrik Werner," in *Bibliographie Heiner Müller*, vol. 2, *1993–1995*, ed. Ingo Schmidt and Florian Vaßen (Bielefeld: Haux, 1996), 335–46.

37. "Die erste ist ein Gang auf den Friedhof mit meiner Großmutter. Da stand ein Denkmal für Gefallene des Ersten Weltkriegs, aus Porphyr, eine gewaltige Figur, eine Mutter. Für mich verband sich das Kriegerdenkmal jahrelang mit einem lila Mutterbild, mit Angst besetzt, auch vor der Großmutter vielleicht, die mich über den Friedhof führte": Müller, *Krieg ohne Schlacht*, 18.

38. Oskar Negt and Alexander Kluge, *Öffentlichkeit und Erfahrung: Zur Organisationsanalyse von bürgerlicher Öffentlichkeit* (Frankfurt: Suhrkamp, 1972), 447.

39. Klaus Theweleit, *Heiner Müller: Traumtext* (Basel: Stroemfeld, 1996), 26.

40. Hans-Thies Lehmann, "Theater der Blicke: Zu Heiner Müllers Bildbeschreibung," in *Dramatik der DDR*, ed. Ulrich Profitlich (Frankfurt: Suhrkamp, 1987), 186–202.

41. Müller, *Rotwelsch*, 72.

42. "Objekt von Geschichte": Müller, *Rotwelsch*, 67; "Gegenstand von Politik": Müller, *Gesammelte Irrtümer 2*, 170. Compare Walter Benjamin, "Über einige Motive bei Baudelaire," GS, 1.2:611, and Heiner Müller, *"Ich bin ein Neger": Diskussion mit Heiner Müller* (Darmstadt: Georg Buechner, 1986), 28 and 35.

43. Heiner Müller, *Gesammelte Irrtümer* (Frankfurt: Verlag der Autoren, 1989), 31–35.

44. Theodor Reik, *Der überraschte Psychologe: Über Erraten und Verstehen unbewußter Vorgänge* (Leiden: n.p., 1935), 132.

45. "Das Vergessen ist kein Gegenteil des Erinnerns, denn dessen Gegenteil wäre vollkommener Ausfall, einer, an dem gar nichts betrifft, an dem keine Mahnung statthat, zu dem überhaupt kein besinnender Weg führen kann. Das Vergessen ist aus gleichem Grund auch kein Gegenteil des Hoffnungs-Eingedenkens, vielmehr: Vergessen ist ein Modus der Erinnerung wie des Eingedenkens, ist jenes Defiziens, das im Gedächtnis Verlassen, im Eingedenken Verrat heißt. Vergessen ist so Mangel an Treue und wieder nicht einer Treue gegen Erloschenes, sondern gegen Unabgegoltenes": Ernst Bloch, "Tübinger Einleitung in die Philosophie," *Werkausgabe*, vol. 13 (Frankfurt: Suhrkamp, 1970), 282.

46. Reinhart Koselleck, "Einleitung," in *Der politische Totenkult: Kriegerdenkmäler in der Moderne*, ed. R. Kosellek and Michael Jeismann (Munich: Fink, 1994), 20.

47. Hans-Thies Lehmann even claims that the figure of a remainder, a supplementary excess is constitutive for Müller's manifold contradictions and could only be articulated appropriately with Jacques Derrida's *De la grammatologie*. See Hans-Thies Lehmann, "Raum-Zeit," *Text und Kritik* 73 (1982): 81, n. 11.

48. Frank-Michael Raddatz, *Dämonen unterm Roten Stern: Zu Geschichtsphilosophie und Ästhetik Heiner Müllers* (Stuttgart: Metzler, 1991), 24.

49. See Heiner Müller, *Theater-Arbeit* (Berlin: Rotbuch, 1975), 7.

50. Heiner Müller, *Medeaspiel*, in *Die Umsiedlerin oder Das Leben auf dem Lande* (Berlin: Rotbuch, 1975), 17.

51. Heiner Müller, *Verkommenes Ufer Medeamaterial Landschaft mit Argonauten* (Bochum: Theater 1983), 92.

52. Marianne Streisand, "'Mein Platz, wenn mein Drama noch stattfinden würde, wäre auf beiden Seiten der Front, zwischen den Fronten, darüber': Über das Arbeitsprinzip der Gleichzeitigkeit bei Heiner Müller," *Weimarer Beiträge* 37, no. 4 (1991): 485–508; and Matias Mieth, "Zur Rezeption von Heiner Müller in DDR und BRD: Eine Erinnerung an das Verhältnis von politischer und ästhetischer Wertung," *Weimarer Beiträge* 37, no. 4 (1991): 604–14. Compare Marianne Streisand, "'Das Theater braucht den Widerstand der Literatur': Heiner Müllers Beitrag zu Veränderungen des Verständnisses von Theater in der DDR," *Weimarer Beiträge* 34, no. 7 (1988): 1156–79.

53. Heiner Müller, *Shakespeare Factory 2* (Berlin: Rotbuch, 1989), 216; see Norbert-Otto Eke, "'Der Neger schreibt ein andres Alphabet': Anmerkungen zu Heiner Müllers dialektischem Denk-Spiel Anatomie Titus Fall of Rome ein Shakespearekommentar," *Zeitschrift für Deutsche Philologie* 110, no. 2 (1991): 294–315.

54. See Klaus Theweleit, *Männerphantasien*, vol. 1, *Frauen, Fluten, Körper, Geschichte* (Frankfurt: Suhrkamp, 1977), 135ff.

55. Käthe Kollwitz, *"Ich will wirken in dieser Zeit": Auswahl* (Berlin: Siedler, 1981), 54–73. Later styled as a pacifist, Kollwitz in fact glorified war and sacrifice: "Das Denkmal

soll Peters Gestalt haben . . . , es soll dem Opfertod der jungen Kriegsfreiwilligen gelten. Es ist ein wundervolles Ziel" (55; "The memorial should have Peter's look . . . it is supposed to be devoted to the sacrificial death of the young war volunteers. It is a wonderful goal"). About her necrophiliac tendencies, see Sigrid Weigel, "Pathologie und Normalisierung," in *Vom Nutzen des Vergessens,* ed. Gary Smith and Hinderk Emrich (Leipzig: Akademie Verlag, 1996), 256–61, and Sibylle Tönnies: "Armer Peter, armes Deutschland," *Merkur* 6 (1994): 491–500.

56. Reinhart Koselleck, "Kriegerdenkmale als Identitätstiftungen der Überlebenden," in *Identität,* ed. Odo Marquard and Karlheinz Stierle, *Poetik und Hermeneutik 8* (Munich: Fink, 1979), 255–75.

57. Heiner Müller, *Frankfurter Allgemeine Zeitung,* 26 October 1995.

58. Heiner Müller, *Süddeutsche Zeitung,* 30 October 1995.

59. Müller, here again makes allusion to Benjamin's *Theses on the Philosophy of History.*

60. Kluge and Müller, *"Ich bin ein Landvermesser,"* 178.

61. Walter Benjamin, "Traumkitsch," GS, 2.2:620–22.

62. Walter Benjamin, "Zu Grenzgebieten: Einiges zur Volkskunst," GS, 6:187.

63. Bernhard Sorg, "Mythos Geschichte: Erzählen nach dem realen Sozialismus," in *Literaturkritik und erzählerische Praxis: Deutschsprachige Erzähler der Gegenwart,* ed. Herbert Herzmann (Tübingen: Stauffenburg, 1995), 15–23.

64. Müller, "Beschreibung einer Lektüre," 41–43.

65. Peter Sloterdijk, *Kritik der zynischen Vernunft* (Frankfurt: Suhrkamp, 1983), 2:760.

66. For the illegitimate grip of state and mother on the dead, see Müller, *Jenseits der Nation,* 49–50; Müller, *Zur Lage der Nation: Heiner Müller im Interview mit Frank M. Raddatz* (Berlin: Rotbuch, 1990), 56; Müller, *Krieg ohne Schlacht,* 321; Müller, *"Ich schulde der Welt einen Toten": Gespräche mit Alexander Kluge* (Hamburg: Rowohlt, 1995), 106.

67. Heiner Müller, "Mommsens Block," in *Drucksache 1 des Berliner Ensembles* (Berlin: Berliner Ensemble, 1993), 8.

68. Norbert-Otto Eke, "'Deutschland ortlos': Dekonstruktionen des Nationalen bei Heiner Müller," in *Dichter und ihre Nation,* ed. Helmut Scheuer (Frankfurt: Suhrkamp, 1993), 490–506.

69. Heiner Müller, "Quartett," *Filmkritik* no. 293 (1993), 206.

70. Uwe Wittstock, "'Zehn Deutsche sind dummer als fünf': Gespräch mit dem Dramatiker Heiner Müller," *Neue Rundschau* 103 (1992): 66–78.

71. Wolfgang Emmerich, "Orpheus in der DDR: Heiner Müllers Autorschaft," in *Metamorphosen des Dichters: Das Rollenverstandnis deutscher Schriftsteller vom Barock bis zur Gegenwart,* ed. Gunter Grimm (Frankfurt: Fischer, 1992), 286–301.

72. Müller, *Jenseits der Nation,* 23.

73. "Gedächtnis ist ja für Leute, die Kunst machen, etwas ganz anderes. Es geht nicht primär um das Erinnern von Ereignissen. Das können Maschinen letztlich vielleicht besser: das Erinnern von Fakten. Es geht um das Erinnern von Emotionen, von Affekten, die im Zusammenhang mit Ereignissen stehen. Um ein emotionales Gedächtnis. Und das ist es, was das Erinnerte zu Material in dem Sinne macht, daß man über dieses emotionale Gedächtnis Traditionen bilden und Erfahrungen tradieren kann. Da geht es

gar nicht um Fakten. Das ist auch der Punkt, wo es im Grunde irrelevant wird, ob im historischen Roman oder Drama Ereignisse in der Folge abgebildet werden, in der sie aufgetreten sind, oder ob man die Chronologie ändert: der Unterschied zwischen der empirischen Wahrheit und der historischen. Die historische ist manchmal gar nicht identisch mit der empirischen, weil die Ereignisse, wenn sie manifest werden, oft schon vorbei sind. Sie sind vorher passiert, die eigentliche Bewegung hat längst stattgefunden": Müller, "Verwaltungsakte produzieren keine Erfahrungen," in *Bibliographie Heiner Müller*, 342.

74. This is echoed in Heiner Müller's cultural-conservative commentary: "die ganze Technik drängt auf Auslöschung von Erinnerung" (*Jenseits der Nation*, 70).

75. In "Shakespeare eine Differenz," Heiner Müller writes: "Unsre Aufgabe, oder der Rest wird Statistik sein und eine Sache der Computer, ist die Arbeit an der Differenz": *Shakespeare Factory 1* (Berlin: Rotbuch, 1985). See Roland Petersohn, *Heiner Müllers Shakespeare-Rezeption: Texte und Kontexte* (Frankfurt: Peter Lang, 1992).

76. Walter Benjamin, "Kriegerdenkmal," GS, 4.1:121.

77. Hans-Thies Lehmann, "Über Heiner Müllers Arbeit," *Merkur* 7 (1996): 541.

78. "Müller hinterläßt uns ein Revolutionspanoptikum über das eine große romantische Thema: die verratene Revolution. Verrat Verrat Verrat—das ist das immer gleiche Garn, mit dem er alle seine Stoffe zusammengenäht hat. Ein hübsches Thema für germanistische Doktorarbeiten": Wolf Biermann, "Die Müller-Maschine," *Der Spiegel* 2 (1996): 161 ("Müller leaves us a revolutionary panopticon about the grand romantic theme: treason of the revolution. Treason treason treason—that is the ever same yarn with which he has stitched together all his material. A nice topic for German doctoral theses"). A good example is Hendrik Werner, *Im Namen des Verrats: Heiner Müllers Gedächtnis der Texte* (Würzburg: Königshausen und Neumann, 2001).

79. "Hinter ihm schwemmt Vergangenheit an, schütte Geröll auf Flügel und Schultern, mit Lärm wie von begrabnen Trommeln, während vor ihm die Zukunft staut, seine Augen eindrückt, die Augäpfel sprengt wie ein Stern, das Wort umdreht zum tönenden Knebel, ihn würgt mit seinem Atem. Eine Zeit lang sieht man noch sein Flügelschlagen, hört in das Rauschen die Steinschläge vor über hinter ihm niedergehn, lauter je heftiger die vergebliche Bewegung, vereinzelt, wenn sie langsamer wird. Dann schließt sich über ihm der Augenblick: auf dem schnell verschütteten Stehplatz kommt der glücklose Engel zur Ruhe, wartend auf Geschichte in der Versteinerung von Flug Blick Atem. Bis das erneute Rauschen mächtiger Flügelschläge sich in Wellen durch den Stein fortpflanzt und seinen Flug anzeigt": Heiner Müller, "Der glücklose Engel," in *Heiner Müller Material*, ed. Hörnigk, 8 (my translation). See Frank Hörnigk, "Texte, die auf Geschichte warten: Zum Geschichtsbegriff Heiner Müllers," in *Heiner Müller Material*, ed. Hörnigk, 123–37.

4. ANDY'S WEDDING

1. This chapter grew out of a research project on answering machines begun in 1995 at Konstanz University, and it was first presented in July 1996 at the University of Aberdeen. The heritage of Konstanz (from Jauss and Stierle to Lachmann and Assmann) is strongly audible in it, and ever since then, it has found itself under surveillance. The

constellation of my work between Samuel Beckett's *Dernière Bande (Krapp's Last Tape)*, my rather *cherché* Proust citation, and the even more obscure Gadamer quote, has repeatedly found itself broadcast elsewhere, and the tape of appropriation is still running. Such is the anonymous character of media. An early, shorter version of this text was published as "Andy's Wedding: Reading Warhol," in *Sensual Reading: New Approaches to Reading in Its Relations to the Senses,* ed. Ian MacLachlan and Michael Syrotinski (Lewisburg, PA: Bucknell University Press, 2000), 295–310.

2. Both citations from Gretchen Berg, "Nothing to Lose: Interview with Andy Warhol," *Cahiers du Cinema in English* 10 (May 1967): 30.

3. Jordan Mekas, "Notes after Reseeing the Movies of Andy Warhol," in *Andy Warhol*, ed. J. Coplans (New York: New York Graphic Society, 1970), 146; compare also Andy Warhol, "Why I Love to Live Fast," *High Times* 33 (May 1978).

4. Theodor W. Adorno, "Aufzeichnungen zu Kafka," in *Versuch das Endspiel zu verstehen* (Frankfurt: Suhrkamp, 1973), 138. English as "Notes on Kafka" in *Prisms* (Boston: MIT Press, 1981), 245–71.

5. Theodor W. Adorno, "Freudian Theory and the Pattern of Fascist Propaganda," in *The Essential Frankfurt School Reader,* ed. Andrew Arato and Eike Gebhardt (New York: Continuum, 1982), 133; Max Horkheimer and Theodor W. Adorno, *Dialectic of Enlightenment* (New York: Continuum, 1972), 172. Warhol's delight in repetition is perhaps best illustrated by his 4 times 15 minutes of nothing but "Uh yes. Uh no" in a loop, recorded on CD with an introduction by Ivan Karp (Pittsburgh: Sooj Records, 1996).

6. Karl Heinz Haag, "Das Unwiederholbare," in *Zeugnisse: Theodor W. Adorno zum sechzigsten Geburtstag,* ed. Max Horkheimer (Frankfurt: Europäische Verlagsanstalt 1963), 152–61. See Gianni Vattimo, "L'impossible oubli," in *Usages de l'Oubli: Colloque de Royaumont* (Paris: Seuil, 1988), 83: "Je dirai que l'art . . . se découvre de plus en plus lié aux mecanismes du marché, à la vie quotidienne, et qu'on voit disparaître la distinction entre art 'haut' et mode, création du consensus social, *Kitsch* peut-être" ("I might say that art finds itself more and more bound up with market mechanisms, everyday life, and that one can see the distinctions disappear between 'high' art and fashion, creation of social consensus, even kitsch").

7. Kenneth E. Silver, "Déjà Vu: Warhols Kunst des Industriell Naiven," in *Andy Warhol Retrospektive,* ed. Zdenek Felix (Stuttgart: Galerie, 1993), 15–31.

8. Hans Georg Gadamer, "Der 'eminente' Text und seine Wahrheit," *Sprache und Literatur in Wissenschaft und Unterricht* 57 (1986): 6: "Ein geschriebener Text soll nicht einfach wie ein Taperecorder Gesprochenes als solches festhalten, das zwar als Gesprochenes verständlich sein möchte, aber in bloßer Fixierung der Rede an die Grenze der Unverständlichkeit gerät." Gadamer presented this argument in Minneapolis in 1985; a footnote confirms that before it went into print, it had to be "completed" for the sake of such "comprehensibility."

9. See Jacques Derrida, *Speech and Phenomena, and Other Essays on Husserl's Theory of Signs* (Evanston: Northwestern University Press, 1973), 80–87.

10. Andy Warhol, *The Philosophy of Andy Warhol from A to B and Back Again* (London: Picador, 1975), 32. See anon., "Briefly Noted: Andy Warhol, *a: a novel,*" *New Yorker* (4 January 1969), 82.

11. Pat Hackett, ed., *The Andy Warhol Diaries* (New York: Warner Books, 1989); Andy Warhol and Pat Hackett, *POPism: The Warhol '60s* (London: Hutchinson, 1981).

12. Andy Warhol, *a. a novel* (New York: Grove Press, 1968). (Further references by page numbers in the text.) Extracts from this book, this novel way of writing "a novel," were published in French as "How to become a professional homosexual": *Comment devenir un homosexuel professionnel: Extrait de A* (Paris: Panoplie de l'Amateur, 1979).

13. Niklas Luhmann, "The Form of Writing," in *Problems of Form*, ed. Dirk Baecker (Stanford: Stanford University Press, 1998), 35; Ernst Jünger, *Autor und Autorschaft* (Stuttgart: Klett-Cotta, 1984), 430.

14. "Comme on ne peut pas téléphoner toujours, on lit. On ne lit qu'a la dernière extrémité. On téléphone d'abord beaucoup": Marcel Proust, "Journées de lecture 1907," in *Journées de Lecture* (Paris: 10/18 Editions, 1980), 59–66; compare Walter Benjamin, "Telephon," *Berliner Kindheit um Neunzehnhundert* (Frankfurt: Suhrkamp, 1950), 22–25.

15. Frank O'Hara, "Personism: A Manifesto," in *The Collected Poems of Frank O'Hara*, (New York: Alfred Knopf, 1971), 498–99; Franc Schuerewegen, "A Telephone Conversation," *Diacritics* 25, no. 2 (1995): 32. See Sally Beauman, "a: a novel," *New York Times Book Review* (4 January 1969), 4.

16. Avital Ronell, *The Telephone Book: Technology, Schizophrenia, Electric Speech* (Lincoln: Nebraska University Press, 1989).

17. In a variation on Ovid, "SONY est, qui vivit in illa." See Ovid, *Metamorphoses* (Bloomington: Indiana University Press, 1955), verses 400–401.

18. Warhol, *The Philosophy of Andy Warhol*, 94–95.

19. R. Olivio, "Ondine, New York 16. December 1978," *Köln & 1* (1995). As Bockris reports, even with the aid of chemicals, Warhol and Olivio took four sessions between 1965 and 1967 to complete the project. Victor Bockris, "A: A Glossary," in Andy Warhol, *a. a novel*, repr. ed. (New York: Grove Press, 1998), 253.

20. Paul Carroll, "What's a Warhol," *Playboy* 16, no. 9 (1969): n.p.

21. Warhol, *The Philosophy of Andy Warhol*, 26. Warhol himself was not only casting and staging this, he participated, as for instance in the 1979 film *Cocaine Cowboys*, where he plays the distant, voyeuristic character who always carries a camera or a tape recorder or both. This persona soon was how he was known off screen, too. See Branden W. Joseph, "Nothing Special: Andy Warhol and the Rise of Surveillance," in *CRTL[SPACE]*, ed. Thomas Levin et al. (Boston: MIT Press, 2002), 237–51.

22. Daniel Boorstin, *The Americans: The Democratic Experience* (New York: Vintage, 1974), 359ff.

23. Robert Lucky, *Silicon Dreams: Information, Man, and Machine* (New York: St. Martin's Press, 1991), 202

24. A. R. Luria, *The Mind of a Mnemonist* (New York: Basic Books, 1968), 66. The Art of Forgetting, developed here long before Umberto Eco, took Luria's patient deeply into the realm of screen memories; it is perhaps sufficient to stress here that writing down and burning his notes of what he wanted to forget did not work, contrary to a widespread assumption about this text. (That method is of course already used in Orwell's *1984*.)

25. See Boorstin, *The Americans*, 379, and the biography of Thomas Alva Edison by Robert Conot, *A Streak of Luck* (New York: Seaview, 1980).

26. Tania Grossinger, *The Book of Gadgets* (New York: McKay, 1974), 76–77. Andy Warhol not only graced the cover of the October 1965 issue of *Tape Recording* magazine, he also demonstrated the technical dimension of his gadget love when he told the interviewer: "Really good, synthesized sound is one of the most exciting things about home video tapes. There is no 'double-system' sound or editing needed. The only thing to be careful about is the position of the microphone. A little experimenting before taping is all that's needed." "Pop Goes the Video Tape: An Underground Interview with Andy Warhol," *Tape Recording* 12, no. 5 (1965), 19.

27. As Koch declares, "voyeurism dominates all Warhol's early film and defines their aesthetics": Stephen Koch, *Stargazer: The Life, World, and Films of Andy Warhol* (New York: Marion Boyars, 1991), 42. However, Branden Joseph objects that voyeurism takes as its objects unsuspecting people. Whether Warhol would prefer Debord's spectacle to Foucault's surveillance is a matter of speculation, but certainly his actors can still become the unwitting "victims" of his recording if they are aware of his actions. See Joseph, "Nothing Special," 240, and Stephen Paul Miller, *The Seventies Now: Culture as Surveillance* (Durham: Duke University Press, 1999), esp. 236f.

28. Roland Barthes, *A Lover's Discourse: Fragments* (New York: Hill & Wang, 1981), 115.

29. Steven Lubar, *InfoCulture: The Smithsonian Book of Information Age Inventions* (Boston: Houghton Mifflin, 1993).

30. Cited after the catalogue of *Sammlung Marx: Andy Warhol, Frühe Zeichnungen*, ed. Heiner Bastian (Munich: Galerie, 1996).

31. Friedrich Kittler, "Draculas Vermächtnis," in *ZETA 02 Mit Lacan*, ed. Dieter Hombach (Berlin: Rotation Verlag, 1982), 103–36; translated as "Dracula's Legacy," in *Literature, Media, Information Systems* (Amsterdam: G+B Arts, 1997), 51.

32. Richard Matheson, "Person to Person," in *I Am Legend* (New York: Tom Doherty Associates, 1995), 294–317.

33. Jacques Derrida, *Ulysse Gramophone* (Paris: Galilée, 1987).

34. Olivio, "Ondine, New York 16. December 1978."

35. In 1990, Christopher Hitchens recounted these anecdotes in the *London Review of Books*; see his book *For the Sake of the Argument* (London: Verso, 1993), 282–86.

36. Robert Mazzocco, "aaaaaa..." *New York Review of Books* (8 December 1969).

37. Northrop Frye, *Anatomy of Criticism* (Princeton: Princeton University Press, 1957), 345. (Note how Kierkegaard's take on repetition and happiness stands in sharp contrast to Adorno, the Frankfurt School class president who wrote a dissertation on him. Kierkegaard, coming back home to seek happiness in repetition, found that his servant had changed everything in his rooms and upon the unexpected return of his employer turned very white and shut the door in Kierkegaard's face, so that he felt "treated like a ghost.")

38. Lacan formulates a convergence: "Ainsi Freud se trouve-t-il apporter la solution au problème qui, pour le plus aigu des questionneurs de l'âme avant lui—Kierkegaard—s'etait déjà centré sur la répétition" (Jacques Lacan, *Le Seminaire livre XI: Les quartre concepts fondamentaux de la psychanalyse (1964)* [Paris: Seuil, 1973], 71; "Thus Freud finds himself approaching a problem which for the most acute questioner of the soul before him—Kierkegaard—was already centered around repetition").

39. Laurence Rickels, *Aberrations of Mourning: Writing on German Crypts* (Detroit: Wayne State University Press, 1988), and Laurence Rickels, *The Case of California* (Baltimore: The Johns Hopkins University Press, 1991).

40. Further reading: John Hollander, *The Figure of Echo* (Berkeley: University of California Press, 1981); John Brenkman, "Narcissus in the Text," *Georgia Review* 30 (1976): 310–21; Claire Nouvet, "An Impossible Response: The Disaster of Narcissus," *Yale French Studies* 79 (1991): 103–34; Maurice Blanchot, *The Writing of Disaster* (Lincoln: University of Nebraska Press, 1995); Anne Berger, "The Latest Word from Echo," *New Literary History* 27 (1996): 641–62.

41. Walter Rathenau, *Gesammelte Schriften* (Berlin: S. Fischer, 1929), 4:345.

42. Electronic technology seemed to provide what parapsychological research had been waiting for: a medium people would consider credible. In 1968, Konstantin Raudive took up the recording of spirit voices in his book (*Das Unhörbare wird Hörbar*). See Konstantin Raudive, *Breakthrough: Electronic Communication with the Dead May Be Possible* (New York: Zebra Books, 1971). A report by David Ellis in *Psychic* (February 1974) sifts accounts of possible telekinetic and telepathic interference in the experimental set-up used by Raudive. See Laurence Rickels, "Resistance in Theory," in *Material Events: Paul de Man and the Afterlife of Theory*, ed. Tom Cohen (Minneapolis: University of Minnesota Press, 2001), 153–79. In the open secret of the footnote, I add that Freud's German word "Psychoanalyse," pivoting on the o-a of "fort-da," loses the "o" in French, becoming "psychanalyse"—a psi-kanal, a channeling.

43. On the third day of his experiment, an acquaintance clues him in: "And then Liz Kotz and I rode the subway down together. She she was so nice. Everybody has a really nice side to them and it's just a matter of getting her off of her position and she started talking to me about her dissertation and like all these people who are like all my friends you know, she wanted to know how to meet Hannah Higgins and Dick and Allison, you know, I knew Vito's writings, you know, I knew, you know, all the all the Language people knew Abby Childs, you know, it was like she was talking my game she had a Cage CD in her bag and a Feldman CD she was so happy she had just bought so she's just kind of getting into this. She was battling for the like Language Poetry. It it was really neat. She was really quite quite interesting. Well she knew she was like so you've been reading at the Ear. It was remarkable I was almost it was just amazing she was like a different person, you know? Uh, you know, it was it was really neat. She's writing she was telling me about Warhol's novels which is almost exactly what I'm doing this week. He just had endless conversations and had somebody transcribe them. I mean, who was to even know that he did you know that he even wrote a novel? It was great. Anyway, I'm I'm pretty well exhausted I had like 4 hours sleep" (Kenneth Goldsmith, *Soliloquy* [New York: Granary, 2001], 189–90 [Wednesday]). *Soliloquy* is an unedited "text art" document of every word Kenneth Goldsmith spoke during the week of 15–21 April 1996, from the moment he woke up Monday morning to the moment he went to sleep on Sunday night (he wore a hidden voice-activated tape recorder). He transcribed *Soliloquy* during the summer of 1996 at the Chateau Bionnay in Lacenas, France during a residency there (it took eight weeks, working eight hours a day). *Soliloquy* was first published in an edition of fifty by Editions Bravin Post Lee in February of 1997 on the occasion of the gallery's

installation of *Soliloquy*. In 2001, Granary Books issued a chapbook of the *Soliloquy* index, as well as the complete text in a new trade edition with an essay by Simon Morris and a statement by Kenneth Goldsmith. The Web version of *Soliloquy* contains the exact text from the 281-page original book version, but each chapter is subdivided into ten parts. See http://epc.buffalo.edu/authors/goldsmith/soliloquy.

44. Peter Gidal, *Andy Warhol: Films and Paintings* (London: Studio Vista-Dutton, 1971), 152: "It's the first novel not to have been read by its author." Cited again in the incongruously titled and incoherently written book by Ultra Violet, *Famous for Fifteen Minutes: My Years with Andy Warhol* (New York: Harcourt Brace Jovanovich, 1988). See Victor Bockris, "Andy Warhol: The Writer," in *Who Is Andy Warhol*, ed. C. McCabe (London: BFI, 1997), 17–21.

45. Jacques Lacan, "The Freudian Thing," in *Ecrits*, ed. and trans. Alan Sheridan (New York: Norton, 1977), 141. To Lacan, memory is neither natural nor a human technology; he locates it, as suggested by his distinction between instinct and drive, only within the speaking being. Psychic temporality is that of the symbolic organization of language, not of any other, linear chronology.

46. Jacques Lacan, *The Seminar of Jacques Lacan, Book I (1953–1954): Freud's Papers on Technique* (Cambridge: Cambridge University Press, 1988), 59.

47. Jacques Lacan, "The Function and Field of Speech and Language in Psychoanalysis," in *Ecrits*, 48 and 88.

48. If writing exists for the sole purpose of doubling, as a second system, the first system of *langage*, it is a memory of the voice, its repetition *and* its loss. See Ferdinand de Saussure, *Cours de linguistique generale* (Paris: Presses Universitaires Françaises, 1967), 45.

49. "Lowlier hands need then only play it back and listen, in order to be able to create a media link between tape recorder, headphones, and typewriter, reporting to the master what he has already said. His words, barely spoken, lay before him in typescript, punctually before the beginning of the next seminar": Kittler, "Dracula's Legacy," 50–51. See Hal Foster, "Death in America," *October* no. 75 (1996), reprinted in *Andy Warhol: October Files*, ed. Annette Michelson (Cambridge: MIT Press, 2001), 69–88.

50. Warhol and Hackett, *POP-ism*. See Jacques Lacan, *Television: A Challenge to the Psychoanalytic Establishment* (New York: W. W. Norton, 1990) and "Radiophonie," *Scilicet* 3 (1970).

51. Gretchen Berg, "Andy: My True Story," *Los Angeles Free Press*, 17 March 1967, n.p.

52. Thomas Crow, "Saturday Disasters: Trace and Reference in Early Warhol," in *Andy Warhol: October Files*, ed. Michelson, 50.

53. Jameson considers "the emergence of a new kind of flatness or depthlessness, a new kind of superficiality in the most literal sense, perhaps the supreme formal feature of all the postmodernisms": Fredric Jameson, *Postmodernism, or the Cultural Logic of Late Capitalism* (Durham: Duke University Press, 1991), 9.

54. Jean Baudrillard, *La Seduction* (Paris: Seuil, 1980), 202 and passim.

55. Jameson, *Postmodernism*, 24.

56. Jameson, *Postmodernism*, 9. To clarify, he adds: "Although this kind of death of the world of appearance becomes thematized in certain of Warhol's pieces, most notably the

traffic accidents or the electric chair series, this is not, I think, a matter of content any longer but of some fundamental mutation both in the object world itself—now become a set of texts or simulacra—and in the disposition of the subject."

57. Baudrillard, *La Seduction*, 203.

58. A Lacanian formulation of the acting out can be found in "L'acting-out, réalisation d'une réponse, production de l'inconscient," *Scilicet* 6–7 (1976): 121.

59. Repetition compulsion is "a resistance that has no meaning—and that, moreover, is not a resistance": Jacques Derrida, *Resistances of Psychoanalysis* (Stanford: Stanford University Press, 1998), 23.

60. Patrick de Haas, "Vider la Vue," in *Andy Warhol, Cinema*, ed. Bernard Blistéme and Jean-Michel Bonhours (Paris: Centre Georges Pompidou, 1990), 27–28.

61. Marcel Duchamp, *Boîte Verte* (1934), cited after de Haas, who draws the conclusion that Warhol is a fiction by Duchamp: "Warhol est un personnage de fiction de Duchamp" ("Vider la Vue," 28).

62. Warhol, *a. a novel*, 36; see "Sunday with Mister C: An Audio-Documentary by Andy Warhol Starring Truman Capote," *Rolling Stone* 132 (1973).

63. "A Wonderful Invention—Speech Capable of Indefinite Repetition," as the Scientific American wrote when reporting about Edison a century ago; cited in Oliver Read and Walter L. Welsh, *From Tin Foil to Stereo—Evolution of the Phonograph* (Indianapolis/ New York: H.W. Sams, 1959), 12. Lacan's seminars were saved on tape and transcribed for the next session because, he said, people were not listening, they were trying to understand. Lacan, "Radiophonie," 94.

64. Further reading: Jonathan Goldberg, *Voice Terminal Echo* (London: Methuen, 1986); Ronell, *The Telephone Book*; Garrett Stewart, *Reading Voices* (Berkeley: University of California Press, 1992); and Donald Wesling and Tadeusz Slawek, *Literary Voice: The Calling of Jonah* (New York: SUNY Press, 1995).

65. Kittler, "Dracula's Legacy," 53.

66. Friedrich Kittler, *Grammophon, Film, Typewriter* (Berlin: Brinkmann und Bose, 1986), 55 and 92.

67. See Vattimo, "L'impossible oubli," 84: "Ma thése est que le mélange inextricable entre art (dans ses aspects de création, réception, critique), marché et *mass media* aboutit à une situation dans laquelle la création ne peut plus être oublieuse, voire ne doit plus se proposer de l'être, sous peine de sombrer dans le kitsch; et que cela ouvre des possibilités nouvelles a l'éxperience esthétique" ("My thesis is that the inextricable mix of art [in its aspects of creation, reception, critique], the market, and mass media approaches a situation where creation can no longer be forgetful, can no longer suggest itself as such, or it would appear as kitsch; and that this opens new possibilities for the aesthetic experience"). Precisely in the spirit of such recombination, see Tony Scherman, "Andy Warhol, the Father of Modern-Day Hip-hop Sampling," *New York Times*, 7 November 1999), 46. Regarding this "DJ View," see also the early portrait of Paul D. Miller aka DJ Spooky by Richard Goldstein, "Fear of Spooky," *Village Voice*, 27 May 1997, 60: "It was my way of reconstructing a past that didn't exist."

68. Characteristically, this is a conspiracy theory: Boris Groys, *Logik der Sammlung: Am Ende des musealen Zeitalters* (Vienna: Turia & Kant, 1997), 54.

69. Walter Benjamin, GS, 5.2:1016–27.

70. Cited after Rickels, *The Case of California*, 206. Compare Walter Benjamin, GS, 1:2:614f. (for the trigger: 630).

71. Laurence Rickels, "Giving Up the Ghost of a Fetish: Between the Couples Theory of Marxo-Freudianism and Nazi Psychoanalysis," *South Atlantic Quarterly* 97, no. 2 (1998, "Psycho-Marxism"): 302.

72. Sigmund Freud, "Fetischismus," GW, 14:311–17 (SE, 21:147–57). Compare Sigmund Freud, "Das Medusenhaupt," GW, 17:47 (SE, 18:273–74).

73. Walter Benjamin, GS, 1.2:646–47. Brecht was skeptical about expecting what one looks at to look back, and considered it mystical: Bertolt Brecht, *Arbeitsjournal* 1 (1938–1942), ed. W. Hecht (Frankfurt: Suhrkamp, 1973), 16 (journal entry of 25 July 1938).

74. Benjamin, GS, 5.2:1135. In order to save the term aura for modernity, he switches Baudelaire for Proust and natural correspondences for involuntary memory—that is to say, instead of nostalgia, he focuses on a trace of the future.

75. As Adorno put it, "at the outset there is fetishism and the hunt for the outset remains always subject to it": Theodor W. Adorno, *Negative Dialectics* (New York: Seabury Press, 1979), 111.

76. Benjamin, GS, 5.2:1128.

77. Benjamin, GS, 1.2:537 and 559, as well as 5.1/2, passim.

78. Hans Robert Jauss, "Spur und Aura (Bemerkungen zu Walter Benjamin's Passagen-Werk)," in *Art social und art industriel: Funktionen der Kunst im Zeitalter des Industrialismus*, ed. Helmut Pfeiffer, Hans Robert Jauss, and Françoise Gaillard (Munich: Fink, 1987), 24, 35.

79. Karlheinz Stierle, "Aura, Spur und Benjamins Vergegenwärtigung des 19. Jahrhunderts," in *Art social und art industriel*, ed. Pfeiffer, Jauss, and Gaillard, 39, n. 3.

80. Karl Marx, *Das Kapital*, vol. 1 (Berlin: MEW, 1972), 49–52.

81. Werner Hamacher, *pleroma—zu Genesis und Struktur einer dialektischen Hermeneutik bei Hegel*, in Georg Wilhelm Friedrich Hegel, *Der Geist des Christentums: Schriften 1976–1800*, ed. Werner Hamacher (Frankfurt: Ullstein, 1978), 83. (Now also as Werner Hamacher, *pleroma—Reading in Hegel* [Stanford: Stanford University Press, 1998], 68.)

82. "Freud felt short-changed by a prevailing Marxist 'world view' . . . not only because the party-line had cut off desire but also (and more importantly) because its program could never deliver the group from the auto-destruct course set by unconscious remote control": Laurence A. Rickels, "Psychoanalysis on TV," *Sub Stance* 61 (1990): 39.

83. Again, from the interview with Berg, "Nothing to Lose."

84. Benjamin, GS, 1.2:480, n. 7.

85. Warhol, *The Philosophy of Andy Warhol*, 75. See Samuel Weber, *Mass Mediauras* (Stanford: Stanford University Press, 1998).

86. Stierle, "Aura, Spur," 43. Compare Vattimo, "L'impossible oubli," 88–89: "Le *Kitsch*, c'est peut-être paradoxalement aujourd'hui, l'oeuvre qui se veut encore unique, instantanée, classique; en tout cas exclusive, sur le fond d'une utopie liée à la métaphysique de la présence" ("Today, kitsch is perhaps paradoxically the work which presents itself as unique, an instant classic; exclusive in any case, on the ground of a utopia connected to a metaphysics of presence").

87. Theodor Adorno, "Musik im Hintergrund," in *Werkausgabe*, 18 (Frankfurt: Suhrkamp, 1990): 819–23.

88. Theodor Adorno, "Schlageranalysen," in *Werkausgabe*, 18: 778. For Adorno, of course, kitsch is not an aesthetic concept, but a sociological one: "Unmöglich, die Idee Kitsch freischwebend äsethetisch zu fassen. Das soziale Moment konstituiert sie wesentlich": Theodor Adorno, "Kitsch" (1932), in *Werkausgabe*, 18: 792 ("Impossible to grasp the idea of kitsch in free floating aesthetics. The social moment constitutes it essentially").

89. "Da im Café ja die Melodien als Gespenster umgehen, ist von ihnen keine Störung zu befürchten. und sind sie noch so sehr da; denn sie werden zitiert aus der unbewußten Erinnerung der Hörer, nicht ihnen vorgestellt": Adorno, "Musik im Hintergrund", 822 ("Since melodies haunt the café like ghosts, no disturbance is to be expected from them, even if they are very much there; for they are cited from the unconscious of the listeners, not presented to them").

90. Theodor Adorno, *Minima Moralia* (London: Verso, 1978), 225.

91. Walter Benjamin, *The Arcades Project* (Cambridge: Harvard University Press, 1999), 205, 210–11, and 883.

92. Compare Ernst Bloch, *Spuren* (Frankfurt: Suhrkamp, 1959), 16, citing Benjamin's "Traumkitsch" anonymously [1930], and Ernst Bloch, *Erbschaft dieser Zeit* (Frankfurt: Suhrkamp, 1973), 3 and 381–86 [1935].

93. "Das Wort Kitsch ist vom Wortsinn soweit abgerückt, daß der es bereits wieder aufklären mag. . . . Er bewahrt, verzerrt und als bloßen Schein, das Gedächtnis eben an eine Formobjektivität, die verging": Adorno, "Kitsch," 791 ("The word kitsch is far enough removed from its original meaning that it may already enlighten again. . . . Distorted and as mere appearance, it preserves the memory of such a faded formal objectivity").

94. "So beginnt die Rede vom Kitsch selber kitschig zu werden, indem sie der geschichtlichen Dialektik erliegt, der ihr Gegenstand erliegt": Adorno, "Kitsch," 794 ("So the talk of kitsch itself begins to become kitsch when it suffers the historical dialectics that its object suffers").

95. "The castration of perception by a court of control that denies it any anticipatory desire, forces it thereby into a pattern of helplessly iterating what is already known": Adorno, *Minima Moralia*, 123.

96. Bloch, *Erbschaft dieser Zeit*, 387. I disagree with Stierle, who in his focus on the "readability" of the historical believes that Benjamin did not admit the dialectical unity of trace and aura to himself: Stierle, "Aura, Spur," 45.

97. Toward the end of *Konvolut H*, Benjamin gestures towards this allegorization and the analogous structure of collecting.

98. The German word *Gegenwart*, present time, tempts you to pun on "gegen" (against) and "warten" (waiting, delaying, whiling away).

99. Jacques Derrida, *The Post Card: From Socrates to Freud and Beyond* (Chicago: Chicago University Press, 1987), 197; as I wrote this, I received an uncanny postcard, with a picture of Andy Warhol on the telephone at Silver Factory 1965, photographed by Billy Name. The writing on this card, mentioning Friedrich Kittler as well as the publication of a novel, was started, but then covered over with white sticky tape, and covered with

new text. However, the U.S. Postal Service had found it necessary to stick bar code labels on both sides of the card, obscuring the handwriting as well as the photograph once more.

100. Bernhard Waldenfels, "Hearing Oneself Speak: Derrida's Recording of the Phenomenological Voice," *Southern Journal of Philosophy* 32, supplement (1994).

101. "Under the primacy of the autonomous production process, the purpose of reason dwindles away until it sinks into the fetishism of itself": Adorno, *Minima Moralia*, 123.

102. Walter Benjamin to Gershom Scholem, 20 May 1935, in *The Correspondence of Walter Benjamin and Gershom Scholem, 1932–1940*, ed. G. Scholem (New York: Schocken, 1989), 159.

103. See Niklas Luhmann, *Die Kunst der Gesellschaft* (Frankfurt: Suhrkamp, 1995), 300 and 401.

104. Robert C. Morgan, "The Status of Kitsch," in *The End of the Art World* (New York: Allworth Press, 1998), 26.

105. A relation between kitsch and the doubling-over of time-space is not surprising, given that the ancient ideas involved in mulling over the paradox of time are repeated over centuries. The history of déjà vu presents itself as split between valuing timeless disclosure in art over temporal enclosure on the one hand, and on the other hand tediously self-reflective witticisms like those ascribed to Yogi Berra.

106. This citation and the following from Clement Greenberg, "Avantgarde and Kitsch" (1939), in *Art and Culture: Critical Essays* (Boston: Beacon Press, 1961), 9–15.

107. We must neither take up the defense of either German word, *ersatz* or *kitsch*, regardless of whether they are useless or useful, nor simply point out that a cultural rearguard soon finds itself cannibalizing the same "reservoir of accumulated experience" as that "synthetic art" that he calls kitsch, as Greenberg indeed surmised. But we need to acknowledge the Warholian history lesson taught by Philip Leider, the founding editor of *Artforum*, to Amy Newman, *Challenging Art: Artforum 1962–1974* (New York: Soho Press, 2000).

108. Interview with Clement Greenberg, in *Andy Warhol*, a film directed by Lena Jokel (Oxford: Blackwell, 1974). Cited after Morgan, "The Status of Kitsch."

109. Certainly a generalization and emptying out of the "concept" of the uncanny has taken place, leading, for instance, to such self-consciously "academic" art projects as Mike Kelly's curatorial comments in "Playing with Dead Things," *The Uncanny* (Arnhem: Sonsbeek, 1993).

110. See Neil Hertz, "Medusa's Head," in *The End of the Line* (New York: Columbia University Press, 1985), 161–215, and *Fetishism as Cultural Discourse*, ed. Emily Apter and William Pietz (Ithaca: Cornell University Press, 1993).

5. *UNFORGIVEN*

1. Christian Metz, *The Imaginary Signifier: Psychoanalysis and the Cinema* (Bloomington: Indiana University Press, 1982), 43.

2. The secret of this experience can be figured as a cryptic, "artificial unconscious," presenting the absent other before it has ever been present. Compare Akira Mizuta Lippit, *Electric Animal* (Minneapolis: University of Minnesota Press, 2000), 189, as well

as Nicolas Abraham and Maria Torok, *Cryptonymie: Le Verbier de l'Homme aux loups* (Paris: Flammarion, 1976), and Jacques Derrida, "Fors: The Anglish Words of Nicolas Abraham and Maria Torok," *Georgia Review* 31 (1976): 64–116.

3. Pierre Nora, "Between Memory and History: Les Lieux de Mémoire," *Representations* 26 (spring 1989), 7–8.

4. Giorgio Agamben, "Le Cinéma de Guy Debord," in *Image et Mémoire* (Paris: hoëbeke, 1998), 70: "Or si on y réfléchit, c'est aussi la définition du cinéma. Le cinéma ne fait-il pas toujours ça, transformer le réel en possible, et le possible en réel? On peut définir le *déjà vu* comme le fait de 'percevoir quelque chose de présent comme si cela avait déjà été,' et l'inverse, le fait de percevoir comme préset quelque chose qui a été. Le cinéma a lieu dans cette zone d'indifférence" ("Once you think about it, it is also the definition of cinema. Does not the cinema always do this, transform the real into the possible, and the possible into the real? One can define déjà vu as the fact of 'perceiving something present as if it had already been here,' and the inverse, the fact of perceiving as present something which has been. The cinema takes place in this zone of indifference"). A somewhat unreliable translation of this text (or of an earlier version?) can be found in Tom McDonough, ed. and trans., *Guy Debord and the Situationist International: Texts and Documents* (Cambridge: MIT Press, 2002), 313–19, under the title "Difference and Repetition: On Guy Debord's Films." In contrast with film, Agamben charges TV news with being "a bad form of memory, the kind of memory that produces the man of *ressentiment*" (316).

5. Marie-Claude Ropars-Wuilleumier, "L'image-mémoire, ou l'écriture de l'oubli," *Hors Cadre* 9 (1991, "Film/Mémoire"): 121. Compare Derrida's cinematic déjà vu: "The vision of cinema allows you to see new spectres appear, while keeping in your memory the phantoms that haunt the films already seen (and projecting them onto the screen in turn)." Jacques Derrida, "Le Cinema et ses fantômes," *Cahiers du cinema* 4 (2001): 75–85.

6. Jean-Louis Baudry, "The Apparatus: Metapsychological Approaches to the Impression of Reality in the Cinema," in *Narrative, Apparatus, Ideology: A Film Theory Reader*, ed. Philip Rosen (New York: Columbia University Press, 1986), 315.

7. "According to Freud, haunting belongs in the movies": Laurence Rickels, "Psychoanalysis and the Two Orifices of Film," *American Journal of Semiotics* 5, nos. 3–4 (1987): 433, referring to Sigmund Freud, SE, 13:57.

8. Theodor Adorno, "Commodity Music Analyzed," in *Quasi una Fantasia: Essays on Modern Music* (London: Verso, 1998), 43 ("Gebrauchsmusik," in *Werkausgabe*, vol. 19 [Frankfurt: Suhrkamp, 1990], 445–47).

9. Vivian Sobchack, "The Scene of the Screen: Envisioning Cinematic and Electronic 'Presence,'" in *Materialities of Communication*, ed. Hans U. Gumbrecht and Karl L. Pfeiffer (Stanford: Stanford University Press, 1994), 83.

10. "From this perspective, the most expressive television image of war is the interruption of transmission, the sudden halt of all images: the empty screen immediately documents the explosion of a bomb": Wolfgang Ernst, "Between Real Time and Memory on Demand: Reflections on / of Television," in *Medium Cool* (*South Atlantic Quarterly* 101, no. 3), ed. Andrew McNamara and Peter Krapp (Durham: Duke University Press, 2002), 629.

11. Lev Manovich, "What Is Digital Cinema?" in *The Digital Dialectic: New Essays on New Media*, ed. Peter Lunenfeld (Cambridge: MIT Press, 1999), 177–97.

12. "One might consider these things eternal (e.g., storytelling), but one can also see them as temporal and problematic, dubious. Eternal things in narration. But probably totally new forms. Television, gramophone and so forth make all these things dubious." Walter Benjamin, "Vorstufen zum Erzähler-Essay," GS, 2.3:1282: "Man kann all diese Dinge als ewig ansehen (Erzählen z. B.), man kann sie aber auch als durchaus zeitbedingt und problematisch, bedenklich ansehen. Ewiges im Erzählen. Aber wahrscheinlich ganz neue Formen. Fernsehen, Grammophon etc. machen all diese Dinge bedenklich. Quintessenz: So genau wollen wir's ja garnicht wissen. Warum nicht? Weil wir Furcht haben, begründete: daß das alles desavouiert wird: die Schilderung durch den Fernseher, die Worte des Helden durchs Grammophon, die Moral von der Geschichte durch die nächste Statistik, die Person des Erzählers durch alles, was man von ihr erfährt. . . . *Tant mieux*. Nicht weinen. Der Unsinn der kritischen Prognosen. Film statt Erzählung."

13. *Minority Report* (2002) was written by Scott Frank and Jon Cohen, based on a story by Philip K. Dick, and directed by Steven Spielberg. *Memento* (2000) was written and directed by Christopher Nolan; its tagline is: "Sometimes memories are best forgotten."

14. *Men in Black* (1997), was directed by Barry Sonnenfeld, written by Ed Solomon and Lowell Cunningham. The same team made *Men in Black II* (2002), written by Robert Gordon and Lowell Cunningham.

15. The *Star Wars* series is written by George Lucas (1977–2003); *The Terminator* (1984) and *Terminator 2: Judgment Day* (1991) were written and directed by James Cameron, and *Terminator 3: Rise of the Machines* (2003) is written by John Brancato and directed by John Mostow. Compare Ernst Bloch, "Images of Déjà Vu," in *Literary Essays* (Stanford: Stanford University Press, 1998), 200–09 ("Bilder des Déjà Vu," *Literarische Aufsätze*, in *Werkausgabe*, vol. 9 [Frankfurt: Suhrkamp, 1965], 232–42), and Eli Marcovitz, "The Meaning of Déjà Vu," *Psychoanalytic Quarterly* 21 (1952): 481–89.

16. *Total Recall* (1990) was directed by Paul Verhoeven, based on "We Can Remember It for You Wholesale," a Philip K. Dick story that won a 1966 Nebula award for short science fiction.

17. *Groundhog Day* (1993) was directed by Harold Ramis and written by Danny Rubin. The short film *12:01 PM* (1990) was directed by Jonathan Heap and written by Richard Lupoff and Stephen Tolkin. *12:01*, the remake for TV, was directed by Jack Sholden in 1993.

18. *12 Monkeys* (1995) was directed by Terry Gilliam from a script by David Webb Peoples, giving credit to the original idea by Chris Marker and his film, *La Jetée* (1962).

19. Chris Marker (i.e., Christian-François Bouche-Villeneuve), *La Jétée: Ciné-Roman*. Also published in book form (New York: Zone, 1996).

20. Fredric Jameson, "Postmodernism, or the Cultural Logic of Late Capitalism," *New Left Review* 146 (July–August 1984): 64 (repr. in Fredric Jameson, *Postmodernism, or the Cultural Logic of Late Capitalism* [Durham: Duke University Press, 1991], 1–54).

21. Sobchack, "The Scene of the Screen," 95.

22. "These films can be read as dual symptoms: they show a collective unconscious in the process of trying to identify its own present at the same time that they illuminate

the failure of this attempt, which seems to reduce itself to the recombination of various stereotypes of the past": Jameson, *Postmodernism*, 296.

23. Chris Marker made passages of filmic material from his oeuvre available to manipulation (*file, edit, select, goodies, color, animation*) in the computer installation *Zapping Zone*, part of the Centre Pompidou's exhibition "Passages de l'image" (Paris, 1990). There, the interface of his cuts and montages is subjected to another layer of complexity of cuts and montages. See Raymond Bellour, "Zapping Zones," in *Passages de l'image*, ed. Raymond Bellour, Catherine David, and Christine van Assche (Paris: Centre Pompidou, 1990), 169.

24. Constance Penley, *The Future of an Illusion: Film, Feminism and Psychoanalysis* (Minneapolis: University of Minnesota Press, 1990), 136.

25. Roland Barthes, *Camera Lucida: Reflections on Photography* (New York: Hill and Wang, 1981), 8 and 79.

26. Compare Manovich, "What Is Digital Cinema?" and Lev Manovich, *The Language of New Media* (Cambridge: MIT Press, 2001). Manovich writes a theory that had already been turned into a film before it was written: the cinema Dziga Vertov programs what Manovich has to say about new media in general and digital cinema in particular. And so it is only apt that the Web site that supplements his book would present itself in turn as a prequel, not a sequel, by offering more montage of film footage from 1929. Déjà vu.

27. For the Benjaminian allegory of opening eyes ("Augenaufschlag der Allegorie"), see Samuel Weber, "Mass Mediauras, or: Art, Aura and Media in the Work of Walter Benjamin," in *Mass Mediauras* (Stanford: Stanford University Press, 1998), 76–107.

28. Interestingly, the computer game hit *Myst* (Broderbund Software, 1993) also unfolds its narrative almost exclusively in still images. And Wetzel has traced the elective affinities in the tradecraft of photography, film, and video in works by Bill Viola, Gary Hill, Jeff Wall, and Chris Marker. See Michael Wetzel, *Die Wahrheit nach der Malerei* (Munich: Fink, 1997), and Bruce W. Ferguson, "Déjà Vu and Déjà Lu," in *Gary Hill: Essays*, ed. Chris Bruce (Washington: Hirshhorn / Henry Gallery Association, 1994), 15–21.

29. Paul Ricoeur, *La Mémoire, l'histoire, l'oubli* (Paris: Seuil, 2000), 593. As a further distinction, Ricoeur insists that amnesty seeks to efface psycho-social traces "as if nothing had happened," while *prescription*, in the French legal sense, is only the suspension of any legal or penal consequences of the act committed (610).

30. Nicole Loraux formulates this structure as "faire taire le non-oubli de la mémoire": Nicole Loraux, *La Cité divisée: L'oubli dans la mémoire d'Athènes* (Paris: Payot, 1997), 171.

31. "La proximité sémantique entre amnistie et amnesie signale l'existence d'un pacte secret avec le déni de mémoire qui l'eloigne en vérité du pardon après en avoir proposé la simulation": Ricoeur, *La Mémoire, l'histoire, l'oubli*, 586 ("The semantic proximity of amnesty and amnesia signals the existence of a secret pact with the denial of memory which distances it from forgiveness after first having evoked its simulation").

32. Vladimir Jankelevitch, *L'irreversible et la nostalgie* (Paris: Flammarion, 1974), esp. chapter 4.

33. See Jacques Derrida, *On Cosmopolitanism and Forgiveness* (London: Routledge, 2001), 27–60.

34. For amnesty as an *ars oblivionis*, see Carl Schmitt, "Amnestie oder die Kraft des

Vergessens," in *Staat, Großraum, Nomos* (Berlin: Dunker & Humblot, 1995), 218–21; for a politics of pardon, see Natalie Zemon Davis, *Fiction in the Archives: Pardon Tales and Their Tellers in Sixteenth-Century France* (Stanford: Stanford University Press, 1987). For the risks of inaccurate recollection in a legal system that puts great faith in memory and testimony, see the seminal investigation by L. William Stern, "Zur Psychologie der Aussage: Experimentelle Untersuchungen über Erinnerungstreue," *Zeitschrift für die gesamte Strafwissenschaft* 22, nos. 2–3 (1902): 315–70.

35. "Die Abwehr der Vergangenheit hindert uns sowohl daran, die falschen von den erinnerungswürdigen Werten und Idealen unterscheiden zu lernen, als auch ihren Zusammenhang mit der Gegenwart deutlich erkennen zu können": Margarete Mitscherlich, *Erinnerungsarbeit: Zur Psychoanalyse der Unfähigkeit zu trauern* (Frankfurt: Fischer, 1987), 114, 115–16.

36. "Where, however, what is 'brought closer' is itself already a reproduction—and as such, separated from itself—the closer it comes, the more distant it is": Weber, "Mass Mediauras," 88.

37. Although the difference of repetition and novelty constitutes a condition of possibility for any kind of attention, one might argue that the truly new will only appear as such in repetition. Likewise, the dialectical image of distraction and attention pivots on habit and its interruption: "All attention must end up in habit, if it does not tear one apart; all habit must be disturbed by attention if it is not to hem one in." Walter Benjamin, "Gewohnheit und Aufmerksamkeit," GS, 4.1:407–08.

38. "Distraction as provided by art presents a covert control," as Benjamin wrote, "of the extent to which new tasks have become soluble by apperception": Walter Benjamin, "The Work of Art in the Age of Mechanical Reproduction," in *Illuminations* (New York: Schocken, 1969), 240. (Walter Benjamin, GS, 7.1:350–84.)

39. The original script by David Webb Peoples was written in the 1970s, and *Unforgiven* shows traces of the political criticism of the genre that became important at that time.

40. Walter Benjamin, "The Storyteller," in *Illuminations*, ed. Arendt, 109. (Walter Benjamin, "Der Erzähler," GS, 2.2:465.)

41. An allusion to Horace Greeley, to whom the exhortation "Go west, young man" is attributed. (In fact it was John Babsone Soule who first coined the phrase, in an article for the *Terre Haute Express* in 1851. It became the motto of Manifest Destiny when Horace Greeley reprinted the piece in the *New Yorker*. Although giving Soule full credit, the expression has since been attributed to him—a clear example for parapraxis of memory even under the condition of media archives. Or as Yogi Berra protested: "I really didn't say everything I said.")

42. Klawans even claims that while John Ford made Hellenic Westerns, Clint Eastwood makes "Hebraic" ones: dark, murky, barren, flat. Stuart Klawans, "Unforgiven," *The Nation* 255, no. 7 (1992), 258–60.

43. Michael Sragow, "Outlaws," *New Yorker* 68, no. 25 (1992), 70–73.

44. Another repressed narrative of exploitation: rumors of how wealth is to be won in the West keep the settlers coming, but also attracts contract killers who keep the workers in check.

45. John C. Tibbetts, "Clint Eastwood and the Machinery of Violence," *Literature/Film Quarterly* 21, no. 1 (1993): 11–17.

46. Laurence F. Knapp, *Directed by Eastwood* (Jefferson: McFarland & Company, 1996), 162. In sequels, Eastwood kept revisiting the characters he portrayed; he displays the pot-bellied stove used in *Unforgiven* as decoration in his restaurant, "Mission Ranch" in Carmel, where he was mayor for a number of years. See Richard Combs, "Shadowing the Hero," *Sight and Sound* 2, no. 6 (1992): 15.

47. Len Engel, "Rewriting Western Myths in Clint Eastwood's New 'Old Western,'" *Western American Literature*, 29, no. 3 (1994): 261–69; Philip J. Skerry, "Apocalyptic, Post-revisionist Westerns," in *Beyond the Stars 5: Themes and Ideologies in American Popular Film*, ed. Paul Loukides and Linda K. Fuller (Bowling Green: Bowling Green University Press, 1996), 281–91. Earlier, Skerry had already pronounced the genre dead: "The Western Film: A Sense of an Ending," *New Orleans Review* 17, no. 3 (1989): 13–17.

48. Weber, "Mass Mediauras," 91.

49. Walter Benjamin, "Zentralpark," GS, 1.2:671; see 2.1:309: "Überall, wo ein Handeln selber das Bild aus sich herausstellt und ist, in sich hineinreißt und frißt, wo die Nähe sich selbst aus den Augen sieht, tut dieser gesuchte Bildraum sich auf, die Welt allseitiger und integraler Aktualität" ("Wherever acting itself presents and is the image, incorporates it and eats it up, where proximity looks out of its eyes, this total image space opens up, the world of imnipresent and integral actuality").

50. Knapp, *Directed by Eastwood*, 164.

51. Simone de Beauvoir, *The Second Sex* (New York: Vintage Books, 1989), 599.

52. Leighton Grist, "Unforgiven," in *The Book of Westerns,* ed. Ian Alexander Cameron and Douglas Pye (New York: Continuum, 1996), 294–301; Edward Buscombe, *The BFI Companion to the Western* (London: British Film Institute, 1988), 132.

53. Tibbetts, "Clint Eastwood and the Machinery of Violence," 15. See also William Ian Miller, "Clint Eastwood and Equity: Popular Culture's Theory of Revenge," in *Law in the Domain of Culture*, ed. Austin Sarat and Thomas R. Kearns (Ann Arbor: University of Michigan Press, 1998), 161–202.

54. Maurice Yacowar, "Re-Membering the Western: Eastwood's *Unforgiven,*" *Queens Quarterly* 100, no. 1 (1993): 247.

55. See the documentary by Nick Redman and Brian Jamieson, *A Turning of the Earth: John Ford, John Wayne and the Searchers*, 1999.

56. Sigmund Freud, "Introductory Lectures on Psycho-Analysis," SE, 15:15; "From the History of an Infantile Neurosis," SE, 17:3.

57. Sigmund Freud, "Fragment of an Analysis of a Case of Hysteria," SE, 7:116.

58. David Breskin, *Inner Views: Filmmakers in Conversation* (New York: Da Capo Press, 1997), 376–403; Knapp, *Directed by Eastwood*, 162–78.

59. Sigmund Freud, "The Psychopathology of Everyday Life," SE, 6:xii.

60. This is the inversion that is prostitution—all living women in the movie are whores.

61. Anna Freud, "Eine Form von Altruismus," in *Die Schriften der Anna Freud*, vol. 1, *1922–1936* (Frankfurt: Suhrkamp, 1968), 305–15.

62. Laurence Rickels, *Aberrations of Mourning: Writing on German Crypts* (Detroit: Wayne State University Press, 1988), 253.

63. Laurence Rickels, *The Case of California* (Baltimore: The Johns Hopkins University Press, 1991), 133.

64. "Nicht die einsame Windstille der Angst, sondern der vorm immer nahenden Gericht daherbrausende laute Sturm der Vergebung, gegen den sie nicht ankann": Walter Benjamin, "Die Bedeutung der Zeit in der moralischen Welt," GS, 6:97–98. See Gershom Scholem, *Die jüdische Mystik in ihren Hauptströmungen* (Frankfurt: Suhrkamp, 1967), 258.

65. "Er vergißt das Meiste, um Eins zu thun, er ist ungerecht gegen das, was hinter ihm liegt, und kennt nur ein Recht, das Recht dessen, was jetzt werden soll": Friedrich Nietzsche, "Vom Nutzen und Nachteil der Historie für das Leben," in *Kritische Studienausgabe,* ed. Giorgio Colli and Mazzino Montinari (Munich: DTV, 1988) 1:254.

6. SCREEN MEMORIES

1. Nicholson Baker, "Discards," in *The Size of Thoughts and Other Lumber* (London: Picador, 1996), 125–81; Richard A. Lanham, *The Electronic Word* (Chicago: University of Chicago Press, 1993); Richard J. Finneran, ed., *The Literary Text in the Digital Age* (Ann Arbor: University of Michigan Press, 1996).

2. Leroy George Williams, "An Experiment Testing Hypertext as a Method of Memory Stimulation" (Ph.D. diss., George Mason University, Washington DC, 1995); Josef Wallmannsberger, "Methoden der Interaktion mit virtuellen Textuniversen" (Dissertation, Universität Innsbruck, 1991).

3. Fredric Jameson, *The Political Unconscious* (Ithaca: Cornell University Press, 1980), 60–61.

4. For samples experimenting with nonlinearity, see David Kolb, *Socrates in the Labyrinth* (Cambridge: Eastgate Systems, 1996) and *Hyperproof, Turing's World 4.0,* and *Tarski's World 3.0,* computer-science pedagogy software by Jon Barwise and John Etchemendy (CSLI Stanford: Stanford University Press, 1995).

5. The mathematician Alan Turing became famous for the unsolved test that was to show statistically that the distinction between human language and computer-generated language is beyond human capacity. (Turing usually referred to this as a "game," only twice does he call it a "test." See Alan Turing, "Computing Machinery and Intelligence," *Mind* 59, no. 236 [1950]: 433–60.) Arguably, if this game of imitation is to be decided this side of eternity, it must be stopped by someone who occupies the position of external observer. See Jean Lassegue, "What Kind of Turing Test Did Turing Have in Mind?" *Tekhnema* 3 (1996): 37–58. Turing himself became the literary material, for instance in Ian McEwan, *The Imitation Game,* in *Three Plays for Television* (London: Picador, 1981), or in Alan Hodges, *The Enigma of Intelligence* (London: Allen Unwin, 1983). The artificial intelligence advocate Minsky even published a science fiction novel about Turing: Marvin Minsky, *The Turing Option* (New York: Warner Books, 1992).

6. Friedrich Kittler, "Die künstliche Intelligenz des Weltkriegs: Alan Turing," in *Arsenale der Seele,* ed. F. Kittler and Georg Christoph Tholen (Munich: Fink, 1989), 198. Yet poets have been trying for a few decades to generate experimental computer poetry, referring to William Carlos Williams, who seemed to grant them permission when he wrote: "a poem is a small (or large) / machine made of words."

7. Robert Pinsky, "The Muse in the Machine, or: The Poetics of Zork," *New York Times Book Review*, 19 March 1995.

8. Charles Hartman's program "Prose," somewhat unstable in DOS, but satisfying in its Apple OS version, is found at www.conncoll.edu/ccother/cohar/programs/.

9. Hugh Kenner and Joseph O'Rourke, "A Travesty Generator for Micros," *Byte* 9, no. 12 (1984): 129–31, 449–69. Their fundamental insight is that material is limited; the challenges are posed by technical and economical iteration of connection.

10. A different concept of hypertext was proposed in Gérard Genette, *Palimpseste* (Paris: Gallimard, 1982), who opposes it to hypotext as defining transtextual relations.

11. Theodor Holm Nelson, "Opening Hypertext: A Memoir," in *Literacy Online: The Promise (and Peril) of Reading and Writing with Computers,* ed. Myron C. Tuman (Pittsburgh: University of Pennsylvania Press, 1992), 43–57. See Jacob Nielsen, *Multimedia and Hypertext* (Boston: AP Professional, 1996), 2; Norbert Bolz, "Zur Theorie der Hypermedien," in *Raum und Verfahren* (Basel: Stroemfeld/Roter Stern, 1993), 26.

12. Aleida Assmann and Jan Assmann, "Schrift und Gedächtnis," in *Schrift und Gedächtnis,* ed. Aleida Assmann, Jan Assmann, and C. Hardmeier (Munich: Fink, 1983), 277 and 281.

13. Joseph Tabbi, "Review of Books in the Age of their Technological Obsolescence," *American Bookreview* 17, no. 2 (1995–96): 31.

14. George P. Landow, "Changing Texts, Changing Readers: Hypertext in Literary Education, Criticism, and Scholarship," in *Reorientations: Critical Theories & Pedagogies,* ed. Bruce Henricksen and Thais E. Morgan (Urbana: Illinois University Press, 1990), 133–61; George P. Landow, ed., *Hyper/Text/Theory* (Baltimore: Johns Hopkins University Press, 1994). See also Paul Edwards, "Hypertext and Hypertension: Post-Structuralist Critical Theory, Social Studies of Science, and Software," *Social Studies of Science* 24, no. 2 (1994): 229–78.

15. Daniel Ferrer, "Hypertextual Representation of Literary Working Papers," *Journal of the Association for Literary and Linguistic Computing* 10, no. 2 (1995): 143–45; Tim William Machan, "Chaucer's Poetry, Versioning, and Hypertext," *Philological Quarterly* 73, no. 3 (1994): 299–316.

16. Edward Barrett, ed., *The Society of Text* (Cambridge: MIT Press, 1989); Charles Platt, "Why Hypertext Doesn't Really Work," *The New York Review of Science Fiction* 72 (August 1994): 1–5; Stuart Moulthrop, "You Say You Want a Revolution? Hypertext & the Laws of Media," in *Essays in Postmodern Culture,* ed. Eyal Amiran and John Unworth (Oxford: Oxford University Press, 1993), 69–97; Robert Markley, ed., *Virtual Reality and Its Discontents* (Baltimore: Johns Hopkins University Press, 1996).

17. Jacques Lacan, "Psychanalyse et cybernétique, ou de la nature du langage," in *Le Seminaire, Livre II: Le moi dans la théorie de Freud et dans la technique de la psychanalyse* (Paris: Seuil, 1978), 339–54; see Laurence Rickels, "Cyber-Lacan," in *Nazi Psychoanalysis,* vol. 2 (Minneapolis: University of Minnesota Press, 2002), 60–62.

18. Darryl Laferte, "Hypertext and Hypermedia: Toward a Rhizorhetorical Investigation of Communication," *Readerly/Writerly Texts: Essays on Literature, Literary/Textual Criticism, and Pedagogy* 3, no. 1 (1995): 51–68.

19. Samuel Weber, *Mass Mediauras* (Stanford: Stanford University Press, 1998), 3.

20. George P. Landow, "Hypertext, Metatext, and the Electronic Canon," in *Literacy Online*, ed. Tuman, 67–94.

21. Jacques Derrida, *Glas* (Paris: Galilée, Collection Débats, 1974); *Glas* (Paris: Denöel/Gonthier, Bibliothèque mediations, 1981); *Glas*, trans. John P. Leavey, Jr., and Richard Rand (Lincoln: University of Nebraska Press, 1986). My Web site http://www.hydra.umn.edu/derrida/ assembles glossaries and related material.

22. George P. Landow, *Hypertext: The Convergence of Contemporary Critical Theory and Technology* (Baltimore: Johns Hopkins University Press, 1992), 2.

23. J. Hillis Miller, "Literary Theory, Telecommunications, and the Making of History," in *Scholarship and Technology in the Humanities,* ed. May Katzen (New York: Bowker-Saur, 1991), 11–20.

24. *Glas,* as Derrida put it, clamps the boundaries between *coupure* and *crochet,* digest and vomit.

25. Bolz, "Zur Theorie der Hypermedien," 17.

26. Richard Rorty, *Philosophical Papers,* vol. 2 (Cambridge: Cambridge University Press, 1991), 100.

27. Mark Taylor and Esa Saarinen, *Imagologies* (London: Routledge, 1994), Simcult 2–3.

28. Richard Rorty, *Consequences of Pragmatism* (Minneapolis: University of Minnesota Press, 1982), 187.

29. "Il y a–toujours–déjà–plus d'un–glas. Il faut lire *Glas* comme singulier pluriel (chute de l'or dans la double séance). Il a son bris en lui-même, il s'affecte et résonne aussitôt de ce dégàt litteral": Derrida, *Glas,* 170bi, see 1b and 150b.

30. Gayatri Chakravorty Spivak, "Glas-Piece: A Compte Rendu," *Diacritics* 7 (1977): 22–43.

31. Derrida, *Glas,* 233bi; one ironic attempt is my Glasweb, see http://www.hydra.umn.edu/derrida. On 6 May 1998 (around 10 A.M. PST), at the very same time I presented an early version of this text at a conference of the International Association for Philosophy and Literature at UC Irvine (in Derrida's presence), someone emailed a *Glas*-discussion list I had set up and claimed there that Derrida had died in a car accident. The fallout of this stupid prank was the end of that discussion list, and the end of my work on *Glas* in particular and on Derrida's texts altogether. See Jacques Derrida's account in *La Contre-Allée* (Paris: La Quinzaine Littéraire, 1999), 274.

32. Derrida, *Glas,* 16ai; see Hubertus von Amelunxen, "Wieder-Gabe und Wieder-gang," in *Der Entzug der Bilder: Visuelle Realitäten,* ed. Herta Wolf and Michael Wetzel (Munich: Fink, 1994), 297–314; Holger Briel, "Derridas Hyperkarte: Glas," *Weimarer Beiträge* 38, no. 4 (1992), 485–505; Pierre Pachet, "Le Plus Récent Texte de Jacques Derrida: Une entreprise troublante," *Quinzaine Littéraire* 197 (November 1974): 19–20: "une machine à lire." This cue is taken up by Hartman's influential work on *Glas*: "A deconstructive machine that sings: Glas." Geoffrey Hartman, *Saving the Text: Literature, Derrida, Philosophy* (Baltimore: Johns Hopkins University Press, 1981), 24. Hegel would have considered a machine that functions without submitting to reappropriation a pure loss.

33. Michael Riffaterre, "Syllepsis," *Critical Inquiry* 6 (1980): 636; see Riffaterre, "La Trace de l'intertexte," *La Pensee* 215 (1980): 4–18, as well as "Intertextuality vs. Hyper-textuality," *New Literary History* 25 (1995): 779–88.

34. Eugenio Donato, "'Here Now'/'Always Already': Incidental Remarks on Some Recent Characterizations of the Text," *Diacritics* 6, no. 3 (1976): 24–29 (on Derrida, *Glas*, 26).

35. Derrida, *Glas*, 188: "ils ne savent pas qu'en fait ils décapitent, pour ainsi dire, l'hydre" ("They do not know that they decapitate the hydra, so to say"). See Aleida Assmann, "Der Eigen-Kommentar," in *Text und Kommentar*, ed. Jan Assmann and Burkhart Gladigow (Munich: Fink, 1995), 357. Hydrapoetics is a term coined by Nicholas Royle: "the thought of a critical glossolalia, a poetico-telephony or computer network operating multiple channels simultaneously" (Nicholas Royle, *After Derrida* [Manchester: Manchester University Press, 1995], 40). This may lead us back to Heiner Müller's *Herakles 2 oder die Hydra*.

36. The contributions to *Hegel after Derrida*, ed. Stuart Barnett (London: Routledge, 1998) all but ignore *Glas* on Genet, while the texts assembled in a special issue on Genet for *Yale French Studies*, ed. Scott Durham, 91 (1997) manage to do without Hegel.

37. Derrida says if it had been possible at that time to calculate the effects of *Glas* by computer and write a bicolumnar text, he would not have done it. (Conversation with Jacques Derrida, April 1998, Irvine, CA; written up in an e-mail to my *Glas* discussion list, 30 April 1998, http://glas.lake.de, Glasweb & Discussion glas-list@glas.lake.de. This list has long been defunct; see www.hydra.umn.edu/derrida/may.html).

38. Here Derrida reads Hegel on Mendelsohn's "Jerusalem oder über religiöse Macht und Judentum" (1783).

39. John P. Leavey, "Jacques Derrida's *Glas*: A Translated Selection and Some Comments on an Absent Colossus," *Clio* 11, no. 4 (1984): 327–37.

40. Jacques Derrida, *Aporias* (Stanford: Stanford University Press, 1994), 15.

41. Jacques Derrida, *Dissemination* (Chicago: University of Chicago Press, 1981), 15 and 279.

42. Jacques Derrida, *Margins of Philosophy* (Chicago: University of Chicago Press, 1982), 325 n. 5.

43. G. W. F. Hegel, *Wissenschaft der Logik*, in *Werke*, vol. 5 (Frankfurt: Suhrkamp, 1969), 275.

44. Consider the Hegelian mutual forgetting of consciousness and its content: "If there is self-consciousness, then it must fall prey to a consciousness of forgetting" (Werner Hamacher, "(The End of Art with the Mask)," in *Hegel after Derrida*, ed. Barnett, 113.

45. See Hegel, *Wissenschaft der Logik*, 113–15.

46. G. W. F. Hegel, *Vorlesung über die Philosophie der Weltgeschichte*, in *Werke*, vol. 1 (Frankfurt: Suhrkamp, 1966), 183.

47. Hegel tried to close the gap between the deep storage of memory and the individually appropriated recollection by way of a philosophy of history. Arguing against the dead principle of the apparatus, he nevertheless relied on one: his apparatus of notes. For Hegel's "Zettel," see Karl Rosenkranz, *Georg Wilhelm Friedrich Hegels Leben* (Berlin, 1844), 12f., and Hermann Schmitz, "Hegels Begriff der Erinnerung," *Archiv für Begriffsgeschichte* 9 (1964), 37–44. Compare also Friedrich Kittler, *Die Nacht der Substanz* (Bern: Bentali, 1989), 18f.

48. Gabriella Baptist, "Wem schlägt die Stunde in Derridas *Glas*?" *Hegel-Studien* 23 (1988): 140.

49. Baptist, "Wem schlägt die Stunde in Derridas *Glas?*" 168.

50. Arguably, this is what Sartre does: "Genet is related to that family of people who are nowadays referred to as *passéistes*. An accident riveted him to a childhood memory, and this memory became sacred" (Jean-Paul Sartre, *Saint Genet* [New York: Mentor, 1964], 9).

51. Hartman, *Saving the Text*, 22; compare Thoreau's "Funeral Bell": "Flower-bells toll not / Their echoes roll not / Upon my ear; / There still, perchance, / That gentle spirit haunts / A fragrant bier" (*The Writings of Thoreau*, vol. 5 [London: Houghton and Mifflin, 1946], 405).

52. "I am sufficiently convinced that *Glas*, like *Finnegans Wake*, introduces our consciousness to a dimension it will not forget": Geoffrey Hartman, "Crossing Over: Literary Commentary as Literature," *Comparative Literature* 28, no. 3 (1976): 268. "A work whose untranslatability must compare only to *Finnegans Wake*": James Arnt Aune, "Review of *Glas*," *Quarterly Journal of Speech* 75 (1989): 356. Landow, *Hypertext*, 10: "implicit hypertext in nonelectronic form. Again, take Joyce's *Ulysses* as an example."

53. Baptist, "Wem schlägt die Stunde in Derridas *Glas?*" 161; see H. C. Lucas, "Zwischen Antigone und Christiane: Die Rolle der Schwester in Hegels Biographie und Philosophie und in Derridas *Glas*," *Hegel-Jahrbuch 1984–1985* (1988): 433: "ein Leseerlebnis, das wohl nur dem von Arno Schmidts *Zettels Traum* oder von James Joyces *Finnegans Wake* vergleichbar ist" ("a reading experience comparable only to Arno Schmidt's *Zettels Traum* or James Joyce's *Finnegans Wake*").

54. Hartman, *Saving the Text*, 2 and 79.

55. Vincent D. Leitch, *Deconstructive Criticism: An Advanced Introduction* (New York: Columbia University Press, 1983), 205.

56. "Cherchent du complet et du cohérent dans une pensée aussi fondamentalement inconsistante et vaine que celle de Derrida! TRISTES IMBECILES!" (My translations from French and German.) Cited after the copy at the Konstanz University library: Derrida, *Glas*, pht 670 dg 51/t74. The publisher must have suffered, since Derrida believes he almost bankrupted them with endless cuts and montages, galleys and revisions (conversation with Derrida, Chateau de Cerisy, summer 1997).

57. Cited after Robert Moynihan, *A Recent Imagining: Interviews with Harold Bloom, Geoffrey Hartman, J. Hillis Miller, Paul de Man* (Hamden: Archon Books, 1986), xi.

58. Derrida, *Glas*, 97b, 53b.

59. René Wellek, "Destroying Literary Studies," *New Criterion* 2, no. 4 (1983): 1–8.

60. John Llewelyn, "Glasnostalgia," *Bulletin of the Hegel Society of Great Britain* 18 (1988): 33–38; see Derrida, *Glas*, 231ai.

61. Merleau-Ponty used the term *écart* to denote the gap not between language and thing but between signifier and meaning. Derrida refers to this difference, but while *écart* for Merleau-Ponty is based on continuity, Derrida uses the same term for a discontinuous difference. Compare Maurice Merleau-Ponty, *Le Visible et l'invisible* (Paris: Gallimard, 1966), 116, and Jacques Derrida, *La Voix et le phénomene* (Paris: Presses Universitaires Françaises, 1967), 77, as well as Derrida, *Spurs: Nietzsche's Styles* (Chicago: University of Chicago Press, 1979), 138: "il faut écrire dans l'écart entre plusieurs styles" ("one must write in the gap between several styles").

62. Renate Lachmann, *Gedächtnis und Literatur* (Frankfurt: Suhrkamp, 1990), 35.

63. "Das differentielle Netzwerk des Hypertextes erzeugt also gerade nicht das Gefühl von Aufschub und Nachträglichkeit, sondern suggeriert die Immersion in eine dauernde Gegenwart der Textbewegung": Bolz, "Zur Theorie der Hypermedien," 29 ("The differential network of hypertext generates not the feeling of delay and Nachträglichkeit, but suggests immersion into a continuous presence of textual motion").

64. Samuel Weber, *Freud-Legende: Drei Studien zum psychoanalytischen Denken* (Freiburg: Olten, 1979), 139.

65. G. F. Hasel, *The Remnant–The History and Theology of the Remnant Idea from Genesis to Isaiah* (Berrien Springs, MI: Religio, 1972), 51; W. E. Müller and H. D. Preuss, *Die Vorstellung vom Rest im alten Testament* (Neukirchen: Vluyn, 1973), 46.

66. Cited after Charles O. Hartman, *The Virtual Muse* (Hanover: University Press of New Hampshire, 1996), 105; see J. Hillis Miller, "The Ethics of Hypertext," *Diacritics* 25, no. 3 (1995): 37: "it could be argued that hypertexts do no more (although that is quite a lot) than make materially embodied and more easily available in a new technological mechanism what has always been the case about linguistic assemblages."

67. Heiko Idensen, "Die Poesie soll von allen gemacht werden! Von literarischen Hypertexten zu virtuellen Schreibräumen der Netzweltkultur," in *Literatur im Informationszeitalter*, ed. Dirk Matejowski and Friedrich Kittler (Frankfurt: Campus, 1996), 157. See Heiko Idensen and Mathias Krohn, "Kunst-Netzwerke: Ideen als Objekte," in *Digitaler Schein: Ästhetik der Medien*, ed. Florian Rötzer (Frankfurt: Suhrkamp, 1991), 384.

68. Vilém Flusser, *Schrift* (Düsseldorf: Bollmann, 1995), 79.

69. "Computervorläufer Babbage": Friedrich Kittler, "Geschichte der Kommunikationmedien," in *Raum und Verfahren* (Basel: Stroemfeld/Roter Stern, 1993), 183 and 186.

70. Derrida, *Grammatologie*, 275.

71. Derrida, *Glas*, 132bi, 148bi, 186bi. The fold of so-called metalanguage is irreducible like a pocket or cyst that incessantly forms anew. Derrida suggests that for this theoretical question, no other word is possible: *Glas*, 189b.

72. Derrida, *Glas*, 309a: "l'absolu du déjà-là du pas-encore ou de l'encore du déjá plus" ("The absolute of the already-there, of the no-longer, or of the again of the once more"). Elsewhere, he went on record saying that the horizon is the "*toujours-déjà-là* of a future that keeps the indeterminacy of infinite openness intact": Derrida, *Introduction à 'L'Origine de la géométrie de Husserl'* (Paris: Presses Universitaires Françaises, 1962), 123.

73. Michael Joyce, *Afternoon* (Cambridge: Eastgate Systems, n.d.); see Jay David Bolter, "Literature in the Electronic Space," in *Literacy Online: The Promise (and Peril) of Reading and Writing with Computers*, ed. Myron C. Tuman (Pittsburgh: University of Pennsylvania Press, 1992), 31.

74. Julian Cowley, "Hypertext: Electronic Writing and Its Literary Tradition," *Moderna Sprak* 87, no. 2 (1993): 129–35; David Burnley, "Scribes and Hypertext", *Yearbook of English Studies* 25 (1995): 41–62.

75. Michael Ryan, *Marxism and Deconstruction: A Critical Articulation* (Baltimore: Johns Hopkins University Press, 1982), 66, referring to Derrida, *Glas*, 168a/b.

76. Ryan, *Marxism and Deconstruction*, 74.

77. Ryan, *Marxism and Deconstruction*, 156.

78. "In 1979, I wrote *The Post Card* on an electric typewriter (even though I talk a lot there about the computer and computer programs), but *Glas*, where the page layout was also presented as a short treatise on the organ by sketching a history of organology up to the present, was composed on a little manual Olivetti": Jacques Derrida, "Word Processing," trans. Peggy Kamuf, *Oxford Literary Review* 21 (2000): 10.

79. Ferdinand de Saussure, *Cours de linguistique générale* (Paris: Presses Universitaires Françaises, 1967), 102.

80. In Culler's introduction to his volume on puns, we find Saussure in close proximity to what *Glas* had to say about the contamination of any internal system of language. Jonathan Culler, "The Call of the Phoneme," in *On Puns–The Foundation of Letters* (Oxford: Blackwell, 1988), 13.

81. *Glas* might be the first place where Derrida's position on metalanguage is articulated: as a constantly regenerated fold for which Derrida chose to keep the old name, considering no other word possible. Žižek accuses Derrida of theoreticism, practicing the denial of metalanguage with the means of metalanguage and thus being "too theoretical." Such supposed access through excess opens the field of theory for considerations of linguistic material at close range. The necessary impossibility, and consequently the pivotal experience of the impossibility of a metalanguage, revolve around an age-old theorem. The "position from which the deconstructivist can always make sure that *there is no metalanguage*, that no utterance can say precisely what it intended to say" is what Žižek triumphantly identifies as "the position of metalanguage in its purest form": Slavoj Žižek, *The Sublime Object of Ideology* (London: Verso, 1999), 153–55. Here we might also locate one of the reasons why Derrida felt compelled to shy away from annotation, to neglect the scholarly genre of footnotes. The dissection of GL effects between Genet and Hegel parallels what Derrida found in Mallarmé's "Or" (where gold, money, now, then, the zero, and the musical sound of the very syllable *or* constitute an orchestrated, subsemantic effect beyond logics and semantics, *hors-texte*); see Derrida, "La double séance," in *La Dissémination* (Paris: Seuil, 1972), 294, and Derrida, "This Is Not an Oral Footnote," in *Annotation and Its Texts*, ed. Stephen A. Barney (Oxford: Oxford University Press, 1991), 192–205.

82. Jacques Derrida, *Of Grammatology* (Baltimore: Johns Hopkins University Press, 1976), 66.

83. "No-one has ever been able to show," as Geoff Bennington emphasizes in an unpublished paper, "that Derrida has *ever* needed to renounce or repudiate *any* substantive argument from earlier work, and one of the many strange features of 'Derrida's work' is just that, its resistance to organisation into the shape of a career or a history, its extraordinary and paradoxical *consistency* or *constancy:* it would be nice one day for a biographer to track back to a moment of originary insight about the non-originarity of origins and originary insights, about an irreducible originary complexity. On this view, we might then reasonably want to claim some modest credit for making a *discovery,* something to inscribe in the archives of 'Derrida scholarship,' indubitable proof that he not only might sometimes *forget* an earlier assertion, but that that forgetting might be motivated by the need to forget": Geoffrey Bennington, "Forever Friends," presentation delivered to a conference on "Politics, Friendship and *Democracy to come,*" London: ICA, 29 November 1997.

84. Jacques Derrida, "Living On: Borderlines," in *Deconstruction and Criticism,* ed. Geoffrey Hartman (London: Routledge and Kegan Paul, 1979), 164b; and Jacques Derrida, "Two Words for Joyce," in *Post-Structuralist Joyce: Essays from the French,* ed. Daniel Ferrer and Derek Attridge (Cambridge: Cambridge University Press, 1984), 150.

85. "non-subjectivité dans l'experience du deuil, c'est que j'ai tenté de decrire dans *Glas*": Jacques Derrida, "Il faut bien manger," *Cahiers Confrontation* 20 (winter 1989): 102 ("Non-subjectivity of the experience of mourning, that is what I have tried to describe in *Glas*").

86. Jacques Derrida, "Between Brackets I," in *Points... Interviews, 1974–1994,* ed. Elisabeth Weber (Stanford: Stanford University Press, 1995), 19–20; Derrida cites Nicolas Abraham and Imre Hermann, as well as from the Littré: "everything comes down to living in the hook {'crochet'; also bracket} of the cripple; the cluster, the grapnel are a kind of hooked matrix. 'Grappe' . . . E. Picardy and env. 'crape'; provenc. 'grapa,' hook; Span. 'grapo,' hook; Ital. 'grappo,' hook; low Latin 'grapa,' 'grappa' in Quicherat's 'Addenda'; from the old High-German 'chrapfo,' hook, mod. German 'Krappen'; cp. Cymric 'crap.' The 'grappe' {grape cluster} has been so called because it has a hooked or grappled quality (Littré)." Compare Derrida, *Glas,* 216–17.

87. Derrida, "Between Brackets I," 21.

88. "Écrire, c'est produire une marque qui constituera une sorte de machine à son tour productrice, que ma disparition future n'empêchera pas principiellement de fonctionner et de donner, de se donner à lire et à reécrire": Jacques Derrida, "Signature Événement Contexte," in *Marges de la Philosophie* (Paris: Minuit, 1972), 376 ("Writing that is producing a mark which constitutes a kind of machine which in turn is productive, and which my future disappearance will not prevent from functioning in principle, nor from giving itself to read and to rewrite").

89. Geoffrey Bennington, "Derridabase," in *Jacques Derrida* (Paris: Seuil, 1991), 291: "cette machine est déjà en place, elle est le déjà même."

90. Wilhelm Dilthey, "Archive der Literatur in ihrer Bedeutung für das Studium der Geschichte der Philosophie" (1889), in *Gesammelte Schriften,* vol. 4 (Stuttgart: Teubner, 1959), 574. (Translations from the German are mine unless otherwise marked.) Of course, Derrida's texts put the supreme reign of an objective spirit into question; see Jacques Derrida, *Edmund Husserl's Origin of Geometry: An Introduction* (Lincoln: University of Nebraska Press, 1989), 63.

91. See Mark Poster, "Theorizing the Virtual," in *What's the Matter with the Internet?* (Minneapolis: University of Minnesota Press, 2001), 129.

92. Gregory Ulmer, *Applied Grammatology* (Baltimore: Johns Hopkins University Press, 1985), 303; Mark Poster, *The Mode of Information* (Berkeley: University of California Press, 1990), 128.

93. Taylor and Saarinen, *Imagologies,* "Telewriting," 9.

94. Peter Krapp, *"Screen Memory*: Hypertext und Deckerinnerung," *in Deutsche Vierteljahresschrift für Literaturwissenschaft und Geistesgeschichte* 72: "Medien des Gedächtnisses" (Stuttgart: Metzler, 1998), 279–96.

95. Miller, "The Ethics of Hypertext," 31.

96. Not that there was nothing on "Derrida" or, for that matter, on "deconstruction"

online; search engines will point users to the archives of an e-mail discussion list and to various e-zine articles in Seulemonde, Postmodern Culture, and Foreign Body, to name but few.

97. See the interview conducted in Paris in August 1993 to mark the publication of Derrida's *Spectres de Marx* (Paris: Galilée, 1993), first published in the monthly review *Passages* in September 1994, and in English as "The Deconstruction of Actuality," *Radical Philosophy* 68 (autumn 1994): 28–41.

98. See E. M. Henning, "Foucault and Derrida: Archeology and Deconstruction," *Stanford French Review* (fall 1981): 247–64; extended repr. as E. M. Henning, "Archeology, Deconstruction, and Intellectual History," in *Modern European Intellectual History: Reappraisals and New Perspectives*, ed. Stephen Kaplan and Dominick LaCapra (London: Routledge, 1982), 153–96.

99. Geoffrey Bennington, "Derridabase," in G. Bennington and Jacques Derrida, *Jacques Derrida* (Chicago: Chicago University Press, 1993), 1, 14, and 313–16.

100. Copyright infringement in digital media is a complex issue. As Derrida demonstrates, there is a distinction between good and bad repetition, and one can always parasite the other. For instance, in September 1995, parts of my Derrida Web site www.lake. de/home/lake/hydra/ were duplicated and rebroadcast under a different address, but with my name carefully erased. A simple link would have provided the same information without changing the documents. Several lawyers contacted me online and suggested that although it might not be worth filing a suit, I should certainly put a copyright notice on the site even if, theoretically, every document published after 1 April 1989 is automatically copyrighted, whether it has a notice or not. (Exemptions are made for fair use.) Had the documents remained intact, the copied site would merely have been considered a "mirror"; in the wake of this event, I established www.hydra.umn.edu as a mirror; it is now the main hub. Exhibit two for how bad repetition can always parasite good repetition: the paraphrase of my argument (published as "'Screen Memory': Hypertext und Deckerinnerung," in *Deutsche Vierteljahresschrift für Literaturwissenschaft und Geistesgeschichte* 72, special issue: *Medien des Gedächtnisses*, ed. Aleida Assmann [Stuttgart: Metzler, 1998], 279–96) by E. Schumacher in *Die Adresse des Mediums*, ed. Stefan Andriopoulos (Cologne: DuMont, 2001), 121–35.

101. Jacques Derrida, *The Post Card: From Socrates to Freud and Beyond* (Chicago: Chicago University Press, 1987), 197.

102. Derrida, *The Post Card*, 27 and 105.

103. Jacques Derrida, *Résistances de la psychanalyse* (Paris: Galilée, 1996), 66: "*Off the record*, cela veut dire hors enregistrement, hors archive. Nous voilà donc reconduits à la difficile question du *record*, de l'histoire et de l'archive. Y a-t-il du *hors-archive*? Impossible, mais l'impossible c'est l'affaire de la déconstruction" ("Off the record, that is to say beyond recording, beyond the archive. We return here to the difficult question of record, of history and the archive. Is there anything without archive? Impossible, but the impossible is the business of deconstruction").

104. Jacques Derrida, *Mémoires: For Paul de Man* (New York: Columbia University Press, 1989), 35–38.

105. See Friedrich Kittler, "Vergessen," in *Texthermeneutik. Aktualität, Geschichte, Kritik,*

ed. Ulrich Nassen (Paderborn: UTB, 1979), 195–221; in English as "Forgetting," *Discourse: Berkeley Journal for Theoretical Studies in Media and Culture* 3 (1981): 88–121.

106. *Les Fins de l'homme: à partir du travail de Jacques Derrida*, ed. Philippe Lacoue-Labarthe and Jean-Luc Nancy (Paris: Galilée, 1981), 486; see Timothy Clark, "Computers as Universal Mimics: Derrida's Question of Mimesis and the Status of Artificial Intelligence," *Philosophy Today* (winter 1985): 302–18.

107. Jacques Derrida, "Archive Fever," *Diacritics* 25, no. 2 (1995): 45 and 27; repr. as *Archive Fever: A Freudian Impression* (Chicago: University of Chicago Press, 1996), 76 and 36.

108. Compare Derrida, "Archive Fever," 50 (*Archive Fever*, 77), and Jacques Derrida, *The Gift of Death* (Chicago: University of Chicago Press, 1995), 82; compare Derrida, *The Post Card*, 267, and Jacques Derrida, "Ja, ou le faux bond," *Digraphe* 2 (1977); compare "Archive Fever," 49 (*Archive Fever*, 74), and Derrida, *Glas*, 82a (i.e., 95a in the French edition).

109. Jacques Derrida, "Dialangues," in *Points... Interviews 1974–1994*, ed. Weber, 142.

110. See Heiner Müller, "Deutschland ist Hamlet," *Die Deutsche Bühne* 7 (1986), 10; Heiner Müller, *Ein Gespenst verläßt Europa* (Berlin: Rotbuch, 1990).

111. See Peter Krapp, "Die Kunst des Unmöglichen–Interesse, Aktualität, Differenz," in *Theorie-Politik: Selbstreflexion und Politisierung kulturwissenschaftlicher Theorien*, ed. Marcus Hahn (Tübingen: Gunter Narr, 2002), 151–70.

112. The feasibility of this allegation is tested in Peter Krapp, "Wer zitiert sich selbst? Notizen zum Suizitat," in *Anführen—Vorführen—Aufführen: Das Zitat in Literatur und Theorie*, ed. Nils Plath and Volker Pantenburg (Bielefeld: Aisthesis, 2002), 105–28.

113. Hans-Thies Lehmann, "Raum-Zeit," *Text und Kritik* 73 (1982): 71–81.

114. As Jacques Derrida writes, in his text "Out of Joint":

I never met Heiner Müller.

Yet—dare I say it, and did he ever know it—he is one of my greatest and best friends.

I speak here neither of my admiration for him, nor of my gratitude, nor of his work. Only of the singular trace that he left in my life and about which I will think until the end, an enigma that is larger than me, a signature that history has inscribed, at countertime, into the body of a spectral friendship.

After the publication of *Spectres de Marx* (haunted by the figure of Hamlet and the anachronism of "The time is out of joint"), we were to meet in Berlin (now East Berlin), Heiner and I, for a public discussion. Everything seemed to call for such a meeting and to predestine it. It put me, in advance, in a disturbed, crepuscular mood. I had reread *Hamlet Machine* on the plane. On my arrival I am told—first counter-time ("The time is out of joint")—Heiner was hospitalized. He would not participate in the discussion, and regretted it. Me too, and I begin to fear the worst. His shadow is very present over the session that takes place without him, yet with him. All the historical and political countertime of which we talked everywhere, he and I, are staged on this evening in Berlin by his illness.

Another meeting is arranged, for the day he feels better. I look forward to it and prepare for it, read him and collect all signs, texts, and images, that can bring me closer to him.

This entire phase of countertime is marked by political events that were all earth-quakes—and by travels, changes of scenery, an erring that takes us both from one end of the world to the other.

Separating us without separating.

One evening, in Italy, my wife calls me: "Heiner Müller is dead, his friends will call you, he has asked before dying that you speak at his grave, or for a last word in the last moment."

After a deliberation that in fact could have been endless and will have to remain endless, I decide, without deciding, that I cannot, that I should not, that it would be in every way impossible for me, for infinitely many obscure reasons that I cannot identify or analyze here, to speak like that, of him, for him, before him, after his death, since I had never met him, this great friend, this friend who was so great, during his lifetime.

Of course, I will never be able to justify my negative response that I gave right away to the friends who called to confirm his request. A feeling of treason, the worst, infinite treason. Treason of a dead friend, thus of an infinitely vulnerable one. Unfounded treason that consists in not saying yes to a single request, the last, that a great friend, a friend who was so great, made of me.

And I know, I presume, he would have thought like me that it was too late to ask him for pardon, him who will be the only one from whom such a demand for pardon would have made any sense.

And yet something tells me that this treason remains faithful. Not only because Heiner perhaps would have understood my withdrawal, perhaps in advance understood and staged it. But because this moment remains more unforgettable, more deeply inscribed in my heart, more faithfully turned toward him than if I had pronounced some words in public in the big Berlin theater of solemn mourning.

Here, I write this very fast, without thinking too long, without rereading it, without cutting, before I depart in a few hours for America, to another one of our common places and nonplaces.

What remains to be said, or to be read, our mutual friends could, if they wished to, find in that public space of remains that one calls writing, images, theater.

Jacques Derrida
Ris Orangis, September 20, 1998

(Jacques Derrida, "Aus den Fugen," French manuscript, personal transmission of the author, 17 December 1998 [my trans.]; published only in German, translated into German by Sigrid Vagt, in *Heiner Müller Archiv*, Stiftung Archiv der Akademie der Künste [Düsseldorf: Kulturstiftung der Länder, 1998], 17–18.)

115. Jacques Derrida, *Specters of Marx: The State of the Debt, the Work of Mourning, and the New International* (London: Routledge, 1994), 12–16. Further references by page number in the text.

116. What will have happened to an updated, reinforced, reexamined, newly informed theory of the déjà vu, or rather after déjà vu: would it amount to anything more than considering the recognizably new always already familiar?

117. Nicholas Royle, "Déjà Vu," in *Post-Theory: New Directions in Criticism,* ed. Martin McQuillan (Edinburgh: Edinburgh University Press, 1999), 3–20.

118. Derrida, *Glas*, 192b.

119. "una certa amnesia a darmi questo gusto, che si può considerare una forza o una debolezza. Non dirò que so dimenticare, ma so che dimentico, e che non è solo né sempre un male": Jacques Derrida and Maurizio Ferraris, *Il gusto del segreto* (Rome: Laterza, 1997), 43.

120. "S'il y a une mnémotechnologie déconstructionniste, comme je suis en train de l'affirmer, elle dépendrait sûrement d'une certaine rapidité de réponse, la capacité d'avoir des informations, comme on dit, sur le bout de doigt": David Wills, "JD-ROM," in *Passions de la Litterature: Avec Jacques Derrida*, ed. Michel Lisse (Paris: Galilée, 1996), 220.

121. "In die Eroberungen des Neuen schmilzt sich auf vertrackte Weise das Alte ein. Das Gegenwärtige wird dadurch zu einer Form unbewußten Erinnerns oder symptomatischer Verkörperung. Dies ist aber auch eine Art Vergessen. Cyberspace ist eine gewaltige Maschine nicht-kenntlichen Vergessens oder unbewußten Erinnerns": Hartmut Böhme, "Über Geschwindigkeit und Wiederholung im Cyberspace: das Alte im Neuen," in *Metamorphosen: Gedächtnismedien im Computerzeitalter*, ed. Götz-Lothar Darsow (Stuttgart: Frommann-Holzboog, 2000), 41 ("The old insinuates itself in complex ways in the conquests of the new. The present thus turns into a form of unconscious remembering or symptomatic embodiment. But this is also a kind of forgetting. Cyberspace is a powerful machine of unrecognizable forgetting or unconscious recollection").

122. Derrida, *Of Grammatology*, 70.

123. Florian Brody, "The Medium Is the Memory," in *The Digital Dialectic: New Essays on New Media*, ed. Peter Lunenfeld (Cambridge: MIT Press, 1999), 146.

124. See Jacques Derrida, "Language: *Le Monde* on the Telephone," in *Points . . . Interviews 1974–1994*, ed. Weber, 171–80. See also Jacques Derrida, "Le toucher: Touch/to touch him," *Paragraph* 16, no. 2 (1993), 124–57: "Tangent IV (a supplementary touch or past retouching, long ago left stalled on my computer, that is, in a place where the relation between thought, weight, language, and digital touch will have undergone in the last ten years an essential mutation of ex-scribing. A description would be necessary of the surfaces, the volumes, and the limits of this new magic writing pad which exscription touches on in another way, from the keyboard to the memory of a disk said to be 'hard')."

125. Jacques Derrida and Bernard Stiegler, *Échographies–de la television: Entretiens filmes* (Paris: Galilée-INA, 1996), 45.

126. Derrida, *Mémoires*, 123.

127. Jacques Derrida and Elisabeth Weber, "Im Grenzland der Schrift: Randgänge zwischen Philosophie und Literatur," *Spuren in Kunst und Gesellschaft* 34–35, no. 4 (1990): 58-70; trans. as "Passages–from Traumatism to Promise," in *Points . . . Interviews 1974–1994*, ed. Weber, 372–95.

128. Derrida and Weber, "Im Grenzland der Schrift," 70: "Dieser Beitrag stellt den vervollständigten Text einer Einführung und eines Gespräches dar, das am 22. Mai 1990 im *Abendstudio* des Hessischen Rundfunks gesendet wurde": ("This contribution represents the completed text of an introduction and conversation broadcast on May 22 1990 from the program 'Abendstudio' of the Hessischer Rundfunk"). The missing, or additional, passage would have been at the end of the first column on page 65.

129. Derrida and Weber, "Passages–from Traumatism to Promise," 382–83.

130. Saving the text: the computer-age metaphor suggests that this can be accomplished by pushing a button. Jacques Derrida's "Epreuves d'écriture" and Jean-François Lyotard's comments "Notes du traducteur" were published in *Revue philosophique* 2 (April–June 1990): 269–84.

131. Derrida, "Archive Fever," 17 and 22 (*Archive Fever*, 16 and 25–26); repetition can, as Freud has it, push itself to the front as a resistance against remembering.

132. This fold announces itself early on: "since everything begins in the folds of citation (you will later learn how to read this word), the inside of the text will always have been outside it. . . . Everything 'begins,' then, with citation, in the creases [faux plis] of a certain veil" (Derrida, *Dissemination* [Chicago: University of Chicago Press, 1981]), 316.

133. Derrida, *Dissemination*, 108–11; see Jacques Derrida, "Freud and the Scene of Writing," in *Writing and Difference* (Chicago: University of Chicago Press, 1978), 228.

134. *From Memex to Hypertext: Vannevar Bush and the Mind's Machine*, ed. James M. Nyce and Paul Kahn (Boston: Academic Press, 1991). See *Hyper/Text/Theory*, ed. Landow, and Hilmar Schmundt, "Autor ex machina. Electronic Hyperfictions: Utopian Poststructuralism and the Romanticism of the Computer Age," *Arbeiten aus Anglistik und Amerikanistik* 19, no. 2 (1994): 223–46.

135. Theodor Holm Nelson, "The Transclusion Paradigm," d8, Project Xanadu/Sapporo Hyperlab 1995; compare Nelson, "A File Structure for the Complex, the Changing and the Indeterminate," in *Proceedings of the ACM 20th National Conference*, ed. Lewis Winner (New York: ACM, 1965); and Nelson, "What Is Literature?" in *Literary Machines: The Report on, and of, Project Xanadu* (Berrien Springs: Nelson, 1987).

136. Theodor Nelson, "Hypertext Is Ready: HTML for Home and Office," *New Media* 5, no. 8 (1995): 17.

137. Geoffrey Bennington, Interview with the *Seulemonde* Online Journal, Tampa, Florida 1994: www.cas.usf.edu/journal/bennington/gbennington.html.

138. Jürgen Fohrmann, "Misreadings Revisited: Eine Kritik des Konzepts von Paul de Man," in *Ästhetik und Rhetorik: Lektüren zu Paul de Man*, ed. Karl-Heinz Bohrer (Frankfurt: Suhrkamp, 1993), 95.

139. See Catherine Liu, "Doing It Like a Machine," in *Copying Machines: Taking Notes for the Automaton* (Minneapolis: University of Minnesota Press, 2000), 1–20, and "De Man on Rousseau: The Reading Machine," ibid., 127–54. Another reading of de Man on Rousseau can be found in Jacques Derrida, "Typewiter Ribbon: Limited Ink (2) ('within such limits')," in *Material Events: Paul de Man and the Afterlife of Theory*, ed. Tom Cohen (Minneapolis: University of Minnesota Press, 2001), 277–360.

140. Derrida, "Word Processing," 3. Compare Elisabeth Weber's interview with Derrida, "Zeugnis, Gabe," in *Jüdisches Denken in Frankreich*, ed. Elisabeth Weber (Frankfurt: Jüdischer Verlag, 1994), 77–78.

141. Derrida, *Mémoires*, 140.

142. "[W]ithout taking into account the obvious fact that deconstruction is inseparable from a general questioning of *tekhné* and technicist reasoning, that deconstruction is nothing without this interrogation, and that it is anything *but* a set of technical and systematic procedures," as Derrida warns, "certain impatient Marxists nevertheless accuse deconstruction of deriving its 'power' from the 'technicality of its procedure'": Derrida,

Mémoires, 16; we add, with Derrida, that "Socrate" is the name of a corpus of system routines (*The Post Card*, 242).

143. Nelson, "The Transclusion Paradigm," 4; other neologisms after Nelson, "Opening Hypertext: A Memoir."

144. Jacques Derrida, *Limited Inc* (Evanston: Northwestern University Press, 1988), 21.

145. See Derrida, "Freud and the Scene of Writing," 202, and Derrida, *Dissemination*, 63.

146. Royle, *After Derrida*, 40. This formulation harks back to the interminable network of listening lines that compels reckoning with the patch, in *Glas*, 118b: "interminable réseau de branchements d'écoute *en allo* qui oblige à compter avec la pièce rapportée" ("interminable network of interruptions of listening—hello—which obliges you to count on the hang-up"). I should add that www.dejavu.org is an amusing and instructive Scandinavian project to archive the genealogy of the World Wide Web as it unfolds.

7. WRAPPING IT UP

1. Examples from Barbara Lazerson Hunt, "Déjà Vu," *American Speech* 69, no. 3 (1994): 285–93; see also William Safire, "On Language," *New York Times Magazine*, 15 October 1989, 18. I also want to record that perhaps the most exciting thing during my time in Santa Barbara was meeting David Crosby at a marine biology reception; compare C. G. Gottlieb, *Long Time Gone: The Autobiography of David Crosby* (London: Mandarin, 1988), and David Crosby, *Déjà Vu* (New York: Guerilla Music, 1970, Crosby Stills Nash & Young).

2. "Um zu wissen, was Krieg ist, brauchen wir nicht mehr die *Ilias* oder Jünger zu lesen, und nicht einmal mehr die Zeitung. Wir können ihn in technischer Schwerelosigkeit aus der Hertzschen Teledistanz in Echtzeit erleben": Elisabeth Lenk, "Achronie," in *Interventionen*, vol. 4 (Basel: Stroemfeld, 1995), 179.

3. Lenk combines a deep appreciation for surrealism with an attempt to bring critical theory up to speed with the Gulf War on CNN. See also Paul Virilio, *L'ecran du desert* (Paris: Galilée, 1991), and Paul Virilio, *L'insecurité du territoire* (Paris: Stock, 1976).

4. This is a threat to literature if the latter is the medium of man's expansion in time. See H. Meyerhoff, *Time in Literature* (Berkeley: University of California Press, 1955), 109.

5. As Valéry reminded us, "le passé oublie qu'il est passé" ("The past forgets that it passed"). See Ernst Robert Curtius, *Europäische Literatur und Lateinisches Mittelalter* (Bern: Francke, 1948), 24: "Für die Literatur ist alle Vergangenheit Gegenwart" ("For literature, all past is present"). Literature may be said to resemble the unconscious, insofar as it is not subject to the temporality of time. In this sense, I quote Lenk, "Achronie," 189: "Ausdruck dessen, was seit der Zeitrechnung aus der Zeit vertrieben wurde" ("Expression of what was expelled from time since the beginning of time-keeping").

6. Joseph Heller, *Catch-22* (New York: Scribner, 1955). See John Wain, "A New Novel About Old Troubles," *Critical Quarterly* 5 (1963): 169, on Yossarian's leap outside the circular catch-22.

7. Readerly expectations about time-space are warped in Heller's depiction of the three-dimensional experiences of his bomber pilot protagonist Yossarian within the two dimensions of a book. As Robbe-Grillet wrote, the new novel is in "absolute need of the

reader's cooperation, an active, conscious, *creative* assistance": Alain Robbe-Grillet, *For a New Novel* (New York: Books for Libraries Press, 1970), 156.

8. Ideally, Yossarian's dialogue with the chaplain in chapter 25 should be reproduced here in full.

9. All quotes from Heller, *Catch-22*, chapter 25.

10. "We presume that the psychical trauma—or more precisely the memory of the trauma—acts like a foreign body which long after its entry must be continued to be regarded as an agent that is still at work": Sigmund Freud and Josef Breuer, "Studies on Hysteria," SE, 2:6. See James M. Mellard, "*Catch-22*: Déjà Vu and the Labyrinth of Memory," *Bucknell Review* 16, no. 2 (1968): 29–44.

11. In the tradition of Hobbes's *Leviathan*, Freud talks of nation-states as "Großindividuen," large individuals, to draw analogies between anthropological theories of aggression and modern war: the social macrostructure exhibits the mechanisms of regression and identification psychoanalysts find in individuals. If nations repeat the development of individuals, even today one encounters them in early degrees of development, and war and peace are not right and wrong, good and bad, nonviolent and violent, but different manifestations of a potential aggression that in peace only takes a different appearance. Sigmund Freud, "Thoughts for the Times on War and Death," SE, 14:275.

12. While writing this, I received an e-mail from the Philippines, from friends who met with Tony Bosch, a Filipino with German ancestors, and anthropologist Raul Pertierra. During fieldwork in Filippine Studies, he found a village where people believe that German men live in couples and always lack one of their extremities. The origin of this assumption was that after the great war, two German veterans settled in a neighboring village, one of whom had lost his right arm, the other his left arm. Whether the interpretation was based on the heroic tales of the two soldiers or not, the villagers never assumed that they had been born that way: they suspected a rite of initiation, in which German men have one of their extremities cut off. The villagers developed the idea that German men can only survive in a couple, because they will complement each other. The same evening Tony Bosch and my friends heard this story from the anthropologist, they spotted a dog on the road who only had three legs, and Raul Pertierra suggested it might in fact be a German dog. I sign this note with my left hand, and thank Dr. Wigan Salazar.

13. Scheler claimed that war, as "Gesamterlebnis" or holistic experience, is the strongest creator of community in history, "der stärkste Gemeinschaftsbildner": Max Scheler, "Der Genius des Krieges und das Gesamterlebnis unseres Krieges," in *Der grosse Krieg als Erlebnis und Erfahrung*, ed. Ernst Jaeckh (Gotha: NP, 1916), 285.

14. Andreas Huyssen, *Twilight Memories* (New York: Routledge, 1995), 249.

15. Theodor W. Adorno, "Weit vom Schuß," in *Minima Moralia* (Frankfurt: Suhrkamp, 197), 60. In 1914, the Germans hoped for a war-experienced nation created out of the molten heap of European civilization. Once the First World War had been lost, they were unable to handle the loss: as the losing party, everything they believed was tied up in the loss; they clung to it. Ernst Jünger and Friedrich Gundolf, but also Thomas Mann and Georg Simmel kept hoping that war was going to be purifying. Mann argued that German "style, form, bearing, taste, a mental organization in the world," went to war against

"skepticism, leniency, dissolution" in the rest of Europe. Thomas Mann, "Gedanken im Kriege," *Neue Rundschau* 25 (1914): 1471–84.

16. Thus the war was lost in a double sense, as Walter Benjamin diagnosed: the winner takes all, yet the loser cannot lose the loss. Walter Benjamin, "Theorien des deutschen Faschismus," GS, 3:238–50.

17. Don Delillo, *White Noise* (New York: Viking, 1985). Further references by page number in the text.

18. Henri Lefebvre, *The Production of Space* (London: Blackwell, 1991), 25. There is an element of paramnesia in the surreptitious return of Benjamin and Bloch in déjà vu as a caption for an inversion in home design: "Déjà Mood: An Elegant Urban Condo Recaptures the Ambiance of a Suburban Home," *Chicago Tribune Magazine*, 30 September 1990, 60.

19. "Wo Erfahrung im strikten Sinn obwaltet, treten im Gedächtnis gewisse Inhalte der individuellen Vergangenheit mit solchen der kollektiven in Konjunktion": Walter Benjamin, "Charles Baudelaire: Ein Lyriker im Zeitalter des Hochkapitalismus," GS, 1.2:611 ("Where experience reigns in the strict sense, certain contents of the individual past enter into conjunction in memory with those of the collective past").

20. Sigfried Giedeon, *Bauen in Frankreich, Bauen in Eisen, Bauen in Eisenbeton* (Leipzig: Klinkhardt & Biermann, 1928), 6.

21. See Freud's letter to Romain Rolland, "A Disturbance of Memory on the Acropolis," SE, 22:239–50. Musing on Freud's aversion from the Acropolis, I note by way of an aside that the largest chain of strip clubs in the United States bears the name Déjà Vu.

22. Quintilian, *Institutio oratoria* 11:2, 11–16; Cicero, *De oratore* 2, 351–53.

23. The mnemotechnical capabilities of Simonides—and his greed—are attested to by Plutarch, chapter 5 of *An seni sit gerenda res publica (Moralia* 786B); see Aristotle, *Rhetoric* 2, 1405b 23–28; and Egon Friedell, *Kulturgeschichte Griechenlands* (Munich: C. H. Beck, 1949), 143.

24. "eine historische Deckerinnerung": Stefan Goldmann, "Statt Totenklage Gedächtnis: Zur Erfindung der Mnemotechnik durch Simonides von Keos," *Poetica* 21, nos. 1–2 (1989): 45. As Goldmann demonstrates in detail (64f.), Simonides becomes the inventor of mnemotechnics only in the third century. This tradition is taken up by Louis Marin, "Le Trou de mémoire de Simonide," in *Lectures traversières* (Paris: Seuil, 1992), 197–209.

25. Jesper Svenbro, *La Parole et le marbre: Aux origines de la poétique grecque* (Lund: Sverige, 1976), 171; see Georg Busolt, *Griechische Staatskunde*, vol. 1 (Munich: C. H. Beck, 1920), 489.

26. Cecil Bowra, *Greek Lyric Poetry from Alcman to Simonides* (Oxford: Oxford University Press, 1936), 360.

27. In an essay on architecture, Wellmer expresses "curiosity" about a "puzzling experience" and a "strong sense of the unique" that is "like a déjà vu" and harks back to his reading Knut Hamsun, and to repressed associations with ideology and Second World War atrocities. Albrecht Wellmer, "Architecture and Territory" (1988), in *Endgames: The Irreconcilable Nature of Modernity* (Boston: MIT, 1998), 269.

28. David Gelman, "A Fresh View of Déjà Vu—Here It Comes Again," *Newsweek*, 7 January 1991, 62.

29. Anthony Vidler, *The Architectural Uncanny: Essays in the Modern Unhomely* (Cambridge: MIT Press, 1992), 13. Further references by page number in the text.

30. Cited after Vidler, *The Architectural Uncanny*, 26–27.

31. Paolo Portoghesi, *After Modern Architecture* (New York: Rizzoli, 1982), 13.

32. David Kolb, *Postmodern Sophistications: Philosophy, Architecture and Tradition* (Chicago: Chicago University Press, 1990), 89.

33. See André Bazin, "The Ontology of the Photographic Image," in *What Is Cinema?* (Berkeley: University of California Press, 1990), 9–16. (See *Qu'est-ce que le cinéma* [Paris: Editions du Cerf, 1985].) It is no coincidence that even neuroscientific contributions on aberrations of memory often refer to film, whether they mention Kurosawa or Schwarzenegger. See Daniel Schacter, "Memory Distortion: History and Current Status," in *Memory Distortion: How Minds, Brains, and Societies Reconstruct the Past*, ed. Daniel Schacter (Cambridge: Harvard University Press, 1995), 1–43.

34. If reference is made to Benjamin in this context, then it is usually to his reading of Carl Bötticher's theory of architecture as a theory of history "in which the unconscious serves as a generative and productive source" challenging existing modes of representation. Detlev Mertins, "Walter Benjamin and the Tectonic Unconscious: Using Architecture as an Optical Instrument," in *The Optic of Walter Benjamin*, ed. Alex Coles (London: de-, dis-, ex-, 1999), 196–221.

35. Benjamin's interpretation of Sigfried Giedeon gave him the opportunity to exemplify his theory of the optical unconscious as analogous to his articulation of a theory of photography. Explications of the unfinished Arcades project in this light keep gaining popularity. See Irving Wohlfahrt, "'Construction has the Role of the Unconscious': Phantasmagorias of the Master Builder," in *Nietzsche and "An Architecture of our Minds,"* ed. André Kostka and Irving Wohlfahrt (Los Angeles: Getty Research Institute, 1999), 141–98.

36. Walter Benjamin, "The Work of Art in the Age of Mechanical Reproduction," in *Illuminations*, ed. Hannah Arendt (New York: Schocken Books, 1969), 239. Shierry Weber Nicholsen and others have called attention to "the 'passage' in relation to the grave or tomb" and the possibility of a secret or interior architecture in Benjamin's work. Shierry Weber Nicholsen, "Translator's Introduction," in Pierre Missac, *Walter Benjamin's Passages* (Cambridge: MIT Press, 1995), xii and xv.

37. What Benjamin called the "caesura in the motion of thought" is a place of suspension between stand-still and thought-movement, or between the split and the self-application of text. Where thinking comes to a halt, sated with tensions, there appears the dialectical image. Walter Benjamin, "Das Passagenwerk," GS, 5.1:594.

38. The masses seek distraction in art, while the connoisseur approaches art in the mode of "Sammlung" (focus or collection). The individual tries to enter the artwork, but the masses draw the work into them; thus architecture is for Benjamin the work of art whose reception takes place in collective distraction. Benjamin, "Das Kunstwerk im Zeitalter seiner technischen Reproduzierbarkeit," GS, 1.2:464.

39. Paul Virilio, *The Vision Machine* (Bloomington: Indiana University Press, 1994), chapter 1.

40. Friedrich A. Kittler, "Medien und Drogen in Pynchons Zweitem Weltkrieg," in *Die unvollendete Vernunft: Moderne vs. Postmoderne*, ed. Dietmar Kamper and Willem van

Reijen (Frankfurt: Suhrkamp, 1987), 247. See also David Gross, *Lost Time: On Remembering and Forgetting in Late Modern Culture* (Amherst: University of Massachusetts Press, 2000).

41. Theodor W. Adorno, "Aufzeichungen zu Kafka," in *Versuch das Endspiel zu verstehen* (Frankfurt: Suhrkamp, 1973), 127–66, here 139. See Kittler, "Medien und Drogen," 251, and his "Romantik—Psychoanalyse—Film: eine Doppelgängergeschichte," in *Eingebildete Texte: Affairen zwischen Psychoanalyse und Literaturwissenschaft*, ed. Jochen Hörisch and Georg Christoph Tholen (Munich: Fink, 1985), 118–35.

42. Plato, *Politeia* 617dff., and Aristotle, *Poetics* 1448b. Compounded historical evidence notwithstanding, see Umberto Eco, "An Ars Oblivionalis? Forget It," *PMLA* 103 (1988): 254–61, and Yosef Hayim Yerushalmi, "Réflexions sur l'oubli," in *Usages de l'Oubli: Colloque de Royaumont* (Paris: Seuil, 1988), 7–21.

43. Adorno, "Aufzeichungen zu Kafka," 137. Nothing could make the transition from Victorian fears to postmodern effects of (intentionally false) recognition more obvious: contrast the analysis in Amanda Anderson, "Dying Twice: Victorian Theories of Déjà Vu," in *Disciplinarity at the Fin de Siècle*, ed. Joseph Valente (Princeton, NJ: Princeton University Press, 2002), 196–218, with the fact that a large beverage company now markets bottled water called Deja Blue.

44. Ernst Bloch, "Bilder des Déjà Vu," *Literarische Aufsätze*, in *Werkausgabe*, vol. 9 (Frankfurt: Suhrkamp, 1965), 235. ("Images of Déjà Vu," in *Literary Essays* [Stanford: Stanford University Press, 1998], 203.

45. "Freud was the first to always arrive late: *Nachträglichkeit* in turn secured a past or context for psychoanalytic structures of thought endopsychically recorded and stored at every stage of a coterminous genealogy featuring the nuclear family and media technology": Laurence Rickels, *The Case of California* (Baltimore: Johns Hopkins University Press, 1991), 133.

46. "Im nackten offenkundigen Bestand des Faktischen gibt das Ursprüngliche sich niemals zu erkennen, und einzig einer Doppelansicht steht seine Rhythmik offen. Sie will als Restauration, als Wiederherstellung einerseits, als eben darin Unvollendetes, Unabgeschlossenes andererseits erkannt sein": Walter Benjamin, *Ursprung des deutschen Trauerspiels* (Frankfurt: Suhrkamp, 1969), 30.

INDEX

Adorno, Theodor W., x, 13, 50, 58, 59, 71–72, 98, 119, 146, 153, 156, 168, 169, 175, 176, 178, 183, 190, 211, 214
adultery, 26–27, 110
Agamben, Giorgio, 98–99
akrasia, xvii–xix, xxvii, 10
amnesia, x, xi, xvi, 3, 18
amnesty, 101–3, 194
anteriority, xiii, 210
anticipation, x, xi, xxvii, 5, 18–20, 144
anxiety, xvi, xii, 15, 83, 145, 150–53, 159, 210
architecture, 146–52, 212, 213, 214
archive, xxi, 131–42
Arendt, Hannah, 46, 167, 175
Aristotle, xvii–xviii, xxvii, 160, 161, 170
Assmann, Aleida, vii
attention, xi, xxiv, 3, 20, 89 121
Augustine, xi, 13, 145
aura, xiv–xv, 90–95, 152

bad faith, 12, 15–18, 23, 168–69
Barth, John, xxii
Barthes, Roland, xviii, 78, 163, 185, 194
Baudelaire, Charles, 38, 56, 59
Baudrillard, Jean, 83, 187
Beckett, Samuel, 84
belief, 18, 163–64
Bell, Alexander Graham, 76–77
Benjamin, Walter, ix, x, xiv, xxv, xxvi, xxvii, xxviii, 31–51, 54, 56, 58–60, 62, 65–66, 68–69, 76, 86, 87, 88, 92, 99, 105, 107, 109, 114, 147, 171, 172, 173,

174, 175, 176; *Berlin Childhood*, 31, 34, 46; on collective consciousness, 33; on echo, 31–32, 151; on folk art, 36, 40; on the future, 32, 35; on hiding, 43–45; on history, 32, 44, 50; on Kafka, 44, 46, 48, 51; on kitsch, 36, 39, 40; on Marx, 36–41; *One-Way Street*, 43–44; on shock, 31
Bennington, Geoffrey, 133, 137, 140, 166–67, 203, 204, 209
Bergson, Henri, ix, xvii, 54, 160
Bloch, Ernst, xxv, 42, 63, 92–93, 100, 164, 174, 180, 190, 193, 214
Bolz, Norbert, 123, 128, 198
Brecht, Bertolt, xxv, 57, 60, 64, 178
Brentano, Clemens, 49
Burroughs, William, xxii

Carroll, Lewis, vii
Cavell, Stanley, xxvi
childhood, xix, 31–51, 64–66
collective memory, xix, xxi, 146, 162
critical distance, xiii, 57
Crow, Thomas, 82

daydream, 26–27
Deleuze, Gilles, 122, 158
Delillo, Don, 146, 212
delusion, xv, xxvi, 10
de Man, Paul, 140, 156, 166, 209
depersonalization, 27–28
Derrida, Jacques, vii, 122–42, 156, 158, 164, 199–210; on archives, 133–35; on

215

PETER KRAPP is assistant professor of new media in the Department of Film and Media at the University of California, Irvine. He coedited *Medium Cool*, a special issue of *South Atlantic Quarterly* on contemporary media theory, and is the editor of the Hydra Web site for theories of literature and media, www.hydra.umn.edu.